Lecture Notes in Economics and Mathematical Systems

Managing Editors: M. Beckmann and H. P. Künzi

154

Problems and Instruments of Business Cycle Analysis

A Selection of Papers Presented at
the 13th CIRET Conference
Proceedings, Munich 1977

Edited by Werner H. Strigel
IFO Institute for Economic Research, Munich

Springer-Verlag
Berlin Heidelberg New York 1978

Managing Editors
Prof. Dr. M. Beckmann
Brown University
Providence, RI 02912/USA

Prof. Dr. H. P. Künzi
Universität Zürich
8090 Zürich/Schweiz

Editor
Werner H. Strigel
IFO Institute for Economic Research
Munich/FRG

ISBN 3-540-08664-1 Springer-Verlag Berlin Heidelberg New York
ISBN 0-387-08664-1 Springer-Verlag New York Heidelberg Berlin

Printing and binding: Beltz Offsetdruck, Hemsbach/Bergstr.
2142/3140-543210

PREFACE

Every two years the members of CIRET (= Centre for International Research on Economic Tendency Surveys) meet at conferences in order to promote the scientific discussion and to encourage the exchange of ideas. CIRET is an international study group for research in the field of business cycle surveys. CIRET was founded in 1960 and has at present about 350 full and corresponding members in 35 different countries. The members either carry out business, investment or consumer surveys[1] or are working on a practical or methodological level with the results of such surveys.

The most important topics of the CIRET conferences are

- the predictive value of survey data as trade cycle indicators,
- the utilization of qualitative data in econometric models,
- forecasts of capital expenditures based on plans of private companies,
- the usefulness of consumer surveys for trade cycle analyses.

In September 1977 the 13th CIRET Conference took place in Munich. On the occasion of the three-day conference 27 papers were presented. 180 economists from 30 different countries participated in the conference[2].

In the past, the papers presented at the CIRET conferences have been published separately by the authors at different places. This time it was decided in view of the great demand for the papers of the CIRET conferences to edit some of the CIRET papers in the form of proceedings. For reasons of economy it was, however, only possible to publish about half of the papers in the present volume. A full list of the papers given at the 13th CIRET Conference in Munich will be found in annex A. The reader who wishes to have a clear idea of the papers not printed in this volume should refer to the CIRET Study No. 25 which contains summaries of all papers presented at the Munich CIRET Conference (see annex B).

Munich, January 1978 W. H. Strigel

---

1 See No. 146 of Lecture Notes in Economic and Mathematical Systems: In Search of Economic Indicators. Essays on Business Surveys. Edited by W. H. Strigel, Berlin - Heidelberg - New York 1977.

2 See also the explanations on CIRET as well as the summary of the institutions carrying out trade cycle surveys in "In Search of Economic Indicators", op.cit., pp. 190-196.

CONTENTS

W. A. JÖHR
HOCHSCHULE ST. GALLEN FÜR WIRTSCHAFTS- UND
SOZIALWISSENSCHAFTEN
ST. GALLEN

PSYCHOLOGICAL INFECTION, A CAUSE OF BUSINESS FLUCTUATIONS

Psychological Infection

A Cause of Business Fluctuations *)

Walter Adolf Jöhr
Hochschule St.Gallen für Wirtschafts- und Sozialwissenschaften

Introduction

The recession, which began in mid-May 1974, and from which we are still suffering (May 1977), does not only present serious problems to entrepreneurs and finance ministers, but also to the large number of economists who believed that a serious decline in economic activity is no longer a threat to us. The high degree in which economists were surprised by the recession was shown by an investigation which the present writer carried out during a project-oriented course last winter at the Hochschule St.Gallen.

The specific topic of my course was: To what extent was the recession, which began in 1974, predicted? The investigation dealt with 29 forecasting institutions. Among these were 10 institutes from different European countries, all belonging to the Association d'Instituts Européens de Conjoncture Economique. In addition, there were 4 similar organisations from the Federal Republic of Germany, 8 from France, 1 from Britain, and 5 from the United States. Out of the multitude of data provided by the Institutes previously mentioned, we chose that which seemed to us to be most representative of the course of economic activity, namely the growth rate of the real gross national (or gross domestic) product. Since particular institutes published more than one prognosis for any given year, the number of prognoses was bigger than the corresponding number of institutes. The prognoses presented in the following table refer to either the pre-recession year 1973 or to 1974 or 1975. They were published in the four quarters of the pre-

*) For helping with the English version of my paper I should like to thank my colleague Mr. Ronald Ewart.

Table 1: Deviation of the predicted growth rates of real gross national product (or gross domestic product) from actual growth rates *)

deviation in percentage points	1973	1974	1975
-5.0 - -4.1		1	
-4.0 - -3.1			
-3.0 - -2.1			1
-2.0 - -1.1		1	
-1.0 - -0.1	12	2	2
0.0 - 0.9	8	3	1
1.0 - 1.9	3	9	1
2.0 - 2.9		12	2
3.0 - 3.9		1	6
4.0 - 4.9	1	7	4
5.0 - 5.9		1	9
6.0 - 6.9		2	8
7.0 - 7.9			4
8.0 - 8.9			
9.0 - 9.9			
10.0 - 10.9			
11.0 - 11.9			1
total of prognoses	24	39	39

*) Included are only prognoses which did not appear later than the first quarter of the year to which the prognosis refers

ceding year or in the first quarter of the year for which the prognosis was made. The prognoses for the pre-recession year 1973 show only a slight deviation from the actual course of economic activity. 12 prognoses present an underestimation of the actual course ranging from 1.0 to 0.1 percentage points, whilst another 8 prognoses show an overestimation ranging from 0.0 to 0.9 percentage points. For 1974, as the preceding table makes clear, not only is the range of dispersion in the prognoses significantly bigger, but also the prognoses themselves show considerably larger deviation from the actual course of business activity. Out of 39 prognoses, 29 made an overestimation of between 1.0 and 4.9 percentage points. A similar dispersion is shown in the predictions for 1975, where the majority of prognoses fall in the deviation range of 3.0 to 6.9 percentage points.

We come to the conclusion that in spite of all the reservations that can be made concerning our investigation, which should certainly have been performed on a bigger scale, it can be maintained that the severity of the recession was, as a rule, not foreseen by the consulted institutions. Among the exceptions figures "The Economist", which as early as the 1st of June 1974 wrote "The world's rich countries are digging the foundations for a major world depression." And about two months later, it announced that "The world recession is no longer just a threat. It has arrived."

The difficulty of the forecasters' task of predicting the course of business activity is shown in another respect. Only five years ago one could admit with a certain confidence that government would be in a position, thanks to a policy of increasing the stream of income, not only to stop a process of contraction, but to transform it into a new process of expansion. That confidence was based on the belief that the doctrine of Keynesianism would be applicable without difficulties. The new fact, however, is the general tendency to an accelerated inflation. When such a tendency exists, then the effectiveness of a Keynesian anti-recession policy is called into doubt in two respects [1]. Firstly, the higher the inflation rates in a period of accelerating inflation, then the more important becomes the aim of fighting inflation in political life. This has the consequence that the government can no longer dare to embark on a policy of increasing the stream of money incomes, which would be necessary for an effective stimulation of business activity and for raising the level of employment. Secondly, even if we suppose that in spite of the reservations mentioned already, such a Keynesian policy is carried out in conditions of accelerating inflation, there is a serious danger that it will be at least partly ineffective because the prevailing expectation of further price increases would have its effect in an increase of prices and nominal wages instead of in higher employment of production factors.

By the fact that the Keynesian policy of high employment - a policy which relies upon influencing the stream of incomes - has suffered a significant set-back in its effectiveness, the theory of business fluctuations, considered by many authors during the period of post-war prosperity to be out of date, is now experiencing increased relevance and at the same time increased interest on the part of the public and economists [2].

In attempting to elaborate some of the main problems of the theory of business fluctuations, I hope at the same time to bring about a better understanding of the actual situation of the world economy to-day. At the centre of my contribution, I place psychological infection, but, according to the agreement with the organiser of the CIRET-Conference, Dr. Strigel, I shall not restrict myself to psychological infection alone, but will discuss it in a larger context, so that I can do full justice to its problems. But I do not pretend in any way to offer a complete exposition of the factors responsible for business fluctuations. Therefore, I shall not deal with the impulses, which, in the classical period of business fluctuations from the Napoleonic Wars to the First World War, were such phenomena as discoveries of gold, opening up of new markets, irregularities in agricultural yields and technological advances. Nor shall I attempt to discuss historical and cultural conditions which affect economic activity - although they have a definite influence on business fluctuations. I limit myself to the following points:

1) the self-reinforcing processes of expansion and contraction,
2) the socio-psychological process of infection,
3) the floating equilibrium of under-employment.

1. The self-reinforcing processes of expansion and contraction

In order to understand business fluctuations, it is very important to realize that they can take on the character of self-reinforcing processes. These processes play a big role not only in economic life, but also in all parts of human existence as well as in the natural world, a much bigger role in fact than is usually supposed. These processes are well known under other names. For example, sometimes they are called "cumulative" processes, or "explosive" processes; when the situation is deteriorating, the process is called "circulus vitiosus" (or "Teufelskreis"). If the situation is improving, than we sometimes find the term "circulus virtuosus". Cybernetics has contributed a further term: "positive feedback", an expression which might be confusing for the lay man since the positive feedback in a deteriorating situation has negative effects *).

These self-reinforcing processes are ubiquitous: i.e. we find them in all disciplines. Having been convinced for a long time that the human psyche is subject to such self-reinforcing pro-

*) It must also be kept in mind that in the long run a positive feed-back in an up-swing spiral will produce negative effects too.

cesses, I was happy to come by chance upon the doctrine of the Viennese psychiatrist Victor Frankl, who qualifies anxiety neuroses and compulsion neuroses as self-reinforcing processes. He reports on the following case. A patient suffers from an over-function of the thyroid gland which produces a certain susceptibility to anxieties: "A symptom, which in itself is harmless and temporary, produces in the patient an obsessive fear of its return. This expectation - anxiety - increases the symptom and finally the symptom, thus intensified, confirms the patient's phobia. The vicious circle is completed, which the patient has spun around himself as a cocoon" 3).

In physical medecine also, such processes are well known, which, when they are allowed to run without control or with insufficient control, can lead to death. A doctor acquaintance 4) kindly provided the following example: because of a heart infarct, the performance of the heart muscle is reduced. This leads to a decline in the pumping function of the heart, which reduces the performance of the heart itself, so that in turn the pumping function of the heart deteriorates further. This vicious circle can repeat itself until it produces complete heart failure.

An example taken from engineering: a turbine, whose axle is slightly off centre will, through continual use, accentuate this defect until it cracks 5).

Another self-reinforcing process, which occurs at such extraordinary speed that one usually does not think that it implies a process at all, is an explosion. The fuse that causes an explosion in a barrel of gun powder only lights a very small portion of that powder. And that small spark leads to the burning of the nearest parts of the powder. This process not only continues but accelerates, because of the rising temperature, until all the powder is alight.

In a similar way, the process of nuclear fission, e.g. an atomic explosion, can be described. Neutron bombardment leads to the splitting of atomic nuclei. Neutrons, which are scattered by this division, can produce new nuclear fissions. Thus, the process is one of self-acceleration.

These five examples suffice to show the general importance of self-reinforcing processes. It would be extremely valuable, if comprehensive interdisciplinary studies documented knowledge of the most important of them, taking into account all scientific disciplines. Such work is up to now unknown to me.

Knowledge of the great importance of self-reinforcement processes for explanation of business fluctuations was generally accepted in previous decades. This is particularly evident in the investigation made by Gottfried Haberler for the League of Nations (1937). Based on a critical analysis of the most important approaches to the theory of business fluctuations, he attempts a synthesis of the existing theories. For him the idea, that in the upswing as well as in the downswing of business activity self-reinforcing processes play a decisive role, was of central importance. He writes: "We assume that the process of expansion (or contraction) has been started in one manner or another and we investigate what is meant by saying that the process is cumulative and self-reinforcing, and on what factors this cumulative quality depends" [6].

How was this idea lost? I mean the idea that business expansion and contraction are shaped to a high degree by self-reinforcing processes. Different factors have contributed to bring about this loss. In the first place, I refer to Keynes' theory. Shortly before the League of Nations published Haberlers' book, Keynes' "General Theory" appeared. This work not only gave a new orientation to discussion of the theory of business fluctuations and employment policy, but has dominated economic thinking for many of the following decades. In the chapter "Notes on the Trade Cycle" (inserted in the "General Theory"), however, we still find the following sentence:

> "By a cyclical movement we mean that as the system progresses in, e.g., the upward direction, the forces propelling it upwards at first gather force and have a cumulative effect on one another but gradually lose their strength until at a certain point they tend to be replaced by forces operating in the opposite direction" 7).

But in his system of simultaneously determined equations of macro-variables(developed particularly by his adherents and followers out of the network of his many sided and complex arguments) the concept of cumulative process plays no part at all.

In the post-Second World War period, which lasted up to 1973 - Hayek implies that it will enter history with the name of "The Great Prosperity" 8) - prosperity and growth seemed to be so assured that interest in the theory of business fluctuations vanished. Economic theory concentrated its interest on the growth process and endeavoured to show that growth can follow an equilibrium path in the long run. From this viewpoint, the recessions of the post-war period before 1974 appeared no longer as phenomena of business fluctuations, but as growth cycles or even only as temporary disturbances of the growth process.

Furthermore - and it might well appear paradoxical - what could be considered as the summit of the theory of the cumulative processes has helped to bring about the final interment of this theory. What we have in mind will be substantiated by a concrete example, which is moreover the most important example. By combining the acceleration principle (which is one of the most obvious factors causing self-reinforcment of business fluctuations) with the multiplier, Samuelson showed that oscillations of economic activity can result - oscillations which, according to the coefficient values employed (accelerator and propensity to consume) can be self-restricting or self-enlarging [9]. By refining the acceleration principle and by superimposing Samuelson's approach on Harrod's growth theory, Hicks succeeded in making an important contribution to the building of mechanical models of business cycles [10]. In basically the same way, factors of self-reinforcement and factors of self-restriction have been inserted into econometric models. This resulted in pre-determined cycles of economic activity, which were used for purposes of prediction.

In fact, the number of self-reinforcing factors is considerably bigger than the number of those factors which are usually built into econometric models. This may be confirmed by the following list which shows the most important self-reinforcing factors [11]:

<u>List of self-reinforcing factors</u>

a) based on differences in time needed for adaptation
   (1) acceleration principle in the field of changing production capacity
   (2) acceleration principle in the field of changing stocks
   (3) v. Zwiedineck's law of the consecutiveness of the flow of money income and the flow of products
   (4) effect of fixed costs
   (5) inverse reaction of family farms in agricultural production
b) based on monopolistic conditions
   (6) lag of wages compared to prices of products
c) based on specific psychological qualities of entrepreneurs and consumers
   (7) limited transparence
   (8) fulfilment of expectations as a clue to future development
   (9) the mood of thinking and feeling (Stimmung) as a factor determining economic activity and determined by economic activity
   (10) the struggle of entrepreneurs to get ahead of their competitors

(11) faulty calculation which leads to too big profits in times of inflation and to too big losses in times of deflation

(12) socio-psychological infection process

d) effects leading to a change in the flow of money

(13) possibility of the destruction or creation of money, being induced by changes in economic activity

(14) possibility of piling up savings or reducing accumulated savings, being induced by changes in economic activity

(15) possibility of hoarding or dishoarding money, being induced by changes in economic activity.

Unfortunately, this is not the place in which to give a full explanation of the way in which the different factors operate. But we shall make an exception in the case of socio-psychological infection which will be discussed in the following pages. Two preliminary remarks are necessary. Firstly, the term "psychological qualities" of economic agents should be clarified. In accordance with other authors' practice, we shall use this expression only to qualify those attitudes and actions of economic agents which differ from the corresponding postulates of the model of perfect competition - postulates which are usually, though not quite correctly, bundled together under the catch phrase of "economic man" [12)]. Secondly, we do not wish to question in principle the ability of econometric models to represent business fluctuations. But they have their limits and this can be seen clearly when we remember the task of predicting the course of business activity from 1974 on. As a matter of fact, the self-reinforcement processes listed before and a considerable number of processes of self-dampening are locked together in continually changing ways. Thus, one would do more justice to specific economic situations and specific theoretical and forecasting tasks, if one did not definitively knit together these factors, and not assign specific roles to them.

2. The socio-psychological infection process

We have now reached the point where the subject indicated by the title of my contribution may be treated. The general significance of the socio-psychological infection process may be illustrated by an example from the Middle Ages. During the two hundred years from the end of the 11th to the end of the 13th century there were seven great crusades from Western Europe to the Orient. They were partly motivated by idealism and religion and partly by political and economic aims. About a decade after the beginning of the fourth crusade, the following events took place,which we can quote as an example of an extraordinary socio-psychological infection process. We refer to the Children's Crusades [13). Im May 1212, a twelve year old shepherd boy went to the French king's palace and said that while he was looking after the sheep, Christ appeared to him and called him to preach for a new crusade. The king ordered the boy to go home, but the boy did not lose courage and this is what he preached: he would lead a children's crusade to save Christendom. The sea would dry up before them as the Red Sea had done for Moses and they would be able to cross into the Holy Land on foot. His words raised great enthusiasm. Many thousands of children gathered in the middle of France and set out from there towards the Mediterranean coast. And in the Rhineland also, raised by the words of an equally young boy, a similarly motivated crusade formed and marched over the Alps. But when the columns of children reached the sea, and when the expected miracle did not take place, their disillusion was bitter and great. Many turned back; others, however, embarked on ships for the Holy Land; many of these were drowned in ship wrecks and many were sold as slaves. And of the other children, a great number died on their way from exhaustion or disease.

These two crusades originated from the preaching of two charismatically gifted boys, one in France and one in the Rhineland. But they would never have taken place if there had not been a mutually increasing enthusiasm for their holy endeavours on the part of the growing number of children and also of many adults. So, the Children's Crusades can be seen as one of the most impressive and also most touching examples of the extraordinary power of the process of socio-psychological infection.

History presents us with many other similar examples. In particular, revolutionary periods are full of such events. These provided the material out of which Gustave Le Bon formulated his famous book "Psychologie des Foules" (1895) [14]. Le Bon came to the conclusion that the crowd (used in the sense of mass psychology) does not represent an average of the qualities of its members, but creates new qualities: lust for power, suggestibility, lowering of cultural levels. Worth remembering also is a book by the psychiatrist Willy Hellpach, whom the oldest of our German colleagues will remember as the candidate of the German Democratic Party for the post of Reichspräsident. The book quoted is entitled "Die geistigen Epidemien" (1906) [15]. According to Hellpach, the infection of psyche A by what occurs in psyche B can take place in three different ways: through persuasion (Einredung), empathy (Einfühlung) and suggestion (Eingebung). Hellpach, in this very interesting work, deals above all with the spreading of phenomena of mental sickness and its consequences.

Of course, in the economic field, we also find similar eruptive processes just as in revolutionary periods in the political field. We also see similar outbursts of the exalted behaviour of an increasing crowd, such as were dealt with by Hellpach. Examples are the Gold Rush, which followed on the discovery of gold in California, excesses of speculation, and runs on banks. But a decisive characteristic of the socio-psychological infection process in the economic sphere is that it does not show itself only in dramatic events, lasting for hours, days or weeks, but in everyday life, including the ebb and flow of business activity.

Half a century ago, Lord Robbins stated in connection with the theme "Economics and Psychology" that "the borderlands of Economics are the happy hunting-ground of minds averse to the effort of exact thought" [16]. Nevertheless, eminent economists such as Jevons [17] and Pigou have spent much time on considering the significance of the infection processes for changes in business activity. Pigou, in fact, succeeded in formulating the socio-psychological infection process in poetic form:

"One with another, soul with soul
They kindle fire from fire" [18].

In my work published in 1952, entitled "Die Konjunkturschwankungen", I also attempted to break a lance for the socio-psychological explanation of business fluctuations [19]. But I met with only very limited success. I could explain this by the fact that in economics, which is dominated by the ideal of natural sciences, the obligation to construct mathematically formulated models is still almost generally accepted. This has the result that the conditions for psychologically oriented models, whose results leave considerable room for uncertainty, are unfavourable. Also my attempt to integrate socio-psychological infection processes in business games [20] and my endeavour to use the diffusion theory to formulate the spread of influences relevant to business activity [21] brought about no substantial change in economists' attitudes to this question. Consequently, I still look for support for this approach from other sides.

Quite recently, I came upon a valuable piece of research which is also an important contribution to the theory of the socio-psychological infection process, though it does not use this term. I am referring to the article by Elisabeth Noelle-Neumann "Die Schweigespirale. Ueber die Entstehung der öffentlichen Meinung" [22]. According to Mrs. Noelle, public opinion is formed by a process consisting of interactions between individuals. For this process, it is important that the individual, as a rule, has a strong desire not to be isolated, but to consider himself in harmony with the future majority, thus gaining security and self-confidence. At the beginning of her work on this subject, Mrs. Noelle treated the expression (or non-expression) of opinion on public issue as a function of the feeling of belonging to the majority (or to the minority). Later, she considered it as a function of the expectation that a certain opinion would be the winner or be the loser in the future. For the effect of this second possibility, Mrs. Noelle coined the expression "Schweigespirale" (spiral of non-expression). The expectation that they will belong to the losing party increases the readiness of its supporters to stay silent and this, in turn, leads to a reduction of the number of supporters, so that expectations for the future are further deteriorated. The opposite effect is produced by a self-reinforcing process, related to the belief that one will be on the winning side in the future. One might term this a"spiral of opinion expression" (as a term corresponding to the previously used "spiral of non-expression"). Mrs. Noelle's approach is very interesting, and the question arises whether it could not be used in a modified form for purposes of business fluctuation theory or diagnoses of the course of economic activity. This seems even more justified, since in the process of business fluctuations public opinion on the future course of economic activity is an important element.

Now let us turn to the role of the socio-psychological infection process in business fluctuations. Since I have only a limited space at my disposal, I must present my socio-psychological approach in a certain number of points [23]:

(1) Regarding his decisions about the direction and the volume of production and investment, the view of the entrepreneur over many of the most important data for his decisions will be clouded by a veil of uncertainty.

(2) The uncertainty about the foundations for decision makes the

entrepreneur susceptible to influences of optimism and pessimism and to indications of what might happen.

(3) These influences and indications come largely from other entrepreneurs, who are facing similar problems of decision.

(4) An equal orientation of business activity can be produced in manyfold ways:

- through motive adoption
- through arousal of ideas
- through imitation
- through adoption of feelings
- through influencing moods (optimism, pessimism).

(5) The endeavour to act in a similar way to others will be increased if their attempts to get ahead of competitors become visible.

(6) In so far as the entrepreneurs themselves form a mass, i.e.: the individual entrepreneurs consider themselves to be more or less anonymous to each other, then the reaction to the socio-psychological influences will be increased.

(7) Although explanations of the self-reinforcing factors constituted by psychological elements(as indicated under (7) to (11) on the list of self-reinforcing factors given before) show an equal orientation of attitudes and activities, produced by the economic process and affecting this process again (see Fig. I), the process of socio-psychological infection is more complex. We can see that the entrepreneurs have a mutual influence on each other, so that an effect of rapid self-reinforcement is possible (Fig. II).

(8) If we wish to do justice, however, to modern economic reality, we should not content ourselves with the model of the socio-psychological infection process which was described in points (1) to (7).

Figure I

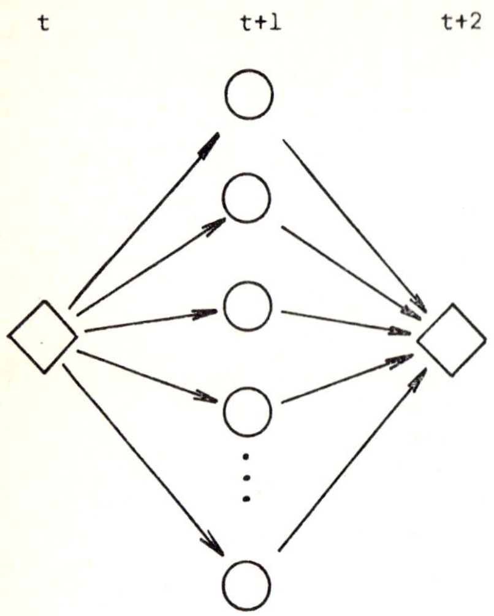

Figure II

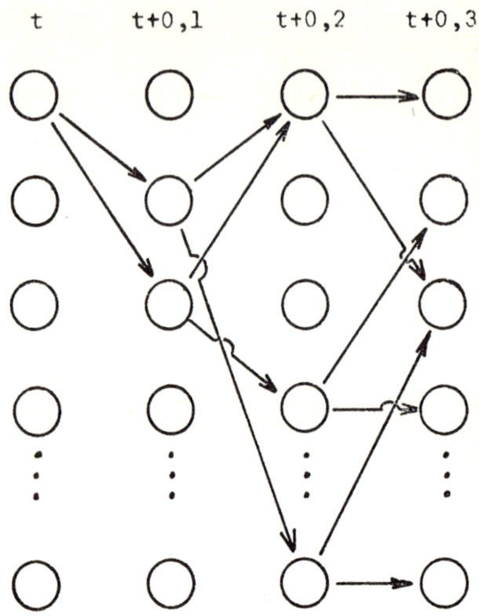

 = process of expansion

 = entrepreneur

That model treated the process as an interaction occurring within a group of entrepreneurs. We must take into account, however, that a whole series of other agents is also involved in producing this process. The following enumeration indicates some of these agents; it does not pretend to be complete. To the entrepreneurs of a given country, we have to add:

- economic organisations
- government
- central bank and commercial banks
- economists and forecasting institutes
- mass media.

Nor should we limit ourselves to considering the socio-psychological infection as a process which takes place fully within the boundaries of one country. The agents mentioned before are interwoven in an international process of socio-psychological infection. Naturally, the degree of dependence on the behaviour of economic agents from other countries differs from case to case.

(9) The infection - or, in other words, the transfer of a certain attitude or a certain way of acting - can make itself felt in minutes, hours, days or weeks. The transmission to other agents of received impulses can proceed also within minutes, hours, days or weeks. But under certain conditions the impulses can be stored, lying dormant until the time comes for them to affect other agents. This is so if the impulses affect decisions concerning production and investment. In these cases, the time period involved may be measured in months, quarters or even years. It is extremely important to realise that the storing of impulses is part of the socio-psychological infection process. Business fluctuations are shaped by it to a significant extent.

(10) Wherever socio-psychological infection processes, produced

by interaction among economic agents, occur, they proceed erratically. As we have seen, socio-psychological infection is among the factors producing business fluctuations. And this explains many of the irregularities of the actual course of business fluctuations.

(11) Therefore, socio-psychological infection also renders significantly more difficult the task of forecasting business fluctuations.

(12) To eliminate any misunderstandings, it should be stressed that the socio-psychological infection process is an important factor in producing business fluctuations, but it is not the only one. It operates together with a series of different impulses, with numerous factors of self-reinforcement, changes of direction (transforming an up-swing into a down-swing or vice versa) and self-dampening factors; but also together with factors which influence conditions affecting business fluctuations positively or negatively in other ways.

3. The floating equilibrium of under-employment

At the present moment (May 1977), the world economy is experiencing a peculiar situation of floating equilibrium with considerable unemployment [24)]. The up-swing, which was observed during 1975 and the beginning of 1976, has not maintained its progress. Every one hopes for a new up-swing, but we are still uncertain if our hope will be justified.

This situation brings to mind an observation made by Keynes in his "General Theory", concerning the "economic system" in which we live. He wrote: "... it is not violently unstable. Indeed it seems capable of remaining in a chronic condition of sub-normal activity for a considerable period without any marked tendency either towards recovery or towards complete collapse" [25)]. Keynes, of course, was referring to the British economy in the second half of the twenties and in the first half of the thirties. However, at the same time he succeeded in showing with the aid of his theoretical model how such a situation of stagnation can result. His expressed intention was to demonstrate that an equilibrium with under-employment can be deduced from his premises whilst the so-called classical theory admitted only an equilibrium with full employment (including frictional unemployment). The factor responsible for the level of employment is - for Keynes - the size of investment [26)].

In the monetarist camp also a concept has been developed which at first sight seems to be a near relation to Keynes's equilibrium with under-employment. Milton Friedman has formulated a concept of the "natural rate of unemployment". He did it with the aid of the Phillips curve [27)]. In the long run, this curve falls perpendicularly. Its distance from the vertical axis is equal to the natural rate of unemployment. The following definition, however, proves that Friedman's concept is only a refined version of frictional unemployment: "The 'natural rate of unemployment', in other words, is the level that would be ground out by the Walrasian system of general equilibrium equations, provided there is imbedded in them the actual structural characteristics of the labour and commodity markets, including market imperfections, stochastic variability in demands and supplies, the cost of gathering information about job vacancies and labour availabilities, the costs of mobility, and so on" [28)]. So Friedman does not help us to explain what we understand by floating equilibrium with under-employment.

As we showed in the preceding section, we can deduce a process of expansion or contraction from the premises of our model if we make use of the concept of socio-psychological infection. And we can conclude that this also explains these processes in the real world. But this concept also enables us - and this has been frequently overlooked - to deduce or explain a stable or a floating equilibrium. This is the case because infection may not only confirm and spread the opinion that business activity is on the up-swing or down-swing, but also the opinion that the present situation will continue. In so far as the entrepreneurs act according to this belief in making their decisions about production and investment, then the impulses mentioned previously are stored for a certain period of time. This has the consequence that the floating equilibrium can continue, not only for months, but even for years.

An example of such a period of equilibrium is the period of high prosperity after the Second World War up to 1974. An example of a floating equilibrium on a very low level was seen in the years 1932 and 1933.

The situation today, however, is characterised by a floating equilibrium on a moderate level of unemployment. A similar situation - currently overlooked - occurred in the United States in 1938/39. The great advantage of the concept of socio-psychological infection is that such floating equilibria can easily be explained with its help. In my book "Konjunkturschwankungen" I proposed a new term for a situation in which both expansion and contraction balance each other, meaning that business must be aware that one of these two processes will become dominant in the future. This new term I called "Buridan's state", in memory of the medieval philosopher Buridan who explained the problem of free will, using as an example a donkey between two piles of hay, each at an equal distance from it [29]. Having reconsidered the problem, I have come to the conclusion that the infection process can also strengthen the tendency to maintain the given situation or to produce small up-swings and down-swings in the course of a continuous long run movement of expansion or contraction. I, therefore, would like to propose a new term for this floating equilibrium. According to a vision of hovering witches, which Goethe brought to the readers' eyes in Faust's words:

"Was weben die dort um den Rabenstein?
.....
Schweben auf, schweben ab, neigen sich, beugen sich!" *)

I propose that this type of floating equilibrium be called the Rabenstein equilibrium.

Conclusions

The socio-psychological approach is useful to economists in different respects.

(1) It facilitates to a considerable extent the task of explaining business fluctuations. With the aid of the previously expounded socio-psychological approach, we are able to explain in an easy way a number of movements and situations in business activity and certain qualities of these movements and situations: processes of expansion and contraction, floating equilibria of high, moderate and low levels, erratic changes of processes and situations.

(2) It also throws new light on business forecasting. If one accepts the significant role played by psychological factors in business activity, one also recognises the great possibilities offered by the method of submitting questionnaires to economic agents. Compared with the data coming from official statistics, such as produced quantities, realised prices, building projects, this method of questioning economic agents has some definite advantages. By asking for opinions on the situation of individual firms or of the general business conditions, by asking for intentions concerning the volume of production and investment in the future, or concerning the future course of economic activity in the whole economy, a better and an earlier picture of the factors determining the level of business activity is provided. In this respect, one can see

*) English version: "What weave they there round the raven-stone?
.....
Soaring up, sweeping down, bowing and bending!"
Translation by B. Taylor, Boston 1871, p. 291.

that the socio-psychological explanation of business fluctuations and the efforts of the Ifo-Institute [30] and the other members of the CIRET (Centre for International Research on Economic Tendency Surveys) are converging. There is also a convergence with the approach developed by George Katona [31] (his Survey Research Center of the University of Michigan is also a member of CIRET) -, an approach which attempts to give - using consumers' questionnaires - a better picture of their role in influencing economic activity.

(3) The socio-psychological approach is also important for the policy of stabilising business activity. To be able to do this, one must know the relations of cause and effect so that one is able to apply corrective measures appropriately. The socio-psychological approach provides a clear answer to this question of cause and effect relationships, although it must be kept in mind that it does not in any way pretend to offer a mono-causal explanation of business fluctuations. As has already been expressed, other factors play their part. Regarding the relevance of what has been said for a stabilisation policy, one must be aware of the possibility of drawing false conclusions. One should not conclude that,as a result of adopting this approach, moral suasion should be the primary weapon of stabilisation policy. It is unsuitable, not because it attacks on the wrong front, but because it is too weak. And this is the case because moral suasion alone will not find the necessary credibility among entrepreneurs and consumers - the credibility which would be necessary to bring about the wanted change of orientation of the economic agents. At the time when the Keynesian policy of stabilisation through regulating the income flow was still fully effective, government was able to influence opinions and behaviour of the economic agents by introducing this policy and promising to maintain it deliberately in the future. But under the conditions of an accelerating inflation - conditions which prevailed until recently in the Western world - it is probable that an anti-recession policy (based on an increase of the in-

come flow) will have the following effect: the additional money expended will not set in motion additional factors of production but will only raise prices. Therefore, a successful fight against inflation is an important prerequisite for an effective anti-recession policy.

(4) The theory of the socio-psychological infection process and of the floating equilibrium determined by it is not only significant in regard to business fluctuations. It is also of general economic significance. It suffices to mention, as relevant and common examples, the international movements of capital under the system of fixed (but adjustable) exchange rates, stock exchange and commodities speculation and the spread of fashion. It is to be hoped, therefore, that an intensified study of the socio-psychological infection process will throw a new light on these and other economic phenomena.

(5) A similar hope exists in regard to other social and political movements, which obviously also have the character of socio-psychological infection. Among these disturbing phenomena, we can include the youth rebellion of the late 1960's, the hippies, the spreading of drug taking, and the increase of criminality and of terrorist activity. Also worth mentioning are new currents of thought, such as the revival of Neo-Marxism, the increased consciousness of the environment and the so-called wave of nostalgia.

Notes and References

1) cf. W.A. Jöhr, Wenn Keynes' Waffen stumpf geworden sind .... Zur Keynesianischen Beschäftigungspolitik in der Welt der siebziger Jahre, in: Schweizerische Handelszeitung, 18th September 1975.

2) cf. E.-M. Claassen, Brauchen wir eine neue Konjunkturtheorie? Unorthodoxe Gedanken zu einem alten Thema, in: Neue Zürcher Zeitung, 2nd/3rd April 1977.

3) V.E. Frankl, Der Mensch auf der Suche nach Sinn. Zur Rehumanisierung der Psychotherapie, 5th ed., Stuttgart/Freiburg i.Br. 1976, p. 54. cf. also p. 79 and 94, and V.E. Frankl, Psychotherapie für den Laien. Rundfunkvorträge über Seelenheilkunde, 5th ed., Freiburg i.Br. 1975, p. 67.

4) Dr. F. Kopp, Zürich, gave me the quoted information.

5) I discussed the following examples in the field of mechanics, chemistry, and nuclear physics with my colleague at the School of Economics and Public Administration St.Gall, W. Weber, Professor of Technology.

6) G. Haberler, Prosperity and Depression. A Theoretical Analysis of Cyclical Movements, Geneva 1937, p. 185.

7) J.M. Keynes, The General Theory of Employment, Interest and Money, New York 1936, p. 313.

8) F.A. Hayek, Full Employment at any Price, London 1975, p. 15.

9) P. Samuelson, Interactions between the Multiplier Analysis and the Principle of Acceleration, in: The Review of Economic Statistics,1939.

10) J.R. Hicks, A Contribution to the Theory of the Trade Cycle, Oxford 1950.

11) The following list is based on W.A. Jöhr, Die Konjunkturschwankungen, Tübingen und Zürich 1952.

12) cf. W.A. Jöhr, Zur Rolle des psychologischen Faktors in der Konjunkturtheorie, in: Ifo-Studien, 1972, Fasc. 2, p. 157 et seq.

13) S. Runciman, Geschichte der Kreuzzüge, Volume III, München 1960, p. 144 (translated from the English) - R. Röhricht, Der Kinderkreuzzug, 1212, in: Historische Zeitschrift, ed. H.v.Sybel, München 1876 - P. Alphandéri, Les Croisades d'Enfants, in: Revue de l'Histoire des Religions, 1916, p. 259 et seq. - D.C. Munro, The Children's Crusade, in: The American Historical Review, October 1913, p. 516 et seq.

14) G. Le Bon, Psychologie der Massen, 6th ed., Leipzig 1932 (translated from the French).

15) W. Hellpach, Die geistigen Epidemien, Frankfurt a.M. 1906 - L.-F. Calmeil, De la folie, considérée sous le point de vue pathologique, philosophique, historique et judiciaire, depuis la renaissance des sciences en Europe jusqu'au dix-neuvième siècle; description des grandes épidémies de délire, simple ou compliqué, qui ont atteint les populations d'autrefois et régné dans les monastères. Exposé des condamnations auxquelles la folie méconnue a souvent donné lieu, Paris 1845 (2 vol.).

16) L. Robbins, An Essay on the Nature and Significance of Economic Science, 2nd ed., 1937, p. 83.

17) W.St. Jevons, Politische Oekonomie (translated from the English), reprinted in: Ausgewählte Lesestücke zum Studium der Politischen Oekonomie, ed. K. Diehl and P. Mombert, Volume 7, 1913, p. 196 et seq.

18) A.C. Pigou, Industrial Fluctuations, London 1927, p. 79.

19) W.A. Jöhr, Die Konjunkturschwankungen, p. 589 et seq.

20) W.A. Jöhr, Spiel zur Simulation von Konjunkturprozessen, in: Zeitschrift für Nationalökonomie, 1965, Fasc. 1-2, p. 99 et seq. - There is another game of mine as yet unpublished which gives the participants the chance to act as speculators on the Stock Exchange in varying conditions. To bring into existence the socio-psychological infection process, at certain stages of the game I inserted a kind of cocktail party conversation involving all players.

21) W.A. Jöhr, Zur Rolle des psychologischen Faktors in der Konjunkturtheorie, p. 176 et seq.

22) E. Noelle-Neumann, Die Schweigespirale. Ueber die Entstehung der öffentlichen Meinung, in: Oeffentlichkeit als Bedrohung. Beiträge zur empirischen Kommunikationsforschung, Freiburg i.Br. and München 1977.

23) The following exposition is an abbreviated version of the theory developed in my book "Die Konjunkturschwankungen", p. 596 et seq.

24) The unemployment figures (December 1976, in millions) for some leading countries of the Western world were: USA 7.56; Great Britain 1.33; German Federal Republic 1.02; Japan 0.96; France 0.93; Italy 0.78 (Source OECD).

25) J.M. Keynes, op. cit., p. 249.

26) J.M. Keynes, op. cit., p. 27.

27) M. Friedman, Price Theory, Chicago 1976, p. 218 and 227.

28) M. Friedman, The Optimum Quantity of Money and Other Essays, London 1969, p. 102.

29) W.A. Jöhr, Die Konjunkturschwankungen, p. 604.

30) A comprehensive survey of the approach of the Ifo-Institute is given by W. Strigel, Der Finger am Puls der Wirtschaft. Entwicklung und Bedeutung der Ifo-Umfragen, in: Wirtschaftskonjunktur, Monatsbericht des Ifo-Institutes, 1964, Fasc. 3.

31) G. Katona in his book "Psychological Economics", New York 1975, presents his earlier work and new contributions in his principal field of research.

G. KATONA
UNIVERSITY OF MICHIGAN
ANN ARBOR

B. STRÜMPEL
FREIE UNIVERSITÄT
BERLIN

CONSUMER SENTIMENT AND ECONOMIC TRENDS

CONSUMER SENTIMENT AND ECONOMIC TRENDS
The Outlook Over Several Years

by George Katona and Burkhard Strumpel

The authors believe that the analysis of middle-range trends of the economy is necessary and possible. By middle-range trends they mean a time span of approximately ten years.

As is well known, short-range forecasts represent the principal preoccupation of a large part of the economic community. In these studies the analysis of cyclical fluctuations results in predictions over the next several months, a year, or at the most, two years. Long-range forecasts such as predicting the conditions twenty-five or fifty years hence have also been prepared by extrapolating past trends. Especially for population studies, but also for a number of economic purposes, it is important to know what conditions would ensue if current growth rates were to continue unchanged over several decades. Yet extrapolation is obviously not a reliable method of forecasting because economic processes are characterized by feedback from results to behavior and also by discontinuities.

The importance of middle-range forecasting may be apparent by mentioning just two major questions the answers to which would greatly facilitate the task of social and economic planning. Will GNP or national income, in real terms, grow fast or slowly, or stay about where they are now, or decline during the next ten years? Will cyclical fluctuations in the next decade be frequent or rare, with high peaks and low troughs, or will they exhibit a small amplitude of change?

The major reason why middle-range forecasting is seldom undertaken consists, we believe, of the absence of reliable methods for this task. To be sure, rates of growth or other economic trends may be extrapolated and at certain times may yield interesting data. To illustrate by referring to recent American developments: In the first twenty-five years after World War II (1945-70) growth rates were very much higher than in the first seven years of the present decade. In those twenty-five years extensive prosperous periods were occasionally interrupted by short recessions, while in the 1970s there were approximately the same number of quarters of upswing and of downswing. Is it possible to draw conclusions from these well-known facts about the probable economic trends in the next ten years? Or should one attribute the record of the past several years to unique developments, such as the worldwide recession and inflation, perhaps caused or worsened by the OPEC cartel? Obviously, it is far from easy to answer these questions.

Neglecting cyclical changes, it appears that the climate for private investment in manufacturing has indeed deteriorated during the last five or ten years. This diagnosis is based on evidence presented in Table 1, revealing many similarities between the United States and Germany:

--The rate of profit of large corporations has declined significantly since 1961.

--Lower profit rates have left their imprint on corporate balance sheets. Symptomatic is the deterioration of the "dynamic debt ratio," the ratio of debt to cash flow.

--Until the late 1960s the production of goods benefited from a decline in the relative prices of energy and raw materials. The index for raw material prices on the world market started to rise faster than the general price level in the early 1970s, long before the oil embargo. Since that time the era of cheap raw materials has ended.

In addition, the environment is increasingly overwhelmed by the wastes and pollutants of a "throughput-intensive" economy which has been doubling its energy and materials use every ten to fifteen years.

Table 1

MEASURES OF THE CLIMATE FOR BUSINESS INVESTMENT: UNITED STATES AND WEST GERMANY

	Profit after Taxes[a] % of capital	% of sales	Dynamic Debt Ratio[b]	
	U.S.	Germany	U.S.	Germany
1961-1965	8.3%	4.0%	6.3%	6.1%
1966-1970	7.7	3.2	7.4	7.3
1971-1973	5.6	3.4	8.5	10.6

[a]U.S. data from William D. Nordhaus, "The Falling Share of Profits," Brookings Papers on Economic Activity, 1974, p. 180. German data from Horst Albach, "Zue Entwicklung der Kapitalstruktur duetscher Unternehmen," in Zeitschrift fuer Betriebswirtschaft, Vol. 45, 1975, p. 9.

[b]Corporate debt ÷ annual cash flow, averaged U.S. data from Hyman P. Minsky, "Financial Resources in a Fragile Financial Environment, Challenge, July/August 1975, pp. 6ff. German data from Albach, ibid., p. 3.

The impact of these changes in the operating conditions of the industrial sector was greatly reinforced by psychological factors, in particular a shift toward pessimism and disorientation on the part of businessmen, experts, and the public at large.

A study of changes in the attitudes and values held by the people provides some clues for an analysis of middle-range trends. There are two types of subjective belief systems that influence behavior and can be ascertained by survey research. Some attitudes and expectations about personal finances and business conditions may change greatly even within a period of a few months, while others change so slowly that they can best be determined by comparing data collected at intervals of two or even five years. The former have been used for more than twenty-five years by the Survey Research Center of The University of Michigan for the purpose of short-run forecasting. It was postulated that short-range attitudes and expectations indicate changes in consumers' willingness to buy, which, together with their ability to buy, determine the greatly fluctuating discretionary expenditures of consumers. The Index of Consumer Sentiment prepared by the Center declined sharply in 1973 and thus made it possible to predict the 1974 recession far in advance. After reaching a trough in December 1974 the Index advanced greatly, pointing toward the cyclical recovery. Chart 1 shows the movement of the Index of Consumer Sentiment in relation to the two recessions of the 1970s.

(Chart 1 about here)

By the autumn of 1976 the Index of Consumer Sentiment had reached its 1972 level and thus recovered its losses during the preceding cyclical downturn. Even though the Survey Research Center also collects extensive data about the reasons for the improvement or deterioration of consumer attitudes at a given time, the available information does not provide indications beyond a time span of nine or twelve months.

In this paper we shall enumerate a number of survey findings that may open up a much longer perspective. Each single item presented may perhaps be questioned as resulting from accidental circumstances or as being of little import. Taken together, however, the items appear impressive and suggest significant conclusions.

Chart 1

INDEX OF CONSUMER SENTIMENT*

February 1966 = 100

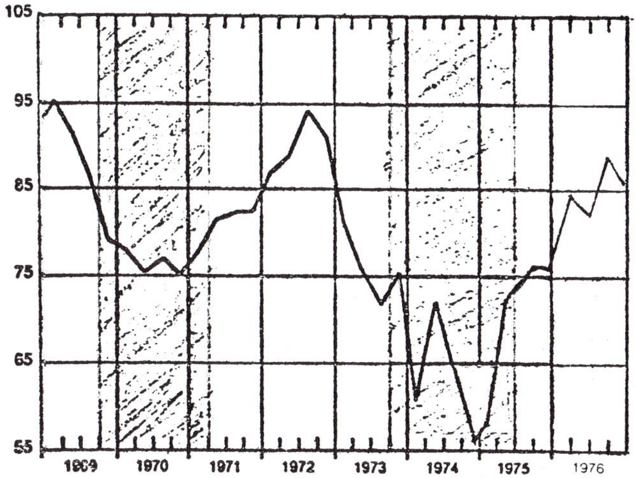

Shaded portions indicate recessions.

*of the Survey Research Center, University of Michigan.

The findings relate to a huge proportion of consumers and businessmen, sometimes most of them, sometimes the majority, at least the modal group, including well-to-do and highly-educated people. Most available data have been collected in the United States, although many of the points listed below also apply to West Germany and other highly industrialized countries. Quantitative data will not be presented here. We shall use the short time at our disposal to present a great variety of indications rather than to present details about a few of them. The documentation of the points made will follow in a book that will be published soon.

For briefness' sake we shall use two shorthand expressions: The expression "earlier" relates to the 1950s and 1960s, and most aptly to the years between 1955 and 1965; the expression "at present" or "today" relates to the 1970s, most particularly to 1973-76.

1. Earlier what was thought to be possible and what most people believed the government had a good chance to accomplish was price stability and full employment. Today inflation is thought to be inevitable and full employment impossible to attain. At present we ask only whether inflation will be rapid or slow, and whether unemployment will be large or small.

Consumers are especially concerned with the rising prices of energy, industrial raw materials and food. They also believe that they themselves have no means to resist price increases, while the business world no longer hesitates to raise prices even beyond increases in costs. Most Americans think that price increases are larger than those of wages and salaries.

The belief in the persistence of unemployment was greatly strengthened by the fact that in the recovery years of 1972-73 or 1975-76 there was but a relatively weak correlation between rising employment and declining unemployment. Business apparently prefers to increase the hours worked rather than to hire inexperienced workers, or workers who might possibly have to be laid off later. Those who are hit by the new type of unemployment are primarily young as well as old people, and blacks.

2. Earlier growth and a continuous improvement in the standard of living were taken for granted and viewed as our natural destiny. We live better than our parents did, and our children will live better than we do, so said the majority of American families. Very many middle- and lower-income families acquired their own homes as well as cars, appliances, and numerous gadgets that represented luxuries owned only by upper-income people in bygone years. The more people accomplished, the higher they raised their aspirations.

Today most people know that they must struggle in order not to lose ground, that is, to keep up with the increase in prices. Disappointment of expectations through an absence of real growth proved to be a painful experience in the last few years. Many younger workers, even those with high levels of education and steady jobs, feel virtually excluded from the market for one-family houses because of the high prices and high interest rates.

Education has ceased to be an easily marketable commodity or the major strategy for upward social mobility. Many young people who enter institutions of higher learning do so not knowing whether later they will be able to work in their field of interest and skill. While during most of the postwar years the labor market favored the worker and permitted him to exchange an unsatisfactory job for a more interesting or rewarding one, his freedom of choice has been greatly impaired in the 1970s.

Few people are aware, of course, of the limits-to-growth discussion, but doubt regarding the continued availability of material resources and, first of all, of energy has spread. Shortages are seen as possible.

3. "The rich get richer and the poor get poorer." This statement is often made and there are some objective data supporting it. The wages of the highest-paid blue-collar workers (employed in the steel and automobile industries) rose much more during the last few years than the wages of the lowest-paid workers (for instance, in the laundry and hotel industries). Similar differences are also often demonstrated among white-collar workers; very many people are aware of some professional people and corporation executives earning several hundred thousand dollars a year.

Feelings of inequity have grown. An increasing proportion of Americans believe that the compensation their job or occupation provides is less than they deserve.

In surveys with representative samples, family heads have frequently been asked whether they were better or worse off financially than a few years ago and whether they expected to be better or worse off a few years later. Upper-income people have always given more favorable answers to these questions than lower-income people. But the gap in the answers of these income groups has increased very greatly during the last few years.

4. In 1975-76 expectations about business conditions in the more distant future (say, five years from now) improved much less than expectations about the near future. Attitudes toward the government and big business improved little. Trust in the government, impaired primarily by Vietnam and Watergate, has not been restored. The ability of the government to fight inflation and unemployment successfully is now doubted by the majority

of people. Thirty years ago big business was admired by the great majority of Americans, but today it is widely viewed as profiteering or even corrupt.

5. There have been great changes in the prevailing work ethic. Confidence in the success of hard work has declined; the belief that one is in control of one's fate has been impaired. At the same time, a great many people demand more from their jobs than at earlier times. It is not enough that the job should provide adequate earnings; it also must be interesting and contribute to "self-fulfillment."

The growing desire for self-expression on the job extends beyond the insistence on interesting work; it is also directed toward more autonomy and less direct supervision. However, young workers frequently do not find what they desire. There are disquieting symptoms of a fading sense of being appropriately rewarded for one's work effort.

Strikingly similar changes in the work ethic are found in Germany. The traditional virtues of polite demeanor, subordination, diligence, modesty and respect for private property have lost ground. And in Germany too the feeling of control over one's fate has been diminishing, together with the conviction that hard work pays off; the proportion of those who prefer "a life without work" has grown.

The major change may be viewed as a shift from "early-industrial" values of discipline and hard work to "post-industrial" values of work involvement and satisfying work. No doubt this shift presents a grave challenge to existing work arrangements, leadership styles, and government employment programs. In our highly mechanized economy, many jobs have not become intrinsically more attractive; and the increasing number of workers who feel they have little to say suggests that changes in values and expectations are by no means fully accommodated by changes in the jobs.

6. Earlier economic developments were easily understood. During World War II full employment was understood as having resulted from the production of war materials. In the 1950s and 1960s the production of the many goods and services needed and wanted by consumers was thought to make the wheels turn and put money in people's pockets.

Today the rapid economic fluctuations appear ununderstandable. Within the span of just three years American automobile production fell from an annual rate of 10 1/2 million cars to 6 million and then rose again to 10 million. Why economic conditions and prospects appeared rosy one year and hopeless a year later--this could not be understood by the public, and the experts offered them no help.

Similarly regarding inflation and unemployment. Laymen were told for many years that there was a trade-off between the two. Then when unprecedented rates of inflation and very high unemployment occurred together, many people learned that the two reflected the same sickness. Yet in 1976 or 1977 numerous experts were quoted saying that fighting unemployment was fraught with danger because it would stimulate inflation.

7. Lack of understanding breeds uncertainty and stress. It also arouses quick and excessive reactions to new developments. A steady course of action and adherence to long-run plans are possible only when the future is seen with some degree of assurance. Today's disoriented consumers are volatile and shift from elation to dejection within a short time.

In the 1950s and 1960s, when the same respondents were asked the same questions about their economic expectations at six-month intervals, there was a high correlation between the two sets of answers. In 1975-77, however, there was practically no correlation. Within six months a substantial proportion shifted toward greater optimism, and another substantial proportion toward greater pessimism. Zigzag movements were also apparent in the Index of Consumer Sentiment as shown in Chart 1 and, more dramatically in contrast to the small fluctuations prior to the 1970s, in Chart 2. Between 1975 and 1977 the increase in consumer expenditures was repeatedly interrupted by plateaus that reflected consumer hesitation.

(Chart 2 about here)

8. During the last ten years there have been great changes in people's priorities. Americans are no longer concerned exclusively or even mainly with an increase in their level of consumption. On the list of priorities of the average family other concerns have gained in importance: a secure job; continuous income even in case of sickness, disability, and old age; appropriate forms of job and career; safety in one's home and on the street; and a neighborhood that does not deteriorate as the result of rapid changes in the human or physical environment. People today have turned their attention toward issues and amenities such as individualized treatment as patients; shopping facilities, public services and helpful neighbors within easy reach; less regimentation on the job. They are also concerned with their freedom to make important decisions for themselves, for instance, about the time of retirement, the timing of vacations and working hours; and also with their ability to correct a mismatch between themselves and their jobs, for instance, by way of adult education and retraining. One can see from the public protests against the construction of nuclear power plants and superhighways in all large industrial countries that the people do not want to be exposed to a barrage of innovations, nor to be confronted with involuntary changes in their physical or social environment.

These new desires are more than a passing fad. They begin to compete with, and even to threaten, the pursuit of more traditional ways

Chart 2

QUARTERLY FLUCTUATIONS OF THE
INDEX OF CONSUMER SENTIMENT

(In percent)

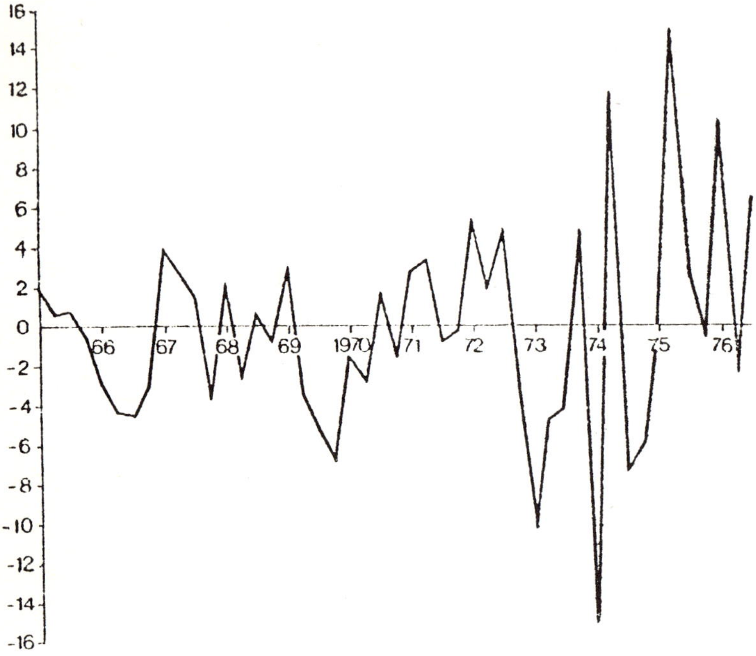

Source: Survey Research Center, University of Michigan.

of progress and growth which made them possible. Much thinking and debate is required in order to find a balance between an unchecked expansion of material production that ignores the new priorities, and an attempt to create a more humane economy that embraces them to the detriment of the present base of production. Rather than deplore these changes or try to legislate them away, we would do far better to adapt to them and structure our future accordingly.

* * *

Thus the current economic problems have deep roots. It appears that in the past few years we have witnessed the beginning of a new economic era in which we must expect a series of rapid fluctuations, periods of recession alternating with periods of recovery in fairly quick succession. Disorientation and uncertainty will end and stability be restored only if and when new constructive goals and strategies have been developed and readily accepted. Until that time ups and downs in the economy brought about by waves of optimism that are soon replaced by waves of pessimism appear more probable than stagnation, overall decline, or further growth.

Summary

We believe that the analysis of middle-range trends of the economy is necessary and possible. By middle-range trends they mean a time span of approximately ten years. The major reason why middle-range forecasting is seldom undertaken consists, we believe, of the absence of reliable methods for this task.

Neglecting cyclical changes, it appears that the climate for private investment in manufacturing has indeed deteriorated during the last five or ten years. This diagnosis is based on evidence revealing many similarities between the United States and Germany:

- The rate of profit of large corporations has declined significantly since 1961.

- Lower profit rates have left their imprint on corporate balance sheets. Symptomatic is the deterioration of the "dynamic debt ratio", the ratio of debt to cash flow.

- Until the late 1960s the production of goods benefited from a decline in the relative prices of energy and raw materials. The index for raw material prices on the world market started to rise faster than the general price level in the early 1970s, long before the oil embargo. Since that time the era of cheap raw materials has ended.

The impact of these changes in the operating conditions of the industrial sector was greatly reinforced by psychological factors, in particular a shift toward pessimism and disorientation on the part of businessmen, experts, and the public at large.

A study of changes in the attitudes and values held by the people provides some clues for an analysis of middle-range trends. There are two types of subjective belief systems that influence behavior and can be ascertained by survey research.

In this paper we shall enumerate a number of survey findings that may open up a much longer perspective.

1. Today inflation is thought to be inevitable and full employment impossible to attain.

2. We live better than our parents did, and our children will live better than we do.

3. Feelings of inequity have grown.

4. Expectations about business conditions in the more distant future improved much less than expectations about the near future.

5. Confidence in the success of hard work has declined.

6. Today the rapid economic fluctuations appear ununderstandable.

7. Lack of understanding breeds uncertainty and stress.

8. During the last ten years there have been great changes in people's priorities.

Thus the current economic problems have deep roots. It appears that in the past few years we have witnessed the beginning of a new economic aera in which we must expect a series of rapid fluctuations, periods of recession alternating with periods of recovery in fairly quick succession. Disorientation and uncertainty will end and stability be restored only if and when new constructive goals and strategies have been developed and readily accepted. Until that time ups and downs in the economy brought about by waves of optimism that are soon replaced by waves of pessimism appear more probable than stagnation, overall decline, or further growth.

J.T. BRIMER
UNIVERSITY OF NIGERIA
NSUKKA

THE CAUSAL STRUCTURE OF EXPECTATIONS IN THE CONFEDERATION OF BRITISH INDUSTRY INDUSTRIAL TRENDS SURVEY

ection 1 Introduction

This paper is part of a long term search for a odel that would describe the way businessmen formulate eir operational plans. The results reported here are entative and comments are invited.

.1 Definitions

An expectation, $\overline{X}$, represents a psychological attiude relating to the future course of an economic time eries, X, called the referent series. X is controllable f it can be influenced by an expecter's action. Expecttions are of two kinds: (a) forecasts or predictions elative to a series X which is not controllable by the xpecter, and (b) plans or intentions relative to a eries X which is controllable. (Theil, 1958)

.2 A Theory of Expectation Formulation

Figure 1 displays the basic elements of expectation ormulation as it relates to decision making. Expec- tions are based upon (a) information available ncerning factors causing changes in X which the excter cannot control and controllable factors, and (b) sumptions held by the expecter regarding the past be- vior of X and related factors falling under the rubric "general business conditions."

According to this theory, assumptions are the basis r an expectation which is modified in light of availle information. The resulting expectation is data for cision making leading to observed consequences which nstitute information for the next period.

3 Causal Hierarchy of Expectations

Plans are based upon forecasts. This statement plies the existence of a hierarchy of expectations. pectations of order one are forecasts depending upon

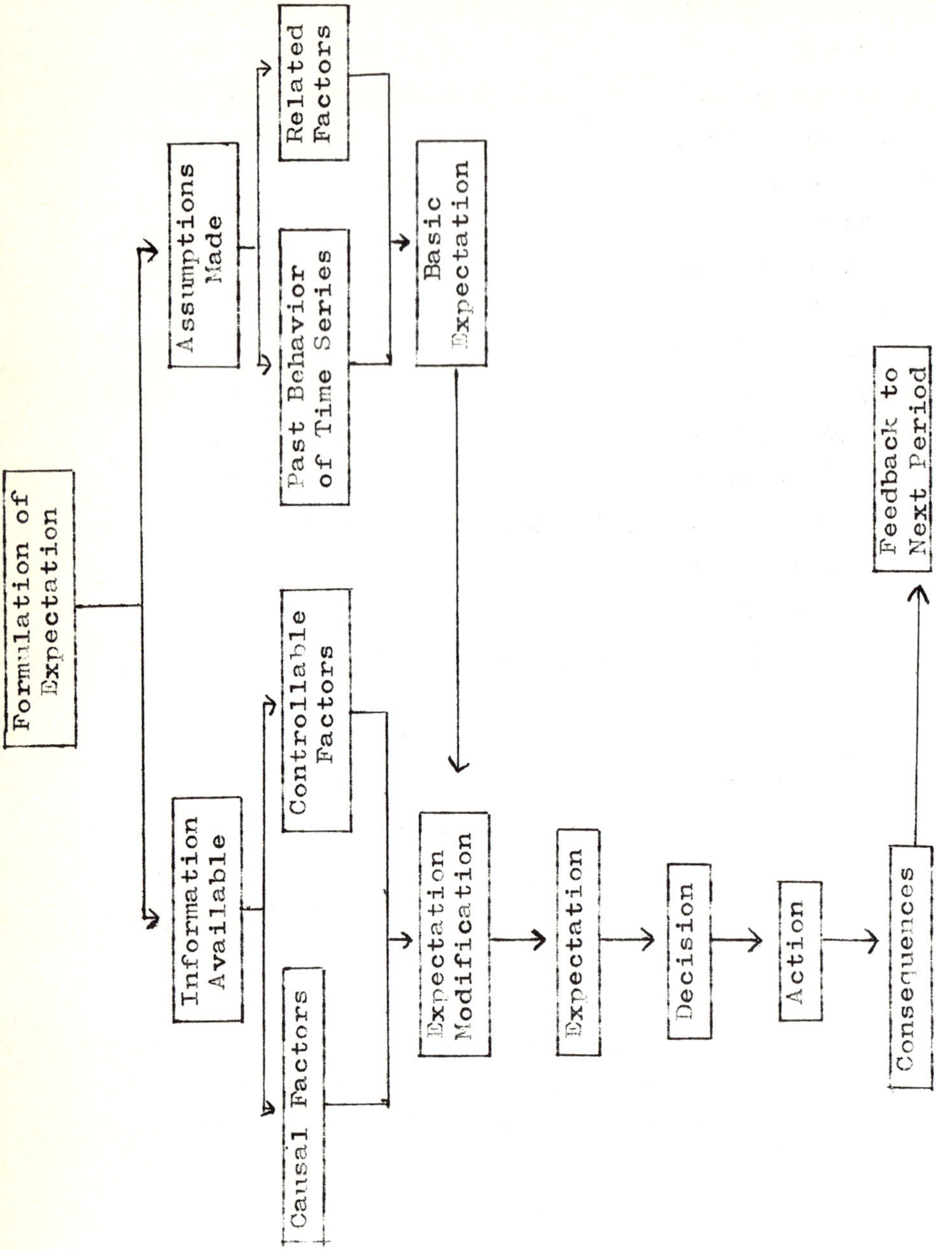
Formulation of Expectation
Assumptions Made
Information Available
Past Behavior of Time Series
Related Factors
Causal Factors
Controllable Factors
Basic Expectation
Expectation Modification
Expectation
Decision
Action
Consequences
Feedback to Next Period

Figure 1

ssumptions and information concerning uncontrollable ausal factors. Expectations of higher orders depend ncreasingly upon expectations of lower orders and controllable factors as well. (Theil, 1958) Expectation ormulation is a cumulative process with expectation uilding upon expectation, as reflected in the following et of expressions:

$\bar{X}_1 = \bar{X}_1$(Assumptions, Information)

$\bar{X}_2 = \bar{X}_2(\bar{X}_1$, Assumptions, Information)

....

....

....

$\bar{X}_n = \bar{X}_n(\bar{X}_1, \ldots \bar{X}_{n-1}$, Assumptions, Information)

here $\bar{X}_i$, i = 1,....,n is an expectation of order n.

4 The CBI Industrial Trends Survey

The data utilized in this study is obtained from e Confederation of British Industries (CBI) Industrial ends Survey. The survey was introduced in 1958 and conducted quarterly during the months of January, ril, July and October. The questions asked in the sury concern the direction of change experienced over the st quarter and expected over the next quarter in terms an increase, decrease, or no change. The data is in e form of percentages weighted according to the size the respondant's labor force.

Information on the following variables is available: mbers employed (E), value of new orders (N), value of tput (Q), stock of raw materials and brought in pplies (HR), stocks of finished goods (HF), average sts per unit of output (C), average prices at which mestic orders are booked (P) and optimism concerning e general business situation in the respondant's dustry (OPT).

Data employed in this paper involves 38 surveys rminating in October, 1976. Some adjustments in the data were necessary. The January, 1971 survey was not held because of the postal strike. To insure continuety in the time series, these values were linearly interpolated. In addition, the inventory question on the October, 1968 questionnaire did not distinguish between HR and HF, so the total was distributed according to average percentages in the immediately preceeding and succeeding surveys.

2.5 Specification of Model for the CBI Data

Applying the ideas developed above to the variables covered in the CBI survey, a model of expectation formulation can be postulated as follows:

$$\overline{P}=B_{11}N+B_{12}OPT+B_{13}C+B_{14}P+B_{15}(P_{-1}-\overline{P}_{-1})+B_{16}(P-\overline{P}_{-1})+B_{17}t+e_1$$

$$\overline{N}=B_{21}\overline{P}+B_{22}N+B_{23}(N-\overline{N}_{-1})+B_{24}(N-\overline{N}_{-1})+B_{25}t+e_2$$

$$\overline{Q}=B_{31}\overline{P}+B_{32}\overline{N}+B_{33}HF+B_{34}C+B_{35}Q+B_{36}(Q_{-1}-\overline{Q}_{-1})+B_{37}(Q-\overline{Q}_{-1})$$
$$+B_{38}t+e_3$$

$$\overline{HF}=B_{41}\overline{P}+B_{42}\overline{N}+B_{43}\overline{Q}+B_{44}HF+B_{45}(HF_{-1}-\overline{HF}_{-1})+B_{46}(HF-\overline{HF}_{-1})$$
$$+B_{47}t+e_4$$

$$\overline{E}=B_{51}P+B_{52}N+B_{53}Q+B_{54}HF+B_{55}E+B_{56}(E_{-1}-E_{-1})+B_{57}(E-E_{-1})$$
$$+B_{58}t+e_5$$

$$\overline{C}=B_{61}\overline{P}+B_{62}\overline{N}+B_{63}\overline{Q}+B_{64}\overline{HF}+B_{65}\overline{E}+B_{66}HR+B_{67}C+B_{68}(C_{-1}-\overline{C}_{-1})$$
$$+B_{69}(C-\overline{C}_{-1})+B_{610}t+e_6$$

$$\overline{HR}=B_{71}\overline{P}+B_{72}\overline{N}+B_{73}\overline{Q}+B_{74}\overline{HF}+B_{75}\overline{E}+B_{76}\overline{C}+B_{77}HR+B_{78}(HR_{-1}-\overline{HR}_{-1})$$
$$+B_{79}(HR-\overline{HR}_{-1})+B_{710}t+e_7$$

The variables were identified above. A bar over a variable indicates that this variable is an expectation of a referent series. The subscript -1 indicates a one quarter lag. t is a linear time trend variable.

The model specified in this section must be justified on the basis of (a) the ordering of the equations nd (b) the format of the equations.

.6 The Ordering of Expectations in the CBI Survey

The order in which the equations appear is deter-
ined by the order of the expectation which each equation
eeks to explain. Since little is known empitically re-
arding the expectations hierarchy, the order postulated
n the model appearing above is hypothetical and one
spect of the investigation presently underway.

Some considerations regarding the postulated
rdering are the following:

(1) $\overline{P}$ is of order one. Static equilibrum theory
ndicates that price and quantity are determined simul-
aneously. But this need not be true for expectations.
Hastay, 1960) Price is generally considered to be a
ignal variable related to market forces. The degree of
ontrollability of price is limited even in this era of
dministered sticky prices. Much of the inflation
iterature is directed toward analysis of market forces
nich determine price levels.

(2) $\overline{N}$ is considered to be of order two because it
s an indication of demand pressure and should be very
ensitive to price changes. Thus, it is presumed that
would take into account $\overline{P}$ as an indication of demand
ressure.

(3) $\overline{Q}$ is of order three. According to the pro-
uction smoothing hypothesis, the cost of production
nd the cost of holding inventories will be minimized if
roduction is not changes in response to changes in
emand, but rather changes in demand are met by
ncreasing or drawing down inventories. (Modigliani and
ohn, 1955) Inventories are a buffer between demand
d supply changes.

Also, actual interviews with businessmen have in-
cated that a typical reaction to a change in demand

is to wait and see if the change in sales is transitory or permanent. (Eisner, 1960) If the change is transitory, then production plans may remain unaffected as implied by production smoothing.

These arguments imply that in formulating production plans, inventories and production costs must be considered as constraining influences.

(4) $\overline{HF}$ is of order four. The speculative, transactions and precautionary motives for holding inventories imply that selling price expectations and production plans both influence finished goods inventories planning.

(5) $\overline{E}$ is of order five. The "labor hoarding hypothesis" implies that businessmen tend to keep a basic labor fource on hand as a necessary overhead expense to avoid production adjustment costs. Changes in this basic labor force might occur when a sales trend has been percieved as permanent and both production plans and inventory plans must revised. Only then would a change in planned employment follow.

Also, employment plans might be sticky relative to inventory plans because the cost of changing the basic work force may be higher than changing inventories within certain limits imposed by existing capacity. Thus in order for employment plans to change, all possibilities for absorbing transitory sales changes from inventory stocks must have been exhausted.

(6) $\overline{C}$ is of order six. Planned costs change in response to changes in production, inventory and employment plans. This is the conventional short run adjustment by a firm with fixed plant and equipment confronted by a change in demand.

(7) $\overline{HR}$ is of order seven. The primary reason for this hypothesis is that rational businessmen have learned from experience that in times of rising sales

hey must compete against other businessmen for avail-
ble stocks thereby incurring higher raw material costs n the short run. In times of falling sales they can tilize present stocks of raw materials. Thus the raw aterials inventories experience is an important ele- ent in cost plans.

At the same time, cost plans are an element in raw aterials inventory plans because of the short run spec- lative element. Changes in $\overline{C}$ lead to changes in $\overline{HR}$.

.7 Psychological Nature of CBI Data

The above section justified the specified ordering f expectations on the basis of conventional economic heory which rests upon data expressed in absolute num- rical terms and not direction of change data.

Direction of change data represent an initial stage n a mental process which terminates in verbalization of xpectations in numerical terms. No direct economic vidence exists for this proposition, but general support rom psychological literature exists. (Brimer, 1972) hus the use of direction of change data in conjunction ith conventional economic theory employs variables hich are not as highly refined as numerical expressions ıt yet represent the same psychological entities. owever, a methodological question remains unresolved. ould a theory rejected on the basis of direction of hange data also be rejected on the basis of conven- ional data?

.8 Model Specification and the Theory of Expectation Formulation

Viewed from the standpoint of Figure 1, the variables each equation in 2.5 can be classified according to e scheme shown in Figure 2.

The notion of controllability involves the impact new information regarding the referent series upon

Equation Number	Causal Factors	Past Behavior of Referent Series	Related Factors
1	N, C	P	OPT
2	$\overline{P}$	N	
3	HF, C, $\overline{P}$, $\overline{N}$	Q	
4	$\overline{P}$, $\overline{N}$, $\overline{Q}$	HF	
5	$\overline{P}$, $\overline{N}$, $\overline{Q}$, $\overline{HF}$	E	
6	HR, $\overline{N}$, $\overline{Q}$, $\overline{HF}$, $\overline{C}$	C	
7	$\overline{P}$, $\overline{N}$, $\overline{Q}$, $\overline{HF}$, $\overline{E}$, $\overline{C}$		

Figure 2

expectations. If there is little impact and expectations are not influenced, then the referent series is highly controllable in the sense that instrumental variables exist such that the referent series can be corrected and brought into line with expected results. On the other hand, if new information has an impact upon expectations such that a very large adjustment results, then it may be assumed that expected controllability over the referent series is nil. The concept of expected controllability is closely related to the degree of confidence with which expectations are held.

One operational measure of expected controllability rests upon the impact of the quantities $(X_{-1}-\overline{X}_{-1})$ and $(X-\overline{X}_{-1})$ on $\overline{X}$. The former measures the net percent of survey respondants who predict an increase in X at time t-1, and the latter indicates the net percent who predicted an increase in t-1 at time t-1 and realized an increase in time period t. By comparing these two quantities to $\overline{X}$ it is possible to assess the impact of information gained between t-1 and t upon $\overline{X}$. By regressing $\overline{X}$ on $(X_{-1}-\overline{X}_{-1})$ and $\overline{X}$ on $(X-\overline{X}_{-1})$ the coefficients A_1 and A_2 result. A_1 measures the influence of the xpectation made at t-1 on that made at t. A_2 measures he amount and direction of revision in the expectation t t given information about the actual trend. When here is little revision in $\overline{X}$ as indicated by the relaive values of A_1 and A_2, then the degree of controlability is high. Many combinations of A_1 and A_2 are ossible. High controllability is indicated when A_1 nd A_2 are approximately equal or when A_1 is slightly arger than A_2. In other cases the degree of controlability is low in view of a distinct revision pattern.

$A_1 + A_2$ is an indication of the degree of trend eversion present in the set of expectations. (Brimer, 975)

In general, forecasts are good indicators of the ssumptions upon which expectations are based. The ajor influence that existed during the sample period s persistent double digit inflation. Thus, a continal growth in P would be an obvious assumption made by ll expecters in the sample period.

ection 3 Statistical Results

.1 Procedures Employed

Four regression procedures were employed in tempting to fit the model in 3.5. Procedure I inolved using the absolute balance data defined as perent increase response less percent decrease response d OLS applied directly to each equation. Procedure II volved substitution of the predicted balance from ch successive equation for the absolute balance callated directly from the data by use of the estimate uation. Procedure III was the same as Procedure I cept that the relative balance defined as the absolute lance divided by the percent of no change responses s used. Procedure IV was the same as Procedure II cept that relative balances were employed.

3.2 Statistical Results

Tables 1 - 7 present the statistical results. The significance values for testing the null hypothesis are given at the bottom of each table. $F(n_1,n_2)$, $X^2(n)$, $T_1(n_3)$. $T_2(n_4)$ and d_u are for F, b, T, TR, and d respectively. The symbols used in the tables are identified as follows: B is the beta regression coefficient, T is the T statistic for the partial regression coefficient, RT is the T statistic for Spearman's rank correlation coefficient between the indicated independent variable and the residuals e, $\bar{R}^2$ is the adjusted multiple coefficient of determination, F is the F statistic for the equation fit, d is the Durben-Watson statistic, b is Bartletts chi square statistic for multicollinearity. (Farrar and Glauber, 1967) ME is the percentage of variation in the independent variable which is explained by the presence of multicollinearity, (Theil, 1971), and MSE is the mean square error.

Comparing the RT and d statistics with the signicance values T_2 and d_u at the bottom of Tables 1 - 7 indicates that serial correlation and heteroscedasticity are not significant. However, multicollinearity is extreme as indicated by the large values of b relative to the five percent level significance value for $X^2(\ )$. Given the above observation regarding the place of assumptions in formulating expectations, high multicollinearity is predicted by the theory.

Given that the model specified is recursive and since none of the RT's are significant, then the application of OLS in the presence of high multicollinearity yields unbiased B's (Blalock, 1969). Also the application of OLS directly to each equation does not introduce simultaneous equation bias. (Koutsgyiannis, 1973)

3 Choice of Procedure

Inspection of Tables 1 - 7 indicate that the $\bar{R}^2$ atistic is generally low for procedures II and IV mpared to $\bar{R}^2$ for procedures I and II. Except for the w order equation, $\bar{R}^2$ is roughly equilivent for both ocedures. On this basis procedure I and II appear to ovide better fits of the model to the data than produres II and IV.

With respect to multicollinearity, both procedure and III have roughly equal ME figures. The only exptions are the new order equation, where ME for produre I produces a lower ME, and the raw materials ventory equation where the ME for procedure III is wer. As a rough overall measure of relative multillinearity between procedures, the ratio of the erage ME to the average $\bar{R}^2$ for procedures was computed d compared. For both cases, this figure is approxately equal (78 percent).

Looking next at F for procedures I and III it can seen from Tables 1 - 7 that in five out of seven ses F for procedure I is larger than that for produre III. In one case, they are approximately equal. e average value for F for both procedures is equal bout 25.00). The b statistic indicates that in four t of seven cases b for procedure I is lower than for ocedure III. In one case, b is approximately the ne for each procedure. Comparing the average b for th procedures, b for I is a bit lower than that for (208.43 versus 224.34).

Based upon the above observations, procedure I is rginally superior to procedure II.

Note that when the estimated value of the expecion is used as a regressor as was done in procedures and IV, MSE tends to increase. This result is puzzling.

3.4 Discussion of Parameter Results

In the presence of multicollinearity, the probability of rejecting a true hypothesis is increased. To guard against this possibility and since F for procedure I and III is generally significant, then if B for procedure I and II is stable or if T is significant then the variable in question will be considered to exert a significant influence.

Results for each equation can be summarized as follows:

(a) Price equation: significant variables are C, P and t. Controllability is low.

(b) New order equation: N is the only significant variable, a surprising result. Controllability is low.

(c) Value of output equation: significant variables are $\overline{N}$, HF, C and Q. The small value of B for Q indicates production smoothing. Some evidence of controllability exists, but the coefficients are unstable.

(d) Finished goods inventory equation: significant variables are $\overline{N}$ and $\overline{Q}$. $\overline{P}$ appears to have a significant negative influence but its B is very unstable. Controllability is low as implied by the buffer stock motive.

(e) Employment equation: significant variables are $\overline{HF}$ and E as implied by the labor hoarding hypothesis. Controllability would appear to be high.

(f) Unit cost equation: significant variables are $\overline{P}$, $\overline{E}$, HR and C. Controllability appears to be high since the influence of new information is nil, but the coefficient is unstable. The -.00 figure denotes a very small number.

(g) Raw materials equation: significant variables are $\overline{P}$, $\overline{N}$, $\overline{Q}$, $\overline{C}$ and HR possibly. Controllability seems be low.

The interaction pattern of the variables is presented in the following diagram:

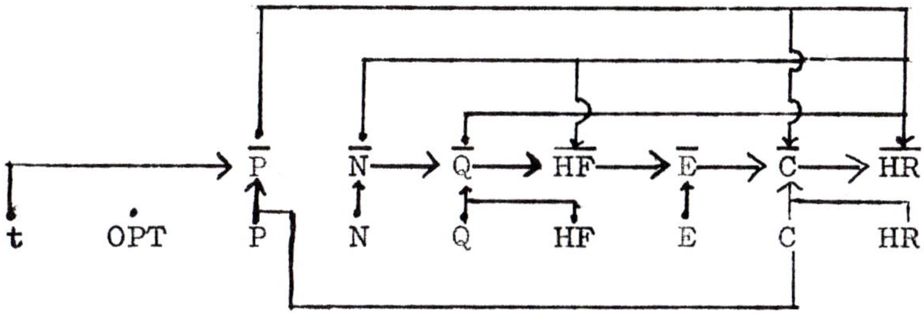

Some remarks regarding this diagram are: (a) $\overline{P}$ seems be discounted as a significant factor in most plans. e element of demand pressure seems to be the principle gnal element. (b) The two inventory variables are ttle affected by past inventory changes. (c) The stulated ordering of expectations appears to be pported. (d) OPT appears to exercise little influence!

ction 4 Conclusions

On the whole, it would appear that the model specied is valid. Yet the presence of multicollinearity ouds the issue and yields unstable coefficients in me cases, and in other cases coefficients are stable d significant. Also, it is difficult to distinguish tween procedure I and III.

Inventory variables tend to be subject to low conollability while other operating variables seem to be ntrollable. The influence of production smoothing, bor hoarding, and inventory price expectation are ident.

TABLE 1 PRICE EQUATION REGRESSION RESULTS

	N	OPT	C	P	$(P_{-1}-\overline{P}_{-1})$	$(P-\overline{P}_{-1})$	t
				Procedure I			
B	.059	.043	.174	.561	-.024	.057	.267
T	.78	.66	.93	2.88	-.41	.89	2.82
RT	-.008	.139	.414	.60	-.07	-1.06	.72
$\overline{R}^2$ = .90, F = 52.10, d = 1.90, b = 155.50, ME = .87, MSE = 41.36							
				Procedure III			
B	-.05	-.14	.24	.19	-.17	.18	.54
T	-.59	-2.04	1.22	.71	-2.36	1.90	4.24
RT	-.49	.21	-1.43	-1.65	1.02	-.57	-.49
$\overline{R}^2$ = .88, F = 41.60, d = 1.68, b = 163.03, ME = .80, MSE = 10.35							

Significance Values at the .05 Level:

$F(30,7) = 5.98$, $X^2(28) = 41.33$, $T_1(30) = 2.04$, $T_2(36) = 2.02$, $d_u = 1.79$

	$\overline{P}$	N	$(N-\overline{N}_{-1})$	$(N-N_{-1})$	t
			Procedure I		
B	.04	.64	-.59	.24	-.05
T	.16	4.31	-3.09	1.13	-.26
RT	.32	-.60	-.14	.43	-.04
$\overline{R}^2$ = .51, F = 9.40, d = 2.34, b = 91.20, ME = .22, MSE = 184.01					
			Procedure II		
B	.12	.68	-.49	.20	.01
T	.95	4.35	-2.61	.88	.05
RT	.39	-.64	.30	.36	-.14
$\overline{R}^2$ = .43, F = 7.13, d = 2.01, b = 49.5, ME = .12, MSE = 206.71					
			Procedure III		
B	-.32	.67	-.37	.01	.24
T	-1.31	2.83	1.54	.03	1.05
RT	-.48	-.76	.07	.11	-.01
$\overline{R}^2$ = .40, F = 6.27, d = 2.32, b = 122.13, ME = .28, MSE = 19.03					
			Procedure IV		
B	.02	.67	-.45	.16	.00
T	.14	2.57	-2.08	.49	.00
RT	-1.03	-.44	-.02	.06	-.16
$\overline{R}^2$ = .30, F = 4.52, d = 2.19, b = 76.27, ME = .20, MSE = 19.26					

Significance Values at the .05 Level:

$F(32,5) = 4.50$, $X^2(15) = 24.99$, $T_1(32) = 2.04$, $T_2(36) = 2.02$, $d_u = 1.76$

TABLE 3 VALUE OF OUTPUT EQUATION REGRESSION RESULTS

	$\overline{P}$	$\overline{N}$	HF	C	Q	$(Q_{-1}-\overline{Q}_{-1})$	$(Q-\overline{Q}_{-1})$	t
					Procedure I			
B	.03	.93	.12	.27	.03	.05	.21	-.02
T	.16	11.47	1.60	1.47	.35	.51	2.03	-.17
RT	-.12	.16	-.05	-.12	.01	-.08	.05	-.04
$\overline{R}^2$ = .83, F = 24.90, d = 2.00, b = 173.34, ME = .25, MSE = 54.12								
					Procedure II			
B	-.07	.67	.06	.17	.01	.20	.07	.05
T	2.73	.65	.34	.04	.00	1.00	.31	.19
RT	.62	-.19	.82	-.49	-.79	1.47	1.18	-.64
$\overline{R}^2$ = .25, F = 2.75, d = 1.91, b = 122.07, ME = .25, MSE = 242.51								
					Procedure III			
B	.23	.93	.11	.14	.08	.13	.04	.01
T	1.22	10.49	1.17	.93	.68	1.13	.33	.11
RT	-.37	.63	-.61	-.48	-.53	.48	.01	-.04
$\overline{R}^2$ = .80, F = 20.10, d = 1.86, b = 164.13, ME = .24, MSE = 7.39								
					Procedure IV			
B	-.03	.50	.04	-.04	.01	.35	-.18	.34
T	-.21	1.84	.24	-.17	.03	1.46	-.66	1.29
RT	-1.59	-.98	.46	-.73	-1.29	1.28	.23	-.46
$\overline{R}^2$ = .15, F = 1.96, d = 1.99, b = 127.44, ME = .17, MSE = 31.78								

Significance Values at the .05 Level:

$F(29,8) = 3.08$, $X^2(36) = 55.7$, $T_1(29) = 2.04$, $T_2(36) = 2.02$, $d_u = 1.79$

	$\overline{P}$	$\overline{N}$	$\overline{Q}$	HF	$(HF_{-1}-\overline{HF}_{-1})$	$(HF-\overline{HF}_{-1})$	t
				Procedure I			
B	-.54	-.09	.74	.13	-.23	.12	.11
T	-2.19	-.30	2.33	.74	-.95	.41	.44
RT	-1.58	.46	.10	.68	.52	.51	-.81
$\overline{R}^2$ = .41, F = 5.01, d = 1.84, b = 170.35, ME = .35, MSE = 59.38							
				Procedure II			
B	.11	.03	.32	-.01	-.50	.35	-.32
T	.63	.07	.71	-.06	-1.58	.89	-1.40
RT	.62	-.19	-.50	1.76	.59	1.06	-.77
$\overline{R}^2$ = .08, F = 1.62, d = 1.89, b = 162.91, ME = .12, MSE = 93.33							
				Procedure III			
B	-.174	-.05	.70	-.01	-.21	.11	-.29
T	-.62	-.15	2.31	-.06	-.86	.38	-1.19
RT	-.50	.30	-.27	.67	.73	.56	-.85
$\overline{R}^2$ = .37, F = 4.33, d = 1.72, b = 168.36, ME = .36, MSE = 3.35							
				Procedure IV			
B	.07	.02	.34	-.09	-.39	.25	-.41
T	.40	.05	.81	-.37	-1.21	.65	-1.43
RT	-.42	-.04	-.44	.87	1.05	1.12	-.70
$\overline{R}^2$ = .00, F = 1.14, d = 1.91, b = 150.98, ME = .08, MSE = 5.29							

Significance Values at the .05 Level:

$F(30,7) = 3.38$, $X^2(28) = 41.33$, $T_1(30) = 2.04$, $T_2(36) = 2.02$, $d_u = 1.79$

TABLE 5 EMPLOYMENT EQUATION REGRESSION RESULTS

	$\overline{P}$	$\overline{N}$	$\overline{Q}$	$\overline{HF}$	E	$(E_{-1}-\overline{E}_{-1})$	$(E-\overline{E}_{-1})$	t
				Procedure I				
B	.00	.05	.09	.48	.51	.19	-.03	.02
T	.00	.27	.41	2.11	4.21	1.96	-.26	.16
RT	.52	.07	.49	.91	.40	-.37	.50	.64
$\overline{R}^2$ = .79, F = 19.5, d = 1.86, b = 214.13, ME = .70, MSE = 23.94								
				Procedure II				
B	-.01	-.26	.69	.14	.36	-.05	-.09	-.31
T	-.09	-.55	1.55	.54	1.81	-.22	-.49	-1.21
RT	.99	.18	.39	.63	-.02	.73	-.18	.09
$\overline{R}^2$ = .44, F = 4.91, d = 2.11, b = 187.92, ME = -.06, MSE = 164.95								
				Procedure III				
B	.19	.48	-.11	.22	.54	.19	.01	.02
T	1.15	2.54	-.54	1.21	4.58	2.26	.07	-.10
RT	.81	.30	.08	.24	.27	.07	-.11	-.05
$\overline{R}^2$ = .79, F = 19.3, d = 1.73, b = 204.12, ME = .64, MSE = 2.33								
				Procedure IV				
B	.01	-.23	.60	.28	.44	.02	-.16	-.29
T	.16	-.75	1.73	1.08	2.07	.12	-.9	-1.00
RT	.26	.90	.48	1.27	.41	.38	-.13	.17
$\overline{R}^2$ = .51, F = 6.17, d = 2.14, b = 187.67, ME = .49, MSE = 5.20								

Significance Values at the .05 Level:

$F(29,8) = 3.08$, $X^2(36) = 43.77$, $T_1(29) = 2.04$, $T_2(36) = 2.02$, $d_u = 1.79$

	$\overline{P}$	$\overline{N}$	$\overline{Q}$	$\overline{HF}$	$\overline{E}$	HR	C	$(C_{-1}-\overline{C}_{-1})$	$(C-\overline{C}_{-1})$	t
					Procedure I					
B	.343	.097	-.16	.16	-.17	.12	.51	-.10	-.00	.17
T	1.83	.77	-1.08	1.91	-1.28	.18	3.55	-1.30	-.02	1.22
RT	-.29	.66	.78	1.39	.24	.17	-.69	-.63	-.11	.06
$\overline{R}^2$ = .90, F = 37.91, d = 2.03, b = 305.13, ME = .87, MSE = 23.94										
					Procedure II					
B	-.11	.09	.05	-.06	-.16	.12	.67	-.11	.09	.21
T	-1.94	.56	.14	-.49	-.37	.63	5.50	-1.65	-1.15	.85
RT	-.54	.17	.53	-.25	-.00	-.02	-.46	-.47	.32	.23
$\overline{R}^2$ = .89, F = 33.28, d = 2.14, b = 343.93, ME = .81, MSE = 27.03										
					Procedure III					
B	.34	.15	-.41	.06	-.13	.19	.34	-.17	.24	.36
T	3.01	1.39	-3.99	1.07	-1.31	2.56	1.59	2.76	1.26	3.20
RT	-.15	-.07	.01	.46	-.31	-.24	-.59	.09	-1.20	.18
$\overline{R}^2$ = .94, F = 72.32, d = 2.22, b = 372.57, ME = .88, MSE = 41.36										
					Procedure IV					
B	-.06	-.11	-.01	-.08	.02	.21	.84	-.13	-.17	.32
T	-.99	-.64	-.03	-.46	.05	.98	2.47	-1.33	-.60	.93
RT	.28	.22	.47	-.08	.38	1.45	-1.07	-1.07	-1.83	.22
$\overline{R}^2$ = .86, F = 25.00, d = 1.89, b = 435.92, ME = .86, MSE = 111.98										

Significance Values at the .05 Level:

$F(27,10) = 2.7$, $X^2(55) = 67.5$, $T_1(27) = 2.05$, $T_2(36) = 2.02$, $d_u = 1.76$

TABLE 7 RAW MATERIALS EQUATION REGRESSION RESULTS

	$\overline{P}$	$\overline{N}$	$\overline{Q}$	$\overline{HF}$	$\overline{E}$	$\overline{C}$	HR	$(HR_{-1}-\overline{HR}_{-1})$	$(HR-\overline{HR}_{-1})$	t
					Procedure I					
B	.17	.16	.45	.12	.22	-.32	.16	-.01	-.12	.04
T	.97	.89	2.75	1.25	1.51	-2.06	1.39	-.15	-.93	.32
RT	-.28	-.68	-.32	-.149	.00	-.28	-.09	.77	.29	-.36
$\overline{R}^2$ = .90, F = 34.68, d = 2.34, b = 349.38. ME = .87, MSE = 16.52										
					Procedure II					
B	-.20	-.66	2.47	-.07	-1.74	-.31	.99	-.52	.01	-1.12
T	-1.76	-1.38	2.66	-.26	-1.94	-1.19	2.30	-1.56	.04	-1.99
RT	.90	.01	-.03	.02	-.61	.00	-1.02	-.05	-.01	.10
$\overline{R}^2$ = .58, F = 6.37, d = 2.33, b = 431.39, ME = .38, MSE = 68.04										
					Procedure III					
B	.16	.22	.40	.20	.10	-.31	.22	.08	.10	.04
T	.65	1.03	1.77	1.47	.54	-1.06	1.33	.46	-.58	.26
RT	.90	.80	1.53	.23	.46	1.02	.47	-.12	-.35	.74
$\overline{R}^2$ = .82, F = 18.8, d = 1.99, b = 376.04, ME = .82, MSE = 1.69										
					Procedure IV					
B	-.31	-.56	2.10	.19	-1.45	-.139	.79	-.66	.34	-1.31
T	-2.60	-1.40	2.33	.47	-1.56	-.32	1.71	-1.74	.97	-1.79
RT	-.60	-.73	-.41	-.03	-.73	-.14	-1.20	.06	-.30	-.15
$\overline{R}^2$ = .47, F = 4.53, d = 2.18, b = 455.34, ME = .25, MSE = 5.02										

Significance Values at the .05 Level:

$F(27,10) = 2.7$, $X^2(55) = 67.5$, $T_1(27) = 2.05$, $T_2(36) = 2.02$, $d_u = 1.76$

Summary

This paper specifies and estimates the parameters of recussive model of expectation formulation utilizing ta from the CBI survey.

The model is based upon the concept of an ordering expectations. Forecasts are of order one, while ans are of higher orders. The basic premise is that ans grow out of forecasts. This is the foundation r the model. The model postualtes that price is a rst order expectation. New orders are of order two, llowed in turn by the value of output, finished goods ventories, employment, cost of production and raw terials inventories.

The model was tested using direction of change data. ur regression procedures were followed utilizing two finitions of the data. Prodedure I used the absolute lance. Procedure II utilized the estimated values of pectations derived from procedure I. Procedures III d IV were simular to I and II except that the relative lance was employed. Multicollinearity was found to be problem. Its source is probably the fact that plans e made on the basis of a common set of assumptions. cording to the $\bar{R}^2$ criteria, the model fits the data ry well. Tests for simultaneous equation bias, teroscadisticity, and serial correlation were negative.

The main conclusion of the study is that the model

cannot be rejected by the data. One interesting substantive conclusion which arises from the study is that expecters seem to have discounted price and general business conditions as significant determinants of plans in a time of sever inflation. Also, the results of the study are consistent with other well known results. This lends further weight to the model's validity.

References

·imer, J.T. 1972. The Psychological Smoothing Hypothesis of Forecast Formulation. Ann Arbor: University Microfilms.

·imer, J.T. 1975. The relevance of the adaptive and rational expectations hypothesis in explanations of business tendency survey data. IFO-Studien (forthcoming)

.sner, R. 1960. Coment, The Quality and Economic Significance of Anticipations Data. Edited by C. Holt, F. Modigiliani, and G. Orcutt. PP. 139-142. Princeton: Princeton University Press.

rrar, D.E. and R.R. Glauber. 1967. Multicollinearity in Regression Analysis: The problem revisited. Review of Economics and Statistics, 49. pp.92-107.

stay, Millard. 1960. The Formation of Business Expectations About Operating Variables. The Quality and Economic Significance of Anticipations Data. Edited by C. Holt, F. Modigiliani, and G. Orcutt. pp. 91-139. Princeton: Princeton University Press.

utsoyiannis, A. 1973. Theory of Econometrics. New York: Macmillan.

digiliani, F. and F. M. Hohn. 1958. Production planning over time and the nature of the expectation and planning horizon. Econometrica, 23, pp. 46-66.

eil, H. 1958. Economic Forecasts and Policy. Amsterdan: North Holland Publishing Co.

eil, H. 1971. Principles of Econometrics. New York: Wiley.

K. VOGLER
IFO INSTITUTE FOR ECONOMIC RESEARCH
MUNICH

CONTENT AND DETERMINANTS OF JUDGEMENTAL AND EXPECTATIONAL VARIABLES IN THE IFO BUSINESS SURVEY

1. Introduction

Business surveys, as a rule, work with a minimum of pre-set definitions and methods as regards the wording of questions. This procedure seems necessary in order to obtain unbiassed judgments and anticipations of entrepreneurs. Moreover, the wording of the question is chosen so as to achieve as flexible an adjustment as possible to specific features of the respective branches and enterprises. The form of the survey, too, ultimately calls for brevity because, in the long run, the addressed panel of entrepreneurs and executive employees will hardly be inclined to answer long and complicated questions.

Any interpretation of business survey data may therefore not be based on precisely defined concepts. As a result, we have sometimes a large scope for interpretation. The present study aimed at an empirically significant definition of the contents of concepts, of comparative quantities and determinants of the most important variables of the Ifo Business Survey. This was done by means of a written poll of all participants in the Ifo Business Survey in industry. These questionaires gathered information on the following four groups of problems:

1. The contents of different concepts of the Ifo Business Survey are not clearly defined. This particularly applies to Ifo's specific concept of the "business situation" but also to other terms, such as "orders in hand". The problem thus was to find out the content attached by the respondents of the Business Survey to a specific concept.

2. Changes in entrepreneurial judgments or anticipations, as a rule, have concrete causes. They reflect real processes judged in relation to the aims of the enterprise rather than psychic changes. The question therefore asks for information on the type of process guid-

ing the enterprise in its judgment and on the indicators being used for this purpose.

3. Calculations or estimates of seasonal movements are required for answering individual questions (e.g. capacity utilization, production months accounted for by the order book, production plans, etc). The enterprises were therefore asked as to which procedures and indicators were being used in these calculations.

4. The reliability of the results essentially depends on the staff structure of the panel, i.e. of the position and function of respondents within their enterprise. This structure was to be ascertained and, in addition, some reporting habits of the respondents.

The present CIRET paper essentially contains the data collected for the above set of problems. A first analysis describes the most important results. However, the analysis has not yet been terminated. A first attempt was made to deepen the understanding of the variable "business situation".[1] Other attempts are to follow.

---

1) Cf. K.A. Vogler, The Business Situation. On the Meaning of an Undetermined Survey Variable, in: W.H. Strigel (Ed.) In Search of Economic Indicators, Berlin, 1977

2. Surveying Method

2.1 Written Poll

The information was gathered with the aid of written information so as to obtain representative statements on the entire industrial panel polled by the Ifo Business Survey. This method set narrow limits both with regard to volume and to content of the questions. After several surveys, however, that were based on a small number of interviews it seemed necessary to obtain statistically significant data.

Any written survey is dictated by the demand for brevity. Questionnaires containing very many or even very complicated questions and therefore taking a long time to be answered are obviously less likely to be returned. Yet there are also restrictions with respect to their content, which have made themselves felt especially in the problem posed in this case. For instance, it was inexpedient to inquire for false parameters of influence or bases. The respondents might have assumed that they could be taken into consideration since we asked for them. Moreover, it was impossible to inquire in detail about the background of the formation of judgments and anticipations as both are largely formed by intuition. The chances of bringing these processes up into the cognitive sphere are limited for written questions on which a respondent is prepared to spend only little time. Remarks of participants that some questions will overinterpret the state of affairs or that the assessment is made spontaneously or intuitively do show that these limits had been reached for individual respondents.

2.2 Questionnaire, Time of Survey

The basic requirements for the development of the questionnaire were the interviewsheld with survey participants[1]. The wording of the questions was tested for comprehensibility in a total of 18 pretest interviews. The survey was conducted in May and June of 1976.

2.3 Population, Representation

The unit polled covered the referee of the participating enterprise competent for answering the business test sheets. He had to fill out a questionnaire for all business test sheets handled by him. The unweighted tabulation of the survey results thus furnishes statements on the distribution of variables among the business survey respondents.

This population consisting of the various units polled, however, may be used only in part. It does not disclose the importance of the survey results to the monthly business test data. The individual reponses had to be weighted in accordance with the business test weights they represent in or-/der to show the distribution of the variables within the parent population of the Business Survey. Here, allowance had to be made of the fact that the questionnaires of the special survey represented a varying number of business survey statements and that these business survey statements, on their part, are weighted. These factors are taken into consideration in the weighting described in more detail in section 2.4. The weighted tabulation of survey results furnishes us with information on the distribution of the variables in the weighted business survey statements. The importance of individual responses to the business test data is thus directly revealed.

---

1) These interviews had already been made by W.H. Strigel and G. Neumann in 196o, (Wie beantworten die Unternehmer die Fragen im Konjunkturtest. Merkblatt des Ifo-Instituts IX/9/6o) and also in the course of B. Nitsche's talks with entrepreneurs in 1976 (TU Darmstadt).

The survey only covered enterprises of the processing industry. All important branches were included in the survey, except for the chemical industry and the food and beverages industry. The results are transferable to other branches of the economy only with some reserve.

The questionnaire was sent to all enterprises of the industrial panel surveyed. We may therefore speak of a total poll. As participation was voluntary, however, we did not achieve any complete exploration. The degree of representation calculated on the basis of comparisons between the returned sheets in May 1976 and the number of test sheets represented by the questionnaires is fully satisfactory having reached 84 %. In the branch with the lowest representation it is still 57 % so that the branch results are considered to be sufficiently representative.

2.4 Weighting

The weighting of results aims at a projection of the test results onto the universe of the Business Survey. This survey of industry is supposed to give as accurate a picture as possible of the structures found in the processing industry. This is achieved, on the one hand, by a representative number of products and companies and, on the other hand, by the weighting of the Business Survey responses. This weighting is done in several stages using the market shares of the companies and the gross production values for the individual products of the entire industry. To reproduce this weighting in the survey results, we also required several stages:

a. The individual responses were to be weighted in a way so that the number of test sheets regularly returned by the respondents as well as the respective weights of these statements in the Business Survey would find expression. This operation was based on the answers given in the questionaire summarizing the number of employees for all products (= test sheet) stated by the referee concerned. The weights of the employee size groups were not entirely accorded in accordance with the number of employees, because - with such a weighting - the results would have been determined solely by the "large" statements and any balancing of mistakes using the law of large numbers would have no longer been probable. The difference in the employee size groups were therefore reduced. This procedure largely corresponds to the practice of company weighting used in the Business Survey.

The results were combined at the branch level with the weighting by number of employees. Any further subdivision by product groups was impossible because the statements in the questionnaires frequently applied to several groups simultaneously.

b. The branch results were then summarized to form the results for the main industrial groups and the total result by weighting with the shares of branches in the gross production value. The numerical values given below are weighted values unless mentioned otherwise.

3. Staff Structure of the Panel

During the first six months of 1976, about 4,8oo test sheets were returned every month from the panel covered by the Ifo Business Survey of industry. Considering that a referee on an average answers 1.36 test sheets according to the survey results a total of about 3,5oo persons in the enterprises will probably have become active in the business survey[1). The majority of these persons belong to the management level. 83 % are entrepreneurs, managers or department heads (cf. Table 1, unweighted percentage). This figure is still increased considering that we find almost exclusively authorized signatories among the group "other polls", who usually fulfill executive functions in smaller businesses.

It seems to depend on the size of the enterprise what position in the firm's hierarchy is taken by the person answering the test sheet. In small enterprises (up to 2oo employees) the test sheet is usually, i.e. in about 63 % of returns (unweighted), answered at the management level. In medium-sized (up to 1,ooo employees) and large enterprises (1,ooo and above) the answers are usually given by the department heads. In large enterprises, the management level is rarely competent. Here the test sheets are frequently answered by referees or officials. The department heads (approximately 5o %) are in charge of the sales department. Another 25 % manage market research and statistical departments, which are almost only found in large enterprises. More than 5o % of the referees or officials work in the market research departments. About one quarter of this group works in sales departments.

---

1) After inclusion of the food and beverages industry, the number of test sheets returned rose to 5,4oo on an average during the first 6 months of 1977. The number of referees will have probably risen to 4,ooo.

This result shows that one important prerequisite for reliable business survey responses has been fulfilled: The respondents are highly likely to possess the information about the actual situation of the enterprise and of the special departments of the enterprise necessary to fill out the test sheets. They probably know the general assessment of the business situation in the enterprise and are sufficiently informed about management plans.

The degree of information held by the respondents may also be derived from the results on reporting habits (cf. Table 2). 68 % of the (weighted) responses are given on the basis of written material. Referees and department heads, in particular, fall back on statistics when making their statements. Information is less frequently collected from other persons, however, there is a similar pattern to be observed as regards the referee's position: Again it is the referees and department heads working in the larger enterprises who gather information for answering the test sheet from other sources in their enterprise.

4. Business Situation

The term of "business situation" is used in the Ifo Business Survey in two questions:

a. In the question of appraisal:

"We judge our business situation for (product) XY presently as being
good/satisfactory or normal for this season/bad".

b. In the question of anticipation:

"During the next 6 months, the cyclical trend of our business situation for XY, i.e. excluding purely seasonal fluctuations, will be
somewhat more favourable/remain about the same/
be rather more unfavourable".

The term of "business situation" remains undefined. It is left up to the individual respondent to decide what content he attaches to it. This lack of definition seems to be necessary in order to ascertain the judgment without distortion, i.e. uninfluenced by the wording of the question and the technique used in the survey. However, when interpreting the data on the business situation this has serious disadvantages. We do not know what factors of influence will determine the judgment of the business situation and what facts do form the basis of the respective forecasts. The study decribed here has dealt with the analysis of these problems at great length.

4.1 Assessment of the Business Situation[1)]

Two sets of problems are important to the evaluation of the business situation judgment:

- The content of the term of "business situation" is to be ascertained. The question posed to enterprises therefore asked for the economic variables mainly used as an orientation for judgments of the business situation.

- To be able to form this judgment, i.e. to rate the business situation as good, satisfactory or bad, we need a standard determining the level of aspiration for the individual scale items. The second question therefore reads: what are the scales of comparison used by the respondents when forming their judgments?

---

1) The following will recapitulate the most important results of the analysis mentioned on page 3.

a. Orientation Variables

The interviews have shown that industrial enterprises make almost exclusive use of internal plant data when judging the business situation. In doing so they particularly bear in mind the demand situation. This was clearly confirmed in the written survey. The enterprises, however, do not take their orientation solely from demand. Out of four orientation sectors (order books, production trends, profit situation and liquidity), an average of two were marked each time. Apart from order books,the profit situation was also very frequently mentioned. The trend of production which is often decided by the enterprise itself, and liquidity are clearly less important in their effect on the judgment concerning the business situation.

To discover the varying importance of the individual conceivable influence factors to the assessment of the business situation, participants in the Business Survey were given a catalogue of 9 factors of influence. Each individual factor was to be ranked in accordance with its significance in making the judgment.

The results shown in Figure 1 confirm the observation that several factors converge in the assessment of the business situation. Almost all the orientation variables, with the exception of labour market situation and liquidity, were ranked as being at least significant by the industrial enterprises. The enterprises do not rely on one factor as their sole orientation variable. Thus the concept of "business situation" is multi-dimensional. The most comprehensive expression of business activity and its most important objective is profit. According to the results of the survey, a very significant status among the orientation factors is allotted to this variable. In addition to that, however, the remaining partial factors are also accorded an important influence. The demand variable "incoming orders" is the most important partial factor. The other demand variables "order books" and "turnover" are also regarded as more influential by the average of the surveyed entrepreneurs than capacity utilization, sales prices and costs. Liquidity and the situation on the labour market, on the other hand, are of less importance when enterprises judge their business situation.

Thus, the results of this detailed inquiry into the orientation factors conform with the first mentioned results. It may be stated that the judgment on the business situation is mainly determined by the movement in demand and the trend of profits.

However, this statement is not yet satisfactory since the demand and profit variables do not appear as alternatives to each other. Since the definitions of the two variables overlap it is presumed that the development of demand serves as an indicator of the profit situation. Such an indicating function may also be attributed to the other variables which usually only explain partial aspects of the business situation.

In different branches of industry the weight of individual orientation variables is to some extent clearly divergent. But in all cases the dominating role of the demand and profit variables remains firmly fixed. The differences in the weighting of orientation variables may frequently be explained by technical and organizational market and production conditions in the individual branches. The present market situation, however, also appears to be of influence. This would indicate that the weighting of orientation factors varies in the course of the business cycle.

The enterprises are asked to form a judgment of the <u>present</u> business situation, yet the judging of the present time can be influenced by anticipations concerning the future. According to the survey results, about 6o % of those responding to the test sheet of the Business Survey do state such influences. This means that the business situation is not simply a description of the actual economic situation as seen by the entrepreneurs. It also contains speculations about the future which are oriented predominantly on the previous movements in demand and the current sales negotiations - as revealed by the results on the anticipated trend of the business situation - but which also contain the less concrete "mood in the economy".

b. Scales of Comparison

Participants in the Ifo Business Survey have the possibility of describing the business situation for their particular product area as good, satisfactory or bad. This rating can only be performed by comparison with a level of aspiration, that is a situation regarded as desirable. Thus the judgment of the business situation expresses the degree (and when taken in aggregate: the number of enterprises) in which the level of aspiration is attained. The level of aspiration itself remains unknown.

The comparison between the prevailing business situation and the level of aspiration is partly a time comparison. The participants orient their rating on an earlier business situation which is considered to be good or even very good. But the present business situation is also compared with the expectations and plans adopted for the period under review and they do not necessarily go by an earlier level. The position of competitors or the average in the branch finally serves the enterprises as a third scale of comparison. However, this criterion is only employed as a complement of the first two scales. The rating of the business situation under the features good, satisfactory or bad is, however, not solely undertaken by comparison of the actual business situation with the level of aspiration. The transition from one feature to another is also determined by short-term comparisons with the situation in the previous year or (with minor seasonal fluctuations) also in the previous month. In addition, the fulfilment of short-term plan objectives or the deviations from plan, play a role. These short-term comparisons appear to be necessary in order to be able to undertake some "fine grading".

4.2 Anticipated Trend of the Business Situation

As a complement to the orientation variables for the judgment of the present business situation, the factors used in a forecast of the trend of the business situation were also to be determined. It was assumed that demand was probably the variable of decisive influence on the forecast. This follows from the reasoning that the cost structure during a given forecasting period of 6 months, on the whole, will probably remain constant and that, given the set cost structure and capacities, demand will be the variable determining profit. Moreover, the earlier results on the concept of business situation confirmed the important role played by demand. An empirical study of this hypothesis would have been desirable, however, had to be given up for reasons of space. Instead, we examined a problem which appears to be important to the variables of anticipation: to what extent do the respondents base their forecasts on measurable observations made in their markets or enterprises which are comparable with respect to the course of time and to what extent do they orient themselves on general, external information not referring to the enterprise or on subjective impressions and moods? The respondents were offered a battery of 7 possible answers ranging from the present level of orders in hand to the mood in the economy and thus covering the entire spectrum of possible leads for making a forecast.

It is striking that the respondents will base their judgment rarely on one piece of information alone but will include as many as possible. On an average, they marked three items (cf. Table 3). In doing so, managers of smaller companies will confine themselves more easily to a few informational fields than the department heads or referees (primarily market researchers) in big enterprises. Among the different information used for a forecast of the future business situation preference is given to internal plant data. About 87 % of the forecasts are based on such information, as order books, incoming orders, inquiries from customers and current sales negotiations. External information, such as the business situation of buyers, the overall economic situation and its respective forecasts or the mood of entrepreneurs are also included, but somewhat less frequently (75 %). In that case, however, allowance has to be made for the fact that such external information is of varying relevance to the respective enterprises: business forecasts are highly informative for enterprises with large markets concerning the development of demand to be expected. Overall economic forecasts are considerably less relevant to enterprises with regionally limited markets. The situation is similar for the "business situation of customers". The dependence of sales on the overall economic cyclical fluctuations is higher the higher the volume of sales. As shown by the results the attention paid to business forecasts and to the cyclical situation of the customers will become markedly greater with a growing business size[1].

Among internal plant data entrepreneurs mainly observe incoming orders and their probable future trend on the basis of current sales negotiations. Depending upon the conditions prevailing in a specific branch, incoming orders and order books are of different informativity.

In branches producing frequently for stock without any

---

1) In 1974, F. Neumann arrived at the same result in her study: Nutzung von gesamtwirtschaftlichen Projektionen und Prognosen in der Industrie. Cf. Ifo-Schnelldienst, 13, 1974, p.14-21

orders (e.g. the building materials industry, rubber processing, wood-working, papermaking and the plastics industry, etc.) incoming orders become less important as demand indicators while the current sales negotiations or the inquiries received from customers will gain importance. Whether they are taken into consideration, in turn, depends on the average volume of the respective orders and on the duration of sales negotiations, etc.

The departments of market research and statistics largely rely on their own business statistics so that particularly frequent use is made of the figures of incoming orders and other information is neglected.

The general mood prevailing in a particular branch or in the overall economy is taken into consideration in 37 % of the forecasts. And the situation is by no means such that bigger enterprises refer less to this mood than small ones or that the departments of market research and statistics are more likely to renounce on considering this variable. The results are also almost the same when broken down by the position of the respondent in the firm's hierarchy. Only the authorized signatories who are grouped under "other polls" more frequently refer to the mood.

To sum up, we may state that there is a tendency to forecast the development of the business situation as much as possible on the basis of measurable data. This information is frequently taken from internal plant data. Data referring to the entire branch or the economy as a whole are usually only relevant to large enterprises. In a good third of the enterprises the business anticipations are also influenced by the mood prevailing in that branch or the economy as a whole.

5. Orders in Hand

5.1 Definition

Orders in hand are formed in the great majority of enterprises. Only the basic materials and production goods industry will produce somewhat more frequently without any order. But here too 9o % of the firms will still have orders in hand. The orders taken together by the respondents under this heading may differ in more than one respect (for instance, the safety ascribed to orders in hand may vary due to different rights of can cellation; or the orders do not go into production in uninterrupted periods of time). This survey tried to find out how enterprises will delimit their orders in hand during the production cycle. According to the definition by the Federal Office of Statistics (Statistisches Bundesamt) orders in hand stand for the sum of all given orders placed by other firms, which have been firmly accepted but not yet executed. When determining the amount of orders in hand in case of goods involving long production times, e.g. started ship or bridge structures, that part (measured by suitable standards) is to be deducted which has already been manufactured[1]. The question now was whether this concept may also be applied in case of the Business Survey.

The possibilities of answering were restricted so as to permit determining up to which stage of production the orders are part of the "orders in hand":

from placement of orders
- up to the beginning of production
- up to the end of production
- up to the entry of turnover in the books

---

1) Cf. H. Brandner, Erhebung der Auftragsbestände in der Industrie, in: Wirtschaft und Statistik, 1, 1971, p.lo

The differentiation between beginning and end of production is relevant only if there is a considerable period of time lying between them, as for instance in shipbuilding, mechanical engineering or in the steel and light-metal industries. Yet this period of time is irrelevant in the papermaking or processing industries, the clothing industry, printing industry, etc. Things are similar for the difference in time between end of production and entry of turnover.

In accordance with the varying conditions by branches we also have different results (cf. Table 4). In the investment goods industry orders usually remain in the order books until they are posted as turnover. The results do not show whether or not the enterprise will deduct already produced parts of orders from the total of orders in hand. This is of great importance to the informativity of any order book figures - also at the enterprise level - so that such a procedure may be assumed. In the consumer goods industries and the basic materials and producer goods industries working with considerably smaller units of orders and products, it is true, the entry as turnover in the books frequently remains the decisive threshold. Compared with the investment goods industry, however, orders are usually taken as being in hand only up to the time of the beginning of production.

Apart from the conditions in the respective branches, the definition of orders in hand also depends on the function of the respondent. If he works in the sales department or for market research he will take the entry as turnover as the decisive criterion. Persons working in production, accounting or the management more frequently only include orders in their books up to the end of production. The definition of orders in hand may vary also according to the number of employees. In small enterprises, an order is often no longer considered part of the order book if production has been completed. In large enterprises, the respondents frequently lack the information on the state of production. They will presumably only know about the fulfilment of an order after invoicing. Thus the orders are only taken out of the order book after having been posted as turnover.

5.2 Assessment of Orders in Hand

The Ifo Business Survey asks for the assessment of the orders in hand as follows:

> "Our volume of orders in hand (domestic and foreign) for XY is presently judged to be
> relatively high/sufficient or normal for this season/ too low".

To rate the present level of orders in hand under one of the three items the respondents need a standard rendering their level of aspiration comparable to the present state. According to the results shown in Table 5 the majority of respondents use the factor of production months ensured by the order book. On the whole, 7o % of the respondents[1)] use this quantity. The capital goods industry, in particular, makes use of this factor of ensured production months. Here, orders in hand take over that important buffer function between fluctuating demand and production which in other spheres is fulfilled by the finished goods inventory. Orders in hand are thus highly important to the capital goods fields with their big fluctuations

---

1) This figure is made up of 56% basing their judgment alone or in connection with other factors on the production months ensured by the order book, and another 27 % comparing between the present volume of orders in hand and the present or planned production level. The latter figure is to be reduced by those 13% who have also named the ensured production months in addition to the production level and are therefore already contained in the 56%.

in demand. The factor of production months ensured by the order book establishes the relation to production and therefore informs about the level of the safety cushion against these fluctuations in demand.

In most of the other production branches, too, the judgment is most frequently oriented on the ensured production months. Other comparable quantities, however, become also more important: the comparison with the average or seasonally normal volume of orders in hand is the next item most frequently marked, reaching 41 %. Especially the respondents in small enterprises base their assessment on past experience. More frequently than respondents in medium-sized and large enterprises, they will rely on this comparison alone while the others will usually use the comparison with the past only in connection with some other factors. The relation of orders in hand to the production capacities given in the enterprise plays a special role in individual branches, above all in cases where long-term overcapacities may make themselves felt, as for instance, in the iron-working industry, steelwork and light-metal construction or shipbuilding.

The assessment of the present level of orders in hand of only about one third of the respondents will incorporate anticipations about the future trend of demand. The assessment of orders in hand therefore yields quite another result than the judgment on the business situation.

5.3 Production Months Ensured by the Order Book

The factor of ensured production months covers the ratio of orders in hand to the production volume per time unit (months, days). It is an expression of the period of time that the production capacities are being utilized for given orders.

Any calculation of this factor must therefore be based

on the determination of a certain production volume. Two concepts are conceivable:

a. The one is based on actual production which is presently being run or has been planned for the next few months. The factor of ensured production months thus expresses for the time under review for how long the production plants will be kept busy at the present level of capacity utilization. The orders in hand are in proportion with production.

b. Full employment to plant capacity is assumed. Thus the factor of ensured production months reveals for how long the production plants will be kept running at the maximum usage level. The orders in hand are in proportion with capacity.

Which of the two concepts is to be applied depends on the information it is supposed to convey. The first variant appears to be better suited for a cyclical analysis, because production is covered statistically while the given capacities are only expressed in terms of estimates. The question now was which of the two concepts is being applied by the respondents in the enterprises. The results show that, unfortunately, the respondents do not show any uniformity of action. A little over half (53%) of the respondents assume the normal full capacity usage of the plant and 44 % base their judgment on the actual capacity utilization. Mainly the small and medium-sized enterprises use the concept of full capacity usage. The large enterprises, however, more frequently refer to the actual output. This may be caused by the varying statistical bases used in large and small enterprises. It appears desirable to fix a uniform concept of reference in order to arrive at a greater informativity of the statements on "ensured production months". It is recommended to use the relation between orders in hand and actual output.

6. Judgment of the Finished Goods Inventory

The Ifo Business Survey uses the following wording to determine the judgment of stocks:

> "During the month under review, our stocks of
> unsold finished goods of type XY were
> too small/sufficient or normal for this season/
> too large/stock keeping uncommon"

As in case of the judgment variables already described we were interested in ascertaining those variables used in the assessment of finished goods inventories so as to determine the changes to which an assessment responds. Most frequently, stocks are judged with respect to demand. About 4o % of the respondents orient their rating, among other things, on the expected trend of demand, 35 % go by the present turnover.

An orientation on delivery times is equally guided by demand. It is important to 27 % of the respondents. If these three spheres are adjusted for multiple responses we arrive at a total of 71% who judge their finished goods inventory with respect to the trend in demand.

Past experience is an important variable besides the direct guidance by the trend of demand. 51 % of the respondents take the average or normal stocks in each season solely or together with other variables as a scale of comparison. Moreover, 2o % of the respondents also take liquidity problems into consideration, which are linked up with stock keeping. They are also led by the amount of the capital invested in stocks. The costs involved in stock keeping are only of secondary importance to the judgment of the stocks of finished goods. Price expectations are rarely made part of such judgments.

The importance of the various orientation variables for the judgment of stocks strongly depends on the respective branch conditions (cf. Table 6). In the capital goods industry, the judgment is mainly based on the trend of demand. In that case, delivery times are relatively highly important compared to the other main groups of industry. The average or seasonally normal stocks are used less frequently for comparisons. However, liquidity problems are more important than in the other production branches, above all in those fields where very expensive products are to be stored, such as in electrical engineering, fine-mechanical or mechanical engineering.

In the basic materials and production goods industries, demand is also the most important base. As a result of the shorter terms of delivery the respondents here, however, more frequently orient themselves on the expected trend of demand. Especially in the oligopolystic spheres of the ironworking industry and mineral oil processing, stocks are also judged with an eye to the expected development of prices. Comparisons are based on the average stocks more frequently than in other sectors.

Demand is comparatively less important to manufacturers of consumer goods when judging their level of stocks. In this case, the average of seasonally normal stocks are used relatively more often for comparison purposes. Like in the capital goods industry, the capital tied down in stocks is also a factor of influence.

In a breakdown of results by number of employees and position of the respondent it is shown - as in case of other judgment variables - that the entrepreneurs in small firms fall back on fewer orientation variables than the department heads or referees in the large enterprises. Demand anticipations become more important to large enterprises while small enterprises rather base their judgments on the trend of turnover up to now. The departments of market research and statistics in large companies rely more on statistical data so that in this case the comparisons are remarkably more often based on average stocks.

7. Capacity Utilization

The assessment of capacity utilization by the surveyed enterprises raises a number of problems. The present poll had to be confined to one single question. In line with the previous questions we asked about the type of factors being used by the companies to measure their degree of capacity utilization.

Capacity utilization is the relation of potential to actual output. This definition corresponds to the measurement of capacity utilization in production quantities. According to the poll results (cf. Table 7) 6o % of the Business Survey responses are calculated on the basis of this quantity. As for the other responses, people have to fall back on one or several auxiliary variables . The marked differences by sectors indicate the reasons for the application of auxiliary variables.

In the basic materials and production goods industries enterprises usually manufacture a relatively homogenous line of products - homogenous with respect to the duration of production per product unit which is important to the computation of capacity. In this case, it is therefore possible to base 83 % of the calculations on the quantitative output. Conditions are different in the capital and consumer goods industries. Here the product lines are heterogenous. Usually, different products may be manufactured using the same or almost unmodified production facilities. A product-specific assessment is no longer feasible. But also the plant-specific assessment is faced with difficulties. In case of a varying duration of production per product unit the units of quantity no longer bear any information. Part of the enterprises (a total of 12 %) therefore take recourse to the output value.

However, this may be approximately correct only in case of constant prices and then only if the price conditions of the products will reflect the relations of the production periods more or less correctly. Other auxiliary quantities are the performed manhours or machine hours. About 40% of the assessments are based on them. The factor of manhour is often used in the capital goods industry and here especially in the labour-intensive spheres, such as shipbuilding, steel and light-metal engineering, and mechanical engineering. Machine hours are used in the capital-intensive branches of the consumer goods industry, i.e. in papermaking, the printing industry or in plastics processing.

Both quantities - manhour and machine hour - will meet the theoretical requirements of the assessment of capacity utilization only to a limited extent because they do not make allowance for the fluctuations in labour or capital productivity. If about 11 % of the respondents - above all in small enterprises - use turnover as the assessment quantitiy this value must be considered as an insufficient indicator.

8. Production Plans

The question as to the production plans of enterprises was worded in the Ifo Business Survey as follows:

> "In the course of the next 3 months our production activities for product XY, in cyclical respect, i.e. excluding purely seasonal fluctuations, will probably
>
> increase/remain about the same/decrease".

This wording of the question supposes a view of development as seen in the course of time, i.e. the enterprises shall state the trend of developments in production for the next 3 months, in each case on the basis of their present level. It was known from talks with enterprises that part of the respondents do not consider the course of time but make comparisons with the previous year. The aim therefore was to determine the method by which the enterprises actually proceed when estimating their production activities. Moreover, it is known that the enterprises do not always pay attention to the seasonally adjusted approach, as requested by the wording of the question so that the variable of "production plans" includes seasonal fluctuations. The question was whether and by which means enterprises will recognize seasonal movements and to what extent it is difficult for them to recognize them.

Both questions do not only apply to the variable of "production plans" but may also be transferred to other variables of expectation. For the purpose of this study these problems had to be treated in a concrete manner on the basis of the production plans.

8.1 Base Period

Starting from the wording of the question quoted, then it is correct to take the current months or the months of the immediate past as base period. 78 % of the respondents stated this type of procedure. 29 % of them refer to the current month and 49 % to the past 3 months (cf. Table 8). The comparison with the level of a three-months period is made above all in branches with relatively strong irregular fluctuations in production, for instance, in foundries or the NF metal industry, in many spheres of the capital goods industry, textile industry, etc. In parts of the basic materials and production goods industries reference is perhaps more often made to the current month because of a more continuous method of production. lo % of respondents compare to the corresponding period of the previous year. In the sense of the question wording, this must be termed as wrong but from the point of view of the respondents it will probably have its good reasons. Above all in branches with pronounced seasonal fluctuations (consumer goods industry) the respondents frequently fall back on a comparison with the previous year. As the following section will show, the comparison with the previous year is the most common method for seasonal adjustments applied in that sphere.

Managers and entrepreneurs use the comparison with the previous year somewhat more frequently than do the other respondents.

8.2 Seasonal Adjustment

A total of 2o % of the respondents state that there are no seasonal influences that come to bear during the course of production in their enterprise (cf. Table 9). This share markedly rises in the branches of investment goods, however, only rarely comes close to zero even in the branches marked by a strong dependence on seasons. The seasonal development normal to this branch does not seem to apply to all products and to all enterprises.

9 % of the respondents state that it is difficult for them to make any seasonal adjustment of the production trend. This percentage is surprisingly low considering the difficulties encountered in seasonal adjustments of highly aggregate data. It should therefore be much more difficult to cover the seasonal development at the enterprise level or even in the individual product spheres of an enterprise. However, the respondents have obviously some ideas about seasonal movements although these ideas are probably rarely quantified.

36 % of the respondents base their seasonal adjustments on comparisons with the previous year and 28 % refer to average values of the past. Above all in the consumer

goods industries where seasonal fluctuations may be observed at very regular intervals, the respondents will use the comparison with the previous year. This comparison yields rates of growth. If the respondents wanted to describe the cyclical trend in the course of the next three months by means of these rates of growth they would have to state the change in the rate. This would not exactly correspond to the question posed but would be a statement on the cyclical tendency in the course of the months ahead. The results do not disclose whether and to what extent this is done. However, if a different method is used we may assume that seasonal adjustments are made by comparing with the previous year and this annual rate of growth will then be the answer to our question.

Tables and Figures

Tab. 1: Staff Structure of the Panel

unweighted percentages

	MANUFACTURING INDUSTRY			
	Total	Basic materials and production goods ind.	Capital goods industry	Consumer goods industry
Frequency, unweighted weighted	3050 3050	568 1005	1319 1386	1163 659
Respondent's position:				
enterpreneur, managing direktor	48,2	40,3	43,8	57,1
dept. head	35,1	39,4	36,8	31,1
referee, official	12,1	15,8	14,8	8,3
others	2,6	2,8	2,9	2,2
no response	1,5	1,6	1,7	1,3
sum	99,9	99,9	100,0	100,0

Tab. 2: Reporting habits

weighted percentages

	MANUFACTURING INDUSTRY			
	Total	Basic materials and production goods ind.	Capital goods industry	Consumer goods industry
Frequency, unweighted	3050	568	1319	1163
weighted	3050	1005	1386	659
Do you normally use written data in order to answer the survey questions?				
yes	68,2	65,2	72,7	63,5
no	31,2	34,2	26,7	35,9
no response	0,6	0,6	0,5	0,6
sum	100,0	100,0	99,9	100,0
Do you normally collect information from other persons in order to answer the survey questions? yes	46,7	52,9	46,0	38,8
no	52,8	46,8	53,6	60,2
no response	0,5	0,3	0,4	1,0
sum	100,0	100,0	100,0	100,0
How many different questionnaires do you fill out every month for our Business Survey?				
average	1,36	1,36	1,36	1,35

ORIENTATION VARIABLES FOR JUDGEMENTS ON THE BUSINESS SITUATION

Fig.1

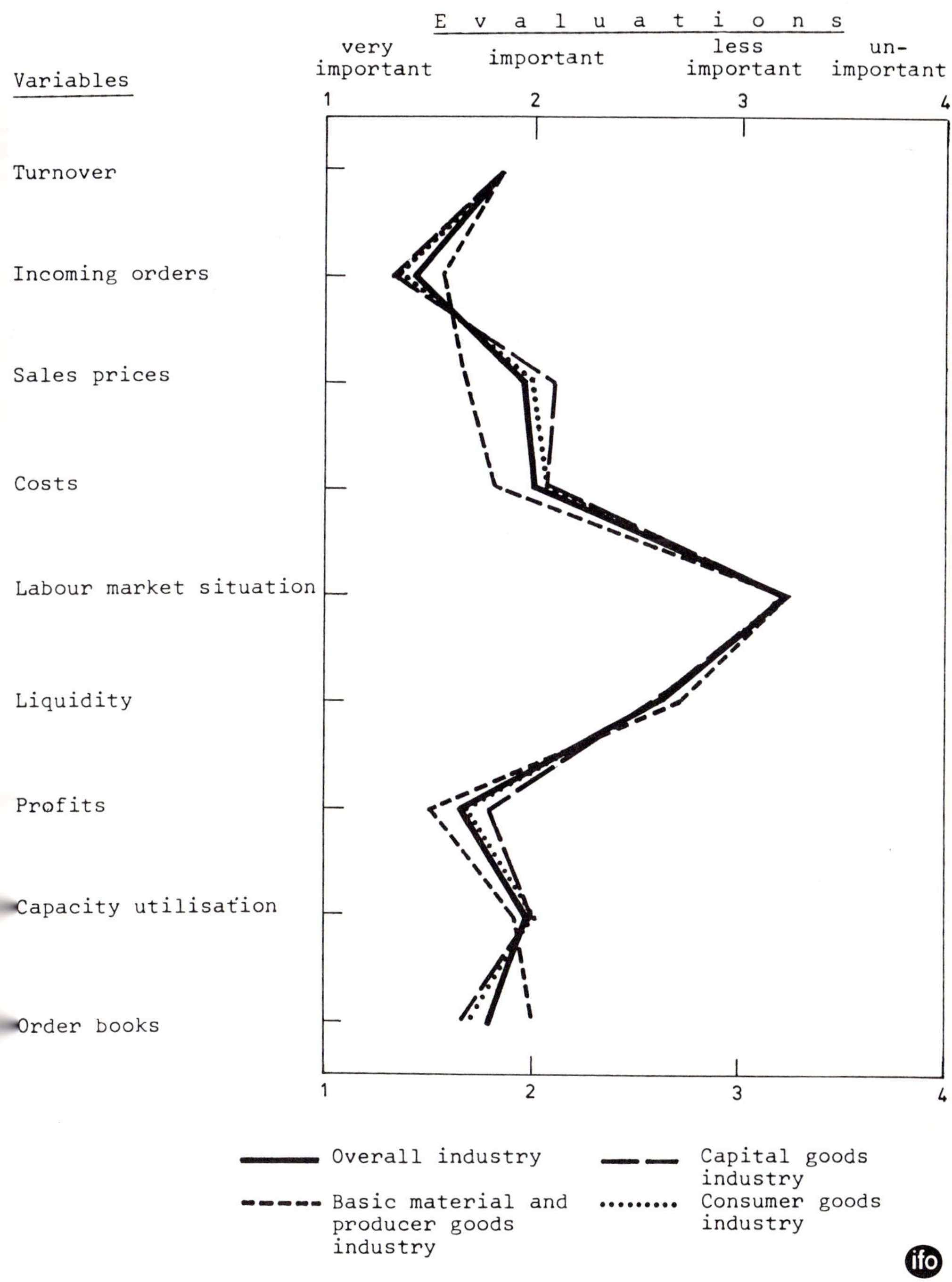

Tab. 3: Business Anticipations

On what do you primarily base your statements on the expected cyclical development of your business situation for the next 6 months?

weighted percentages

	MANUFACTURING INDUSTRY			
	Total	Basic materials and production goods ind.	Capital goods industry	Consumer goods industry
Frequency, unweighted weighted	3050 3050	568 1005	1319 1386	1163 659
We primarily fall back on:				
- current sales negotiations	50,3	48,7	52,7	47,6
- inquiries from our customers	34,8	35,9	37,0	28,2
- incoming orders up to now	58,0	57,7	59,0	56,5
- orders in hand up to now	35,8	31,2	38,2	37,6
- business situation of our customers	49,1	56,7	49,3	37,1
- business forecasts for our branch/the economy as a whole	31,7	37,9	30,9	23,8
- general mood in our branch/ the economy as a whole	37,2	40,5	32,7	41,7
others	1,4	2,4	0,8	1,2
no response	0,2	-	0,4	0,1
sum	298,5	311,0	301,0	273,8

4: Definition of orders in hand

weighted percentages

	MANUFACTURING INDUSTRY			
	Total	Basic materials and production goods ind.	Capital goods industry	Consumer goods industry
ency, unweighted	3050	568	1319	1163
weighted	3050	1005	1386	659
in hand:				
ary	95,2	89,6	98,0	97,7
stomary	4,8	10,4	2,0	2,3
sum	100,0	100,0	100,0	100,0
ncy, weighted in hand customary	2904	900	1358	644
are considered ers in hand from the ent of orders:				
beginning of manufacture	20,3	23,1	16,9	23,6
end of manufacture	22,7	25,8	20,3	23,4
entry as turnover	46,1	40,5	51,8	41,9
others	9,2	8,5	9,1	10,2
no response	1,8	2,1	2,0	0,8
sum	100,1	100,0	100,1	99,9

ab. 5: Judgement on Orders in Hand

What are your main factors of information used when judging the orders in hand, i.e. when you rate whether the amount of orders in hand is relatively high, sufficient or too small?

weighted percentages

	MANUFACTURING INDUSTRY			
	Total	Basic materials and production goods ind.	Capital goods industry	Consumer goods industry
requency, weighted Orders in hand customary	2904	900	1358	644
e primarily orient ourselves n:				
the average/seasonally normal amount of orders in hand in the past	40,8	43,1	37,4	44,7
the present/planned production level	26,7	29,1	28,1	20,4
the present capacity	35,6	42,8	33,4	30,3
the production months accounted for by the order book	55,5	44,0	63,3	55,3
others	0,9	1,6	0,7	0,4
no response	0,8	1,9	0,1	0,6
sum	160,3	162,5	163,0	151,7

: Judgement on stocks of unsold finished goods

Which are the main factors of information used by you to assess whether your stocks of unsold finished goods are too small, sufficient or too big?

weighted percentages

	MANUFACTURING INDUSTRY			
	Total	Basic materials and production goods ind.	Capital goods industry	Consumer goods industry
ency, unweighted weighted	3050 3050	568 1005	1319 1386	1163 659
ks of finished goods				
tomary	70,2	68,1	69,3	75,1
customary	29,8	31,9	30,7	24,9
sum	100,0	100,0	100,0	100,0
uency, weighted: ks of finished goods omary	2141	684	960	495
rimarily orient our- es on:				
e average/seasonally nor- l stocks of the past	51,0	55,6	45,7	54,9
e present turnover	34,5	34,0	36,8	30,9
e expected trend of mand	39,3	42,3	40,8	32,5
e present terms of livery	26,9	19,7	35,7	20,0
e cost of storage	6,1	5,6	6,5	5,9
e expected development sales prices	3,7	7,2	1,7	2,8
e amount of the capital vested in stocks	19,6	11,5	23,2	23,8
others	3,0	3,4	2,8	2,5
no response	1,9	4,4	0,9	0,6
sum	186,0	183,7	194,1	173,9

b. 7: Capacity utilization

Which factors(s) do you use to determine the degree of capacity utilization?

weighted percentages

	MANUFACTURING INDUSTRY			
	Total	Basic materials and production goods ind.	Capital goods industry	Consumer goods industry
Frequency, unweighted weighted	3050 3050	568 1005	1319 1386	1163 659
- output by quantity	59,7	83,0	43,8	57,7
- output by value	11,5	4,4	17,0	10,7
- turnover	10,8	5,0	15,4	9,9
- manhours worked	20,2	6,8	31,2	17,4
- machinehours performed	19,6	13,2	19,6	29,5
- other factor(s)	1,5	1,1	1,7	1,8
no response	1,7	0,4	2,8	1,1
sum	125,0	113,9	131,5	128,1

: Production plans: Base period

What ist your base period for an advance estimate of whether manufacturing activities will rise, remain about the same or decline in the course of the next 3 months ?

weighted percentages

	MANUFACTURING INDUSTRY			
	Total	Basic materials and production goods ind.	Capital goods industry	Consumer goods industry
ency, unweighted weighted	3050 3050	568 1005	1319 1386	1163 659
current month	28,9	35,3	25,2	26,8
past three months	48,8	44,5	53,9	44,4
corresponding period the previous year	10,2	8,9	8,5	15,8
others	4,0	2,9	4,6	4,5
no response	8,1	8,3	7,8	8,5
sum	100,0	99,9	100,0	100,0

ıb. 9: Seasonal adjustment

How do you eliminate seasonal fluctuations when making an assessment of the manufacturing activities in the next 3 months?

weighted percentages

	MANUFACTURING INDUSTRY			
	Total	Basic materials and production goods ind.	Capital goods industry	Consumer goods industry
requency, unweighted	3050	568	1319	1163
weighted	3050	1005	1386	659
y				
- comparison with the previous year	35,7	39,9	27,4	46,7
- determination of averages	28,4	26,7	29,4	29,0
- some other procedure	4,3	4,2	4,7	3,5
easonal adjustment difficult to make	8,7	11,0	7,8	7,0
easonal influences non existent	19,7	15,6	27,1	10,2
no response	3,2	2,6	3,5	3,5
sum	100,0	100,0	99,9	99,9

Summary

Business surveys work with a minimum of present definations and methods as regards the wording of questions. This seems necessary in order

- to obtain unbiassed judgments and anticipations from the entrepreneurs
- to achieve flexible adjustment to specific features of the respective branches and enterprises
- and to keep questions short.

Any interpretation of business survey data may therefore not be based on precisely defined concepts. As a result, we have sometimes a large scope of interpretation.

In principle there are two ways how to discover the content of business survey variables and their determinants. You either take regression analyses and look for dependencies on the aggregate level or you go down to the micro-level and ask the respondents of your tests, which influence factors are important for their answers. For our inquiry, we took the second way and made a poll of all participants in our business survey in industry. By means of this poll we tried to gain information on 4 groups of problems:

1. Some concepts in the Ifo Business Survey are deliberately not defined clearly, e.g. the concept of the "business situation". The problem was to find out the content attached by the respondents of the survey to a specific concept or question.

2. Changes in entrepreneurial judgments or anticipations, as a rule, have concrete causes. We wanted to know on which factors the respondents to our survey orient their specific judgments and to gain some lead, which real changes are responsible for changes in the judgments of the entrepreneurs.

3. Calculations or estimates of seasonal movements are required for answering individual questions (e.g. capacity utilization). The enterprises were therefore asked as to which procedures and indicators were being used in these calculations.

4. The reliability of the survey-results essentially depends on the staff structure of the panel, i.e. of the position and function of respondents within their enterprise. This structure was to be ascertained and, in addition, some reporting habits of the respondents.

J. LEYLAND
ORGANISATION FOR ECONOMIC CO-OPERATION
AND DEVELOPMENT (OECD)
PARIS

QUALITATIVE INDICATORS IN INTERNATIONAL BUSINESS CYCLE ANALYSIS

QUALITATIVE INDICATORS IN INTERNATIONAL BUSINESS SURVEY ANALYSIS

Introduction

This paper describes the OECD system of cyclical analysis for manufacturing industry. The system has been published since May 1974, i.e. for just over three years, as Part III of the monthly statistical publication 'Main Economic Indicators'. Indicators for eleven countries were initially published and this number was later extended to 18. Qualitative data as well as quantitative data are used and this paper will also attempt to assess the usefulness of qualitative data in the system.

It was not intended, partly for resource reasons, to set up a fully fledged cyclical analysis system for all countries studied. The indicators therefore refer to manufacturing industry only and no attempt has so far been made to construct composite indices.

Background

Work on cyclical analysis started in OECD in the early 1970s. This reflected the growing interest in this type of approach to economic analysis in a number of countries at this time. For several reasons work at the first stage was restricted to manufacturing industry. First because only a limited amount of resources could be devoted to the project making a full scale analysis impossible. Secondly, in virtually all countries a far greater range of statistical data of all types are available for the manufacturing sector than for other sectors in the economy. Thirdly, the evidence available suggests that manufacturing is perhaps among the sectors most influenced by the "business cycle". For these reasons it was felt that the limited resources available would be best used in an analysis of the manufacturing sector.

Traditionally cyclical analysis systems have been based almost exclusively on quantitative data, reflecting perhaps the original development of this analysis in the United States whose statistical system is orientated towards a vast and comprehensive range of quantitative statistics and correspondingly little qualitative data. Qualitative series have however played a major role in the OECD system for a number of reasons. Earlier research within the OECD Statistics Service had indicated that qualitative data might be of value in this regard particularly as leading indicators. This tied in with the results of research on qualitative data and the business cycle carried out by several other institutions. Secondly, in a number of countries, qualitative data can usefully be used to fill in gaps in the range of quantitative statistics.

Perhaps more importantly qualitative surveys can and are often used to measure concepts not easily measurable by the traditional statistical methods. Several examples of this can be given. The level and the change in stocks can be measured by quantitative statistics (though the estimation of stocks in volume terms presents some difficulties). It is not however possible to measure - or at least to measure directly - the extent of the pressure on stock holdings; for example, to take the case of finished products, whether stocks of these are higher than the entrepreneur would wish or would normally hold, indicating a lack of demand relative to productive capacity, or whether these stocks are lower than desired or lower than normal indicating the reverse. This 'state', as it might be called, of stock holdings is nevertheless a concept closely linked with the business cycle. Similar remarks can be made regarding order books. Capacity utilisation provides another example. This is a concept, which while highly important in economic analysis, is in a certain sense somewhat indefinable. Everyone has a general idea of what it means but it is not easy to define sufficiently rigidly to enable a precise quantitative measure to be conceived. Even if it were rigidly defined it would probably prove difficult to measure precisely in quantitative terms. Two types of approach to measuring capacity utilisation have therefore been adopted. One type of approach uses an analysis of other forms of quantitative data. Several methods have been developed here of which the most well known is probably the Wharton system. The other type of approach is to use qualitative surveys. Here the vagueness of the concept does not matter since the basis of a qualitative survey is to obtain impressions rather than precise facts. We therefore obtain series whose absolute level is perhaps not very meaningful but whose evolution over time certainly is; a number of independent assessments have indicated that the evolution of qualitative capacity utilisation data is a valuable guide. Finally, under this section, qualitative surveys provide a unique opportunity for measuring businessmen's overall opinion of the economic situation or for providing some form of 'business climate' indicator.

Another advantage that sometimes - though not always applied - concerns the relative smoothness of qualitative data compared with quantitative. New orders data provide a good example here. In certain cases where qualitative surveys ask businessmen to indicate the direction of change in order-books over the most recent period the result is a much smoother series than that given by quantitative data; in some cases this may be because the survey asks for the change over, say three to four months, which is necessarily smoother than the one month change given by a monthly quantitative survey, but a more general reason may be that respondents consciously or unconsciously tend to "smooth" their replies a little, for example by not taking account of particularly irregular fluctuations, and in so doing render a useful service to the analyst who wishes to detect the short-term trend in the series. It should be pointed out though that while most qualitative new orders series are fairly smooth, one or two countries - for example, the Netherlands - prove exceptions to this rule.

Another potential use of qualitative data concerns the 'forecast' or 'anticipations" questions that most business surveys contain. These can in certain cases be advantageously used, as can be seen later, to provide forecasts of quantitative series.

Finally, two practical advantages of qualitative data can be mentioned. First the processing time is normally short leading to a relatively rapid availability of the data. This is particularly important in some countries given the time lag before publication of certain quantitative indicators. Secondly the series are rarely revised and any revisions that do occur are nearly always minimal. This means that the first figures produced for a particular period are normally the definitive figures which is by no means always the case where quantitative data are concerned. As a secondary effect this also helps the business cycle analyst to assess the series since in examining past data a true picture of the indications given at each moment in time by the series exists.

Obviously a number of disadvantages exist for qualitative data in a cyclical analysis context. The very lack of precision that gives the surveys their characteristic is sometimes - though not always - a drawback. Some surveys do not always include the questions that the cyclical analyst would like to see. Perhaps however the most important drawback is the fact that several surveys are quarterly rather than monthly.

As mentioned earlier the OECD system was never intended to provide a full-scale system of cyclical analysis for all the countries concerned and was because of resource limitations necessarily limited in scope. Because of this no attempt has been made to compile composite indicators from the various series chosen. The aim was firstly to select and present in a meaningful form certain series useful as leading, coincident or lagging indicators. A secondary aim was also to present certain series - notably foreign trade series and price series - who were not in themselves' cyclical indicators' but who are subject to fluctuations that are of particular importance to economic study and which are considered to be at least partially connected with the general business cycle.

Methodology

The OECD system of cyclical analysis is based on what is generally known as the "growth cycle" approach in which the long-term trend is removed from the series used to enable the series to be shown in a detrended form. During the post-war period, cyclical fluctuations have tended (with certain exceptions, e.g. the 1974-1975 recession) to be milder than the fluctuations commonly experienced in the pre-war period. In particular, the 'contraction' or 'recession' phase of the cycle has in many cases manifested itself not as a decline in the absolute level of activity but as a period of slower growth than that of the 'expansion' period. These periods of slower growth (or 'growth recessions') do not show as a contraction phase under traditional cyclical analysis.

In order to identify cyclical fluctuations of this type it is helpful to remove the long-term trend from the series considered. In the OECD system this is done by estimating the long-term trend (using the method described below) and then dividing the original series by this estimated trend to give a series of deviations from the trend or 'ratios to trend'. Under this process all periods showing slower growth than the long-term average show up as declines in the 'deviations' or 'ratio' series. This enables growth recessions to be identified.

The growth cycle approach can also be linked with the classical decomposition of an economic time series into the four components of long-term trend (T), cycle (C), seasonal variation including trading day variations if appropriate (S), and irregular movements (I). All series with a significant seasonal variation are seasonally adjusted before being used in the cyclical analysis. It can therefore be taken that the series consist only of the three other components. It is assumed (though this assumption is perhaps open to question) that the trend is combined multiplicatively with the other two components, i.e. the series can be represented as follows:

$$T \times f(C.I).$$

If this series is divided by its trend (T) the result is

$$f(C,I)$$

the cyclical component together with the irregular. It would be desirable to remove the irregular component to show the cyclical component alone; in practice, however, this is difficult. In order to partly reduce the irregular fluctuations in the case of monthly series, however, a small period moving average (normally a three-month simple moving average) is applied to the original seasonally adjusted series before its division by the trend.

(An alternative hypothesis to the multiplicative relationship of the trend to the other two components would be to assume that it is combined additively, $T+f(C,I)$. In this case the trend should be subtracted from the original series. It can, however, be shown that the difference as regards the designation of peaks and troughs is likely to be minimal providing, as is virtually always the case, that the trend growth rate is not too steep).

The use of the growth cycle approach also enables series with different long-term growth rates to be compared. If the long-term trend is not removed some form of trend adjustment (e.g. the 'reverse-trend adjustment' procedure developed by the United States National Bureau of Economic Research for their United States analysis published in the Business Conditions Digest) should ideally be used to enable the turning points of different series to be compared.

In removing the long-term trend of a series it is necessary to distinguish between what can be considered as the long-term component and what can be considered as the cyclical component. The distinction is not always clear-cut. While the existence of cyclical fluctuations in the economy has always been accepted, economic theory has at various times suggested the existence of different lengths and types of cycles. These range from the Kondratieff long-wave (which suggests cycles of 40 to 60 years) through the building cycle (15 to 20 years) and the normal business cycle to the Mack subcycles (of about 2 years duration). Different definitions of these cycles have also been proposed. The purpose of cyclical analysis, however, can normally be defined as identifying fluctuations associated with the business cycle and the best known definition of this is the Burns-Mitchell definition given in 'Measuring Business Cycles'(1).

(1) 'Measuring Business Cycles', Burns and Mitchell, New York, National Bureau of Economic Research, 1947.

"Business cycles are a type of fluctuation found in the aggregate activity of nations that organise their work mainly in business enterprises; a cycle consists of expansions occurring at about the same time in many economic activities, followed by similarly general recessions, contractions, and revivals which merge into the expansion phase of the next cycle; this sequence of changes is recurrent but not periodic; in duration business cycles vary from more than one year to ten or twelve years; they are not divisible into shorter cycles of similar character with amplitudes approximating their own."

When the purpose of identifying the business cycle is accepted it is unnecessary to distinguish longer period fluctuations, if they exist, from the true long-term trend (which can, of course, be considered as a cycle with infinite period). The object in removing the so-called long-term trend must therefore be to filter out of the original series all fluctuations with a period longer than, say, ten to twelve years.

On this assumption, the removal of trend by simple regression against time becomes inappropriate and some form of moving average method or filter is indicated. The method finally chosen was based on the principle of a ten-year moving regression of the logarithms of the original data (after, of course, seasonal adjustment) against time(1). In deciding the exact application of this method a decision had to be made as to whether to use what may be termed 'current trends' or 'past trends'. Under the current trend method the trend for any particular point in time is estimated using the point under consideration plus data for equidistant periods either side. The trend for the present moment in time is therefore a mixture of the experience for a certain period in the past and for a similar period in the future. The past trend method uses the point under consideration plus previous data only. The trend is therefore essentially based on past experience; thus the present moment in time is compared with past trend only. It is debatable which of the two methods is more appropriate in cyclical analysis. In the event the past trend method was chosen since it was considered more appropriate to compare present data with average experience over the past, which is a known factor, rather than with a mixture of known experience and future or unknown experience.

Following from this the application of the ten-year moving regression was carried out as follows. The logs of the first ten years plus one period (i.e. 121 months or 41 quarters) are regressed against time. The antilog of the last point (i.e. the 121st month or the 41st quarter) of the regression line is taken as the trend value for the last point. The regression is then repeated for the ten-year period starting in the second period for which data are available (i.e. 2nd-122nd month or 2nd-42nd quarter) to give a trend estimate for the

(1) For a fuller description of the method and its justification see, R. Gränzer, 'Cyclical Indicators for Manufacturing Industries', OECD Economic Outlook, Occasional Studies, December 1973.

122nd month or the 42nd quarter. This process is repeated to the end of the series. This process provides trend estimates for all points in the series with the exception of the first ten years, the trend values for which are estimated by a simple ten year logarithmic regression against time.

When forecasts of certain series are used (see below) it is necessary to have trend values for a period 3-6 months ahead of the last known actual value. In this case, each moving regression trend line is extrapolated by the appropriate number of months and a trend estimate obtained not for the last period of the ten years but the last period plus 3 or 6 months.

It can be shown(1) that this method is equivalent to applying a weighted ten-year moving average to the logarithms of the original series and placing the antilog of the results in the last period of the ten years (or the last period plus three or six months if appropriate). The weights of the moving average are determined by the length of the moving regression (in this case ten years) plus the point on the regression line (in this case the last period, or the last period plus 3 or 6 months) it is desired to estimate. The moving average approach to the method is used in practice since it is far more economic in terms of computer time.

This method of trend estimation gave generally very satisfactory results up to about the end of 1974. More recently, however, results, particularly during 1975, have been less satisfactory as the method resulted in a very abrupt decline in the trend growth rate - in certain cases even a small absolute decline. While this does not affect the timing of turning points other than marginally some research is currently being carried out to examine other trend removal methods; it is also planned to use spectral techniques to help develop if possible a more satisfactory system.

Qualitative series are not used in a detrended form. The reason for this is two-fold. First, very few, if any, qualitative series show any sign of strong long-term trend. Secondly, in a number of cases the series can be considered to represent already deviations from a trend. For example, if we take the frequent question "Is your stocks level above normal, about normal, or below normal", the 'normal' position can be taken as equivalent to the 'trend' position. The balance of positive less negative replies can therefore be taken as a measure of the deviation from the long-term trend.

The rest of the analysis is however applied to qualitative data. The series are therefore seasonally adjusted where there is evidence of significant seasonal variation and a three-month simple moving average is applied to the monthly series to smooth out some of the irregular fluctuation.

---

(1) See Annex 1 to Gränzer, op.cit.

Throughout all the three-fold qualitative questions (i.e. those that give a positive, negative or 'about right' answer) have been used in balance form, i.e. the difference between the percentage of positive and the percentage of negative replies has been used. This, while a popular way to use such data, is not, of course the only way, and some research has been carried out into the possibility of taking account of the 'about right' replies as these can on occasion provide for a large proportion of the replies.

Use of qualitative anticipations data for forecasting

Virtually all business surveys contain questions asking entrepreneurs for their future expectations regarding certain items. Common questions in this category are: "Do you expect your selling prices to decrease, increase, or stay the same?", "Do you expect your production to increase, decrease or stay the same?", "Do you expect to increase or reduce your labour force in the near future?". Some previous work carried out in various institutions had indicated that these series could well be used to provide forecasts of traditional quantitative series of prices, employment and production and a method was devised to examine this, as follows(1).

The basic correlation in these cases lies between the growth rate in the quantitative series and the balance of the qualitative data. This stems from the basic theory underlying the use of qualitative data, i.e. that the balance of positive less negative replies while, in strict logic, only indicating the number of firms expecting a certain outcome compared to the number expecting the opposite is also a highly valuable indicator of the extent of the change indicated by the majority.

Accepting this assumption, the question to be decided is how to define the appropriate growth rate in the quantitative series most clearly linked with the qualitative balance. Here one guide is the form of the question in the qualitative survey. If, for example, the question asks entrepreneurs for their expectations over the following three month period we might logically expect to find a good relationship between the response series and the series of three month growth rates derived from the quantitative series. However, the situation is not that simple and two factors in particular have to be taken into account. First, respondents to business surveys may not always have in mind the precise period indicated in the survey - research has shown that they sometimes reply in terms of longer or shorter periods(2). Secondly, where respondents are thinking

(1) See also, Gränzer, op.cit. Annex II.

(2) See, for example: J.K. Shepherd, 'The FBI Industrial Trends Inquiry', National Institute Economic Review, November 1963, London; C. Malhomme, 'L'influence du passé dans les enquêtes de conjoncture: un essai de correction' CIRET paper, Madrid, September 1969; M. Gregory, 'The CBI Industrial Trends survey as a measure of current manufacturing output', National Institute Economic Review, May 1970, London.

generally in terms of a certain period - let us take, for example, three months - they may be comparing the situation three months ahead not with the situation at the exact present moment in time but with the average position in recent periods, i.e. the position not only at the time of responding but also in the recent past. This average position can perhaps best be represented by taking an average of the last few months. For this reason after some experimenting the concept of what may be termed 'average based growth rates' was adopted. This meant that the balance series from the business survey which asks for an expectation relative to month t (i.e. the survey being carried out a few months before t) is compared with the following series:

$$\frac{y_t}{\frac{1}{r-q}\,(y_{t-q} + y_{t-q+1} + \cdots\cdots\, y_{t-r})}$$

where y_t represents the quantitative series at time t. The range (t-q) to (t-r) represents the time period with which entrepreneurs are considered to be intuitively comparing the forecast period. In the case of forecasts relating to employment and production, it was found useful to take q = 18 and r = 6. This gives a twelve month base for the 'average based growth rate'. It also implies, since the mid-point of the time range for the base is t-12, that entrepreneurs have, on average, a 12 month span in mind whatever the form of the question. In the case of employment and production series this length of time has in fact been suggested by the results of several research papers. In the case of prices, the situation is more variable. Various possibilities have been tried. In most cases a three month growth rate (corresponding with the form of the question) was found the most useful but in some cases a six month average based growth rate (q=12,r=0) was found to give the best results.

Once the identities of q and r have been determined, a regression is run to establish a relationship between the average based growth rate and the balance series as follows:

$$\frac{(r-q)\ y_t}{(y_{t-q} + y_{t-q+1} + \cdots\cdots + y_{t-r})} = a_o + a_1 B_t + e_t$$

where a_o and a_1 are the regression coefficients, B_t the balance from the question giving a forecast in respect of period t (i.e. resulting from an enquiry taken a few months before t), and e_t the residual.

From the results of the regression the forecast series $\hat{y}_t$ is constructed as follows:

$$\hat{y}_t = \frac{1}{r-q}\ (a_o + a_1 B_t)(y_{t-q} + y_{t-q+1} + \cdots\cdots y_{t-r})$$

i.e. the forecast series $\hat{y}_t$ is a product of $(a_o + a_1\ B_t)$ and a moving average of length r-q applied to the past series and appropriately lagged.

A complete forecast series $\hat{y}_t$ is thus produced. This series is divided by the trend values of the original series y_t in order to obtain a series of forecast deviations from trend.

Choice of the Reference Cycle

Any system of cyclical analysis has first to define a reference cycle and hence obtain in some form a chronology of turning points. This can in come cases be done simply by selecting a series, or possibly a combination of series (e.g. those selected as coincident indicators) and using the indicated turning points. A more soundly based system is for the cyclical analyst to consider all the evidence available (which would include not only the coincident indicators but any other information that exists) and to form a judgement on the most likely dates to select for a turning point chronology.

In the case of the OECD system, the resource constraints previously mentioned ruled out any calculation of composite indices including a composite coincident index. The more sophisticated way of selecting a reference cycle and turning points was also too heavy on resources. An additional problem lies in the fact that the OECD as an international organisation is automatically not as competent to define reference turning points as national economists and statisticians who have a close and detailed knowledge of economic developments and the strengths, weaknesses and special factors affecting statistical data in their own countries.

For the above reasons a fairly simple solution was indicated. The prime indicator for manufacturing industries is of course the index of manufacturing production. As far as one series alone can be said to represent the overall fluctuations in one sector this does. It was therefore in the circumstances the obvious candidate as a reference cycle indicator. It is furthermore a widely available indicator, and a series which is generally among the more soundly based and more minutiously compiled of statistical indicators. Of the eighteen countries included in the OECD system only one - Denmark - does not compile a production index.

One series alone is, however, always subject to distortion by special events (e.g. strikes, unusual weather, difficulties in the data collection process, etc.) and this is certainly true of production indices. Furthermore, production indices, even if smoothed, are subject to erratic movements. Hence, in examining the series, we see a number of examples of irregular movements including examples of double peaks and double troughs. The production index is not therefore taken as a rigidly defined form of reference cycle and indeed no formal definition of peaks and troughs, is made in the OECD system. It is, however, intended to be an indicator of the reference cycle and is therefore taken as a yardstick for the advance and lagging indicators.

Where possible capacity utilisation indicators are also shown as coincident indicators. The pressure on capacity can be taken as another indication of the cycle (indeed certain cyclical research in the past has started from the principle of defining the cycle using the relation of actual to potential output(1). The inclusion of capacity utilisation is therefore, among other uses, intended as an additional guide to the reference cycle for manufacturing.

As previously mentioned, one of the countries included in the OECD system - i.e. Denmark - does not have an index of production. A deflated index of sales is therefore used instead. (Danmarks Statistik have, in fact, recently considerably extended and changed from a quarterly to a monthly basis their sales indices with the intention that these shall serve as a proxy for a production index.)

Choice of indicators

As mentioned in the previous section the index of production is used as an indicator of the reference cycle with, where possible, some indicator of capacity utilisation as a subsidiary indicator.

In choosing the other indicators it was not possible (or even desirable) to have identical indicators for each country. The choice had to depend both on which series were available and, of course, on the performance of these series as cyclical indicators. The procedure followed was therefore to draw up a list of series - described in the following paragraphs - and to select for each country a choice of series from this list depending on availability and the performance of each series as a cyclical indicator in the country concerned.

Several types of qualitative series are frequently used as leading indicators in the OECD system. The first of these is a 'business climate indicator' if this exists for the country concerned. Various types of business climate indicators are compiled all of them normally good leading indicators. In certain surveys respondents are asked for their opinion on the actual and/or the future general developments in business conditions, either generally or for the respondent's firm. The results of one of these questions can either be used alone (Australia, Finland, France, Italy and the United Kingdom) or, if the respondent's opinion on both the present and future economic climate is asked for, combined together (as in the IFO business climate indicator). Another way of obtaining a 'business climate indicator' is not to ask businessmen's opinions on changes in the general climate directly but to take the results of several questions in the survey and to combine them together. This is how the Swiss 'Business Situation Indicator' and the Belgian 'Courbe Synthétique' are obtained. Generally speaking all business climate series have been found to be useful leading indicators.

---

(1) See for example, 'The Measurement of Domestic Cyclical Fluctuations'; OECD Economic Prospects Division. OECD Economic outlook, Occasional Studies, July 1973.

As mentioned earlier, a common question in business surveys is to ask whether respondents consider their finished goods stocks level to be above normal, about normal, or below normal, or whether they are considered too high, about right or too low. Stocks of finished goods are highly sensitive to the business cycle. During a recession phase entrepreneurs normally find themselves with too many finished products in stock and seek to reduce them. Once, however, the turning point approaches, the first increase in demand is normally met by drawing on existing stocks - the stepping up of production normally occurs at a later stage. Hence, one of the first signs of the end of a recession is often a decrease in the number of firms who consider their finished goods stocks to be too high or above normal. The opposite arguments apply in the case of a peak. The balance of positive less negative replies to such questions on finished goods stocks are therefore often found useful as leading indicators giving a few months lead to the turning point in production. The balance is used in 'inverse' form, i.e. the peak corresponds to a trough in the production index.

Questions on the state of order books, for example: "Are your order stocks above normal, normal or below normal" are also often useful as leading indicators as are questions on order inflow. The latter can be either in the form "Were your new orders during the last month (quarter) above normal, normal or below normal" or in the form "Were the orders you received during the past month (quarter) higher, lower or about the same as those received during the preceding month (quarter)". Questions are also sometimes asked on the expected inflow of new orders. Examples of all these questions on order inflow and order stocks are obvious candidates as leading indicators to the production cycle and are so used in the OECD system though as we shall see later their performance varied from country to country. (The forecast series is used in its original form, i.e. it is not converted to give forecasts of quantitative series as described in the last section but one).

A further type of qualitative series used in the system is that which asks entrepreneurs for an estimate of the anticipated tendency in their production during the next few months. This is used in two ways, either in its straight form, or converted to give forecasts of the actual index of procuction. While on occasion this is a useful leading indicator, it is perhaps in some respects a little disappointing as the turning points in the series do not always precede those in the production index. It would appear that entrepreneurs' replies to this question sometimes reflect the present situation more than the future tendency.

A certain number of quantitative series relating to manufacturing industry are, of course, also used in the OECD system as leading indicators. One obvious choice is quantitative series of new orders. When these are not published in volume terms by the source institute they are deflated by whichever price series seems most appropriate before use.

The stocks/deliveries ratio or stocks/output ratio is sometimes also a candidate for selection as a leading indicator. It is somewhat analogous to the qualitative series of judgements on the state of stocks.

Finally, a range of series sometimes, though not always, found useful as a leading indicator is that of weekly or monthly hours worked. This reflects perhaps the initial reaction of employers to the need to increase or decrease production given the time lags normally involved in recruiting labour or in reducing the labour force.

In 'Main Economic Indicators', the cyclical indicators graphs are shown in two columns side by side. The first column has the chosen leading indicators at the top followed by the reference cycle. At the bottom of the column is a section entitled 'Foreign Trade Indicators'. Series of manufacturing exports and imports are here shown in the form of deviations from their long-term trend. Where possible the series are shown in volume terms; otherwise value terms are used. (The category 'manufacturing' does not, strictly speaking, occur in most trade classifications. Certain countries publish export and import data for special groups which can be considered roughly analogous to manufacturing industry. In other cases data for sections 5 to 8 or 5 to 9 inclusive of the Standard International Trade Classification have been used. In one or two cases, where this was not possible, other methods have been used to obtain a proxy for manufacturing.) The reason for including these indicators was not because they are considered to be cyclical indicators as such but because the relationship between trade flows and cyclical impulses is clearly of the highest interest. In most cases business survey series concerning judgements on either the inflow or the level of export orders are also shown - in certain cases (but not all) these act as leading indicators for the export series.

The second column starts with the coincident indicators. As mentioned earlier, capacity utilisation series figure prominently here. A number of different types of questions on capacity utilisation are used in the business surveys of different countries and hence in the OECD cyclical analysis system. Some of the more common questions are those which ask the firm for a rough estimation of its actual level of capacity utilisation, those which ask the firm if it is working at full capacity or if it could produce more with its existing capacity, those which ask whether the firm considers its technical (as distinct from overall) capacity is sufficient for a specified future period taking account of the backlog of orders on hand and the likely level of future orders during the specified period. In certain cases quantitative series of capacity utilisation are also used where these are available.

A few other questions, varying from country to country, are also sometimes included in the coincident indicators. The most common group of questions relate to manpower shortages.

Finally, the rest of the second column is devoted to a section entitled 'Lagging and Other Indicators'. Essentially four groups of series figure here where possible, investment indicators, employment indicators, wholesale or producer price series, and unit labour cost or an associated series. Not all of these types of series, particularly unit labour cost and, to a lesser extent, investment indicators, are available for all countries. In principle, this section contains mainly lagging indicators. However, it also includes some series, particularly price series, whose classification is dubious and which are included not so much as cyclical indicators, but, in the same way as the foreign trade series, because the relationship between their evolution and general cyclical fluctuations in the economy are of prime interest.

Investment series are a classic lagging indicator. The investment series shown concern either expenditure on plant and equipment or total investment by manufacturers, according to data availability. In a number of cases, investment data are only available annually, and often only available after some time. Where possible, therefore, forecast investment data are also used. Virtually all these forecasts come, unlike the other forecast series used in the OECD system, from quantitative forecast investment series. The published results of these are either used as forecasts directly or adjusted as appropriate, depending on the type of survey and the method of publication (both vary enormously between countries). The percentage deviation of the forecast series from the trend of the actual series is then calculated and plotted.

Manufacturing employment is considered by some authorities to be a coincident indicator, by others a lagging indicator, with respect to production. It was felt that the balance of the evidence - particularly in recent periods - pointed to its being a lagging indicator. Where possible a forecast series, derived as described in the previous section from qualitative anticipations questions, is also shown.

Two wholesale or producer price series are normally shown. One represents prices for manufactured products (or the nearest equivalent), the other either raw materials' prices or intermediate goods. The manufactured products series is normally a lagging indicator while the cycles in raw materials or intermediate goods can be leading, coincident, lagging, variable or unconnected with the main business cycle depending on the country. Forecast series from qualitative data are often shown for the manufactured goods series and are often successful advance indicators.

Finally, unit labour cost or a similar indicator is shown for the few countries which calculate it as a lagging indicator.

Assessment of the Results

We can now look on the results produced by the system - in particular at the performance of the qualitative series. To obtain some idea of the overall quality of business survey data as cyclical indicators we can perhaps examine three countries in detail - one non-European, one E.E.C. country which has used the E.E.C. harmonised business survey, and one European non-E.E.C. country. We shall therefore look at Australia, Sweden and Belgium. In assessing the results, it must be remembered that we shall primarily be looking for the following points. First, how well those series selected as leading indicators predicted the turning points in the fluctuations of the manufacturing production index from its long-term trend. Secondly, how the coincident and lagging indicators performed relative to the index of production, including comparison of the capacity utilisation series and the production series. Thirdly, how well the series of judgement on export orders, when it existed, forecast the fluctuations in exports. As mentioned in the previous section, this comparison is complicated by the difference between value and volume series. For certain countries volume trade data has been shown, for others value. Questions on export orders inflow in business surveys do not always specify whether value or volume terms should be used - even if this is specified respondents may not of course always follow the terms of the question. Fourthly, how well have the forecasts generated by qualitative series performed as predictors of the corresponding quantitative series particularly as regards predicting turning points?

AUSTRALIA

The Australian Business Survey used is run jointly by the 'Associated Chamber of Manufactures of Australia' and the 'Bank of New South Wales'. Results from the survey are available on a consistent quarterly basis from 1966. The survey is quarterly which is a disadvantage. To offset this however it has probably the quickest processing time of any business survey. The survey is taken during the early part of the third month of each quarter and results are published before the end of the same month.

The graph opposite shows the system of indicators produced for Australia. Four series have been used as leading indicators: Firms' judgements on the 'Prospects for the Total Economy', the 'Judgement on the change in the total order inflow over the past three months', the 'Judgement on the change in the order inflow predicted for the next three months', the 'Judgement on the change in production over the last quarter'. The last series should theoretically be a leading indicator as it concerns changes in production - typically series of changes lead 'level' series since one of the first signs of a turning point in a 'level' series is a slowdown in the rate of growth or the rate of decline.

The index of production is shown as a deviation from its long-term trend and the anticipated series of production changes has been used to provide a forecast series (shown as a discontinuous line).

Imports and exports are shown in value terms - the two series of judgements on changes in export deliveries over the past and future three months are shown as advance indicators.

Two series are shown as coincident indicators - the percentage of firms working at full capacity, and the judgement on the change in the difficulty of obtaining labour over the past three months.

Expenditure on plant and equipment in value terms is shown in the 'lagging and other indicators section'. The forecast series is derived not from qualitative data but from a half-yearly quantitative investment forecast survey carried out by the Australian Bureau of Statistics. Employment is also shown in this section with its forecast series derived from qualitative data. Finally, in the absence of a wholesalers' or producer's price index, the qualitative series of 'judgement on selling prices over the past three months' is shown as an indicator of price movements together with the corresponding ex ante series.

Looking at the index of production, which is available from 1963, we can perhaps define troughs and peaks as follows:

Peaks:	December 1964	Troughs::	August 1966
	January 1970		February 1972
	August 1973		June 1975

In a number of cases the existence of double peaks and troughs makes the dating unclear - these have been resolved by reference to the capacity utilisation indicator and also by reference to various cyclical analysis studies carried out in Australia (by the Institute of Applied Economic and Social Research and the Australian Bureau of Statistics).

In examining the performance of the four leading indicators one feature stands out - the performance in the later years is much improved compared with the earlier years.

Looking at the first of the leading indicators, 'change in prospects for the total economy', we see little sign of a consistent cyclical pattern before 1971. Since that date the series has forecast all the three turning points that have occurred - the 1972 trough with a lead of about 2 months and the 1973 peak and 1975 trough with leads of 8 and 9 months respectively.

The ex post series of judgement on total order inflow is a disappointment as a leading indicator and would perhaps more correctly be classed as coincident. With the exception of the May 1975 trough, where a lead of five months was shown,

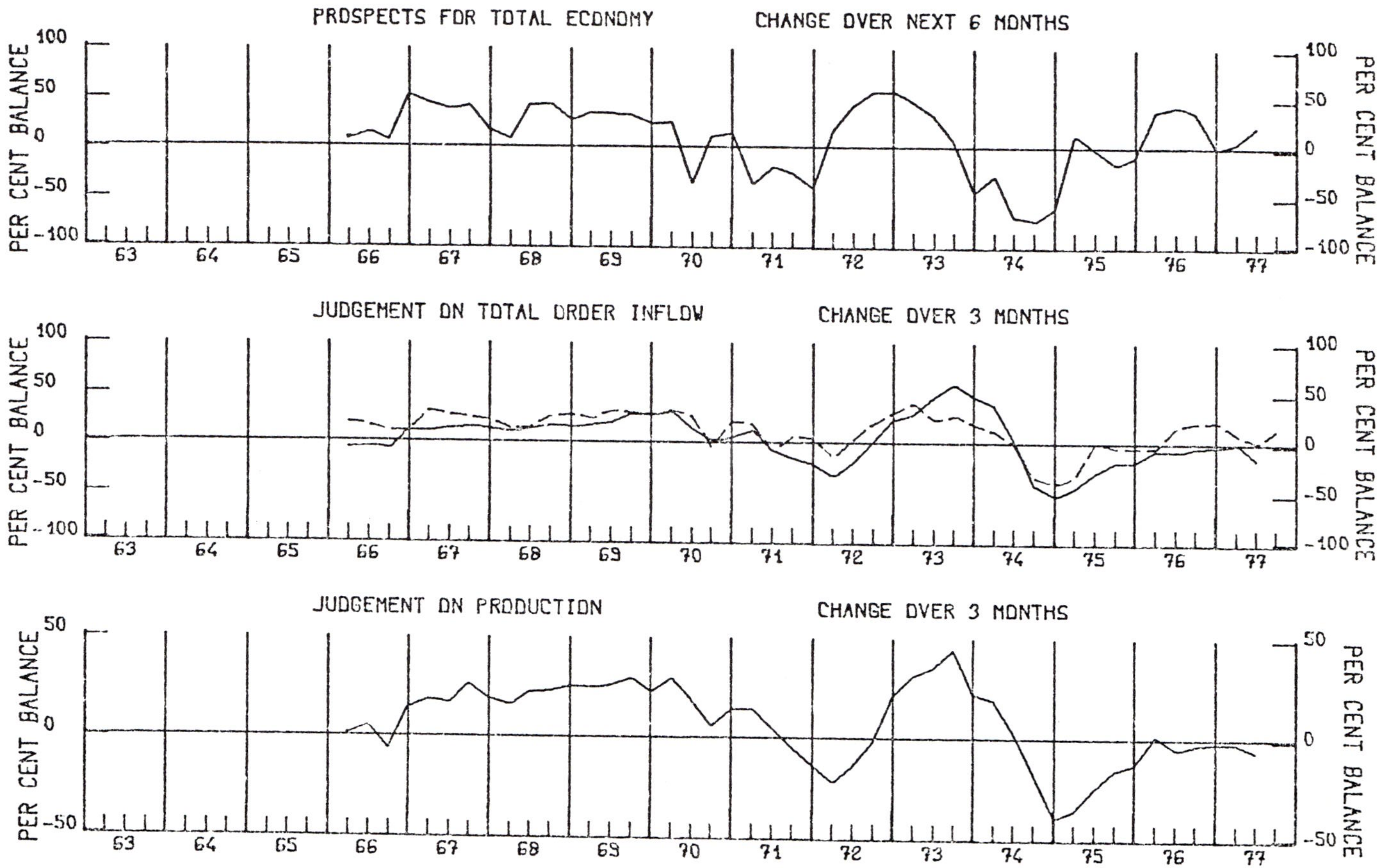

For notes see page 18a

REFERENCE CYCLE

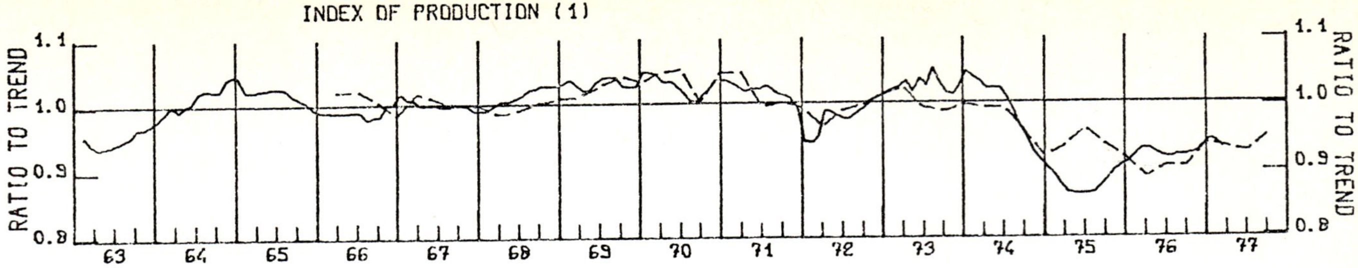

FOREIGN TRADE INDICATORS

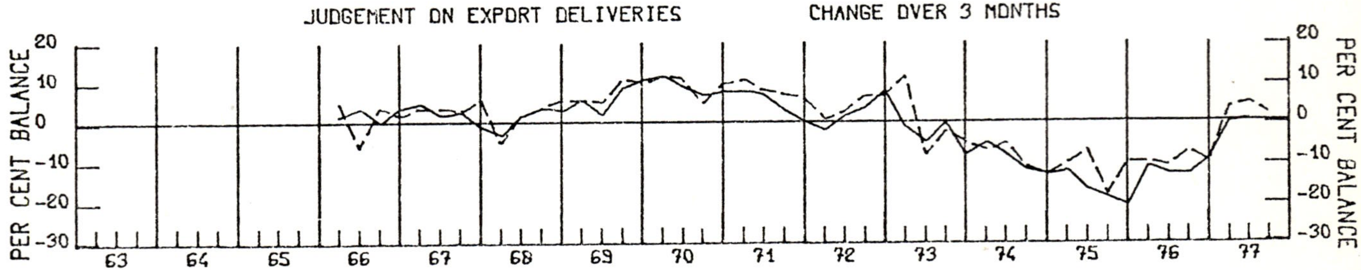

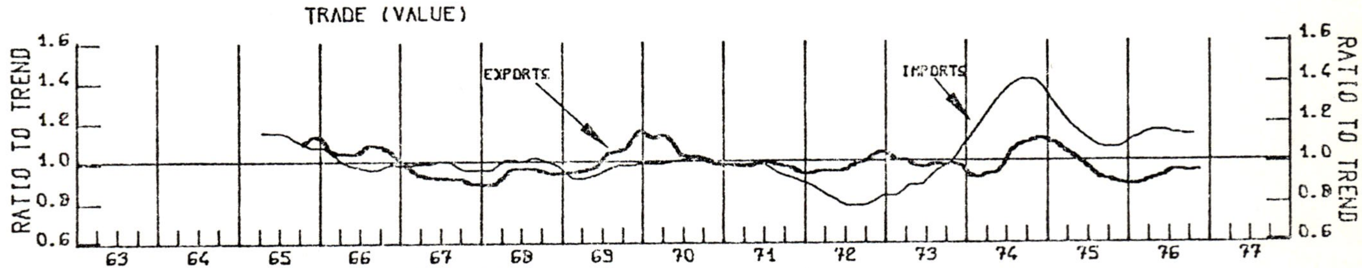

FOR NOTES, SEE NEXT PAGE

JUDGEMENT ON CAPACITY UTILISATION

% OF FIRMS WORKING AT FULL CAPACITY

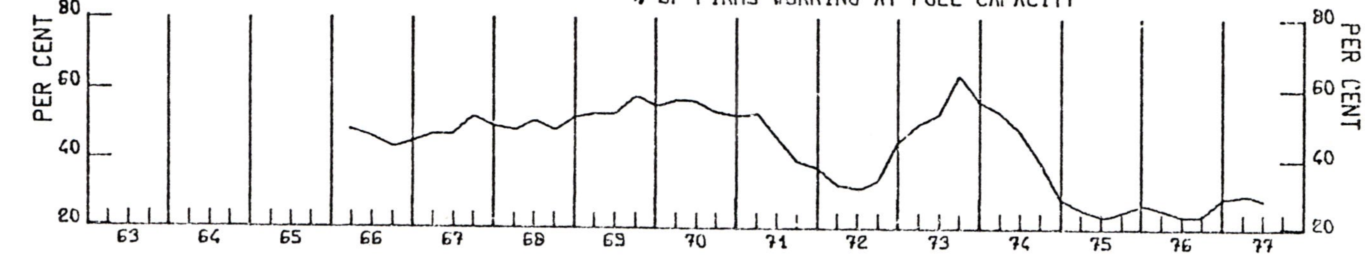

JUDGEMENT ON DIFFICULTY IN OBTAINING LABOUR

CHANGE OVER PAST 3 MONTHS

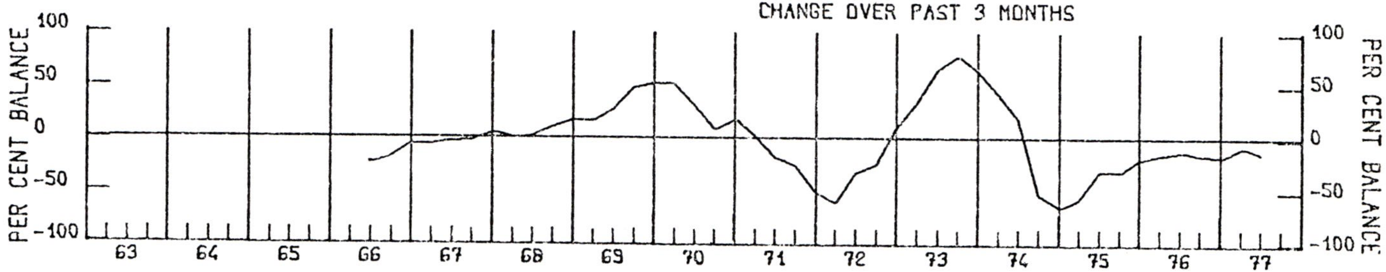

(1) PREDICTIONS BASED ON QUALITATIVE JUDGEMENTS

(2) HALFYEARLY PREDICTIONS BASED ON QUANTITATIVE JUDGEMENTS

SOURCE OF QUALITATIVE DATA: ASSOCIATED CHAMBERS OF MANUFACTURES OF AUSTRALIA AND THE BANK OF NEW SOUTH WALES

——— ACTUAL OR EX POST DATA. - - - PREDICTIONS

LAGGING AND OTHER INDICATORS

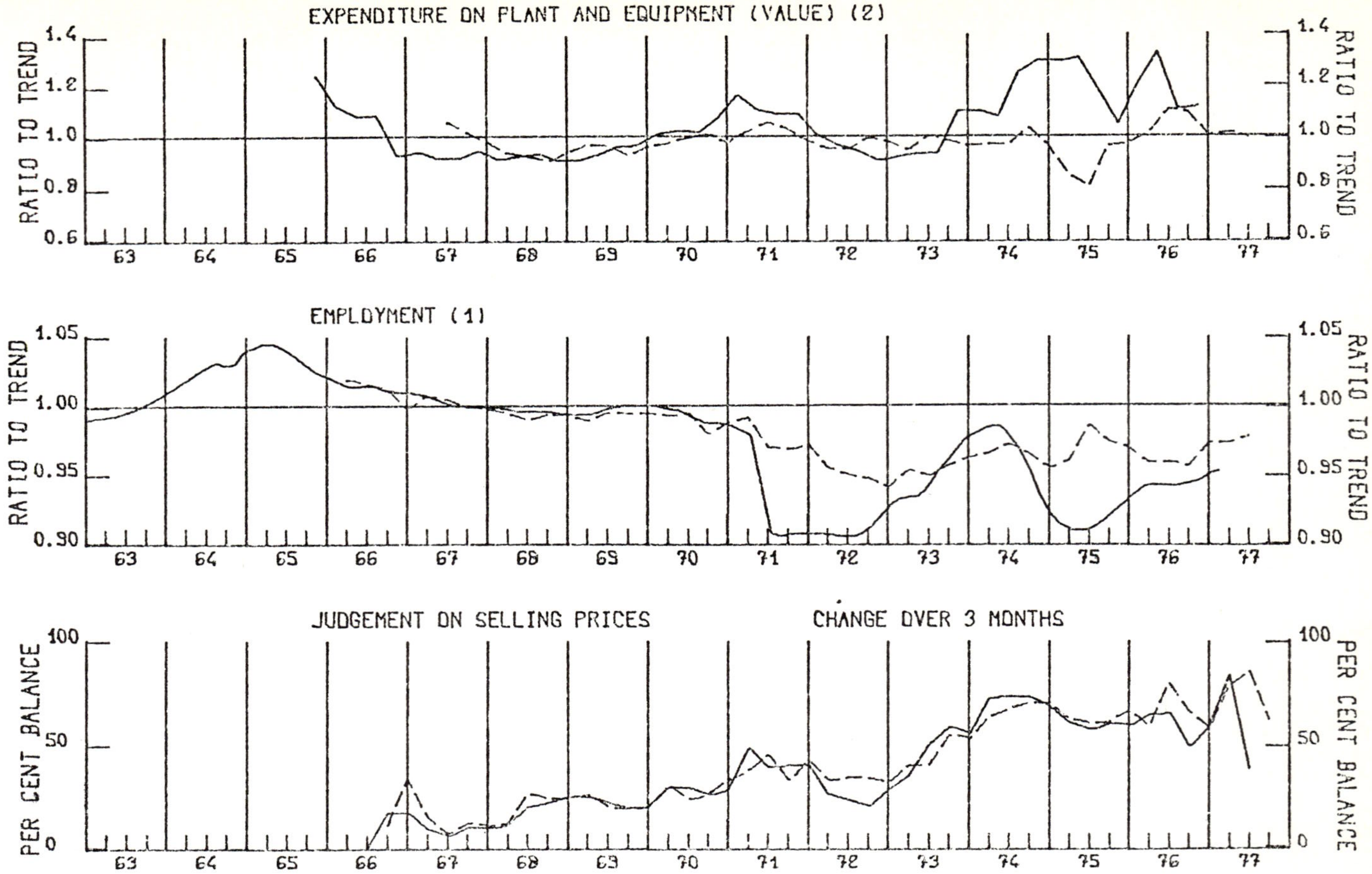

For notes see page 18a

the series has been more or less coincident at turning points. The ex ante series is, however, more useful. In the graph the series is plotted in its forecast position (i.e. since it refers to a three-month change, for the month three months after the survey month). It can be seen that the ex ante series forecast correctly turning points in the ex post series for three out of the four turning points distinguished - for the fourth (September 1973) it placed it six months too early. As a result it gave effective small leads on the reference cycle for the January 1970 and February 1972 turning points and longer leads (seven to eight months) on the two later turning points.

The judgement on the change in production is also disappointing - like the ex post order inflow series it is more of a coincident indicator with the exception of the 1975 trough where a 5 month lead was shown.

Looking at the 'Foreign trade' indicators, the imports series shows a cycle closely connected with the production cycle - with turning points generally lagging by some months. The exports series also appears to show some connection with fluctuations in the production index though an extra cycle appears in 1972/73. It is difficult to find a consistent relationship between either the ex post or the ex ante series of judgements on export deliveries and the exports series.

The series showing the percentage of firms working at full capacity shows a pronounced cyclical pattern. Generally speaking it fulfills its objective in the OECD system of acting as an alternative guide to the reference cycle, in particular in the case of a double trough or peak in the index of production series. The turning points indicated by the capacity utilisation series and the index of production together fit well in general with the results of other cyclical research that has been carried out with respect to Australia.

The qualitative ex ante series - those on changes in production and employment - have been used to provide forecasts of the corresponding quantitative series. The production series treated in this way, generally performed well, correctly anticipating turning points, except in the last few years. As can be seen, however, the employment forecasts produced have been less useful.

SWEDEN

The qualitative data used come from the quarterly survey carried out by the Konjunkturinstitutet (the National Institute of Economic Research) and the quantitative data from normal official statistical sources.

As usual the monthly index of production is used as a reference cycle with capacity utilisation and manpower bottleneck indicators as alternative coincident indicators. Four leading indicators are shown - judgement on the present level of finished goods stocks, judgements on the present level of total orders, and the ex post and ex ante questions on judgement on the change over one quarter in total order inflow.

The Foreign Trade Indicators section shows volume series for imports and exports plus ex post and ex ante series of judgements on the one quarter change in export order inflow. The lagging and other indicators section contains three groups of series: investment showing annual investment data and annual forecast data obtained from the Swedish Central Bureau of Statistics' quantitative forecast survey: employment showing a forecast series derived from a qualitative anticipations question as well as the quantitative series; wholesale prices showing series of manufactured goods and intermediate goods plus, for the manufactured goods price index, a forecast series derived from anticipations data.

The cyclical turning point in the deviation or 'ratio to trend' series for the index of industrial production can perhaps be defined as follows:

Peak:	January 1965	Trough:	February 1968
	April 1970		January 1972
	May 1974		

The Swedish economy avoided strong cyclical fluctuations up to the mid-sixties. The timing of the latest trough is dubious - as can be seen after March 1976 there was first an increase in production then a decrease - at the time of writing it is not yet clear what this episode represents in cyclical terms.

Looking first at the four leading indicators, we can see that the stocks series is generally a good indicator. Four out of the six turning points are well anticipated with leads from 6 to 12 months. The other two showed zero leads but in both cases some prior flattening of the series gave some advance indication.

The judgement on order levels series is also generally good though the leads are shorter - 2 to 4 months - and coincident twice (though once, the January '72 trough, with some prior flattening).

The ex post order inflow series shows consistent leads though the extent of the lead is variable ranging from three months (February 1968 and May 1974) to eleven months (April 1970 and January 1972).

The ex ante order inflow series is slightly more erratic but gives good leads (from eight to twelve months) at the four most recent of the six turning points.

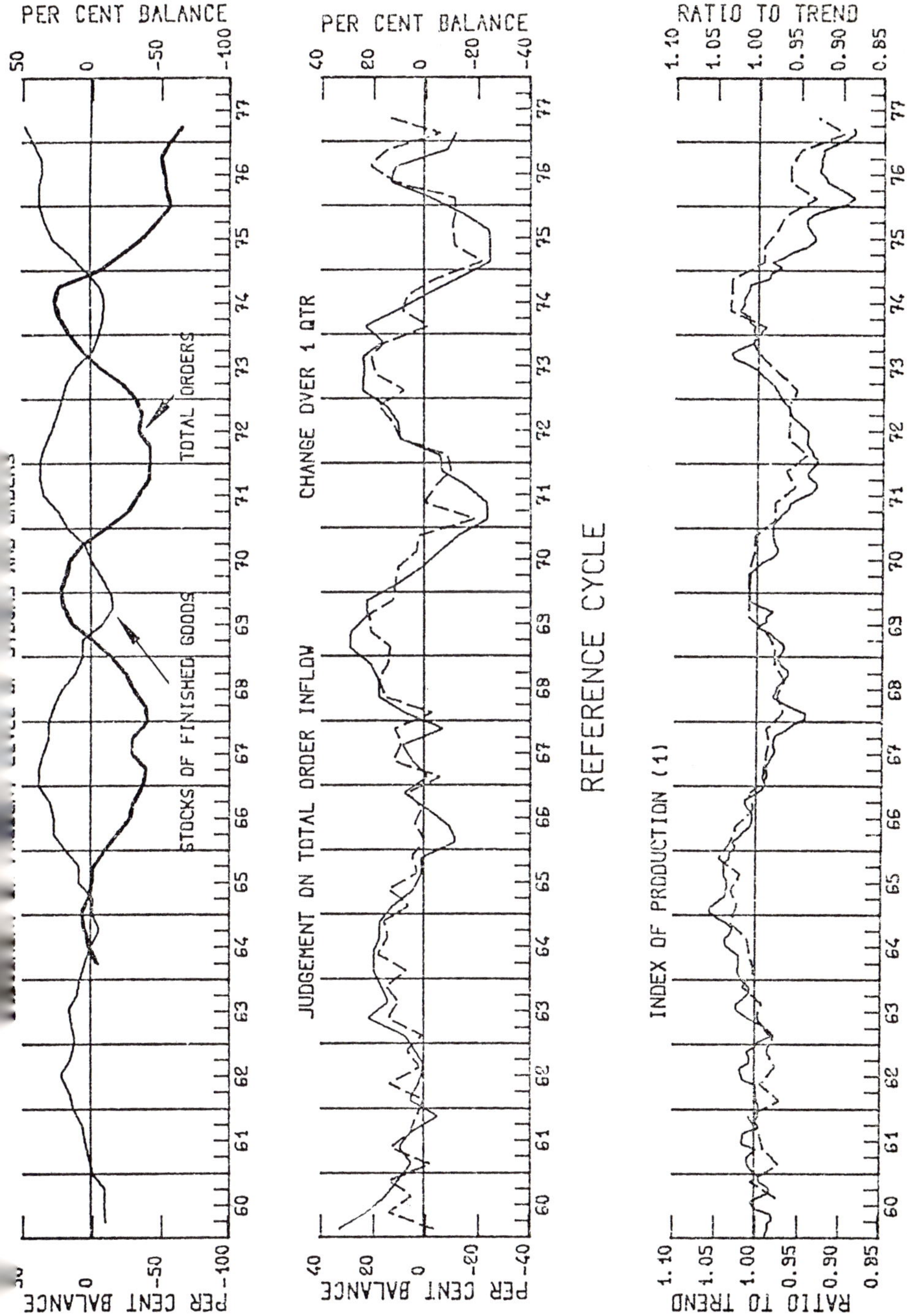

For notes see page 21b

FOREIGN TRADE INDICATORS

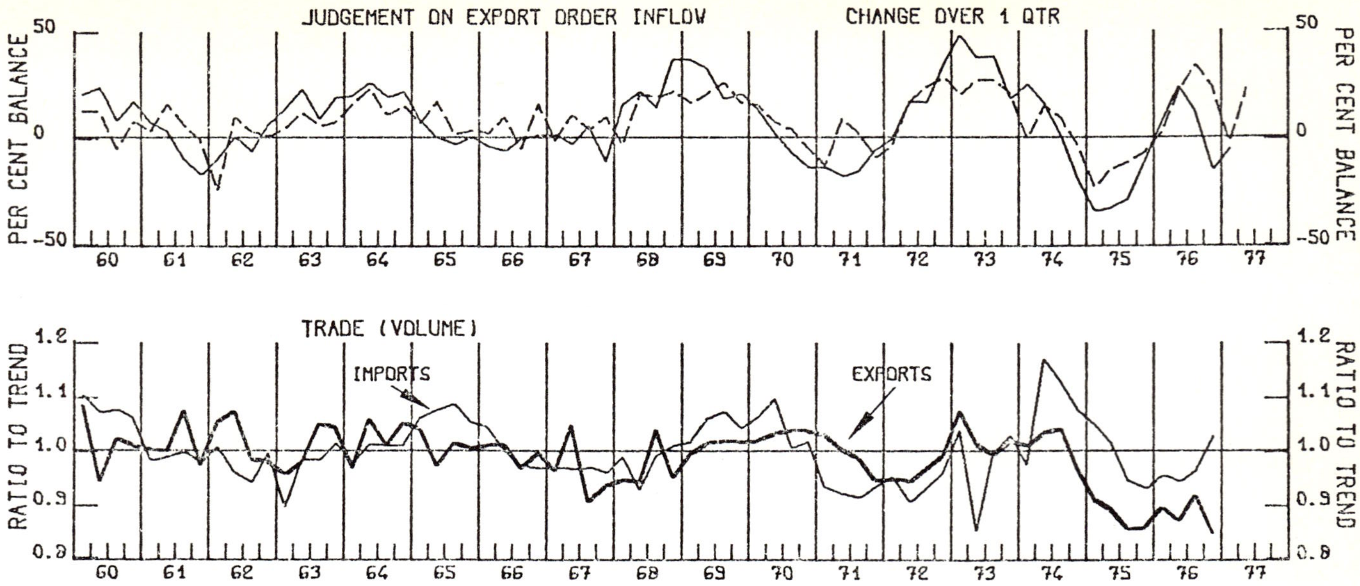

(1)PREDICTIONS BASED ON QUALITATIVE JUDGEMENTS.

SOURCE OF QUALITATIVE DATA: KONJUNKTURINSTITUTET

——— ACTUAL OR EX POST DATA. - - - PREDICTIONS

JUDGEMENT ON UTILISATION OF TECHNICAL CAPACITY

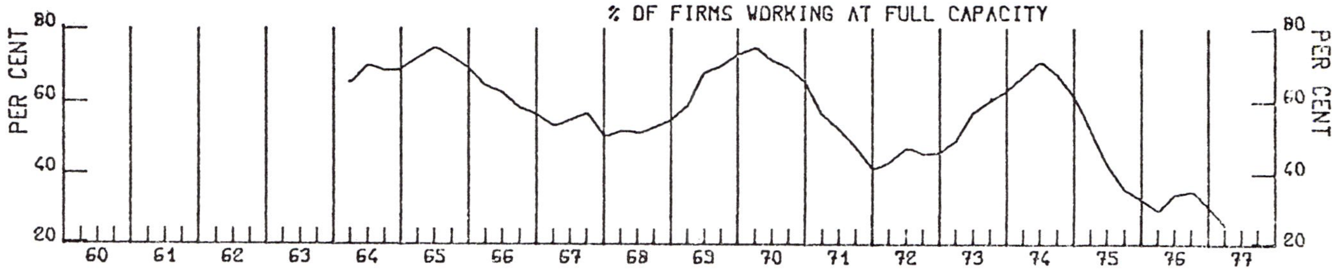

JUDGEMENT ON SKILLED MANPOWER SHORTAGE

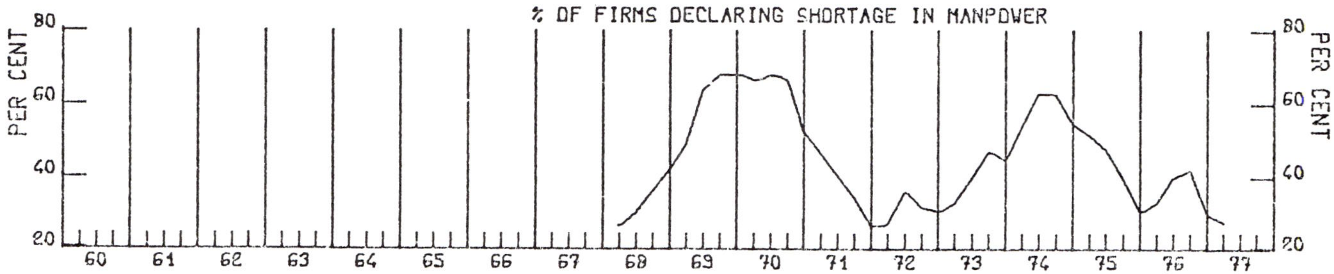

(1)PREDICTIONS BASED ON QUALITATIVE JUDGEMENTS. (2)ANNUAL FIGURES, 4TH PREDICTION COLLECTED IN MAY OF REFERENCE YEAR

SOURCE OF QUALITATIVE DATA: KONJUNKTURINSTITUTET

——— ACTUAL OR EX POST DATA. - - - PREDICTIONS

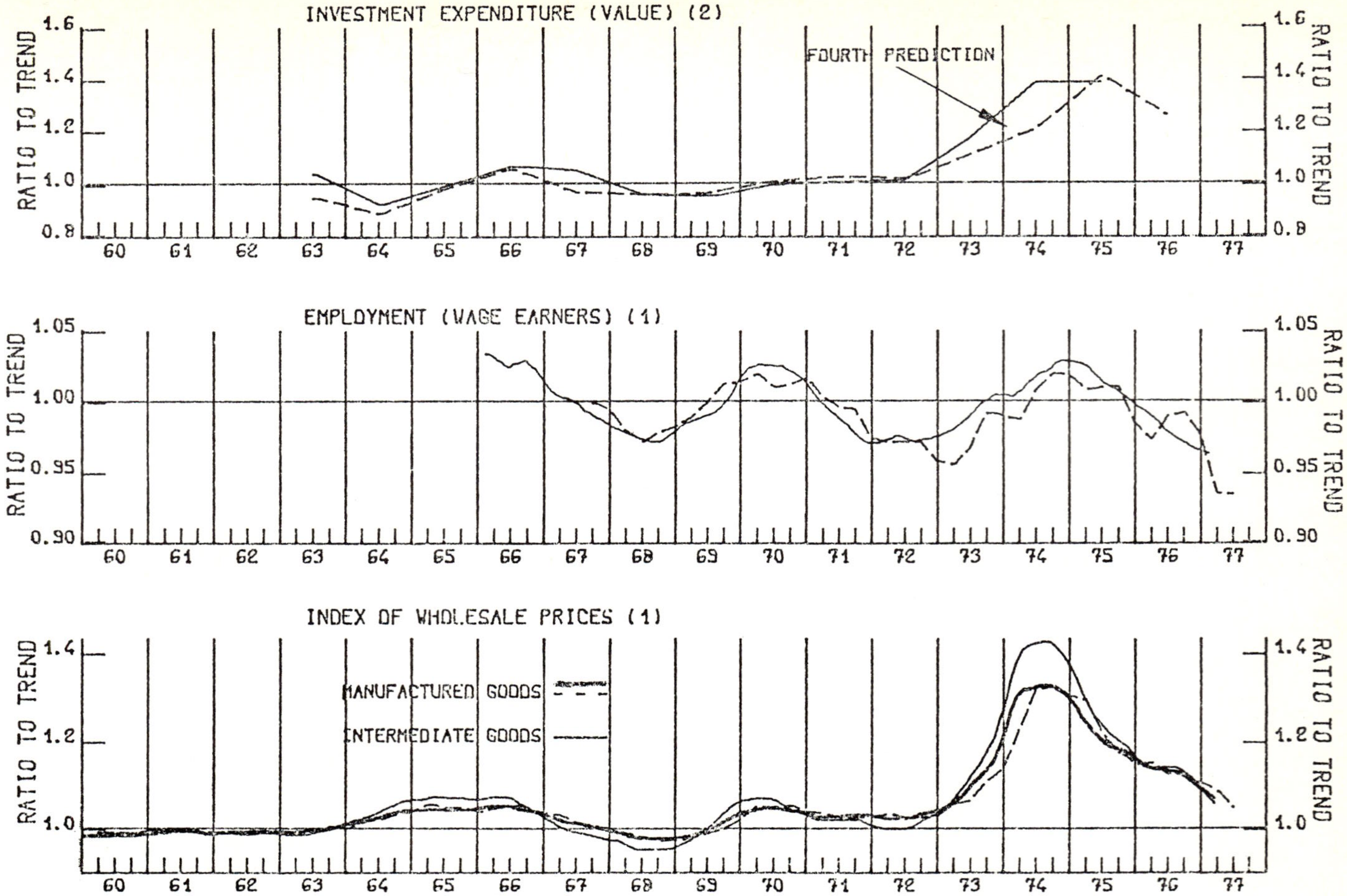

For notes see page 22a

The first two series, the judgements on stock and order levels, are in addition extremely smooth series and give almost no false signals - those that are given being relatively minor. The ex post order inflow series is slightly more erratic and gave some false signals particularly in the earlier period though the series becomes smoother in later years. Only the ex ante order inflow series remains erratic enough to give a number of false signals - this is of course not surprising given the nature of an ex ante question.

Finally, it should be noted that all four series have shown - and have indeed generally forecast - the increase in production in 1976 and the decrease in early 1977.

Looking at the foreign trade section, we find a certain relationship between movements in exports of manufactured goods and the production cycle. In general the exports cycle follows the production cycle and is roughly coincident with it, though erratically so. The imports relationship is perhaps less clear cut though some cyclical movements can also be discerned.

The ex post and ex ante series of judgements on export order inflow both appear generally to forecast - with a reasonable lead - the main cyclical movements in the export series.

Turning to the coincident indicators, the series of the percentage of firms working at full capacity has turning points which correspond well with the index of production cycle. Again, the series is very smooth and the number of false signals correspondingly few and of minor amplitude. The judgement on manpower shortage is almost as good.

The investment cycle in Sweden is, for well-known reasons, less marked than in many other countries. Its determination is, of course, not helped by the use of annual data. Nevertheless what cyclical movement can be discerned shows a lagging cycle as is normally the case for investment.

The employment series shows up as a generally lagging indicator. The forecast series derived from qualitative anticipations data follows the general movements but is rather erratic.

Any cyclical study of price movements is distorted by the sharp movements in the seventies which dwarf earlier movements. Nevertheless, cycles can be distinguished in both the price series shown. The 'manufactured goods' series has on general a small lag relative to the index of production with perhaps - as seems logical - slightly less lag in the case of the intermediate goods series. The forecast series derived from qualitative data is generally good but with an occasional slight lag on turning points.

BELGIUM

The business survey used is the well-established one run by the Banque de Belgique which is attuned to the harmonized E.E.C. survey.

Again the deviation cycle of the index of manufacturing production is taken as the reference cycle. Four leading indicators are used: the 'courbe synthétique', the judgement on the level of finished goods stocks, the judgement on the level of total orders, the judgement on the change in domestic order inflow over the past month. The 'courbe synthétique', as mentioned earlier, is a series derived from a combination of several series from the bank's survey(1). All these four series are monthly and are therefore shown after application of a three-month moving average.

The Foreign Trade Section shows value series of manufacturing exports and imports plus the judgement series on the present level of export orders. Two capacity utilisation series are shown as coincident indicators, the 'percentage of firm's capacity presently utilised' and firms' judgements on the sufficiency or insufficiency of their technical capacity in view of their expected order inflow over the next twelve months. The 'Lagging and other Indicators' section contains two graphs. One shows the index of manhours worked in manufacturing as a substitute for employment. The second shows two wholesale price indices, manufactured goods and raw materials.

Three forecast series are derived from the Business Survey anticipations questions: for production, the manhours index and the index of wholesale prices.

The manufacturing production index shows turning points in the deviations series as follows:

Peaks:	August 1963	Troughs:	July 67
	August 1969		November 1971
	February 1974		July 1975

The 'courbe synthétique' has shown a small, but consistent, lead for all the turning points with the exception of the earliest one in August 1963. The lead ranges from two months (July 1969) to four months (February 1974 and July 1975). The 'judgement on the level of orders' series is less useful -- on most occasions it is almost coincident though it gave a good lead (ten months) for the February 1974 peak. The judgement on finished goods stocks has generally acted as a leading indicator in recent years, with a short lead though it failed to forecast the July 1975 trough. The order inflow series leads all turning points with a mean lead of 4 - 5 months.

(1) See 'Bulletin de la Banque Nationale de Belgique', June 1975.

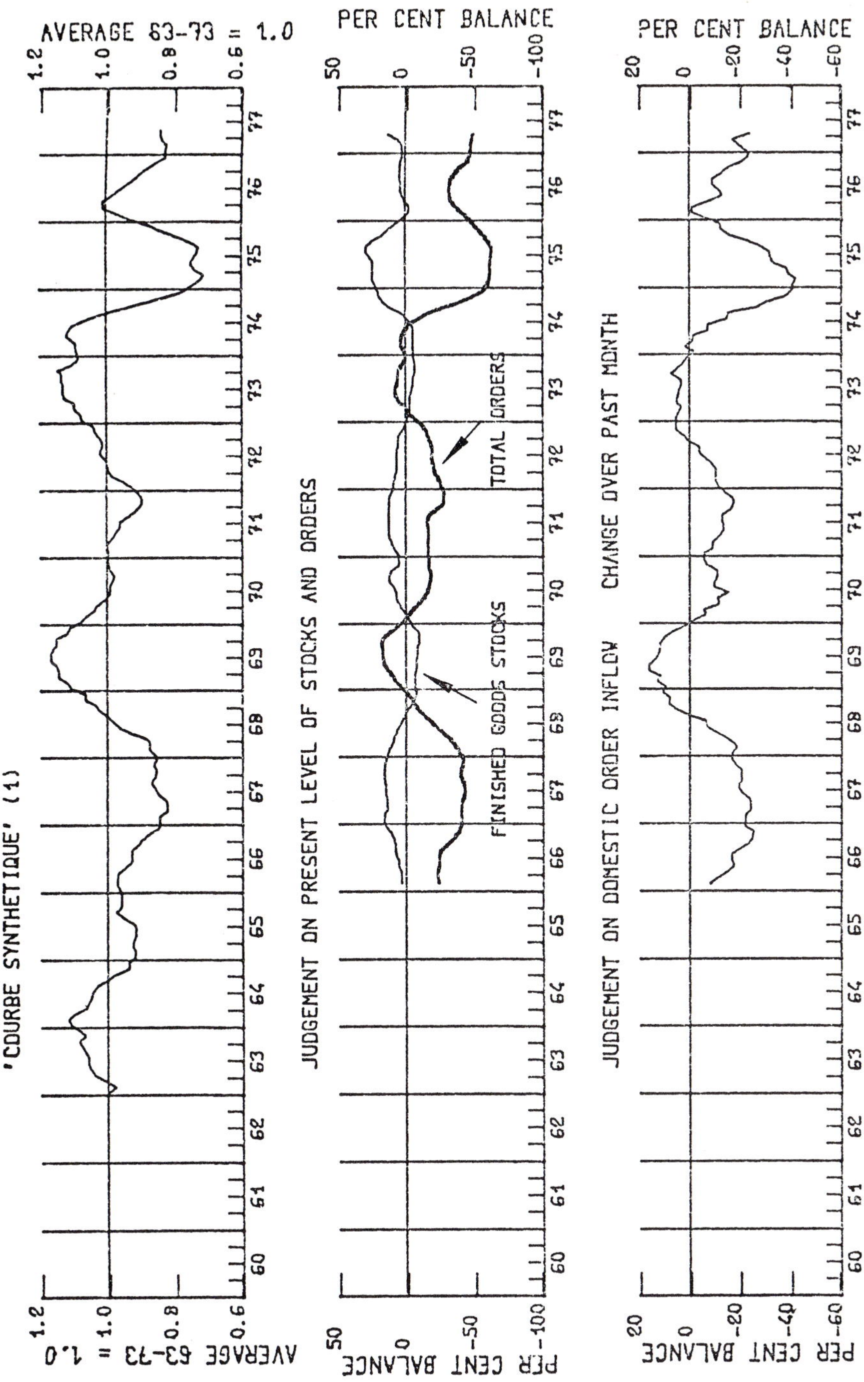
'COURBE SYNTHETIQUE' (1)
AVERAGE 63-73 = 1.0
JUDGEMENT ON PRESENT LEVEL OF STOCKS AND ORDERS
PER CENT BALANCE
TOTAL ORDERS
FINISHED GOODS STOCKS
JUDGEMENT ON DOMESTIC ORDER INFLOW CHANGE OVER PAST MONTH
PER CENT BALANCE

INDEX OF PRODUCTION (2)

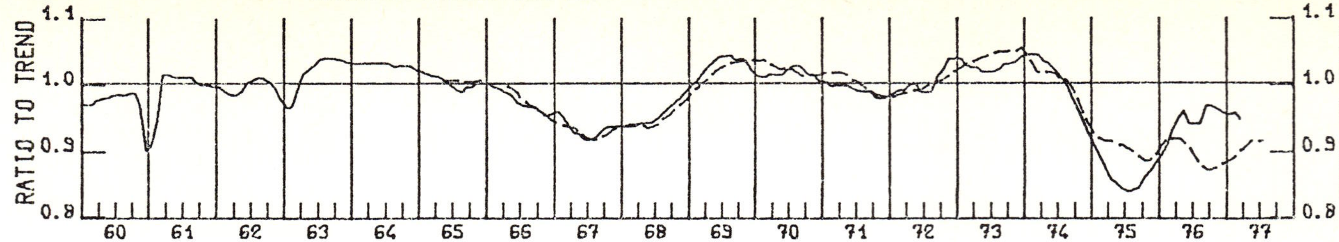

FOREIGN TRADE INDICATORS

JUDGEMENT ON PRESENT LEVEL OF EXPORT ORDERS

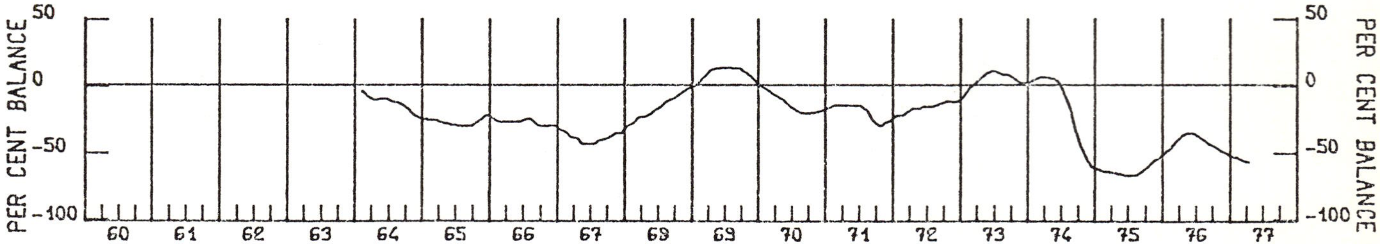

TRADE (VALUE)

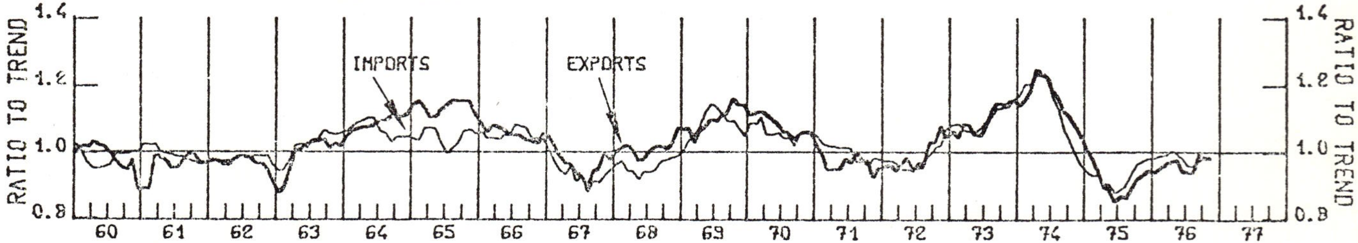

FOR NOTES, SEE NEXT PAGE

COINCIDENT INDICATORS

JUDGEMENT ON CAPACITY UTILISATION

% OF FIRMS CAPACITY PRESENTLY UTILISED

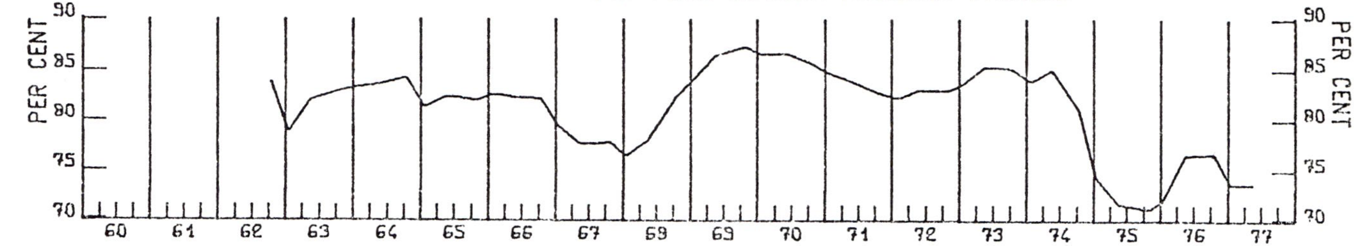

JUDGEMENT ON TECHNICAL CAPACITY

INSUFFICIENCY IN VIEW OF NEXT 12 MONTHS ORDERS

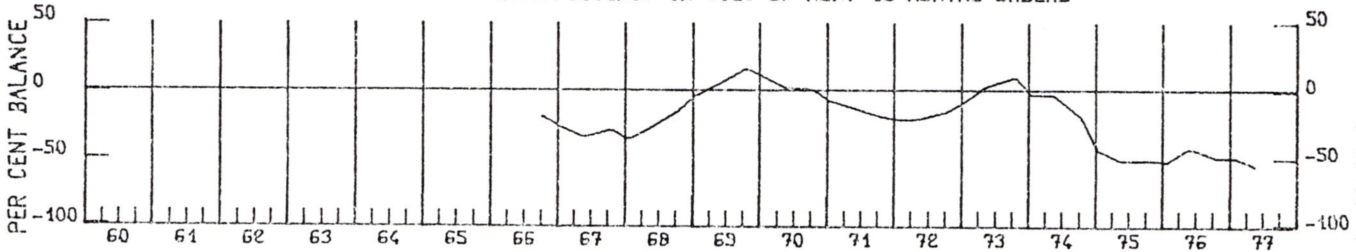

LAGGING AND OTHER INDICATORS

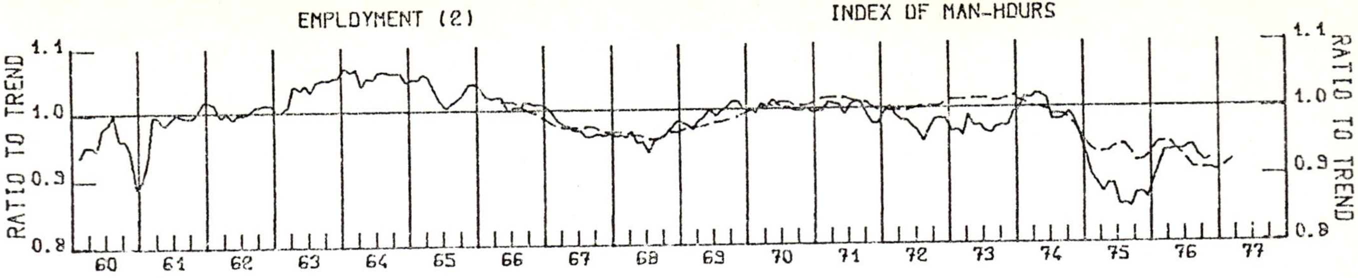

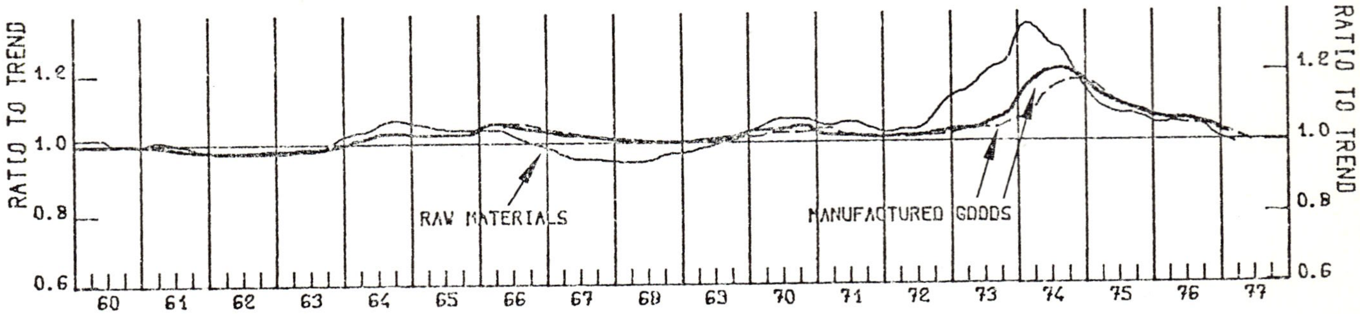

(1) SYNTHESIS OF RESULTS OF SEVERAL SERIES FROM THE SURVEY OF THE 'BANQUE NATIONALE DE BELGIQUE'

(2) PREDICTIONS BASED ON QUALITATIVE JUDGEMENTS

SOURCE OF QUALITATIVE DATA: BANQUE NATIONALE DE BELGIQUE

——— ACTUAL OR EX POST DATA. - - - PREDICTIONS

Again, all four series with the possible exception of order inflow are smooth and comparatively few false signals are given.

An interesting aspect is the behaviour of all the four series during the last year. Three of them indicated a new recession while the fourth indicated a slowing down in the rate of growth. In 1976 the production index certainly slowed down after a period of fast growth to March 1976 - after that date there was a short, sharp decline, a short rise and the most recent data show a gradual decline during the last six months. Interestingly, two of the four leading indicators - the two most in advance - show signs of an upturn again in the very latest data - this would suggest a short decline in the production index followed perhaps by a new upturn but at the time of writing it is too early to forecast with any precision.

Both manufacturing imports and exports have a cyclical movement that bears some resemblance - though not always a close one - to the production cycle. The judgement on export orders series also shows a good general relationship with the exports series though it does not always give an advance indication of turning points.

The two capacity utilisation series are both good coincident indicators with turning points close to those in the production index.

The manhours series is generally a lagging indicator though as an erratic series it is not easy to classify.

As in the case of Sweden the two price indices have cycles which are not always easy to determine during the sixties. Both series, however, seem to lag the production cycle, the raw materials being nevertheless in advance of the manufactured goods series.

The three forecast series have a somewhat erratic behaviour. On occasion all three series give a good fit but they do not always succeed in forecasting turning points in their corresponding quantitative series.

Recent Experience with the Leading Indicators

The 1974/75 recession was unprecedented in post-war experience both as regards its severity and as regards the fact that all 'developed' Western countries were affected more or less simultaneously. The recovery from the recession is also unusual in that it has not been as rapid or as consistent as in the past. It is therefore, perhaps, of interest to look briefly at how the leading indicators in the OECD system forecast the trough and experience since the trough.

It can be seen from the three countries examined that nearly all the leading indicators in fact forecast the trough (including one or two cases where the indicators concerned had not always given good guides in the past). This experience holds good for most of the other countries in the system. Where qualitative indicators were used the majority of series gave an advance indication of the trough - Japan being the only country to provide a consistent exception to this rule. In a few cases the lead given was of one or two months only but in many cases the qualitative series gave leads of several months.

Experience since the trough varies from country to country. In certain countries, the production index has shown a generally steady rise with only minor departures from this trend. In others the initial rise was followed by an uncertain period, in some cases an actual decline. It is difficult to judge at the time of writing the performance of the qualitative indicators since it is, of course, by no means clear what is actually happening at this moment in time. However, in most cases where it can be seen that a noticeable check to the expansion following the trough in the production index occurred this was foretold by the qualitative data. In certain other cases, some interruption to the expansion has recently been indicated by the leading indicators - it remains to be seen what will actually happen.

Some conclusions

Qualitative indicators were used in the OECD system in four main ways: as leading indicators of the production index; as leading indicators of exports; as coincident indicators; as a means of obtaining forecasts of certain quantitative series.

It is difficult to draw overall conclusions on their performance in the four categories as the experience varies both over time and from country to country. Nevertheless certain general points can perhaps be made.

Certain qualitative series are good leading indicators. The exact series vary between countries; some series - for example business climate indicators and judgements on order inflow - are good advance indicators in almost every case while other series - judgements on the level of orders, judgements on the level of finished goods stocks - are good in some countries but not in others. Qualitative series have three additional advantages: their relative smoothness which prevents many false signals; their quick processing time; their lack of revision. The last two points add - and this by no means a negligeable factor - to the effective lead given by series. The main disadvantage of qualitative data generally is that data for a number of countries are quarterly rather than monthly. It is perhaps true to say, though this could be debatable, that qualitative data are generally more useful in this context in European countries - which is where the technique developed - than in non-European.

Qualitative series on capacity utilisation and manpower bottlenecks - in particular the former - are practically always good coincident indicators.

Judgements on export orders or deliveries are sometimes good indicators of fluctuations in exports but the relationship is clouded by problems of data comparability and by other influences and needs to be examined in more detail.

On certain occasions qualitative anticipations questions can be used to give forecasts of corresponding quantitative series. Each case needs however to be examined separately.

Turning to a more wide subject concerning all types of data (not only qualitative data), a question that often arises in international cyclical analysis is how far it is feasible and useful to use similar series for all countries. Clearly in the case of a group of countries such as the OECD Members, there are sufficient similarities in their economic systems to support to some extent the proposition that if one series is a good indicator in one country it will probably be good in others. However while there are similarities between countries' economic systems there are also differences; and these differences can prevent a series being a consistently good or bad indicator of a certain category in all cases. This can be seen in the examination of the three countries above. In addition countries' statistical systems differ enormously; not all series are compiled in every country and the statistical quality of a particular series can vary between countries according to the importance attached to it and the feasibility of the basic data collection and processing resources necessary. Finally legal, financial and tax systems vary and statistics which are derived from these processes naturally reflect the system inherent in the country concerned. All these measures would argue against a blanket adoption of certain series as certain types of indicators.

Finally turning to the OECD system itself the question of its future arises. It is felt that the system is generally useful but it would of course benefit from being extended and developed, in particular to cover the whole economy rather that just manufacturing industry. At the same time any full international system of cyclical analysis would clearly be better developed as a joint project with experts from all countries concerned rather than as a system set up by one organisation on its own. It is hoped that the future development of cyclical analysis in OECD will form part of such a joint project.

The opinions and comments expressed in this paper are the personal responsibility of the author and are not necessarily those of the OECD.

Summary

The OECD Secretariat started work on a cyclical analysis system in the early seventies. Results for 11 countries were first published in graphical form in Part III of the monthly OECD publication 'Main Economic Indicators' in May 1974 - a further 7 countries were added later.

Work so far has been limited to manufacturing industry partly because of the need to have a manageable work programme rather than undertaking a full-scale system for all OECD countries straight away, partly because of the greater range of data available for manufacturing than for other sectors of the economy, partly because manufacturing is one of the sectors most heavily affected by the business cycle, and finally, because of resource limitations in the OECD.

As well as using the more traditional quantitative statistical series substantial use has been made of qualitative data from business surveys for countries for which these are available. This followed previous research carried out both in the OECD and in certain European countries which had suggested that these series might be of potential use as cyclical indicators. Apart from the concepts covered by the series themselves (which often include ideals or principles not easily measured in quantitative statistics), qualitative indicators have certain advantages such as, in many countries, a relatively quick processing time which in the case of leading indicators often increases the effective lead by a few months, lack of revision and the fact that the series produced are relatively smooth. The main disadvantage of qualitative series in this context is that data for certain countries are quarterly rather than monthly.

Because of the impossibility of carrying out a full-scale study no attempt has so far been made to construct composite indices or to establish reference cycle chronologies. The index of manufacturing production has been taken as a reference cycle indicator both because it is perhaps the prime indicator of the cycle in manufacturing and because it is in general a series that is among the most widely available and the most minutely compiled. Leading indicators for each country have been mainly chosen from among the following list: judgement on the general business situation, judgement on the level of finished goods stocks, judgement on the level of order stocks, judgement on the inflow of new orders, judgement on the anticipated change in production (all of which are qualitative series), new orders, stocks/deliveries ratios, hours worked, stock changes and other quantitative series. Capacity utilisation series - either from quantitative or qualitative sources - were used as coincident indicators, as were qualitative series of manpower bottlenecks and recruitment difficulties. Lagging indicators were chosen from: investment series, employment series, producer or wholesale price series for manufactured products, and, where available, unit labour cost. Raw materials and intermediate goods wholesale and producer price series have also been included; these are shown with the output price series though their classification as cyclical indicators varies from country to country and according to the exact nature of the series.
In addition to the above, a section showing exports and imports of manufactured products is included - this is not because these series are good cyclical indicators, but because it is interesting to compare their fluctuations with the business cycle. Qualitative series of export orders or deliveries are often included as advance indicators of exports.

The approach is based on the 'growth cycle' principle - i.e. series are studied in the form of deviations from their long-term trend. The original series is divided by the trend to give a series of deviations from trend to show the growth cycles. In the case of monthly data a three-month moving average is applied to the original series before its division by the trend to dampen the irregular fluctuations.

In general qualitative series used in the analysis have not been de-trended, partly because it is rare that they show any significant long-term trend, partly because in a number of cases the questions from which they result are such that the series can be considered to be in an already de-trended form. The three month moving average is, however, applied to monthly series (1).

A further use is made of qualitative anticipatory data, i.e. responses to questions which ask for entrepreneurs' opinions on future movements in prices, production and employment, as these are used to provide forecast series of the appropriate quantitative ex-post series. This is done essentially by establishing a relationship by regression between the results of the qualitative series and the growth rate in the quantitative series. The derived relationship is then used to generate a forecast series which is then divided by the trend of the quantitative series to provide a forecast series of deviations from the trend.

---

(1) For further details of the methodology see: R. Gränzer, 'Cyclical Indicators for Manufacturing Industry', Occasional Study; Supplement to OECD Economic Outlook, December 1973.

Qualitative data are therefore used in the OECD cyclical analysis system in four ways: as leading indicators of the reference cycle (index of industrial production); as leading indicators of exports; as coincident indicators; as a means of obtaining forecasts of certain qualitative series. In examining their performance in the system it is clear that the experience varies to some extent both over time and from country to country. Some general conclusions can however be drawn.

Certain qualitative series have been found to be almost invariably good leading indicators, in particular business climate or business conditions indicators and judgements on order inflow. Other series - e.g. judgement on order levels or judgements on finished goods stocks - are good (or even very good) leading indicators for some countries but give only very short or zero leads in other cases. Recent experience with all the series selected as leading indicators has however been generally favourable. The 1975/76 trough was well predicted by the majority of qualitative series so used. In addition, the series concerned have also successfully predicted the various movements that have since occurred in different countries' production indices, whether this was a more or less uninterrupted recovery from the trough or a period of recovery followed by a slow-down or even a further decline.

Qualitative series on capacity utilisation and manpower bottlenecks - in particular the former - are practically always good coincident indicators.

Judgements on export orders or deliveries are sometimes good indicators of fluctuations in exports but the relationship is clouded by problems of data comparability and by other influences and needs to be examined in more detail.

On certain occasions qualitative anticipatory questions can be used to give forecasts of corresponding quantitative series. Each case needs, however, to be examined separately.

In conclusion, experience has shown that qualitative series can successfully be used as cyclical indicators in a number of ways. In particular they are in many cases useful leading indicators though experience in this regard varies between countries.

G.H. MOORE
NATIONAL BUREAU OF ECONOMIC RESEARCH
NEW YORK

PH.A. KLEIN
THE PENNSYLVANIA STATE UNIVERSITY
UNIVERSITY PARK

FORECASTING FOREIGN TRADE WITH LEADING INDICATORS

Forecasting Foreign Trade with Leading Indicators

Geoffrey H. Moore and Philip A. Klein*

When the National Bureau of Economic Research began the International Economic Indicator project in 1973 we had two initial objectives. The first was to test the feasibility of employing traditional NBER methods to identify growth cycles in a number of market-oriented economies. The second objective was to see whether the leading, roughly coincident, and lagging indicators, which had proved reliable in analyzing business cycles in the United States, would prove equally useful in analyzing growth cycles in the United States and abroad. Our paper at the 1975 CIRET meetings in Stockholm, as well as other reports, demonstrated that the NBER indicators can be adapted to both these purposes, and we are now engaged in developing a system for monitoring international instability along these lines. In this endeavor we are cooperating with the OECD in establishing a current data bank which we trust will prove helpful for many purposes in all the countries that ultimately can be included.

There is no purpose which suggests itself for experimentation more readily than the effort to forecast foreign trade flows. A country's demand for imports is likely to follow closely fluctuations in its

* Philip A. Klein is on the staff of the National Bureau of Economic Research and Professor of Economics at Pennsylvania State University. Geoffrey H. Moore is Director of Business Cycle Research at the National Bureau and Senior Research Fellow, Hoover Institution, Stanford University. In the research underlying this paper we have had the able assistance of Walter W. Ebanks, research associate at the National Bureau. We are indebted to Chantal Dubrin, Jean Maltz and Elizabeth Wehle for their careful statistical work. The research has been supported by funds from the U.S. Departments of State, Treasury, Commerce, Labor, and Agriculture, The Federal Reserve System, and several American corporations.

domestic economic fortunes. Imported materials are used in domestic production, and imported finished goods are sold directly in domestic markets. The leading indicators include a number of factors pertaining to these demands for imports: orders placed for goods in the importing country; the accumulation or liquidation of inventories; marginal adjustments in the utilization of labor (e.g., by shortening or lengthening the workweek); prices paid for industrial materials; new commitments to invest in plant and equipment; and cost-price relations affecting profit margins. These are not the only elements bearing upon decisions to import, of course, but they are sufficiently important to have a significant relationship to import demand.

Hence the leading indicators can be used either to forecast aggregate dem and the latter used to forecast imports, or they can be used to forecast import directly. We have chosen the direct route in the experiments described below. The system can be applied to exports as well as to imports, provided the exports go to countries represented in the leading indexes. Hence it can be used to obtain forecasts of trade balances among these countries.

The forecasts are of a short-run nature, since the leading indexes do not lead aggregate demand (or imports) by more than four to six months on the average. Nevertheless, the system can be used to obtain forecasts of next year's trade at the end of the preceding year, and of the rate of growth of trade three or four quarters ahead of the latest available data, as will be shown.

We have applied this general line of reasoning to U.S. exports by constructing leading indexes for several of the more important trading partners of the United States, individually and combined by weighting country indexes by the country's GNP in a base year (1970), and using them to forecast subsequent U.S. exports to these countries. In the work presented here we include U.S. exports to the United Kingdom, West Germany, France and Italy. Exports to Canada and Japan are analyzed in a separate report.[1] These countries by no means constitute all of U.S. trade, but they do cover about half of it. The method can, of course, be applied to U.S. exports to other countries as soon as we are able to construct leading indexes for them. It is clear, moreover, that the method can be applied to the exports of any country, to the extent that its exports go to countries for whom leading indexes have been constructed. In this way, it is our hope, the analysis of foreign trade considered here can augment our knowledge of how instability is transmitted internationally and promote efforts to formulate wise economic decisions.

The Methodology

We begin by describing in somewhat greater detail the method employed. The variable we have chosen to forecast is the percent change in U.S. exports. Forecasting change is more challenging than forecasting levels, because the levels are often largely dominated by long-run trends. We have experimented with both annual and quarterly forecasts and report on our efforts for manufactured goods exports as a whole and several commodity groups. Exports can be measured in terms of quantity, unit value, and total value and we have experimented with forecasting all three, but in this paper we concentrate on quantity forecasts.

1 The Development and Use of International Economic Indicators, manuscript, January 1977.

As noted above, the forecasts themselves are generated by the percentage change in the leading index for the country (or countries) to which U.S. exports are going, which is assumed to lead the flow of imports into the area under review by six months.

The percentage change in the leading index is the independent variable. For annual (calendar year) forecasts, the six-month lead implies that changes in the leading index between fiscal years (years ending June 30, overlapping the calendar years by six months) are required. In order to make forecasts before the calendar year has begun (or rather, before data for any part of the calendar year are available), we assume that the fiscal year overlapping the calendar year to be forecast can be approximately represented by the December figure for the leading index. This is (approximately) the central month of the fiscal year. Hence to forecast the percentage change in exports from year 1 to year 2 we use the percentage change between the average value of the leading index for the fiscal year average ending June 30 of year 1 and its value in December of year 1. No data for year 2 are employed in the forecast. We further assume a linear relationship between the percentage changes in exports and in the leading index. Hence our regressions are of the form:

$$\Delta Q_t = a + b\Delta LD_{-1}$$

where ΔQ_t is the percentage change in export quantity from year t-1 to year t, and ΔLD_{-1} is the percentage change in the leading index between the fiscal year average and December of year t-1. A simple adaptation of this scheme to quarterly data is described below.

The leading index for each country includes approximately twelve leading indicators corresponding as nearly as possible to the twelve included in the National Bureau's list as developed in 1966. This list was used in the Department of Commerce's monthly publication, Business Conditions Digest, until May 1975, after which a revised list was substituted. The chief adjustment we have made is to express in constant prices each of the series that was originally in current prices, with the exception of two price indexes (materials prices and common stocks) which are left as is. This adjustment means, of course, that the leading index is more indicative of changes in the real volume of activity. The same adjustment has been made in the new list of indicators presently used by the Department of Commerce, and there is also considerable duplication in content between the new and old lists, though they are not identical.

Wherever we use composite leading indexes for several countries the indexes are weighted by the country's GNP in 1970, expressed in dollars. The broadest group includes six countries: Canada, the United Kingdom, West Germany, France, Italy and Japan. These countries collectively took 51 percent of total U.S. exports in 1970, and 47 percent of U.S. manufactured goods exports. Another group includes only the four European countries in the above list. In Chart I we show the leading index for the United States, for the major trading partners grouped by

Chart I - Leading Indicator Indexes: United States, Canada, Western Europe and Japan

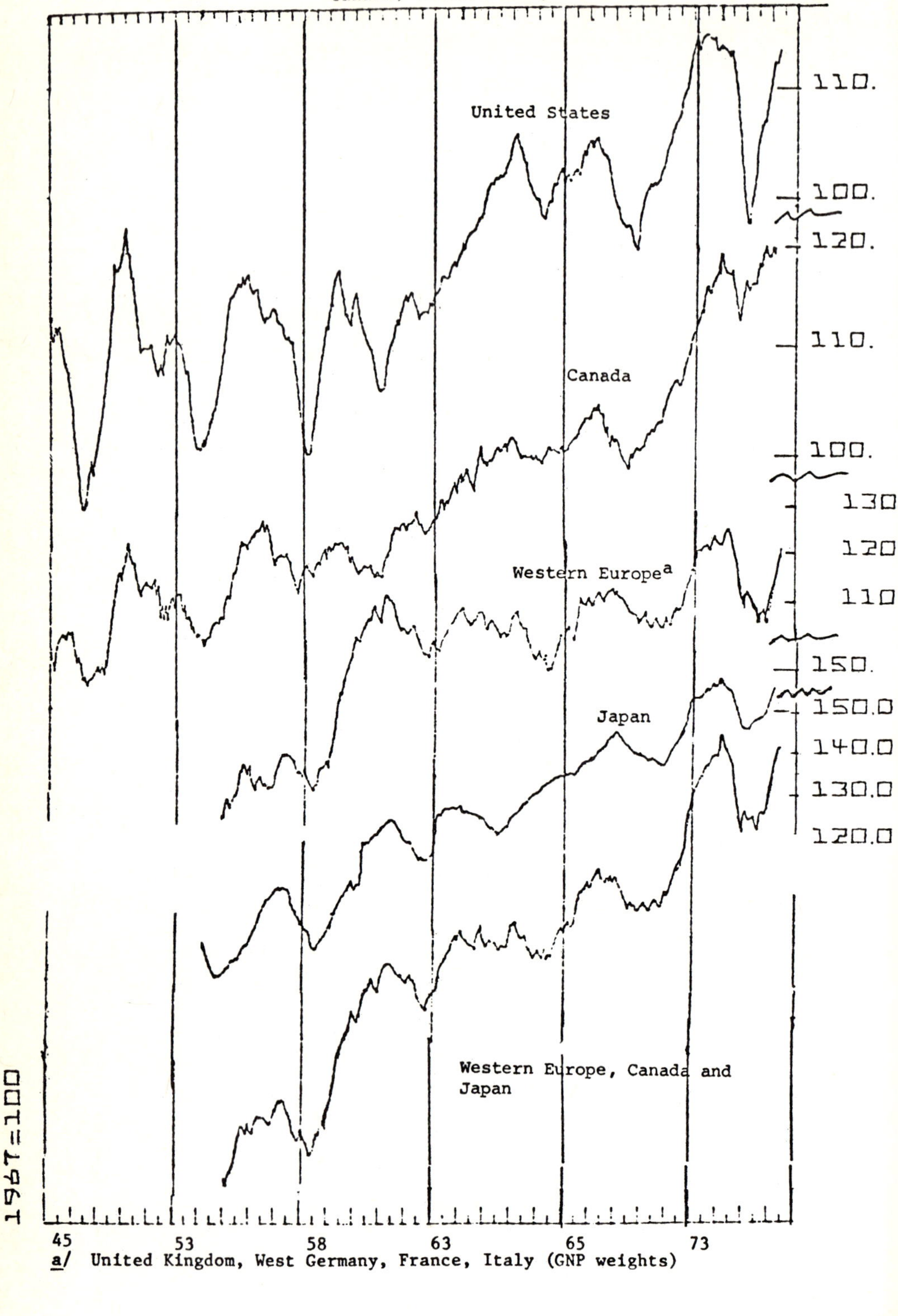

a/ United Kingdom, West Germany, France, Italy (GNP weights)

area, and for all six countries together. Although there are differences in timing, it is clear that the different areas experience many cyclical movements in common.

In sum, by means of the method described we obtain an independent variable based on percent changes in the leading indexes of U.S. trading partners and use it to forecast subsequent percent changes in U.S. exports to these countries. The size and significance of the correlation coefficients and mean errors obtained thereby constitute a measure of the success obtained by this simple forecasting technique.

We have not been able in all instances to match the geographic coverage of the export data with that of the leading indexes. Thus we have used the composite leading index for four Western European countries to forecast exports to all Western European countries. Also, we have used the six-country composite index to forecast total U.S. exports to all countries. This is a possible source of error, therefore, though it is mitigated by the likelihood that some of the countries not covered by our leading indexes may experience cyclical movements similar to those that are covered.

The Results: Manufactured Goods Exports, Annual Data

Forecast and actual year-to-year changes in total quantity of U.S. exports of manufactured goods to Western Europe as a whole are shown in Chart II. The major swings in the rates of change in U.S. exports of manufactured goods to these four countries appear to be fairly well

Chart II

Forecast and Actual Percent Changes in U.S. Exports of Manufactured Goods to Western Europe, Quantity, 1964-76, Using Leading Index for Four Countries,* GNP Weights

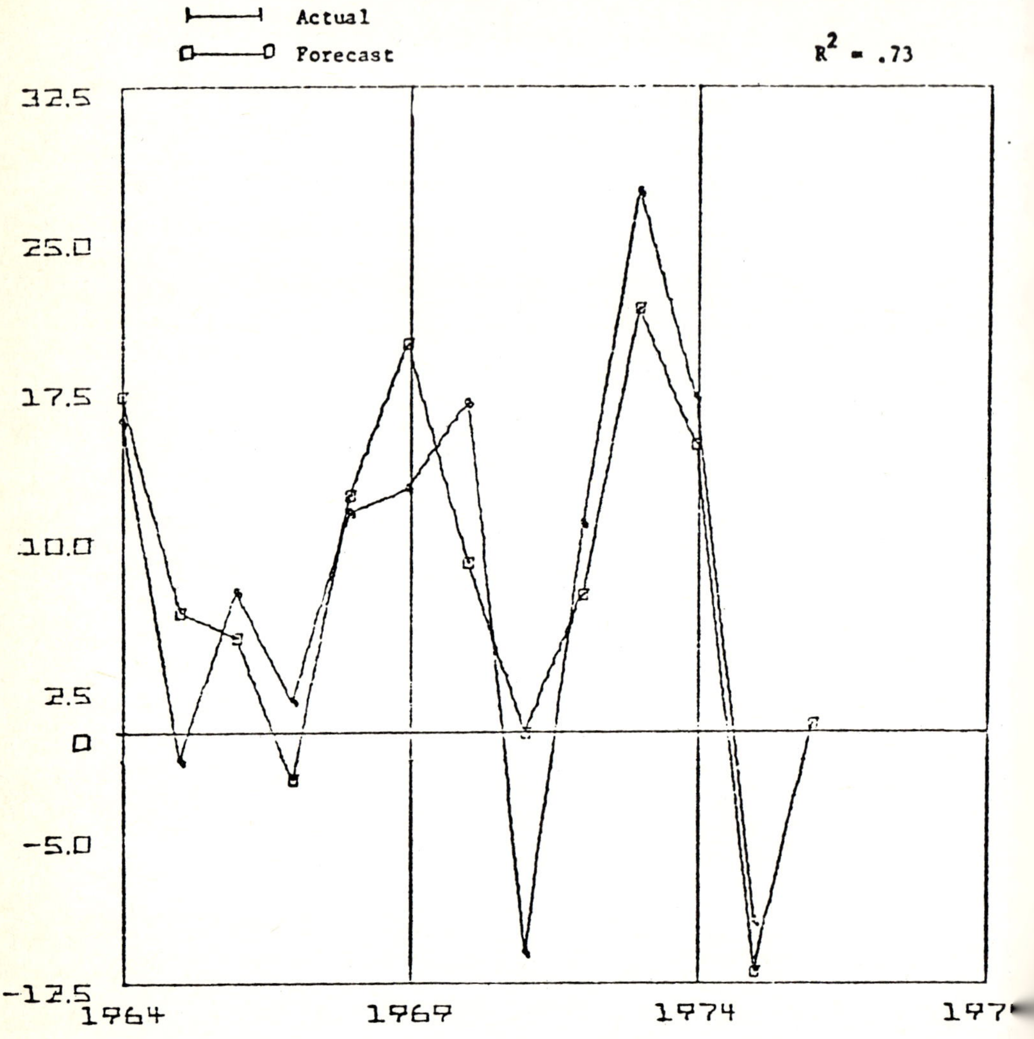

* United Kingdom, West Germany, France, Italy

reflected in the forecasts. The correlation coefficient (R^2) is .73, implying that about three-fourths of the fluctuation in the rates of change is captured by the forecasts. The root mean square error is 5.6 percentage points. The fit seems to be best during the 1973-75 period, but the correspondence is moderately good during the milder swings of the earlier years as well.

When the same method is used to forecast the quantity of U.S. manufactured goods exports to Canada and Japan during the same period, using our leading indexes for Canada and Japan, the R^2 are .71 and .64, respectively, and the root mean square errors are 5.1 and 12.3 percentage points. When the leading index for all six countries combined is used to forecast the quantity of U.S. manufactured goods exports to all countries, the R^2 is .81 and the root mean square error is 4.1 percent. We conclude that the technique can account for roughly two-thirds to four-fifths of the variation in the year-to-year changes in the physical volume of U.S. exports of manufactured goods.

The Results: Selected Manufactured Commodity Exports, Annual Data

The performance of the leading indicators in forecasting changes in total exports of manufactured goods suggests that the method might be useful in forecasting the exports of particular commodity groups as well. We have run a series of regressions using as the dependent variable the year-to-year percent changes in the quantity of U.S. exports of chemicals (SITC group 5); textiles, metal products, and other manufactures classified chiefly by material (SITC group 6); machinery and transportation equipment

(SITC group 7); and miscellaneous manufactures (SITC group 8). These data cover U.S. exports to all countries, so we use the six-country leading index to forecast them since it has the broadest geographic coverage. Charts III through VI present the results together with the correlation coefficients. In each case a moderately good fit is obtained, with R^2 in the range of .5 to .8.

The Results: Quarterly Data

The same method of forecasting year-to-year rates of change in exports that has been illustrated above can be applied on a quarterly basis. Recall that the change in the leading index between its average for a fiscal year and the figure for the following December is used to forecast calendar-year changes in exports. Now calendar-year changes are equivalent to changes in four-quarter averages four quarters apart. Where quarterly data are available these averages can be moved forward one quarter at a time, thereby bringing them more nearly up to date. Similarly, the changes in the leading index can be moved forward three months at a time also, so the forecasts are more up to date as well.

This scheme really accomplished two things. First, it means that the rate of change in exports that is being forecast is a relatively smoothly changing rate. Four-quarter moving averages are smoother than quarterly figures, and the use of a four-quarter interval over which to measure the change in the four-quarter averages tends to emphasize the cyclical swings in the rate of growth as compared with shorter-run erratic movements. A plausible objective of quarterly forecasts is to

Chart III

Forecast and Actual Changes in U.S. Exports of Chemicals (SITC 5), Quantity, 1964-76, Using Leading Index for Six Countries,* GNP Weights

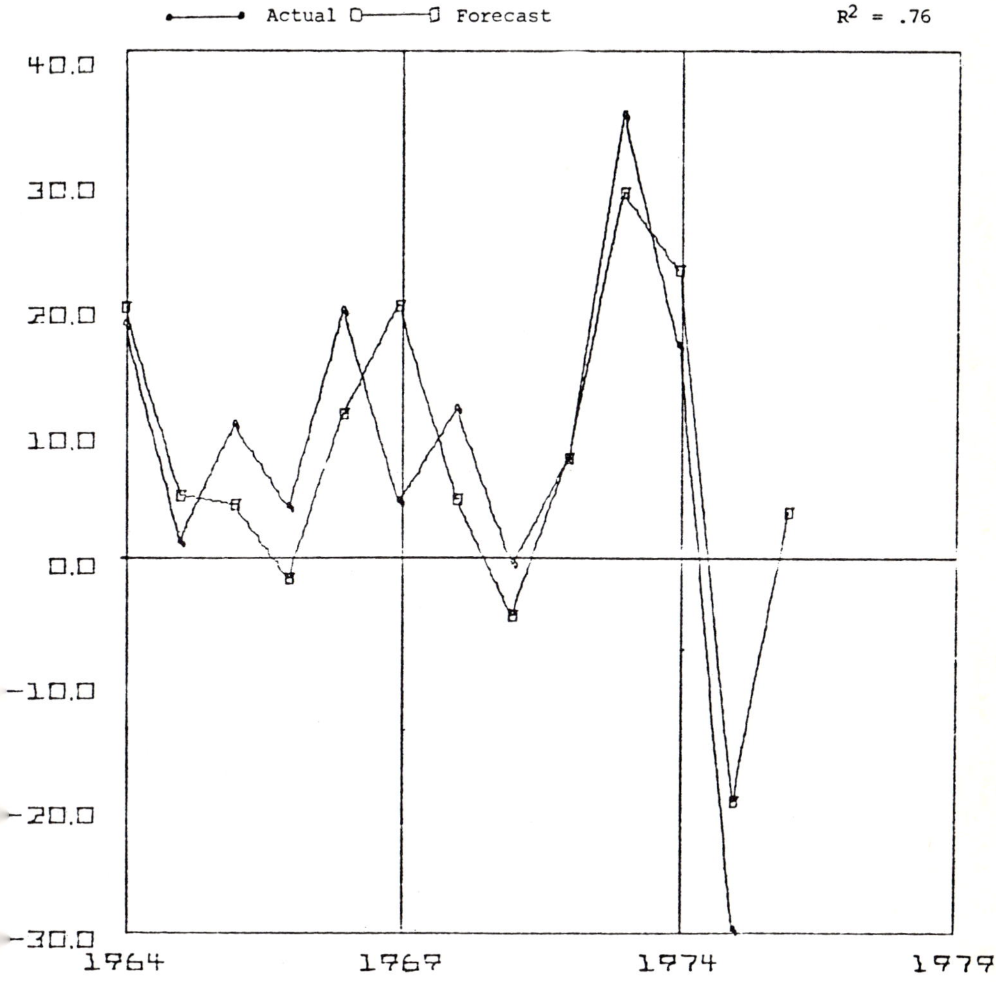

* Canada, United Kingdom, West Germany, France, Italy, Japan

Chart IV

Forecast and Actual Changes in U.S. Exports of Textiles, Metals, etc. (SITC 6), Quantity, 1964-76, Using Leading Index for Six Countries,* GNP Weights

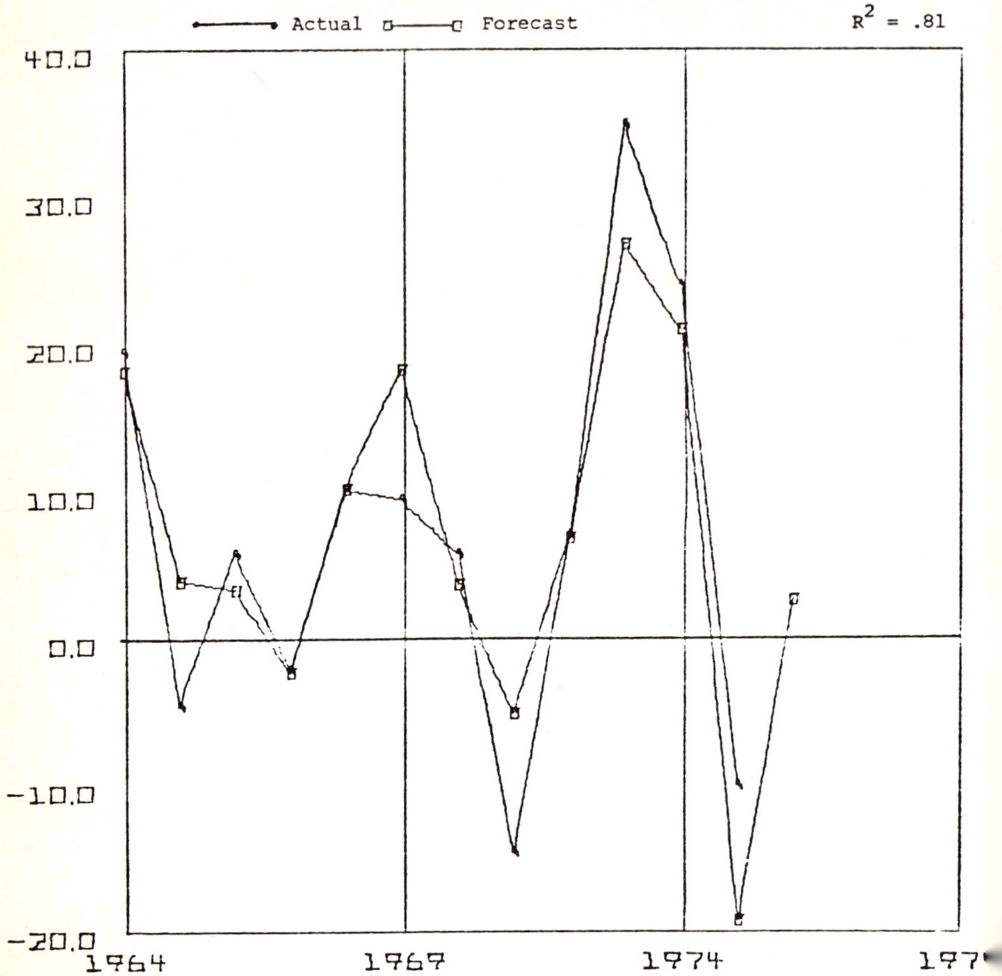

* Canada, United Kingdom, West Germany, France, Italy, Japan

Chart V

Forecast and Actual Changes in U.S. Exports of Machinery and Transportation Equipment (SITC 7), Quantity, 1964-76 Using Leading Index for Six Countries,* GNP Weights

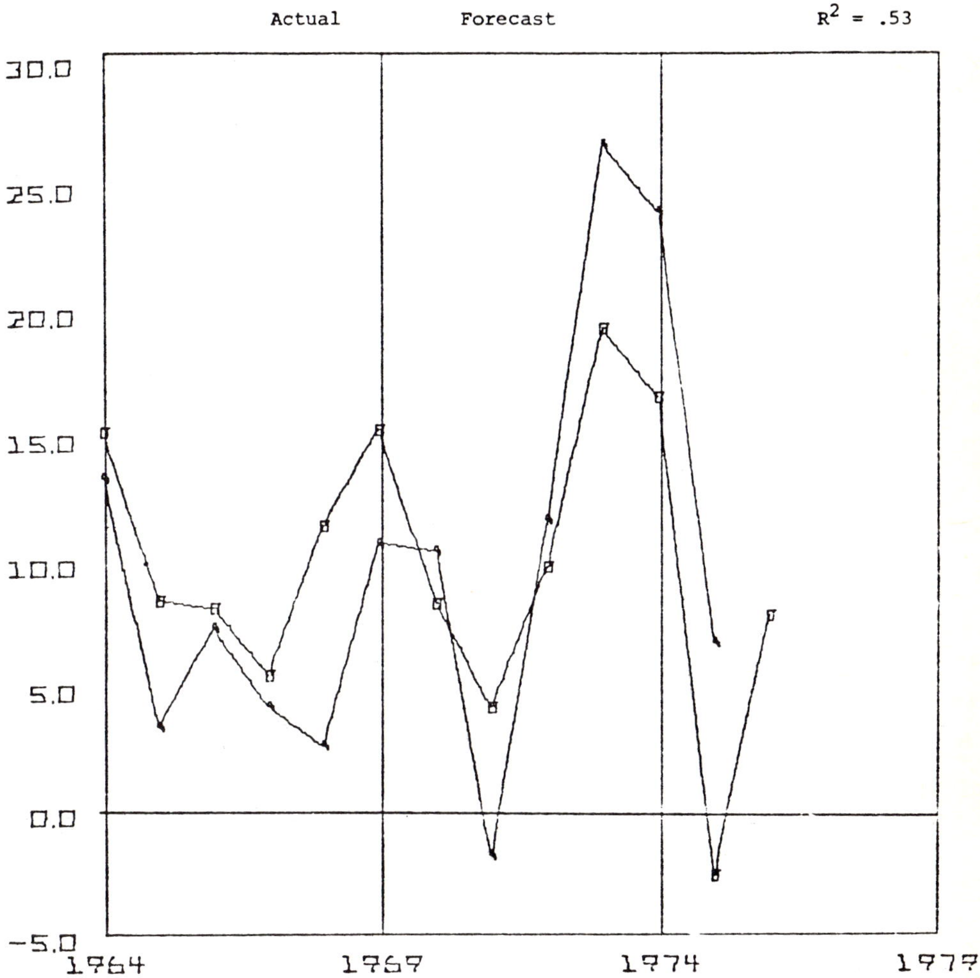

* Canada, United Kingdom, West Germany, France, Italy, Japan

Chart VI

Forecast and Actual Changes in U.S. Exports of Miscellaneous Manufactures (SITC 8), Quantity, 1964-76, Using Leading Index for Six Countries,* GNP Weights

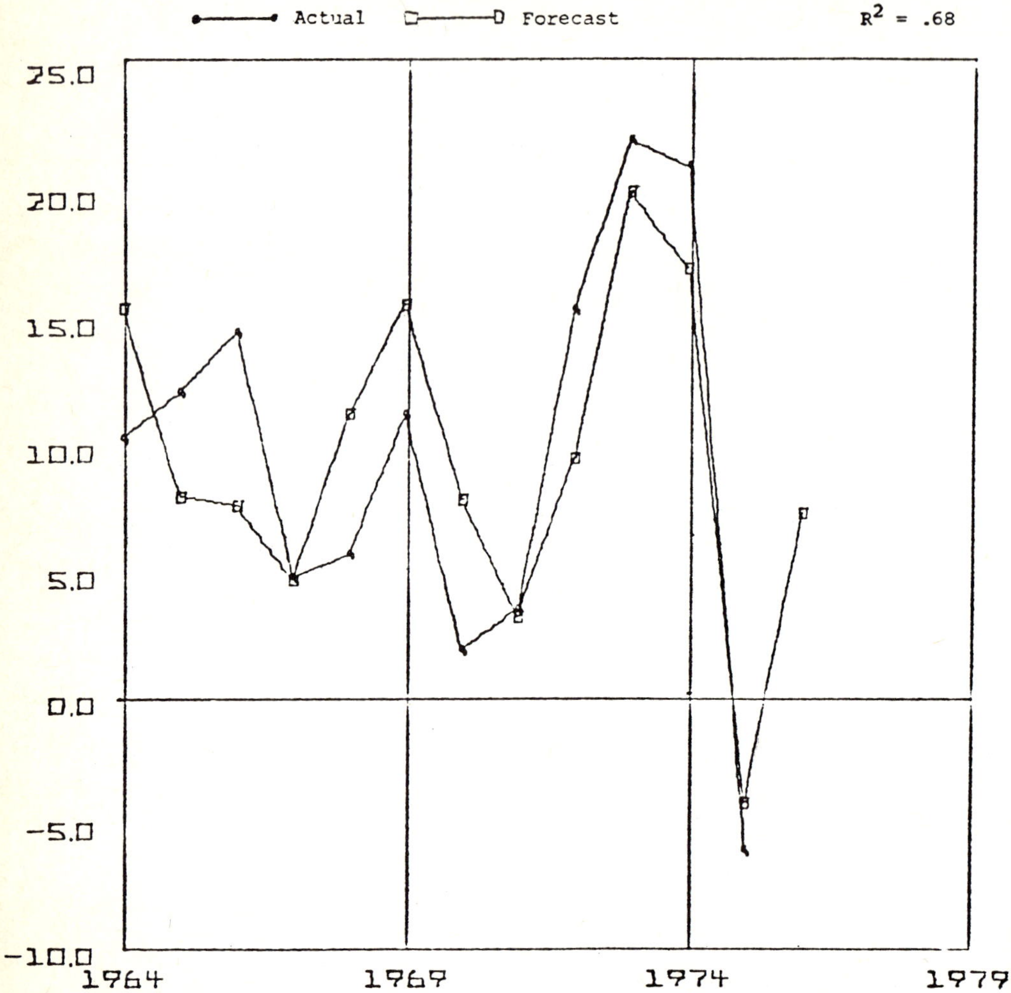

* Canada, United Kingdom, West Germany, France, Italy, Japan

forecast not the actually observed value for a particular quarter but rather a smoothed version of that value. The happenings in a particular quarter, which in the case of trade are dictated by a variety of special factors such as dock strikes, unusual weather, exceptionally large shipments, and lags or other errors in reporting, are ordinarily not of much interest. Of greater interest is the underlying trend of trade. Moreover, one cannot expect cyclical indicators to forecast these special events. Their function is to reveal the underlying trend. We define this trend in terms of rates of change in four-quarter moving averages taken four quarters apart (i.e., without overlapping).

The second thing the scheme accomplishes is that it makes it possible to vary the assumed lag between the leading index and the trade variable being forecast. Prices may have a different lag than quantities, and the lag for values may be something in between. Certain types of exports, such as heavy equipment, may have a different lag than others, such as textiles. Although we have assumed a six-month lag in working with annual data, this can now be varied from one quarter to two, three or more quarters. Indeed, since the leading indexes are available by months, the lag can be adjusted in terms of months, using changes from twelve-month moving averages in the leading index to a monthly figure six months after the twelfth month in the average. The method does not require monthly trade data, though such data can be used if available. The trade data do not need to be seasonally adjusted, since four-quarter or twelve-month averages are used throughout.

In our work to date we have not tested all these possibilities. Our studies of monthly and quarterly forecasts have only just begun. Chart VII shows one of the initial tests, applied to changes in the quantity of U.S. exports of manufactured goods. All the data shown are rates of change over four-quarter intervals. The dotted line is the usual four-quarter change, i.e., change from same quarter a year ago, plotted in the terminal quarter of the span. These rates exhibit considerable erratic movement, since the end points are only one quarter long.[1] When the end points are four quarters long, as in the scheme described above, the rates of change are much smoother. This is shown by the solid line. Here the rates are plotted in the second quarter of the second of the two four-quarter periods compared. For example, the change from calendar year 1963 to calendar year 1964 is plotted in 1964.2. This is the same point at which the change from 1963.2 to 1964.2 (dotted line) is plotted. The positioning is justified by the assumption that the calendar-year average is an estimate of the smoothed value for the second quarter (it could equally well be assumed it is a smoothed value for the third quarter).

The smooth (solid) line is what we attempt to forecast. The line with hollow square points is the forecast, based on the leading index

[1] The extreme erratic movements (dotted line) tend to be inversely correlated one year apart, because the changes overlap at that interval. Compare 1965.1 with 1966.1, 1968.3 with 1969.3, 1969.1 with 1970.1, and 1971.4 with 1972.4. There is a similar tendency in the changes in the four-quarter averages (solid line) for the same reason (compare 1965.2 with 1966.2 and 1970.4 with 1971.4), but the effect is muted because the four-quarter averages are so much smoother than the one-quarter figures.

Chart VII: Quarterly Forecast and Actual Percent Changes,
U.S. Exports of Manufactured Goods, Quantity

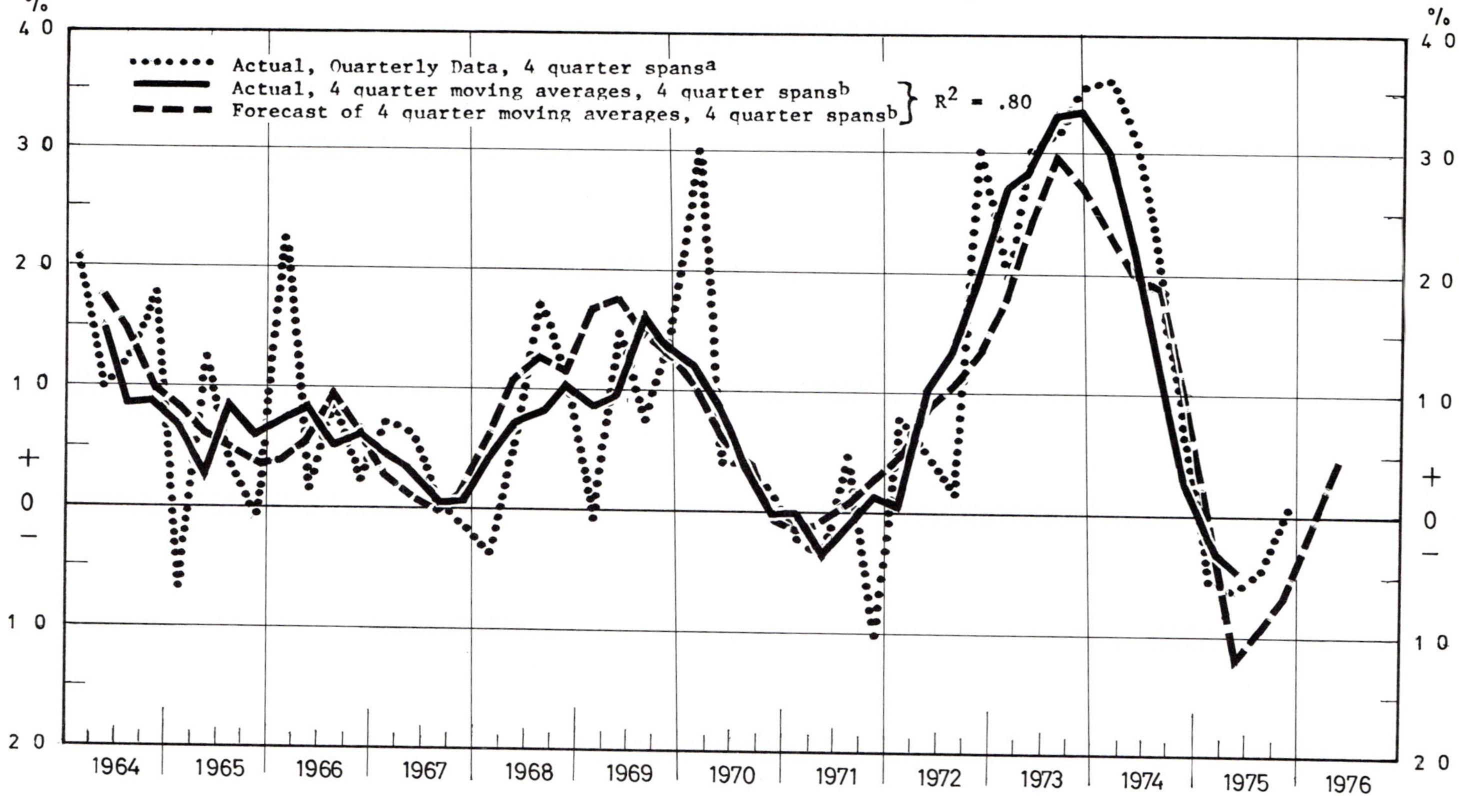

Note: Forecasts are based on six-country leading index, GNP weights.
a/ Plotted in terminal quarter. b/ Plotted in second quarter of terminal year (see text).

for six countries. It traces the major swings in the rate of growth of manufactured goods export quantities with considerable fidelity and identifies the cyclical peaks and troughs in these rates at about the time they occurred. The value of R^2 is .80 and the root mean square error is 4.3 percent. This is approximately the same result as for the annual (calendar year) forecasts (R^2 = .81), as indeed it should be, since the data for one of the four quarters (the second) are the same as those used in the calendar-year forecasts.

Conclusions

Our major conclusion clearly is that forecasting exports by means of a leading index for one's export partners is eminently feasible, although a good deal of testing remains to be done. The application of the technique can be extended in several ways. Although the results reported here have focused on Western Europe and export quantities of manufactured goods, we have indicated that it works as well for exports from the United States to Japan and Canada, and that it can be broadened to cover total exports or restricted to focus on commodity groups. Although price changes introduce various complications, which can be avoided by looking at export quantities, the technique appears to work reasonably well when applied to export values.

Since the technique should prove equally applicable to the import side of the trade flow, we should be able to employ leading indexes to forecast changes in trade balances. That the technique need not be limited to forecasting U.S. exports is, of course, highly likely.

Because we have previously demonstrated that the indicators work with reasonable fidelity in all the major market-oriented economies, there is no reason not to reverse our work -- and use the U.S. leading index, alone or with that of other countries, to forecast the exports of other countries to the United States alone or to all major trading partners.

When the International Economic Indicator Project can broaden its basic coverage beyond the seven countries thus far analyzed (currently we are working on the Netherlands and Belgium) the trade forecasts can, of course, similarly be broadened. One line of experimentation that particularly suggests itself is to test the leading indicator technique of forecasting with the export data of the developing countries. It can, of course, be applied to the export data of any country that exports to the countries for which leading indexes are available. The seven countries that we have already covered import a substantial share of the total exports of the developing countries. Because the demand for such exports must fluctuate with the cycles in the industrialized countries, the developing countries could appraise the immediate future of many of their export markets by means of our technique. Since these countries depend upon exports to a very large extent, and are therefore especially vulnerable to the cyclical fluctuations experienced by their trading partners, improvements in their ability to forecast export fluctuations should prove extremely useful.

By means of such applications and others, it is our hope that the research discussed in this paper, along with other studies planned for the International Economic Indicators Project, will further our understanding of how instability is transmitted internationally, so that public policy in all countries can be developed on the basis of greater understanding and current awareness of the underlying economic interrelationships.

Summary

The International Economic Indicator Project at the National Bureau of Economic Research has previously applied traditional NBER methods to develop leading, roughly coincident, and lagging indicators of growth cycles both in the United States and abroad.

This paper extends the work by utilizing the leading indicators of one country to forecast its imports from another country, a logical extension inasmuch as a country's demand for imports is widely regarded as associated with its domestic business cycle. The technique can be applied to trade in the other direction as well, always using the leading indicators for the importing country, and so ultimately leading indicators can be used to forecast changes in the balance of trade among countries for which leading indexes are available.

We apply the method initially to forecasting U.S. exports to Western Europe, Canada and Japan. The methodology concentrates on forecasting percent changes in U.S. export quantities by relating them to the percentage change in the leading composite index for the other countries. We assume a six-month lead is typical and so estimate that percent changes between calendar years can be forecast from percent changes between fiscal years (ending June 30). To forecast before the calendar year has begun, we assume that the fiscal year overlapping the calendar year can be approximately represented by the December figure for the leading index. The forecasts thus become regressions in the form

$\Delta Q_t = a + b\ \Delta LD_{-1}$ where ΔQ_t is the percentage change in export quantity from calendar year t-1 to year t and ΔLD_{-1} is the percent change in the leading index between the fiscal year average and December of year t.

We have forecast year-to-year percent changes in the total quantity of U.S. exports of manufactured goods to Western Europe as a whole and compared the forecast percent changes with the actual changes, 1964-1975, obtaining a correlation coefficient (r^2) of .73. That is, almost three-fourths of the fluctuation in the rates of change was reflected in the forecast. We applied the same technique to forecasting changes in U.S. exports to Canada and Japan during the same period and obtained r^2 of .71 and .64 respectively.

We have also applied this method to forecasting selected manufactured commodity exports. In particular we ran a series of regressions of actual against forecast changes in U.S. export quantities to all countries, using a composite leading index for six countries (Canada, United Kingdom, West Germany, France, Italy, and Japan) during the period 1964-75. The resulting r^2 were: Chemicals -- .76; textiles and metals -- .81; machinery and transportation equipment -- .53; miscellaneous manufactures -- .68.

Finally we have experimented with applying our method to forecasting quarterly as well as annual percentage changes. Because calendar year changes are actually equivalent to four-quarter averages four quarters apart we experimented by advancing our leading index forecasts one quarter at a time. This yields smoother changes in both the leading index and in the actual quantity of exports than would be achieved by using the quarterly changes alone. The result emphasizes cyclical swings in the rate of growth rather than shorter-run erratic movements. For U.S. manufactured goods export quantities, the quarterly regression yields an r^2 of .80, suggesting that further work of this nature might be productive of useful results.

In the future we should like to apply the method to U.S. imports as well as to trade balances. It can, of course, be applied to the trade of countries other than the United States, i.e., to any country where composite leading indexes can be constructed.

W. SIMON
G. LANGHANS
R. BAUMGÄRTNER
SIEMENS AG
ERLANGEN

APPLICATION OF LEADING INDICATORS WITH REGARD TO INDUSTRIAL PLANNING

I. Introduction

An essay recently published by the Ifo Institute for Economic Research on the subject of "Branch indicators for the future demand of firms"[1] shows by way of several examples how demand indicators specific to a company can be developed from the results of economic tendency survey. These demand indicators are of the nature of projections, since they more or less forecast the sales trends as measured from the amount of incoming orders. The extent to which this forecasting method is used by industry is not generally known[2]. Nevertheless it is reasonable to suspect that in recent years more and more companies have turned to the use of leading indicators as an instrument of sales planning.

II. Leading indicators in the capital goods sector

This paper concerns itself with the "Business climate"[3] trend checked and reported monthly by the Ifo Institute in the Federal Republic of Germany, and its function as a leading indicator for the sale of electrical capital-goods. The paper includes experience gained with similar indicators used in other countries. The examples presented are based on figures of the Power Engineering Group of Siemens AG. The paper also describes an attempt to construct a "Sales climate" which - analogous to the 'Business climate' - gives several month' advance indication of changes expected in the trend of incoming orders.

---

1) See "In Search of Economic Indicators", ed. by W.H. Strigel, Heidelberg 1977, p. 81 et. seq.

2) So far, the authors have only heard of one company, a consumer-goods manufacturer, who has applied this method.

3) See "In Search of Economic Indicators", p. 67 et. seq.

III. The problem

Fluctuations in investment are known to be a major factor in affecting the business cycle. It has been observed over a long period of time that the curve showing orders received is exceptionally steep for the classical capital-goods industries, that is, in mechanical engineering and in electrical equipment.

Order inflow (1962 prices)
Mechanical engineering and electrical capital-goods equipment, in Germany
% Growth rate of moving 12-month totals

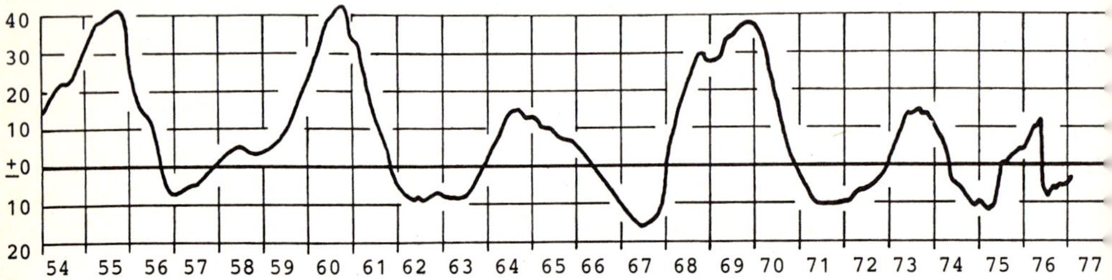

The positive and negative percentage changes are far above the average for all of industry and have probably been exceeded only by fluctuations in the inventory.

The important forecasting problem facing manufacturers of capital goods whose sales depend on these wide cyclical fluctuations, is to recognize sufficiently early the turning-points of order inflow[4]. Stated differently: the primary objective in short-term sales planning is to forecast correctly whether the trend will be a positive or negative one, in other words, to predict a change in the existing trend.

Planning errors due to incorrect forecasting of the turning-points of a trend automatically result in friction losses of a company and are generally incorrigible no matter how quick adjustment is attempted. In contrast, planning errors due to wrongly forecasting the intensity of an upward or downward trend are more amenable to correction.

Information on the "Business climate" has proven to be quite accurate for early recognition of changes (turning-points) in the trend of incoming orders. How can this be explained?

There is obviously a cause-and-effect relationship between the business climate and the demand for capital-goods (specifically, the orders received by capital-goods manufacturers). For example, if there is a lasting improvement in the business climate, that is to say, if the majority of industrial companies take a positive view of things, experience shows that the reason for this improvement in climate is production moving closer to capacity and hopes of better profits. Quite logically, this has a positive effect on investments. But before the desire to invest is translated into actual orders, a certain amount of time devoted to the investment planning process normally passes[5].

---

4) With capital goods requiring relatively long workshop time, forecasting the turning-points of sales depends to a large degree on the pattern of incoming orders. Also, a considerable portion of sales is determined by order-books and their deliveries.

5) In investment planning involving complex plant, the planning process normally starts with inquiries sent to manufacturers of capital goods. Systematic evaluation of these inquiries has shown that there is a lead-lag relationship to order inflow in certain industries as well.

The chain of causation, beginning with the business climate (= propensity to invest), proceeding with investment planning, and ending with orders placed for capital-goods equipment (= orders received by capital-goods manufacturers), is always reaffirmed, according to our observations. Since this process - for technical reasons alone - often requires many month, the lead is usually sufficient to make forecasts on the turning points of order inflow, using as a basis the projected pattern of the business climate curve and allowing for reasonable tolerances.

IV. Examples of applications

1. Leading indicators for the total order inflow Domestic and Export

In order to be able to use the Ifo "Business climate" for forecasting, it is necessary to select a mode of presentation which shows the close relationship between the shape of the "Business climate" curve and the trend of a company's own order inflow. This is done as follows:

The monthly order inflow values are transformed into moving 12-monthly totals to filter out most of the seasonal influences. If a complicated method (such as ASA II 2) for seasonal adjustment were used, the monthly seasonal component could be calculated more accurately. But this would mean the disadvantage of having the last data of the time series produce only provisional values which often enough change subsequently. Therefore, whenever figures are brought up to date, this would necessitate a correction of the last monthly values and thus create a feeling of uncertainty.

The next step is to calculate the "deviation from the trend" on the basis of the moving 12-monthly totals:

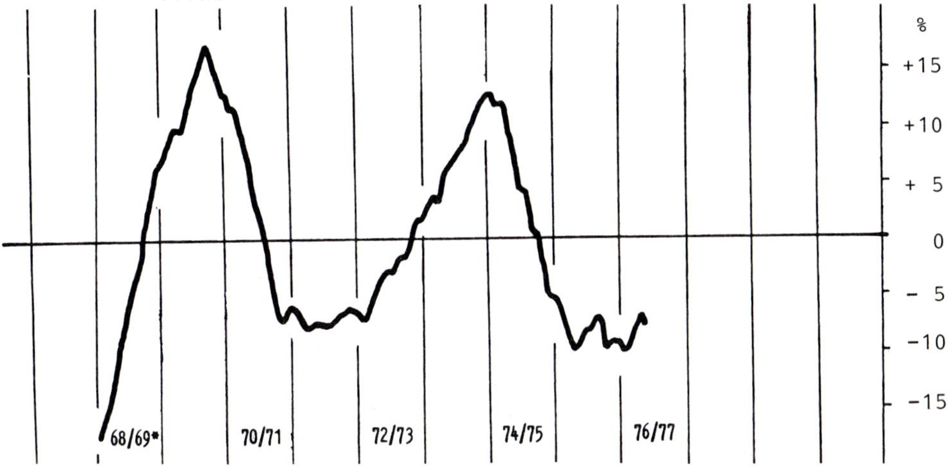

The monthly extrapolation of the trend deviation then reflects the business cycle. While there are still a number of irregular influences contained in this, they are not too bothersome, since we normally know about them, espescially as regards major orders.

This cyclical curve adjusted for trends and season is then placed in relation to the business-climate curve, this being in the form of an indicator band:

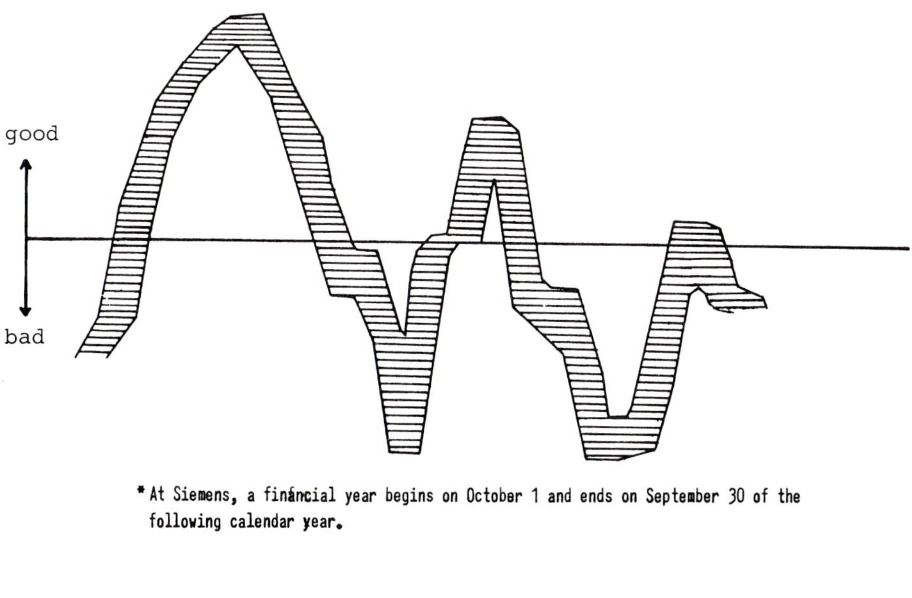

* At Siemens, a financial year begins on October 1 and ends on September 30 of the following calendar year.

The band allows for the fact that the lead of the indicator is not stable, but rather fluctuates between 12 and 18 month in this particular example.

Showing the business climate as a band has the additional advantage of the indicator performing only such directional changes where definite turning-points are involved. The shape of the business-climate curve, more erratic in reality is also smoothed. Displaced in time, this band is plotted over the trend deviation curve:

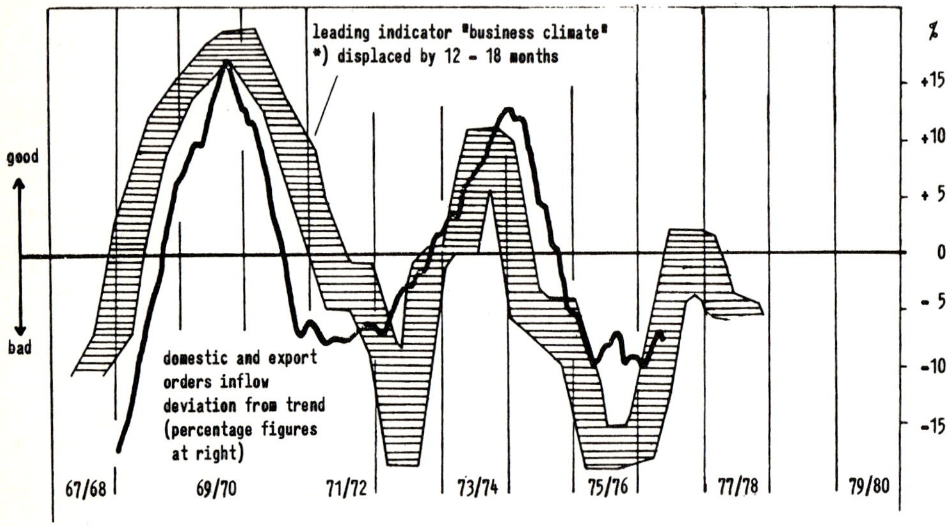

As the graph shows, the lead of the indicator at the peaks is frequently greater and more defined than at the throughs. Since the important thing for company planning is early and accurate recognition of the peaks, the special value of the indicator lies in the practical benefit of its function in signalling necessary slowing down.

2. Leading indicator for the incoming orders of a product group

In addition to its application for the total order inflow, we have used the method described above for some selected product groups as well.

However, with smaller units, the relationship between indicator and cyclical trend of order inflow is not always as close as in the foregoing example. One of the reasons for this is that export figures are subject to wide fluctuations, or that major orders are much more irregular in forthcoming than in the case of a larger unit.

For sub-units, the indicator most suitable in each case is used to obtain absolute forecast figures. This is performed as follows: if the lead of an indicator is 12 month, for example, with regard to the unit to be forecast, the trend shown by the indicator is used as a criterion for predicting order inflow.

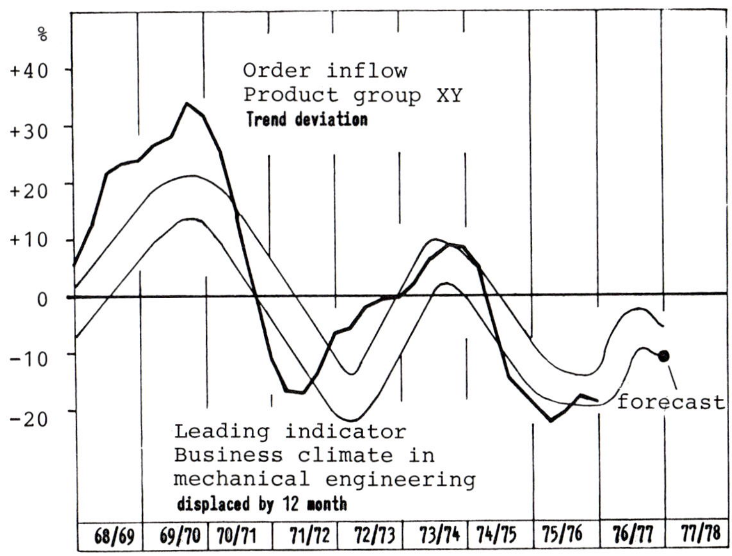

It is assumed, that as in the past, the parallelity of the indicator and order inflow will continue in the next year as well. Of course, the usual special influences which the indicator does not reflect, have to be allowed for in the forecast. The absolute forecast figure for the unit being analysed can be estimated by bringing in the "trend value" of the following financial year and the suspected "trend deviation of order inflow":

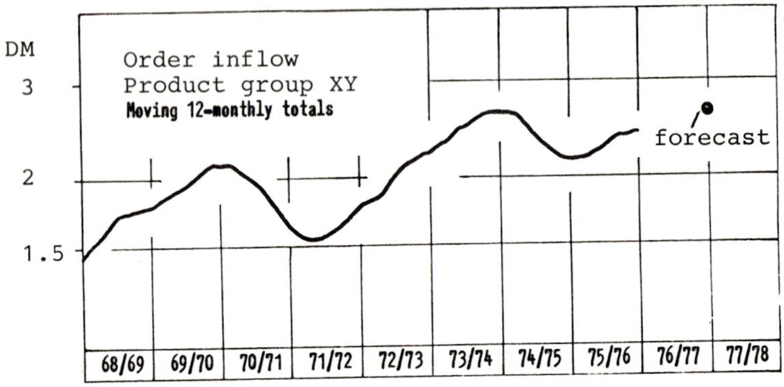

The forecast figures determined in this manner are a solid orientation aid for planning. However, only after certain company objectives such as market shares, have been taken into account, is the target figure established.

3. Leading indicators for a sales sector abroad

Indicators similar to that of the "business climate" may also be used to advantage for the 12-months planning of certain sales sectors abroad.

In Italy, the source of information we use is the monthly questionnaire of ISCO. From this questionnaire, a combination of answers to the questions on the present order situation ("livello degli ordini") and for expected trend of the order inflow for the next 3 - 4 months ("tendenza degli ordini") has proven to be a suitable indicator. We term this combination "demand climate".

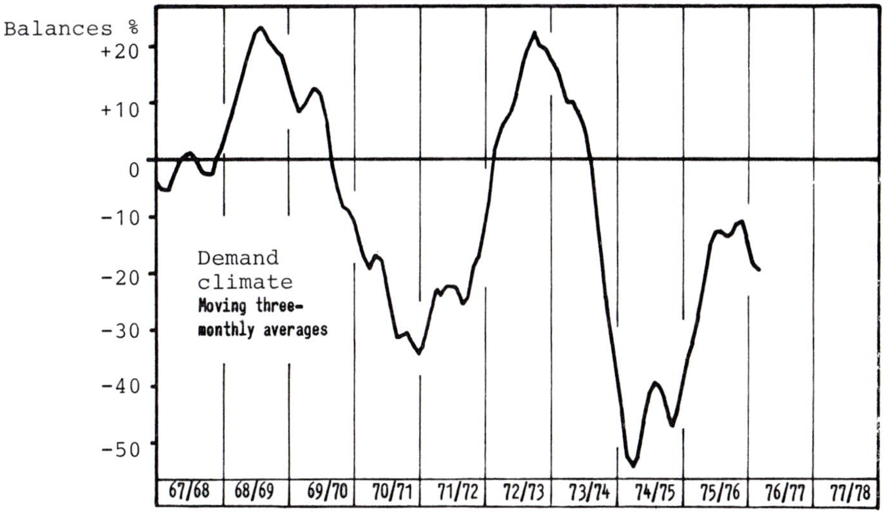

Order inflow of Sales Dept. XY in Italy is the target figure:

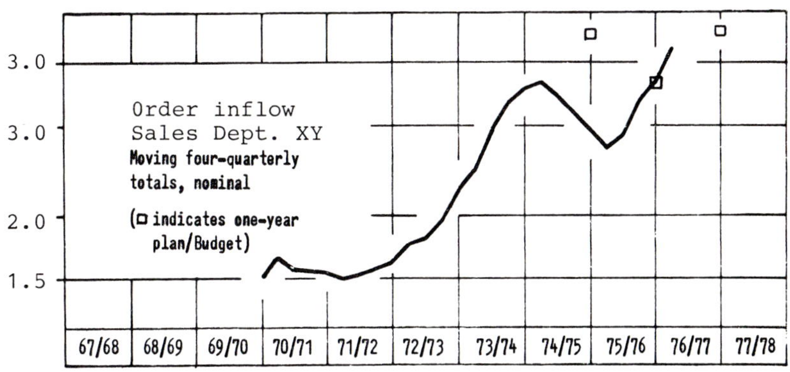

To be able to compare both curves, a few transformations are required here as well. The climate curve contains no price component nor, theoretically, any long-range trend. The order-inflow figures would thus have to be adjusted accordingly. To simplify matters, we have calculated an exponential trend from the nominal values and have shown the percentage deviations from this trend.

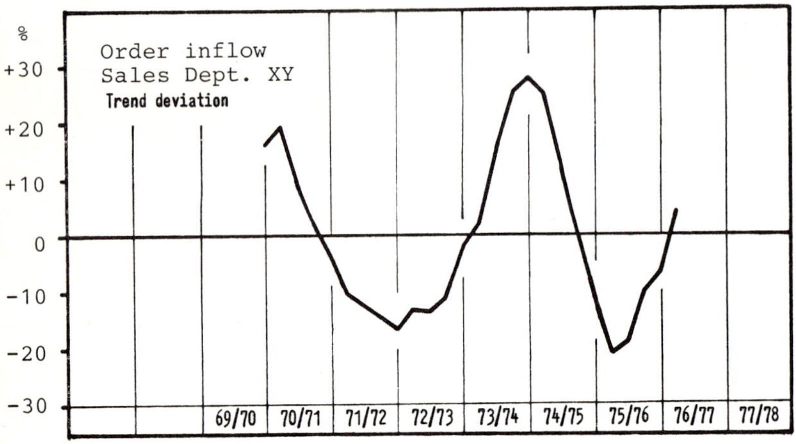

Again, the benefit of the demand climate lies in the fact that it shows a lead compared with the moving four-quarterly totals of our incoming orders. Beginning around 1973, this lead is about one year, by which period of time the indicator is displaced. Since only quarterly values are available for the incoming orders, quarterly averages are formed from the monthly results of the indicator. Finally the assessments seem to dicrease continuously, a fact the (nominal) order inflows do not reflect. Therefore, instead of the original balances, their deviation (in percentage points) from the linear trend is used.

The transformations made are as follows:

Order inflow (nominal):

- Percentage deviation from exponential trend;

Demand climate:

- Positive displacement by 1 year
- Establishing quarterly averages
- Deviation from the linear trend

The time series thus transformed show exceptional parallelism:

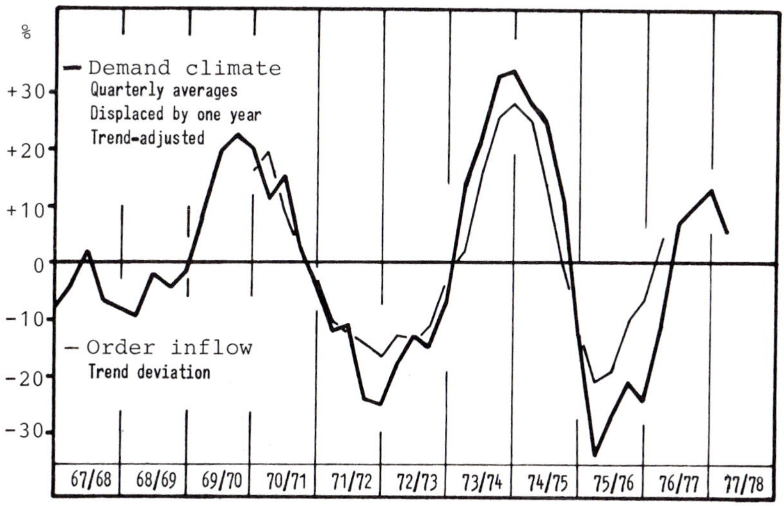

We use this instrument primarily for comprehensive assessment and possible correction of the individual plans added up for this sales sector. Among the three Budget squares shown in the lower graph on page 9, the first one was entered without reference to the indicator, whereas the other two are already influenced by this relationship.

We employ such climate indices as indicators for short-term trends in order inflow in other countries and in other sectors as well. In Austria, for example, we use the results of the tendency survey made by the Österreichisches Institut für Wirtschaftsforschung, in Spain the "Coyuntura Industrial" of the Ministerio de Industria etc. In most cases, the "assessment of order books" and "estimate of production trend" combination of questions produces good results.

In Belgium - to quote another example - we use the "Courbe synthêtique" (synthetic curve) obtained by the Banque Nationale from the results of a survey. Basically, the method we use is the same as that given in the example of Italy, the only difference being that we do not form quarterly averages nor adjust the indicator for its trend, because neither transformation would provide additional information.

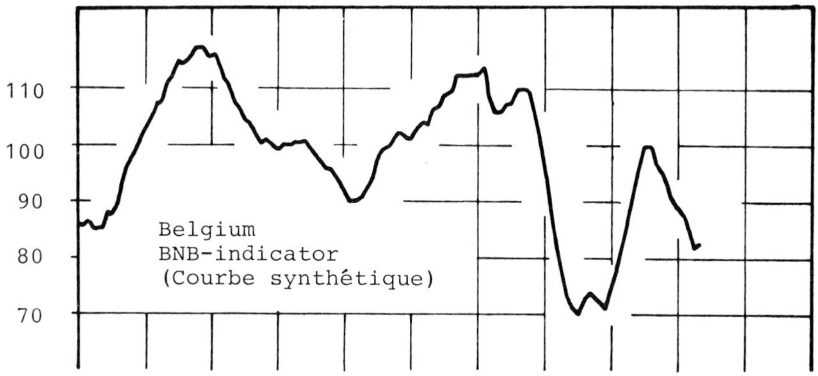
110
100
90
80
70
Belgium
BNB-indicator
(Courbe synthétique)

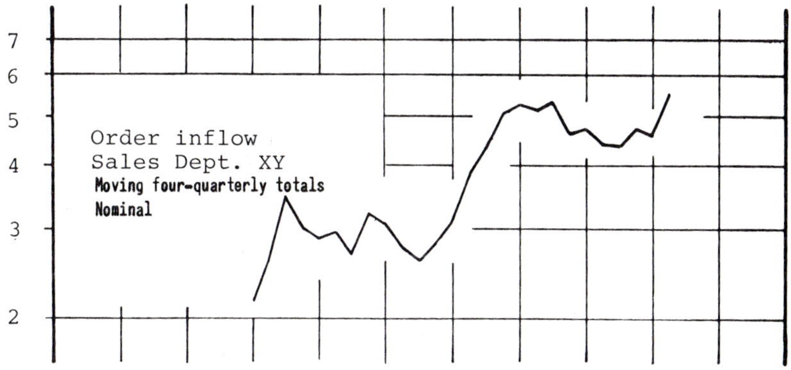
7
6
5
4
3
2
Order inflow
Sales Dept. XY
Moving four-quarterly totals
Nominal

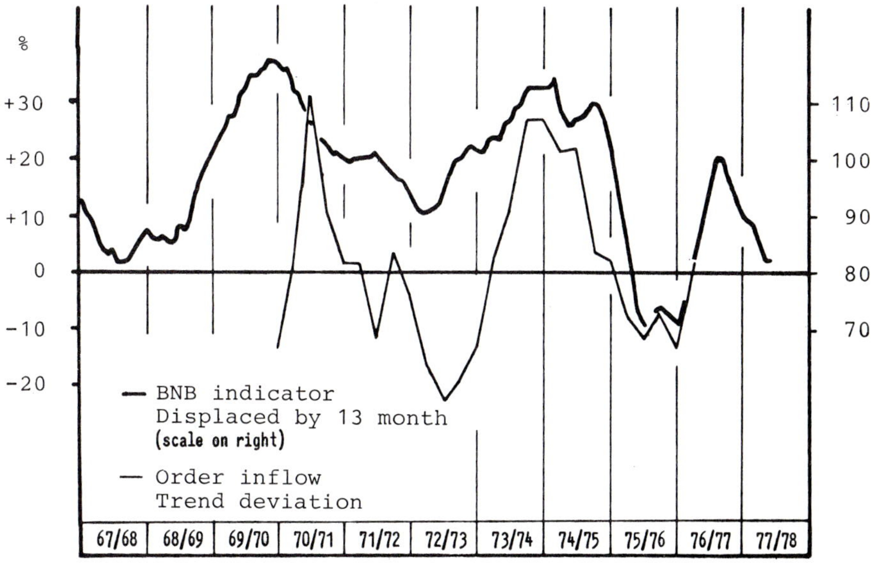
%
+30
+20
+10
0
-10
-20
110
100
90
80
70
BNB indicator
Displaced by 13 month
(scale on right)
Order inflow
Trend deviation
67/68
68/69
69/70
70/71
71/72
72/73
73/74
74/75
75/76
76/77
77/78

The differing periodicity of the curves compared would complicate things only if we wanted to calculate the regression equation. However, we do not intend to perform this calculation, in order to avoid the impression of any functional relationship. Moreover, this would not do justice to the meaning and purpose of this method, which is primarily to give early indication of trend changes.

4. Leading indicators generated by Siemens

Prompted by the good experiences gained with the "business climate" and similar indicators, we have tried to utilise in a survey the closeness of our own field sales network to the market. The sales managers responsible for business involving two product sectors in our branch offices receive monthly questionnaires (see annexed sample) arranged similar to those of the IFO Institute but containing only 4 questions. In contrast to the IFO questionnaire, the two major questions (sales situation and expected sales) allow five answers. Originally, only three answers were possible; but is eventually became apparent that too many of the answers were in the middle.

Evaluation is the same as with "business climate": the balances are formed from the answers weighted with the sales of each branch office, the resulting time series are called "sales climate".

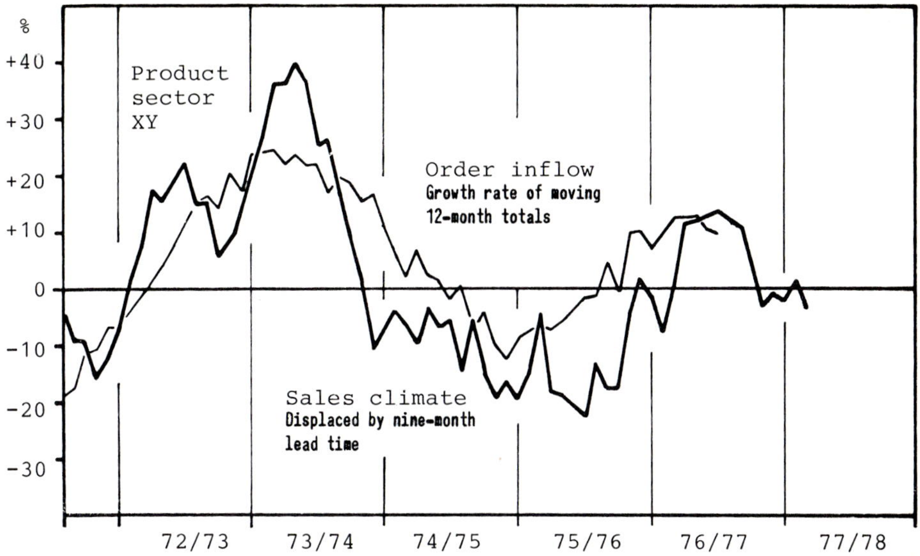

It will be clear that the time lag between "sales climate" and actual receipt of orders has to be shorter than that in the preceding examples, since the target value itself is assessed in the survey.

In seeking relationships between an indicator and a target figure, transformations involving at least one of the two series are usually required - as already shown - in order to obtain optimal results. In the present case, the rates of change in incoming orders (moving 12-monthly totals compared with previous year) are an especially informative element. Since percentage change compared with the previous year is automatically brought in when one-year plans are discussed, this particular relationship provides important information in assessing the plan figure.

Such surveys are not only conducted with our domestic branch offices; the sales units responsible for these product sectors in other European countries participate in similar surveys. The results obtained assist in short-term export forecasting.

Annex

Questionnaire on market situation

Branch office ....

....
Month, year

....
(Name of person completing questionnaire)

	Mark as applicable: XY	YZ
1. We consider our present sales situation to be		
very good	□	□
good	□	□
satisfactory/seasonal	□	□
less satisfactory	□	□
poor	□	□
2. Our sales situation is considered poor for the following reasons:*		
Demand situation/market capacity	□	□
Competition (e.g. prices, quality, deliveries)	□	□
Other reasons (e.g. shortage of personnel)	□	□
3. In the next 6 months, demand for products XY/YZ is expected to		
increase heavily	□	□
increase lightly	□	□
remain static/develop seasonally	□	□
drop slightly	□	□
drop heavily	□	□
4. We estimate customer inventories in products XY/YZ to be		
inadequate	□	□
adequate/seasonal	□	□
above average	□	□

* If several reasons apply, please indicate their order (1 = most important reason, 2 = second most important reason etc.)

G. NERB/W.H. STRIGEL
IFO-INSTITUT FÜR WIRTSCHAFTSFORSCHUNG
MÜNCHEN

ENTREPRENEURS' PERCEPTION OF SOCIAL ENVIRONMENT AND ITS INFLUENCE ON GROWTH EXPECTATIONS

A. Introduction

Other than after the 1966/67 recession there has not been any autonomous or accelerating upswing in West German business after the 1975 recession. Private investment activities, in particular, lacked momentum despite the government programmes to step up business. What is the reason for this disappointing course of business? Is it caused exclusively by objective facts - such as perhaps lower profit margins, greater pressure of international competition, signs of saturation in important fields of consumer goods - or do extra-economic factors play a decisive role, as for instance, the general pessimism about economic growth, socio-political uncertainty or restriction felt as to the entrepreneurial scope, etc.?

The following study will investigate into possibilities to prove that social-psychological factors will influence the behaviour of entrepreneurs.

The authors are indebted to Mr. W. FRIEDRICH for stimulating suggestions and assistance in data-processing.

B. The Role of Social-psychological Factors in a Theory of Entrepreneurial Behaviour

The influence of extra-economic factors may be presented in the following pattern:

S = stimulus, information (in our case, business data)

I = intervening variables (the indeterminate factors which we try to detect in this study)

R = reaction

In simple closed models we have the reaction

$$S \longrightarrow R.$$

It is presumed, however, that the reaction does not have as deterministic causes as that but that it is frequently also induced by the intervention of extra-economic facts In that case,our model will read:

$$S \rightleftarrows I \longrightarrow R$$

The interaction between S and I means that the intervening variables will influence an information already at the reception stage. Intervening variables may have a varying substance. Psychological factors, for instance, are usually of a subjective nature while sociological and political factors are characterized by a preponderance of normative facts.

We should now like to present some of our deliberations without, however, claiming completeness. For further information, the reader is asked to look up the references.[1)]

---

1) All notes are at the end of the paper: see p. 44 et seq.

1. Psychological Factors

It is to be noted that there is only a rudimentary specific psychology of decisions taken with regard to economic processes and hardly any psychology for the category of people of interest to us, namely top executives or managers of the economy. We will therefore have to confine ourselves to general psychological statements on the behaviour in taking decisions.

a) The individual is always faced with the problem of adequately processing the great abundance of information presented to him. As a rule, he will adopt more or less restrictive measures to do this, namely
   - methods of quantitative restriction, and
   - measures of assessing the purport of information.

   In the course of this process of selection and assessment, the original contents of an information may get distorted:
   Fig. 1 is an illustrative example of the manner in which a quantitatively unchanged information on the amount of orders on hand in industry, in the course of time, has been appraised by entrepreneurs entirely differently. While in the fifties, a backlog of orders for three production months was still considered a largely sufficient or normal reserve by industry, the majority of responses in the sixties and, even more so, in the seventies rated such reserves as being too low. Consequently, entrepreneurs have become more cautious in their production plans.[2)]

b) Human decisions are characterized by a "reorientation lag". This means, for instance, that it is not only a single positive stimulus that is required after a phase of bad experience in order to change man's behaviour but a repeated confirmation of this positive

Fig. 1

CHANGING EVALUATIONS AND ANTICIPATIONS IN INDUSTRY[a]

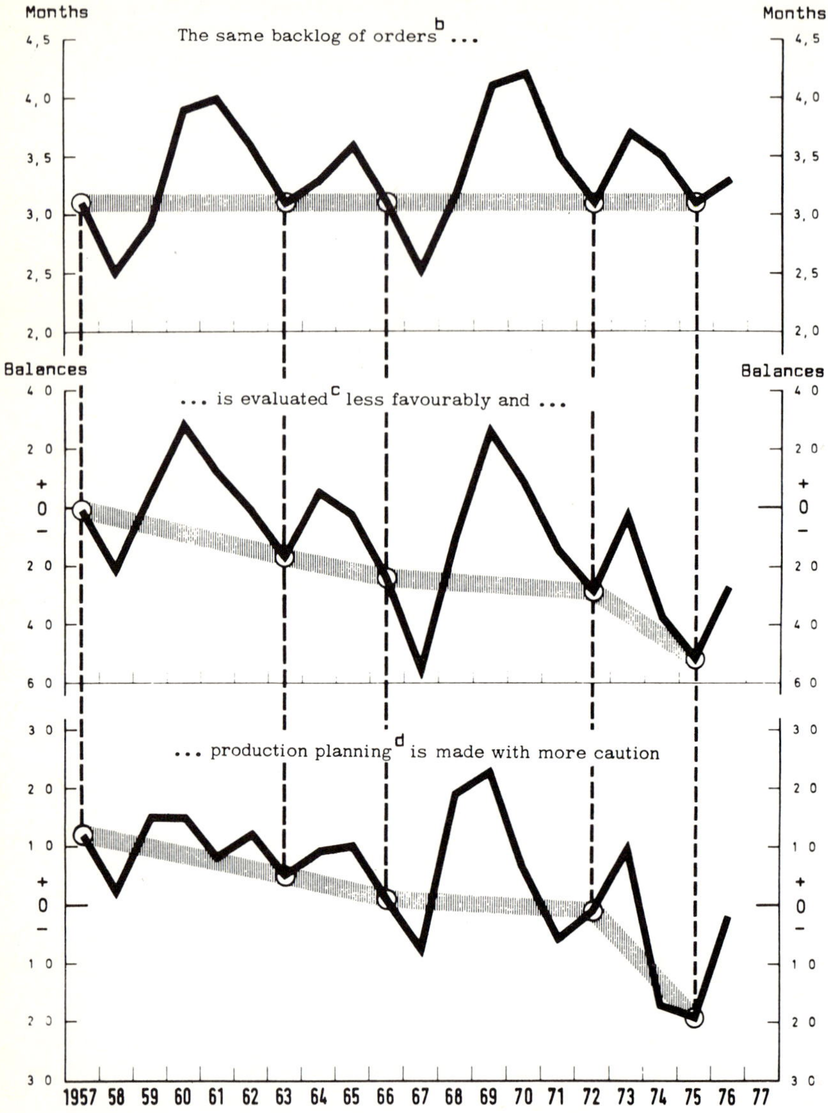

a) Manufacturing industry. - b) Orders on hand measured in months of production; month June. - c) Percentage balances of the responses indicating large or small backlogs of orders; month June. d) Percentage balances of the responses on planned increase and decrease of production; June plans for the third quarter.

experience. This especially applies in case of reorientation after long or extreme periods of bad experience. In the concrete situation we are in, this implies, among other things, that a single increase in profits - as has occurred in 1976 - will not be enough for industry to come out of their reluctance to invest.

The theory following next is also closely connected with this "lag", namely:

c) In (alleged) periods of uncertainty, people are often inclined to be guided by opinion leaders, that is to say, they wait for the others to take the lead and will only then change their own behaviour[3]. This way of behaviour is based on a tendency toward imitation. Katona[4] and Jöhr[5] have pointed out in this connection that entrepreneurs - even more so than consumers - are subject to changes in their expectations which will lead to a largely uniform behaviour induced by a process of cumulation, confirmation and infection. This is due to the fact that entrepreneurs in the whole show a higher receptivity toward information and a closer coherence.

2. Sociological Factors

The perception that values and standards are of decisive importance to entrepreneurial actions is not a recent one. Max Weber, as is well known, has found the motive force of the economic development of capitalism[6] to lie specifically in the conceptions of value of Protestantism. The vigorous growth of the economy during the Period of

Promoterism in Germany was explained by Weber by the following two factors:

- Economic success is considered a favour of God, and
- Protestant asceticism obliges the entrepreneurs to lead a modest life and thus results in a high cumulation of capital.

Today, entrepreneurial actions, however, are in the crossfire of socio-political discussions. As examples we have co-determination, socialization, the debate of energy supply, investment control, etc. It is assumed that the present reluctance to growth is also rooted in such socio-political discussions. The entrepreneur is involved in these discussions as a member of various groups. It is therefore obvious that he will take his decisions not without being influenced by his obligations toward the various roles played by him. The environmental conditions of the entrepreneur as a member of a complex economic, social, political and technological system are schematically shown in Fig. 2. He may take part in some systems actively or may exert a decisive influence on them (family, society, associations, market). However, here the entrepreneur finds himself torn between the differing obligations of his various roles so that conflicting interests may arise. Such conflicting interests are more frequently found when the entrepreneur is confronted with actions of competition, of the political system or of trade unions. Technical progress, too, may cause conflicts (nuclear power). All these influences act as stressors in part positively and in part negatively upon the behaviour of entrepreneurs. The pattern of forces that the entrepreneur is exposed to is, of course, much more complicated in practice. The simplified representation of the interrelations - as shown in Fig. 2 - will, however, do for the purpose of this study.

Within the scope of this paper it is, not possible to relate the empirical results with all theories mentioned. Nevertheless, it seemed necessary briefly to point out the theoretical background forming the basis of our empirical efforts.

Fig. 2

The Entrepreneur in the Pattern of Environmental Forces

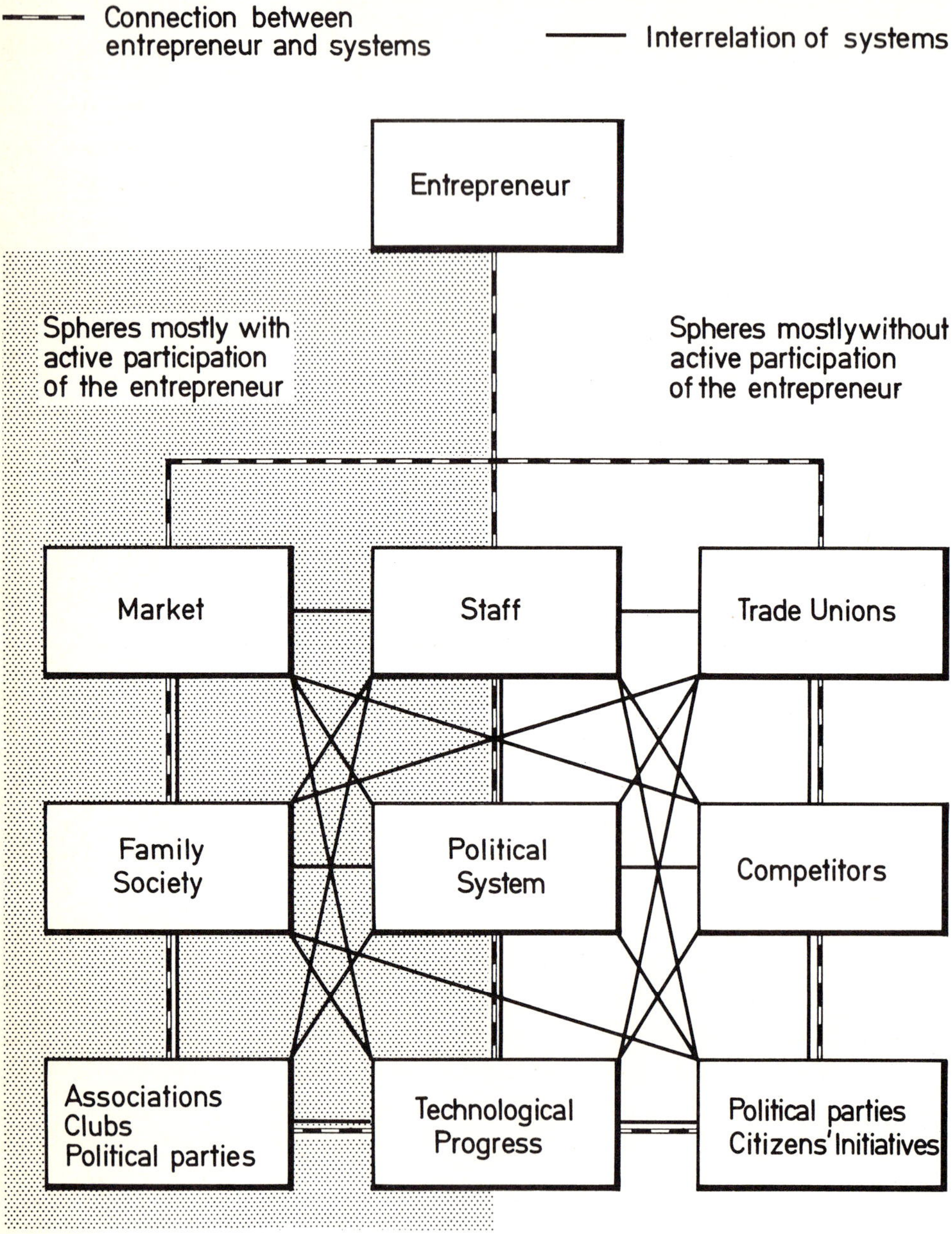

C. Description of Survey Results

1. Structure of the Groups of Respondents

In June 1975 and in November 1976, the Ifo-Institute carried out two special surveys of the economy (industry, construction, trade) with the aim to collect detailed information on the satisfaction of entrepreneurs and execuvtives with their private and vocational fields of activity as well as with their ideas about the future in these fields. The results of the first survey which covered 4,000 executives have already been published[7]. The second survey was conducted on a smaller basis (fewer questions, only 1,500 respondents) and was primarily directed toward determining whether or not and to which extent the negative influences of the 1975 recession upon the responses have lost their importance after 18 months of economic upswing. As the structure of the two responding groups is largely identical despite their differing volume we were able to strike a comparison of the results of the two surveys for comprehensive aggregates (cf. Table 1 on page 12). The differences in the results of the two surveys have statistical significance.

2. Dissatisfaction as a Predominat Tendency

This section mainly deals with the dissatisfaction of executives in certain fields even though, considered as a whole, the majority are satisfied with their <u>general</u> living conditions (cf. the lower part of Fig. 3 on page 13) because, as will be shown later, dissatisfaction in the sphere of politics and the economy takes a significant influence on medium-term entrepreneurial planning. A total of 9 spheres of life were included in the survey (politics, economy, education, private life, health, occuptation,

Table 1

Survey Structure

	1975	1976
Number of evaluated questionnaires of executives	4089	1544
% of responses for		
Sectors		
Industry	55	56
Construction	11	10
Trade	34	34
	100	100
Branches		
Pre-products	22	21
Investment goods	19	21
Consumer goods	59	58
	100	100
Business size		
up to 49 employees	37	35
50 to 1999	32	31
200 to 999	23	25
1,000 bis 4,999	6	7
5,000 and above	2	2
	100	100
Age groups		
20 to 30 years	4	2
31 to 40	24	20
41 to 50	31	32
51 to 60	26	28
over 60	15	18
	100	100
Income		
below DM 36,000	14	9
DM 36,000 to 50,000	32	27
DM 50,000 to 75,000	25	29
DM 75,000 and above	29	35
	100	100
Occupational position		
Senior employees	44	41
Board members, general managers	18	21
Entrepreneurs	38	38
	100	100

Fig. 3

SATISFACTION IN THE ECONOMY

... % of the respondents[a] statet that in July 1975 in the mentioned fields their living conditions were

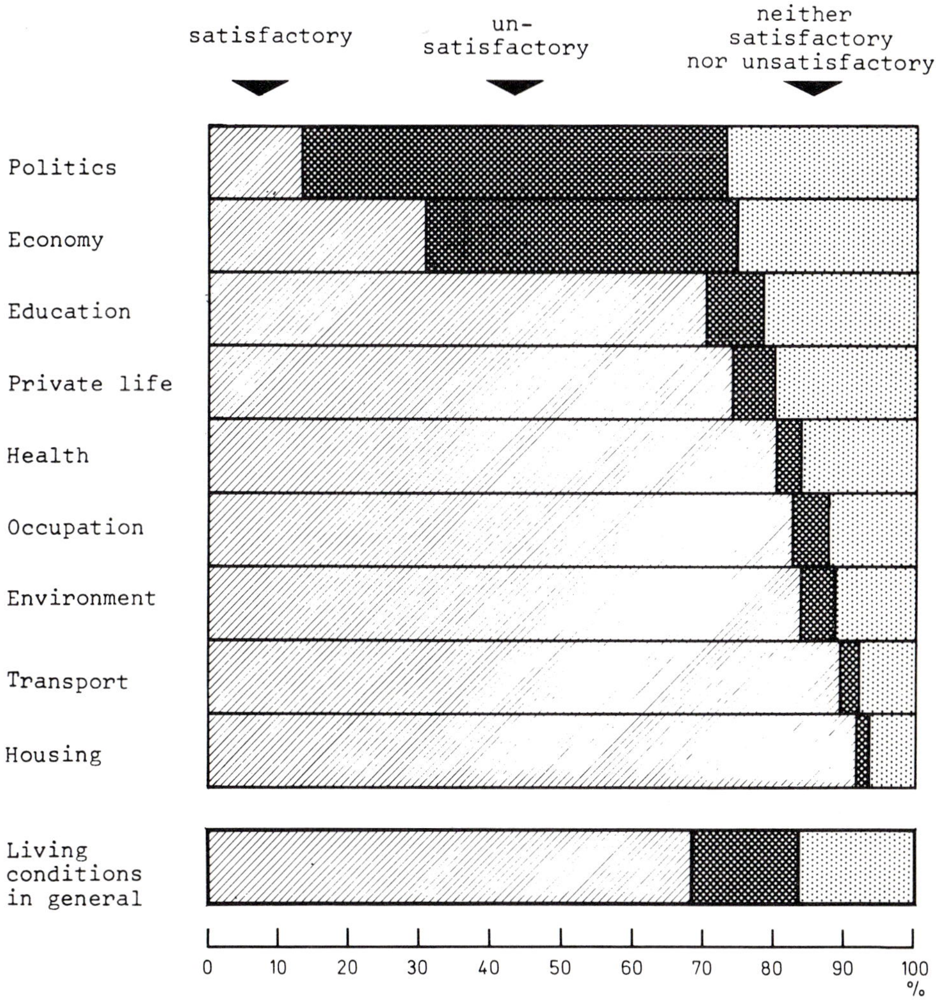

[a] About 4.000 executives and entrepreneurs.

environment, transport, housing). In their answers the executives show the highest degree of dissatisfaction by far with respect to the economic and political situations - that is with those two factors which have to be seen in close interrelation. In 1975, 44 % of the executives polled were dissatisfied with the general economic situation and 6o % with the political situation at the time of the survey. Figure 3 lists the results of the survey for the 9 sectors and for the judgment on the living conditions in general.

As may be assumed on the basis of Fig. 3 the response "dissatisfied with the economic situation" must be linked relatively frequently with the response "dissatisfied with politics". The tabulation results shown in Table 2 will confirm this assumption:

Most frequently we find dissatisfaction with the economic situation linked with a negative judgment on politics. There are considerably less executives who will pass a positive judgment on the economic situation and be dissatisfied with the political conditions. In other words: politics are blamed for an unsatisfactory economic situation.

Table 2

Satisfaction with the Economy and Politics

Key: ++ completely satisfied
+ mainly satisfied
= neither satisfied nor dissatisfied
- mainly dissatisfied
-- completely dissatisfied

		Satisfaction with the Economy					Cases
		++	+	=	-	--	
Satisfact. with Politics	++	12	1	o	o	o	33
	+	31	29	7	4	2	5o6
	=	26	34	44	14	5	1o95
	-	26	32	45	7o	4o	1988
	--	5	4	3	11	53	427
	%	1oo %	1oo %	1oo %	1oo %	1oo %	
Cases		13o	1119	1o3o	1426	344	4o49

In 1975, dissatisfaction with the economic situation among executives was mainly based on the following 3 grounds:

- dissatisfaction with the economic trend
- criticism of social policy and the trade unions
- general uncertainty and lack of confidence

Here again we find economic judgments linked with political ones.

The following table will reveal how little the state of affairs in politics and in the overall economy has corresponded to the ideal conceptions held by the executives:

Table 3

Desired Improvements

... % of executives consider an improvement urgent

	1975	1976
for the economic conditions in the FRG	67	64
for the political conditions inside and outside the FRG	58	56

It is striking that an improvement of the economic sphere is considered to be more pressing than in the political sphere although the political conditions are negatively judged by far more executives than the economic conditions (cf. Fig. 3 and Tab. 8).

As expected, the general economic situation in 1976, the year of upswing, was judged somewhat more positively than at about the middle of 1975, the cyclical low of the past recession. But also at the end of 1976 we were not able to detect any clear preponderance of positive judgments on the economic conditions (cf. Table 4).

Table 4

As Regards the General Economic Conditions in the FRG .... % of the Executives Surveyed were

		1975	1976
completely satisfied	(++)	3	2
mainly satisfied	(+)	28	35
neither satisfied nor dissatisfied	(=)	25	26
mainly dissatisfied	(-)	35	33
completely dissatisfied	(--)	9	4
balance[a)]		-13	+/-o

a) from [(++), (+)] and [(-), (--)]

The continuing pessimistic expectations for the next five years are an indication of the fact that the cyclical upturn starting in autumn 1975 has not been considered also to be the beginning of a far-reaching upward development in the economic and political spheres.

Table 5

Expectations of Business Executives for the Next 5 Years (% of Responses)

Expectation	Economic Situation 1975	Economic Situation 1976	Political Situation 1975	Political Situation 1976
Positive (+)	19	15	15	11
No substantial change	29	42	34	41
Negative (-)	52	43	51	48
Balance from (+) and (-)	-33	-28	-36	-37

As a comparison of Tables 5 and 4 shows, the economic future at the end of 1976 was judged more pessimistically than the present. The close relation of political and economic expectations is reflected by a high correlation coefficient (r - o.71). It is striking that the slight improvement in the balance of economic expectations for the next 5 years from mid-1975 to the end of 1976 is not to be explained by an increase in positive responses but by a decline in negative answers. Compared to 1975, a much larger portion of the executives questioned have taken a position of "wait-and see" ("no change") in their anticipations concerning both the economic and the political development. In view of such a position of "wait-and-see" we may expect relatively rarely that executives will take decisions directed toward an expansion of their own enterprises. This is confirmed by the 1976 survey. Compared to 1975, there has virtually been no change in the answers given to the question about the company strategy to be followed for the next 5 years (expand, keep to thc prcsent level, shrink) (Table 6).

The results of the two surveys show that a good two-thirds of the enterprises still do not intend to expand (cf. "reorientation lag", page 5). Yet a bare third does have such intention. However this percentage seems to low to realize a vigorous growth.

Table 6

Entrepreneurs' strategy regarding size of their own company

	1975		1976	
	% of responses			
Expansion (+)	31		32	
No change (=)	57	69	54	68
Shrinkage[a)] (-)	12		14	
Balance from (+) and (-)	+19		+18	

a) i.e. closing or selling parts of the business

At the end of this section dealing with the subject of "dissatisfaction" we will briefly try to establish the relationship to the theory of entrepreneurial behaviour outlined in Chapter B, as follows:

- The entrepreneur has obviously judged positive information of the economic upswing from mid-1975 to the end of 1976 differently than in earlier phases of a cyclical upward movement. His former scepticism of future chances of development was largely retained (cf. Tables 5 and 6). In addition, the abovementioned "reorientation lag" has presumably become longer. Possibly, the comprehensive discussions about the "limits to growth" have also had their share.

- The socio-political discussions on the position of the entrepreneur in a "social market economy", which have become considerably more lively in the declining phase of economic growth, have caused uncertainty in entrepreneurs. This uncertainty is reflected, on the one hand, by the high percentage of dissatisfaction and, on the other hand, by the wide-spread fear that the political situation will deteriorate in the next few years (cf. Fig. 3 and Tab. 5).

Sections 4 and 5 of this Chapter will try to prove that the component of dissatisfation together with a wide-spread pessimism about growth will take a negative effect on the company strategy.

3. Optimists and Pessimists as Contrastive Groups

For simplicity's sake we shall term executives pursuing an expansive policy for their own enterprise during the next five years as "optimists" and the rest as "pessimists". These terms, however, shall not be construed to imply any judgment[x)]. The questions posed to these groups in both surveys read:

"In the next five years, the enterprise where I work, in my view, should:

---

x) These two groups may have also been termed as "expansionists" and "non-expansionists".

- expand
- maintain its present size
- shrink, i.e. close down or sell unprofitable parts of the enterprise.

Although the 1975 survey took place during the recession and that of 1976 during a phase of upswing we may determine a constancy of ratings for the two surveys as a whole, as was mentioned before (cf. Table 6). Nevertheless, decisive changes in the attitudes of the individual sectors could have taken place. In Table 7, the shares of optimists and pessimists were therefore broken down according to various criteria: while, for instance, the construction industry gave the same rating - the signs here clearly point toward "shrinkage" - the wholesale and retail trade considered the prospects of expansion in 1976 somewhat more positively than industry; in 1975, they still held an almost identical view. Based on the subdivision by branches, consumer goods seem to be marked by a light improvement - however, it may not be overlooked that also in 1976 scepticism ("pessimism") predominates in about two-thirds of the respondents both for the sectors and the branches. Table 7 further shows that in both surveys younger executives were more optimistic than older ones and that larger firms and thus also executives with higher incomes showed a greater propensitiy to expand.

The difference shown in Tables 7 to 13 between "optimists" and "pessimists" are statistically significant, the probability of error being 95 to 99 %.

Table 7

Shares of "Optimists" and "Pessimists" according to Various Criteria

	Optimists		Pessimists	
	1975	1976	1975	1976
Sectors				
Industry	34	32	66	68
Construction	12	12	88	88
Trade	34	38	66	62
Branches				
Pre-products	32	31	68	69
Investment goods	35	31	65	69
Consumer goods	34	37	66	63
Business size				
up to 49 employees	28	3o	72	7o
5o to 199	33	33	67	67
2oo to 999	32	31	68	69
1,ooo to 4,999	4o	37	6o	63
5,ooo and above	46	39	54	61
Age groups				
2o to 3o years	41	47	59	53
31 to 4o	42	42	58	58
41 to 5o	33	37	67	63
51 to 6o	25	28	75	72
over 6o	21	17	79	83
Income				
below DM 36,ooo	22	23	78	77
DM 36,ooo to 5o,ooo	28	26	72	74
DM 51,ooo to 75,ooo	34	32	66	68
DM 75,ooo and above	38	39	62	61
Occupational position				
Senior employees	32	32	68	68
Board members,general managers	36	37	64	63
Entrepreneurs	28	29	72	71

Apart from a few minor differences we may generally state that a cyclical upswing between mid-1975 and the end of 1976 did not bring about any basic change in the structure of optimists and pessimists. This statement is important because later on we shall fall back on the larger sample of the 1975 survey in our investigation into the determinants and because we shall then be able to frame the hypothesis that the survey results are hardly distorted by the 1975 recession and that they are therefore of a more general significance.

4. Differences in Profiles of Satisfaction and Trends

It had to be assumed a priori that the judgments and anticipations of "optimists" and "pessimists" will markedly differ from one another. To characterize these differences we have selected the answers to the following questions posed in the comprehensive set of questions of the 1975 survey:

- Private living conditions
- Occupation
- Economic conditions in the FRG
- Political conditions inside and outside the FRG

a) Present Satisfaction

To get a judgment on the various subjects the executives responded in each case according to a predetermined set of answers as follows:

- completely satisfied
- mainly satisfied
- neither satisfied nor dissatisfied
- mainly dissatisfied
- completely dissatisfied

For the sake of clarity, the following table shows a combination of the first and last two answers in each case.

The satisfaction profiles are always somewhat less favourable with pessimists than with optimists. In the 1976 survey, the satisfaction profils with respect to the economic situation, as expected, have improved in both groups: In case of optimists we now have a preponderance of prositive responses. However, among pessimists we still find the negative judgment more frequently than a "satisfied" rating. These more unfavourable judgments are in part explained by the branch-specific structure of pessimists: This group comprises many medium-sized units of the building trade, for instance, a line where competition is particularly stiff. But the varying age structure is probably also an important factor, for in case of optimists, there are only about one third that are older than 5o years of age while in case of pessimists it is approximately half of them.

The results of Table 8 further show that more than half of the executives, both optimists and pessimists, are dissatisfied with the political situation and that this dissatisfaction is much more pronounced than that concerning the economic situation.

b) Development over the Past Five Years

While there are no big differences between optimists and pessimists as regards their satisfaction with private living conditions and occupation (cf. Table 8) an ex post study (development over the past five years) will reveal big differences between the two groups in these fields: The group of optimists reported considerably more frequently a favourable development in the private and occupational spheres. In both groups, the negative judgments on the economic and political development over the past five years were particularly pronounced (cf. Table 9). In 1976, the ratings have somewhat improved, however, negative tendencies are still predominant.

Table 8

Profiles of Satisfaction

	Optimists		Pessimists	
	% of responses			
	1975	1976[a]	1975	1976[a)]
Private living conditions				
satisfied (+)	76	.	73	.
neither/nor	19	.	21	.
dissatisfied (-)	5	.	6	.
balance from (+) and (-)	+71		+67	
Occupation				
satisfied (+)	85	.	81	.
neither/nor	11	.	13	.
dissatisfied (-)	4	.	6	.
balance from (+) and (-)	+81		+75	
Economy				
satisfied (+)	34	44	3o	34
neither/nor	22	25	27	27
dissatisfied (-)	44	31	43	39
balance from (+) and (-)	-1o	+13	-13	- 5
Politics				
satisfied (+)	15	.	12	.
neither/nor	25	.	28	.
dissatisfied (-)	6o	.	6o	.
balance from (+) and (-)	-45	.	-48	.

---

a) The 1976 survey posed the question of satisfaction only with regard to the economic situation.

Table 9

Development Over the Past Five Years

	Optimists		Pessimists	
	% of responses			
	1975	1976	1975	1976
Private living conditions				
satisfied (+)	43	40	29	27
neither/nor	47	47	57	57
dissatisfied (-)	10	13	14	16
balance from (+) and (-)	+33	+27	+15	+11
Occupation				
satisfied (+)	40	37	24	18
neither/nor	36	43	42	53
dissatisfied (-)	24	20	34	29
balance from (+) and (-)	+16	+17	-10	-11
Economy				
satisfied (+)	9	13	6	7
neither/nor	15	31	12	26
dissatisfied (-)	76	56	82	67
balance from (+) and (-)	-67	-43	-76	-60
Politics				
satisfied (-)	5	7	4	3
neither/nor	22	32	19	30
dissatisfied (-)	73	61	77	67
balance from (+) and (-)	-68	-54	-73	-64

c) Expected Development for the Next Five Years

Optimists and pessimists mark the biggest difference in their anticipation profiles in each of the four fields named. The anticipations of pessimists are always considerably more negative, above all, with respect to occupational and economic developments. This is quite understandable for as shown in this paper the company strategy plans are strongly influenced by considerations of a general economic nature. That we do have the following chain of thought:

▼ unfavourable economic development

▼ defensive company strategy

▼ moderate opportunities of a career

• negative repercussions on private living conditions

This is clearly reflected by the results of the "pessimists".

Table lo

Development for the Next Five Years

	Optimists		Pessimists	
	% of responses			
	1975	1976	1975	1976
Private living conditions				
satisfied (+)	19	22	11	13
neither/nor	64	67	65	71
dissatisfied (-)	17	11	24	16
balance from (+) and (-)	+ 2	+11	-13	- 3
Occupation				
satisfied (+)	23	22	11	lo
neither/nor	61	68	63	7o
dissatisfied (-)	16	lo	26	2o
balance from (+) and (-)	+ 7	+12	-15	-lo
Economy				
satisfied (+)	25	2o	17	13
neither/nor	32	46	28	4o
dissatisfied (-)	43	34	55	47
balance from (+) and (-)	-18	-14	-38	-34
Politics				
satisfied (+)	18	13	14	11
neither/nor	37	46	33	38
dissatisfied (-)	45	41	53	51
balance from (+) and (-)	-27	-28	-39	-4o

An evaluation of responses was made at the micro-level in order to determine whether negative medium-term economic anticipations, as a rule, are coupled with negative political expectations. We found that in case of

optimists, 36 %, and
pessimists, 46 %

of the responses came from the same respondents.

A similar correlation above average we found between the negative medium-term economic expectations (for the next 5 years) and the negative longer-term growth expectations (for the next lo-2o years). Identical, e.g. negative, reports came from

31 % of optimists and
43 % of pessimists.

It is remarkable that optimists think that their occupational situation will rather improve dispite a deterioration of the economic situation. Pessimists, however, do not only rate the future economic opportunities considerably worse but, on the whole, they also expect a deterioration of their occupational and private living conditions.

In the two surveys, entrepreneurs, usually proprietors of medium-sized units, are much more sceptical of the future political development than, say, senior employees, as may be derived from the following figures:

	Senior Employees		Entrepreneurs	
	1975	1976	1975	1976
Judgment of the future political development x)				
Improvement (+)	17	13	12	9
No improvement	39	43	27	36
Deterioration (-)	44	44	61	55
Difference between (+) and (-)	-27	-31	-49	-46

Apart from the occuptational position, there are further features characteristic of the two groups that may be the cause of varying opinions about an "aggressive" or "defensive" company strategy. One of these features is, for instance, as already mentioned above, the size of business: In large companies we find optimists relatively more frequently (cf. Tables 7 and 11).

d) Long-Term Growth Expectations

At the end of this chapter we shall deal in somewhat more detail with the relationship between confidence in the future economic growth and the size of the enterprises employing the executives surveyed:

x) in- and outside FRG

Table 11

Expected Real Growth of GNP during the Next lo to 2o Years
(% of Responses)

Expected annual rate of growth or expected trend	Optimists in enterprises with			Pessimists .... employees		
	up to 49	5o to 999	1ooo and above	up to 49	5o to 999	1ooo and above
3-4 %	2	1	3	1	1	1
1-2 %	4o	47	68	29	34	48
Stagnation	41	38	24	39	4o	35
Decline	17	14	5	31	25	16
	1oo%	1oo%	1oo%	1oo%	1oo%	1oo%

We may derive from this table - which is based on the survey results of 1975 - that executives in larger companies are in general more optimistic about the longer-term economic growth than leading people in smaller businesses. In addition, it is also clearly revealed that pessimists expect a growth of the overall economy considerably more rarely than optimists. In 1975, 49 % of the optimists and 33 % of the pessimists, on an average, expected an overall economic growth of 1 to 4 %, in 1976 the percentages rose to 71 and 54 %, respectively. Weighting the distribution of answers with the actual company size structure of industry, construction and the trade in the FRG we would come to the conclusion that in 1975 about two thirds of the West German enterprises did no longer expect further growth of the economy. This clearly reflects the influence of the recession of that year. In the meantime, the overall economic anticipations have markedly improved (cf. Table 12). Nevertheless, the enterprises have not become more inclined to expand (cf. Table 6), which is probably the effect of the "reorientation lag" referred to earlier. However, it should be retained that only a negligible minority (7%) of the executives in the FRG expect an economic growth for the future, exeeding 2 per cent per annum.

Table 12

Expected Real Growth of GNP during the Next 1o to 2o Years (% of Responses)

Expected annual rate of growth or expected trend	Survey 1975		Survey 1976	
3-4 %	1	38	7	59
1-2 %	37		52	
Stagnation	38		29	
Decline	24		12	

By all probability, however, the results of Table 12 are negatively distorted, an experience that is frequently made in case of questions of such a far ex-ante horizon. Entrepreneurs tend to underestimate the longer-term development. However, these anticipations for the future which, judged objectively, are too negative, obviously take an influence on the present plans of enterprises: Only a bare third of the firms intended to expand (cf. Table 6). Deducting those enterprises ready to shrink there will remain only one-fifth of "optimists". As these expansion plans may be realized only in the course of several years the overall economic momentum of growth of these companies, as this year's experience has shown, is obviously too low.

Like at the end of section 2 we shall now try to relate the tabulation results of section 4 to our theoretical deliberations (Chapter B):

- It is clearly shown that judgments of a general nature as for instance, judgments on the economic conditions in the FRG are frequently influenced by the branch-specific structure of the people surveyed. In part, there are also other influences involved which depend on the size of the business, the occupational position and the age of executives. According to these factors, the same information spectrum which is available to all executives in almost equal amounts, will therefore be judged differently.

- The groups of optimists and pessimists mark the biggest difference in their anticipation structures. Among pessimists, uncertainty as a result of the increasing socio-political discussions finds shape in a significantly more negative assessment of the economic and political prospects for the future (cf. Table lo). Respective fears were uttered most frequently by independent entrepreneurs.

- Despite an markedly more positive assessment of the longer-term chances of growth in FRG at the end of 1976 as compared to mid-1975 (cf. Table 12) there has not been any positive influence on medium-term entrepreneurial planning. In part this may be due to the longer re-orientation lag but in part also to the fact that the cyclical upswing lasting up to the end of 1976 was felt to be too weak. In addition, there has been hardly any abatement of the scepticism about developments in the fields of politics and the economy for the medium-term future (cf. Table 1o).

- Striking a balance of the companies having positive and negative plans (cf. Table 6) and distributing the positive remainder over the 5 years of the period of planning we will obtain only a relatively low percentage which, in view of the generally sceptical attitude toward the future is obviously too low to induce a cumulative process of infection as described by Jöhr.

5. Determinants for a Company Strategy Results of an Analysis of Variance

a) Method Applied

Having so far shown factors of importance to the intended growth of the enterprise in isolation we shall now try to explain the most important factors of influence. This is done using a form of variance analysis also known as "Split"-, "Auspik"- or "Tree"-Analysis.
As the statistical method chosen by us is still relatively rarely applied in economical research the following paragraphs will deal with this method in somewhat more detail. The essence of Tree-Analysis lies in the determination of a hierarchy of variables of influence for a predetermined target variable (dependent variable).

For this purpose, the surveyed characteristics of every independent variable are dichotomized in sub-groups in a way that a particular sub-group will show more homogeneity as the target variable and the heterogeneity between subgroups is as high as possible.

In our Figur A[x] the first split variable("expected economic growth in the FRG during the next lo to 2o years") explains from all other included variables in this dichotomization the variance of the target variable the best.

---

x) See Annex p. 48.

At the next step these subgroups are analyzed in the same way, that means we look for further variables which explain the variance of the precedent subgroup the best. This method is repeated to a defined stop-point. Such stop-points are given for example:

a) if the number of cases in the subgroups is to small
b) the total variance of a subgroup is to small

One of the disadvantages of the procedure chosen lies in the fact that often only a single variable of a number of highly correlating variables is included in the analysis as a sort of representative for other, about equally highly explanatory variables. For further details of this method see footnote 8, for literature footnote 9.

b) Instructions for the Interpretation of Trees

The mean values ($\bar{x}$) in the segments always refer to the dependent variable. The following example is given: The executives shown in Fig. A, segment 4 (aged 5o and above) who anticipate a decline concurrently with the overall economic development for the next lo to 2o years will have a mean value of $\bar{x}$ = 2.o5 with regard to their own company strategy (segment 1), i.e. as the highest possible value (= 3) stands for shrinkage, that this group expects the possibilities of their own enterprise to be particularly bad. The group of executives aged between 2o and 5o (segment 5) is characterized by a mean value

Tree Analysis A for the decision: "Expansion versus stagnation or decrease in own enterprise"
(survey 1975)

Replies:

(1) expansion
(2) stagnation
(3) decrease

Above the dividing line the represented managers are on the average more pessimistic than below the dividing line

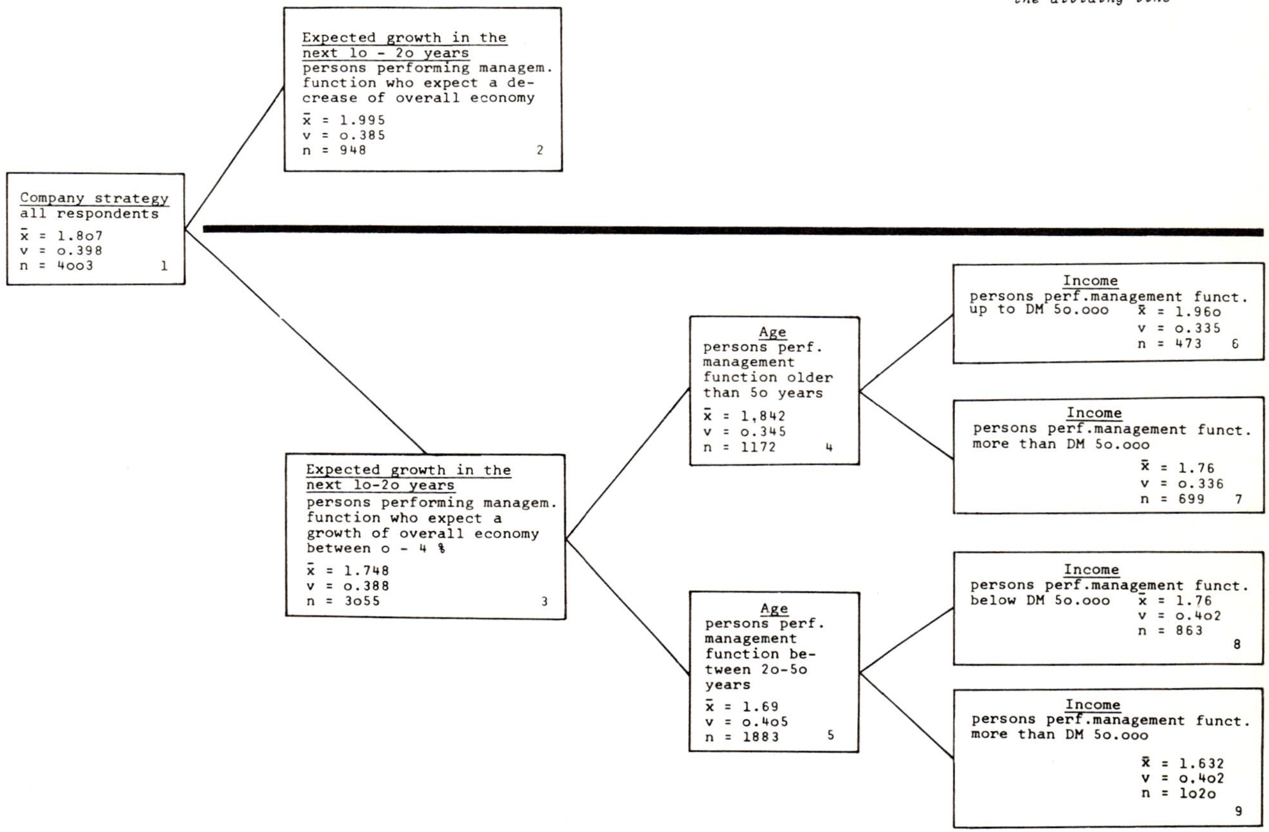

Tree Analysis B for "expected growth of overall economy in the next lo - 2o years" (survey 1975)

Replies:

(1) Annual real growth of the national product by 3-4 %

(2) Increase of the NP by 1-2 %

(3) Stagnation (on the level as up to now)

(4) Decrease of the NP

Above the dividing line the represented managers are on the average more pessimistic than below the dividing line

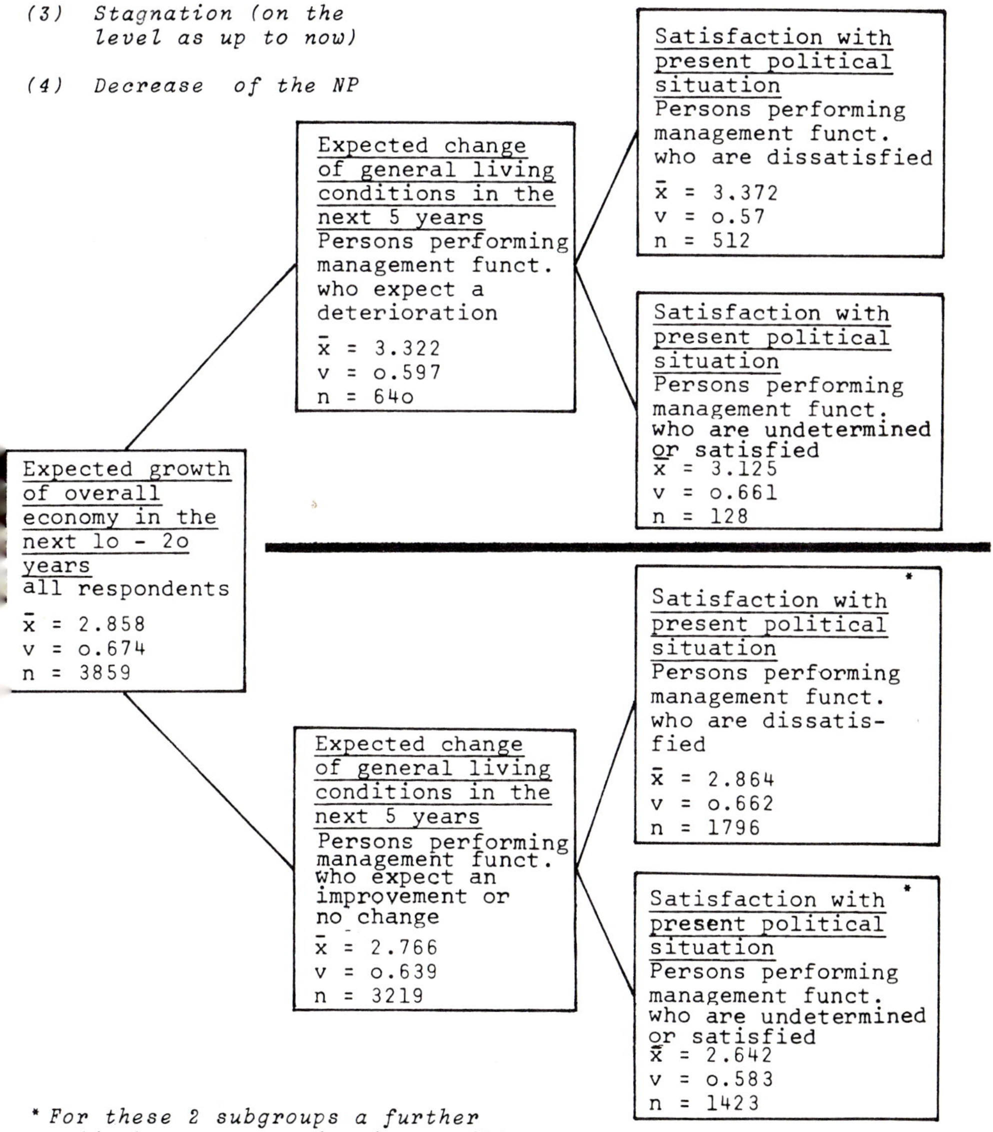

* *For these 2 subgroups a further split by company sEize is possible.*

Tree Analysis C: It represents the field of force which surrounds the entrepreneur when making strategic decisions on expansion or stagnation

Summary of the analyses A and B

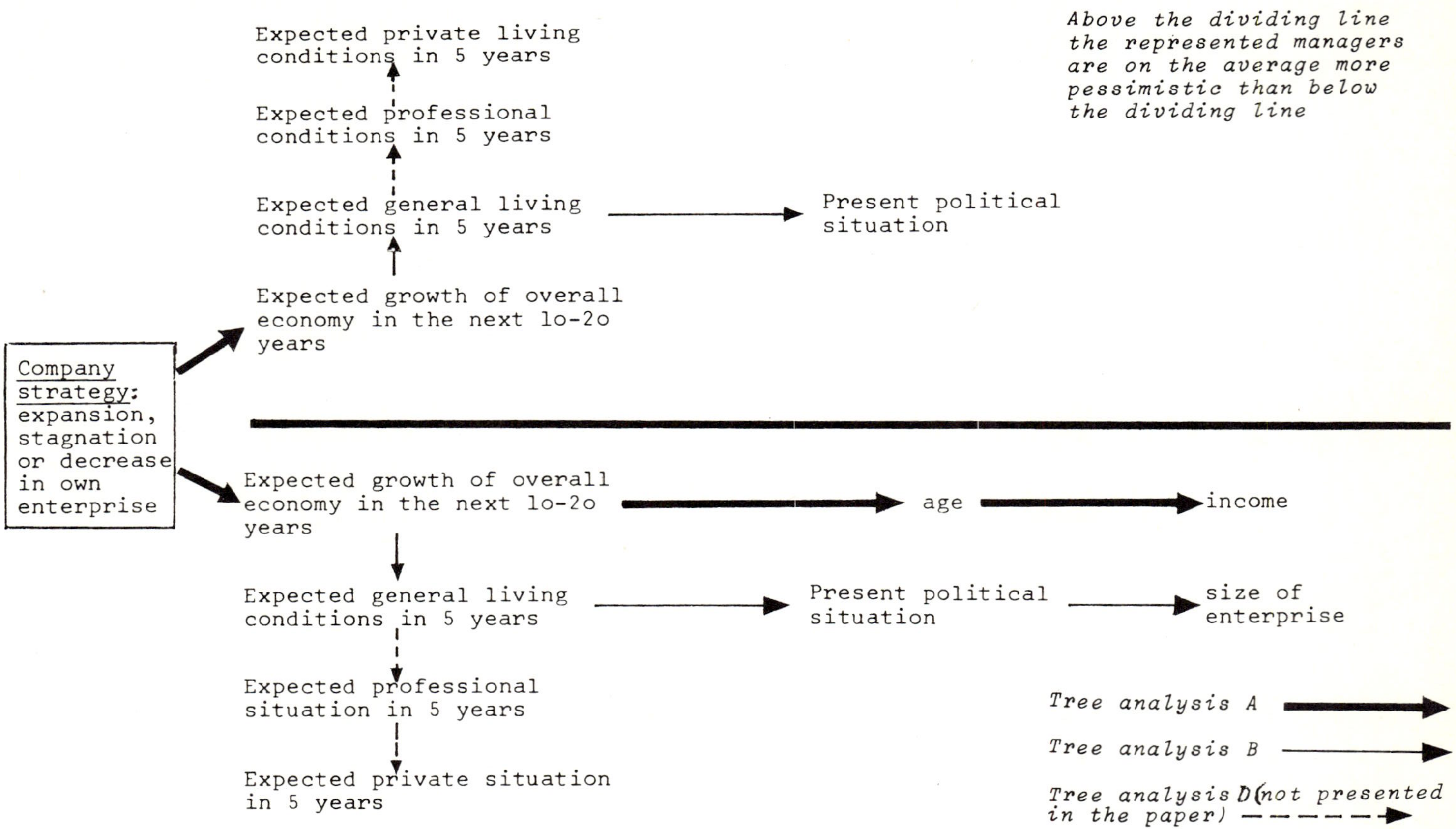

E.J. VAN DER LINDEN
COMMISSION OF THE EUROPEAN COMMUNITIES
BRUSSELS

PRINCIPAL COMPONENT ANALYSES WITH DATA FROM THE EEC-ENTREPRENEURIAL AND CONSUMER SURVEYS

1. INTRODUCTION

This paper does not aim at to give an exhaustive survey of applying principal component analysis to survey data, nor does it propose to elaborate on the technicalities of this method itself. It merely proposes to use this statistical tool in a few cases in order to facilitate the understanding of the underlying dimensions in the replies of economic agents in different countries to conjunctural survey-questions and where possible to use the synthesised information as business-cycle indicators.

On several occasions papers have been presented at CIRET-Conferences with evidence on the application of principal component analysis to different conjunctural surveys [See references (5), (8), (9),(11)]. In this paper we plan to look at two surveys: the first is the monthly business survey and the second is the four-monthly consumer survey. Both surveys are to a high degree harmonised among the participating EEC-member countries and thus supply us with information which is comparable as between those countries.

For cross-section analysis both surveys provide us with enough data. In the case of time-series analysis, the situation is slightly different. The monthly business survey poses no problems, as it has existed in harmonised form since 1963 for most monthly questions and, since 1965 for most four-monthly questions for five member countries (*). The consumer survey, however, is of a more recent date. The harmonised programme started in the second quarter of 1972 in five member-countries and in the second quarter of 1974 all member countries, except Luxembourg, participated.

The consumer survey is carried out three times a year, in January, May and October [see (4)]. This means that by September 1977 we will have a total of 16 observations for five countries and 10 observations for the others. Therefore, the data for Denmark, the United Kingdom and for Ireland will not be analysed in this paper. Until the end of 1975, the sample was 5,000 households and each time attitudinal questions, as well as questions on buying intentions and the possession of durable goods were asked. Since January 1976, the EEC-consumer survey programme has been altered such that in January and in May the sample size is reduced to 2,500 households, i.e. half the original size, and only attitudinal and expectational questions are asked. Once a year, in

...I...

* The Netherlands started the harmonised programme in October 1971, Ireland and the United Kingdom joined the harmonised programme from 1974 onwards.

October, the sample consists of about 5,000 households and questions are concerned with consumer attitudes, expectations as well as buying intentions (buying intentions will, however, only be analysed in this paper in the cross-section-part).

The question can be asked : what is the purpose of applying principal component analysis to survey data? What additional information can this analysis provide us with that may increase our understanding of the conjunctural surveys or at least some aspects of it?

It would be superfluous to enter in detail into the reasons for analysing subjective information in relation to the business cycle. It has been done on many occasions and by well-known researchers after the pioneer-work of Prof. G. Katona in the field of psychological economics [see (7)]. Attitudes and expectations have an important impact on decision-making of all economic agents, consumers as well as businessmen.

One of the different ways of looking at the relations among attitudes and expectations is the technique of principal component analysis. The purpose of principal components analysis is to summarize the information given by a set of variables in a smaller number of uncorrelated variables which describe the greater part of the variance of the original set. More precisely, the original variables are described linearly in terms of new components - each of which a linear transformation of the original set. The new components are pairwise uncorrelated and of which the first will have the maximum possible variance, the second the maximum possible variance among those uncorrelated with the first, and so forth. For practical problems only a few components may be retained if they account for a large proportion of the total variance in the data-set. The analysis starts from the covariance matrix or the correlation matrix. It can easily be proved that the total variation in the variables is given by the sum of the eigenvalues (λi), e.g. the latent roots of the covariance matrix of the original (or standardised) series. The variation explained by the first component then equals the ratio of the first eigenvalue to the sum of the eigenvalues, etc. The correlations between the variables and the components are called the factor loadings. The values of a component at given points in time are called the factor scores (see f.i. [6]).

.../...

This makes principal component analysis an adequate tool for the construction of conjunctural indicators [see (1), (2), (5), (9), (13), (14), (15)]. Of primary interest is the fact that by using this technique attitudes and expectations are grouped in specific dimensions. The principal-component-method has also been applied to look for "waves of optimism and pessimism" in industry. An analysis of survey testbalances for export expectations in the Federal Republic of Germany (i.e. positive minus negative replies) carried out in 1961 showed that changes in the intra-industry consensus were largely different for different industries [see (8)]. We will, however, not analyse this specific topic in this paper.

In the following pages some results of principal component applications will be discussed within the framework of the harmonised business survey and the harmonised EEC-consumer survey. The main purpose of this exercise is to see if, in different member-countries, identical clusters of attitudinal variables can be identified.

2. THE MONTHLY BUSINESS SURVEY

A. A monthly synthetic indicator of economic activity

Attempts of building leading indicators of economic activity go quite far back. One of the first experiments was the Harvard-Barometer which ultimately stopped. However, interest in synthetic or compound indicators of business activity revived and the construction of indicators based on business surveys is even a relatively recent development. Thus, in different EEC- member countries, several such indicators are in existence (cfr. Banque Nationale de Belgique : conjunctural barometer; IFO-Institute in Munich : Geschäftsklima; ISCO-Institute in Rome). They are all monthly indicators and the basic series that constitute the synthetic indicator are generally readily available as compared to "objective" statistical series.

The monthly business survey series that are part of the EEC-programme and that are fully harmonised number five: they are (1) the evaluation of production compared to last month, (2) the evaluation of total order-books, (3) the judgment on the stocks of finished products, (4) production tendencies over the next three to four months and (5) selling price expectations over the next three to four months [see (17)]. The first four of these variables will be analysed in this section.*

Although, clearly the number of variables is rather low, we applied a principal component analysis on the testbalances (i.e. positive minus negative replies) for the Federal Republic of Germany, France, Italy, Belgium and the Netherlands. This exercise is along the same lines as has been done for Italy in [(9)]. The period covered extends from January, 1965 until February, 1977 (the Netherlands only started to participate in October 1971).

An interesting fact is that - when looking at the sample correlation coefficients (see Appendix, table A1) for all five countries, correlation is highest between the replies on the "orderbook situation" and the replies on the "level of stocks of finished products", with a negative sign, due to the nature of the question on stocks of finished products, as this question is "Do you consider that your present stocks of finished products are, for the season : above normal (+), normal (=), below normal (-), no stocks of finished products"? In general, it appears that the judgments businessmen

.../...

* The reply categories are "higher" - "the same" - "lower" for (1) and (4), "above normal" - "normal" - "below normal" for (2) and (3).

make, as well as their expectations for the near future are highly consistent throughout Europe. The relatively high correlations make that the percentage of total variance explained by the first principal component (PC1) ranges from 79 % for Italy to 87 % for France (see Appendix, table A2).

Although the replies to the questions are highly correlated with each other, their behaviour at peaks and troughs shows differences. This characteristic has been shown in many studies on business surveys. Nevertheless, we thought it would be interesting to summarise the information into one synthetic indicator, the factor scores of the first principal component (i.e. the value taken by a factor for each observation), reflecting the evolution in general business climate, just like the above-mentioned "Geschäftsklima" of the IFO-Institute and other business-cycle indicators based on survey-material. Moreover, the weights of the four variables are approximately identical, which suggests that for the sake of constructing a synthetic indicator, it would be sufficient to take the arithmetical average of the standardised variables (see Appendix, table A3). The resulting curves are depicted on graphs 1A to 1E (pp. 4a, 4b, 4c, 4d, 4e) where they are confronted for the period 1970-1976 with year-to-year growth rates of industrial production (excluding food-processing industries and the building sector).* For smoothing a three-month moving average was applied. These graphs show that, in general, as a leading indicator they are not very regular.

B. Non-monthly data in the business survey

As a certain number of questions in the business survey are asked three to four times a year (topics here are (a) production capacity, (b) obstacles to production, (c) the hiring of personel and (d) the number of months needed to complete orders [see (17)]), we were also interested in the relationships among these non-monthly questions on the one hand and the relation between the non-monthly and the monthly data on the other hand. Therefore, we "quarterised" all nine series in the analysis by interpolation of four-monthly series or by averaging of monthly series and applied a principal component analysis on the following series (the letters between brackets indicate the original frequency**):

.../...

* We started the confrontation in 1970/71 as, for most countries, comparable production statistics are delivered from then on by the Statistical Office of the European Communities (S.O.E.C.)

** For the precise wording of the survey questions, see [17].

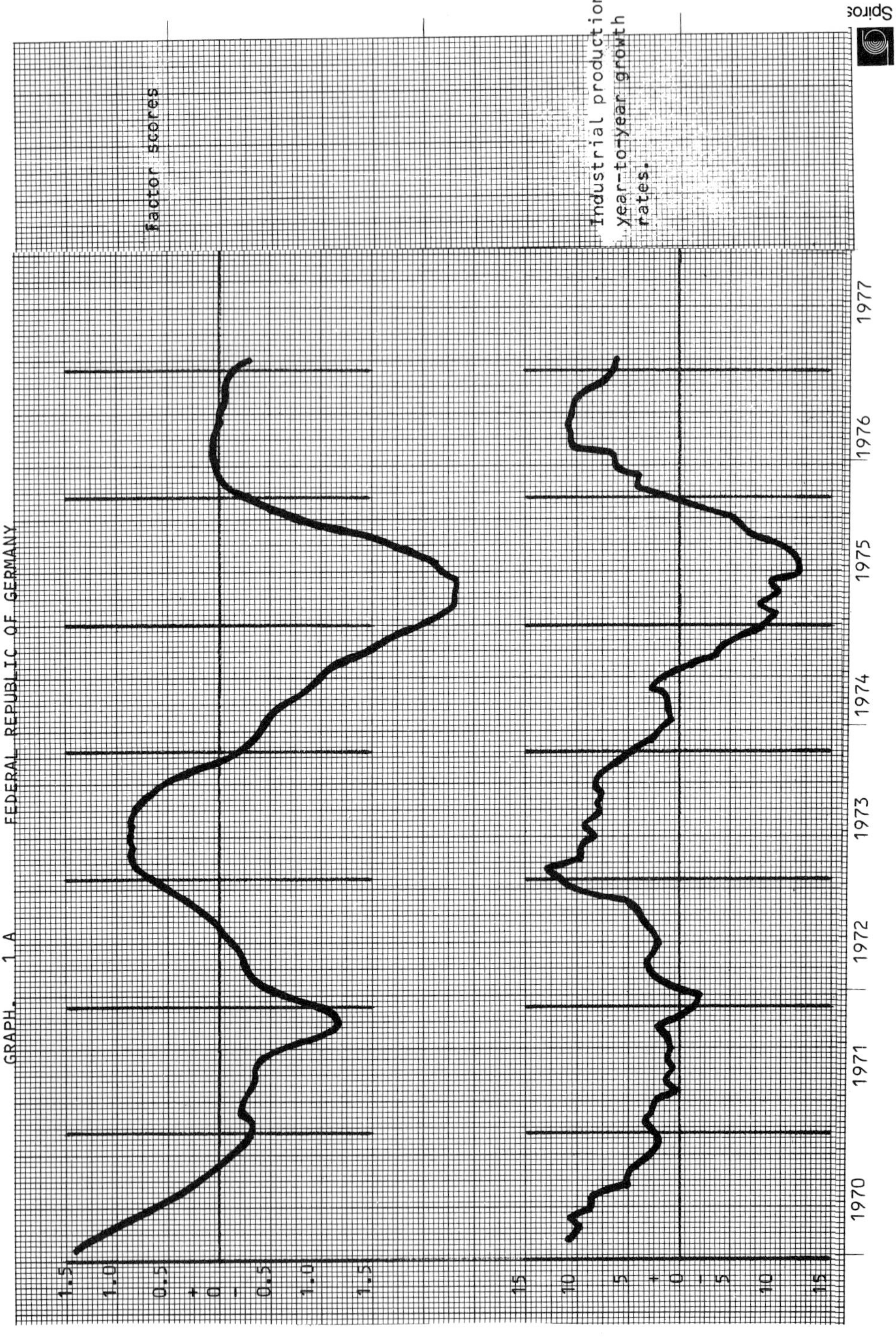

GRAPH 1 A
FEDERAL REPUBLIC OF GERMANY
Factor scores
Industrial production, year-to-year growth rates.
1.5
1.0
0.5
+ 0 −
0.5
1.0
1.5
15
10
5
+ 0 −
5
10
15
1970
1971
1972
1973
1974
1975
1976
1977

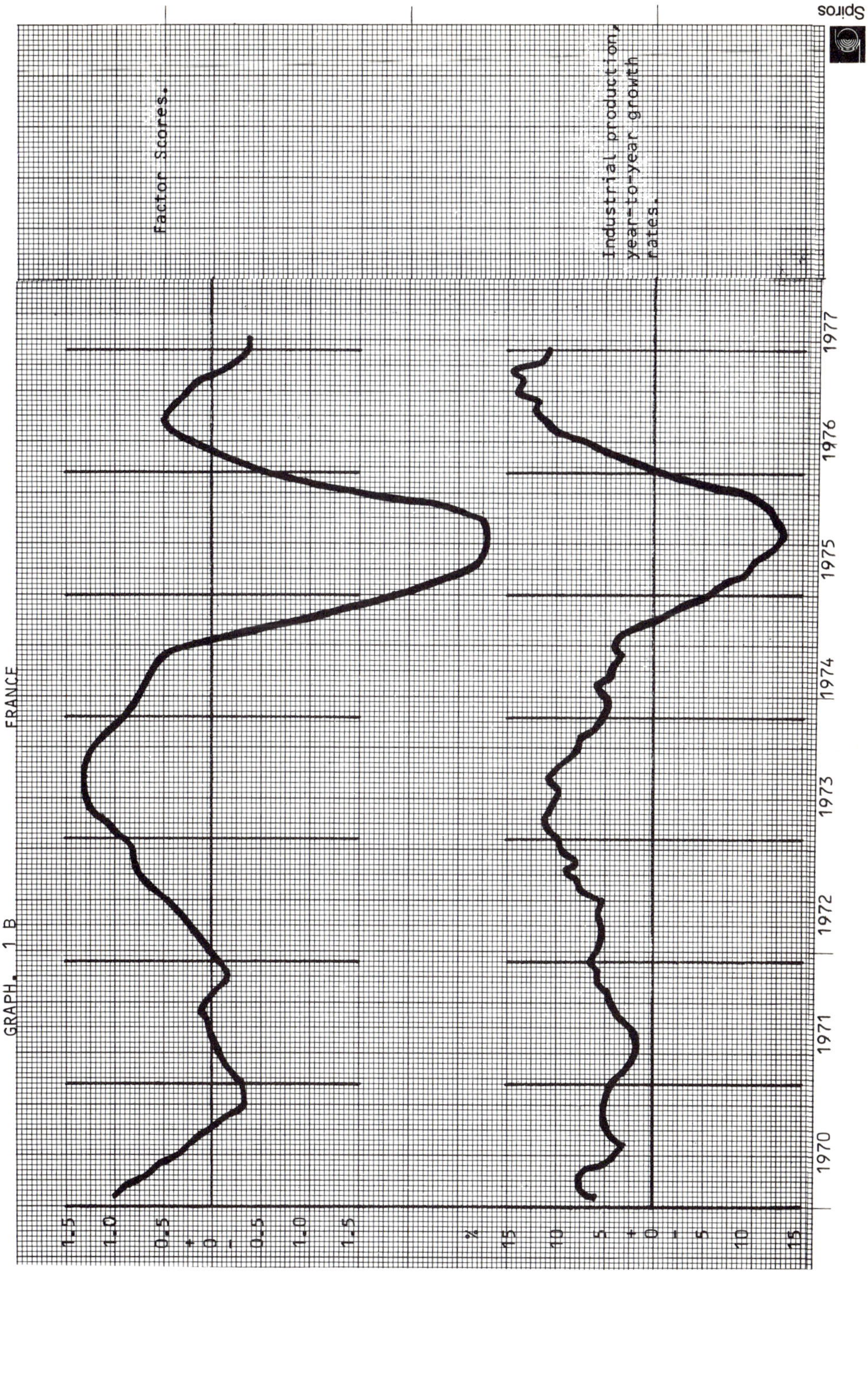
GRAPH. 1 B
FRANCE
Factor Scores.
Industrial production, year-to-year growth rates.
1970
1971
1972
1973
1974
1975
1976
1977
%

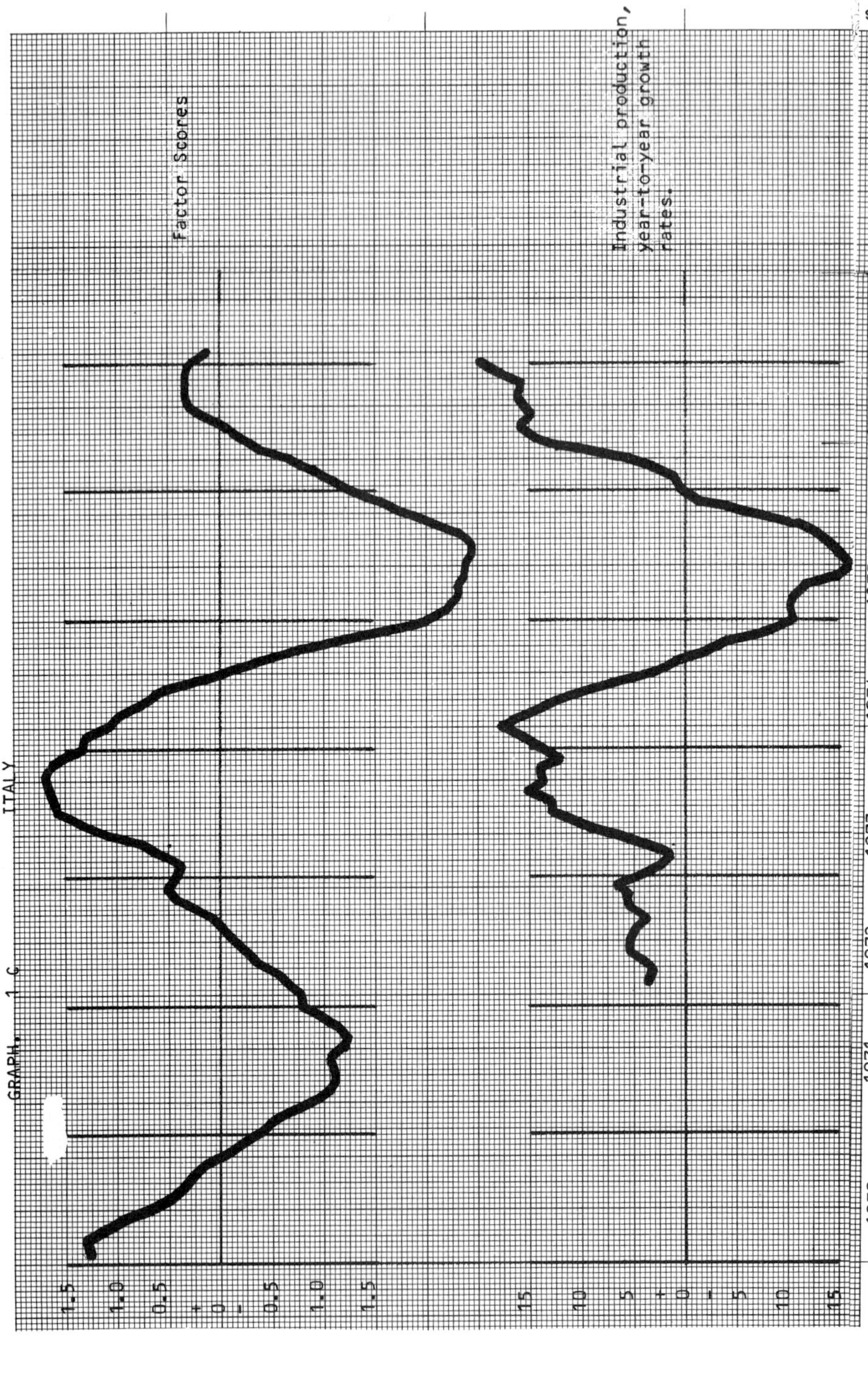
GRAPH 1 C
ITALY
Factor Scores
Industrial production, year-to-year growth rates.
1.5
1.0
0.5
+ 0 -
0.5
1.0
1.5
15
10
5
+ 0 -
5
10
15
1970
1971
1972
1973
1974
1975
1976
1977

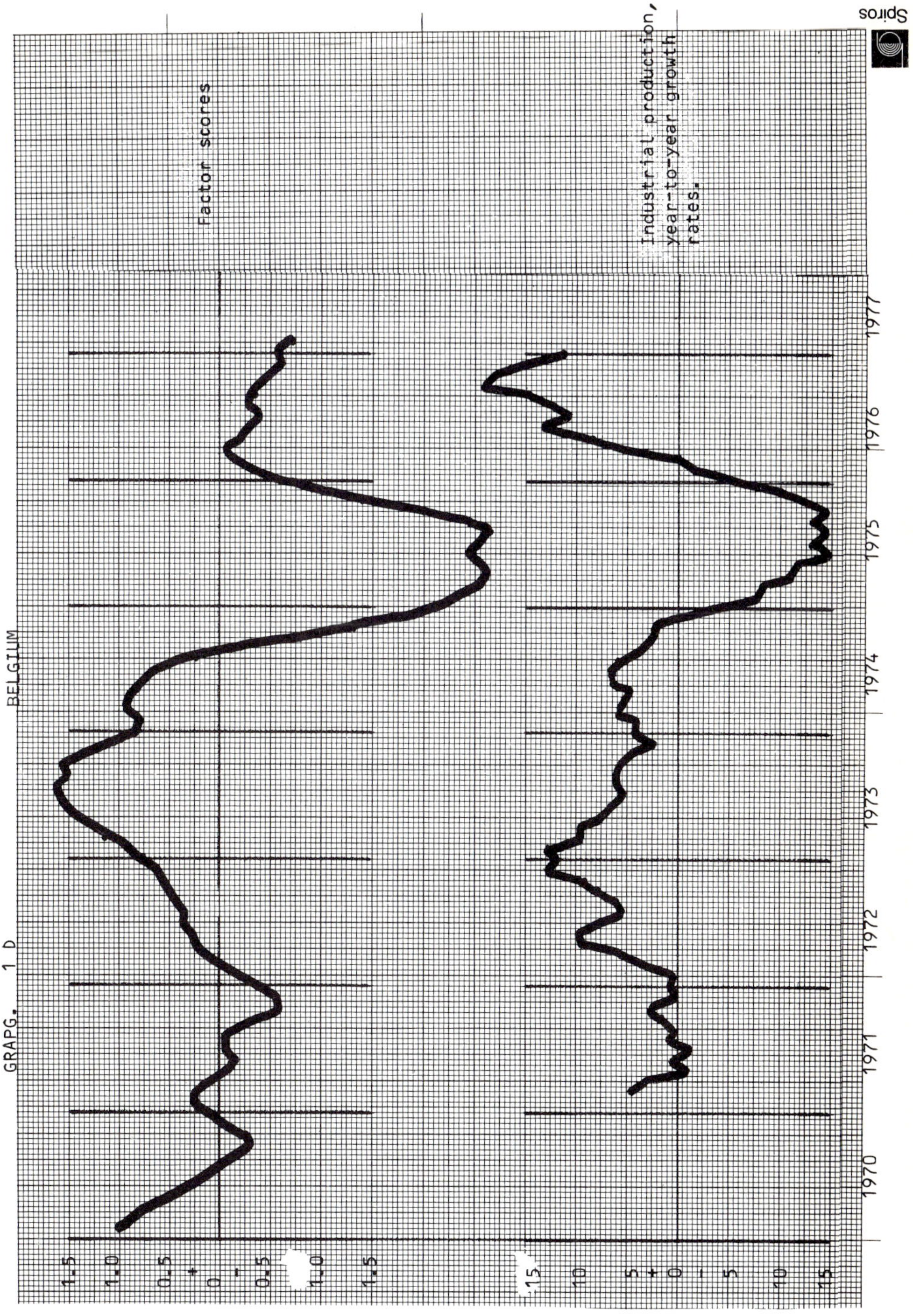
GRAPG. 1 D
BELGIUM
Factor scores
Industrial production, year-to-year growth rates.
1970
1971
1972
1973
1974
1975
1976
1977
1.5
1.0
0.5
+
0
-
0.5
1.0
1.5
15
10
5
+
0
-
5
10
15

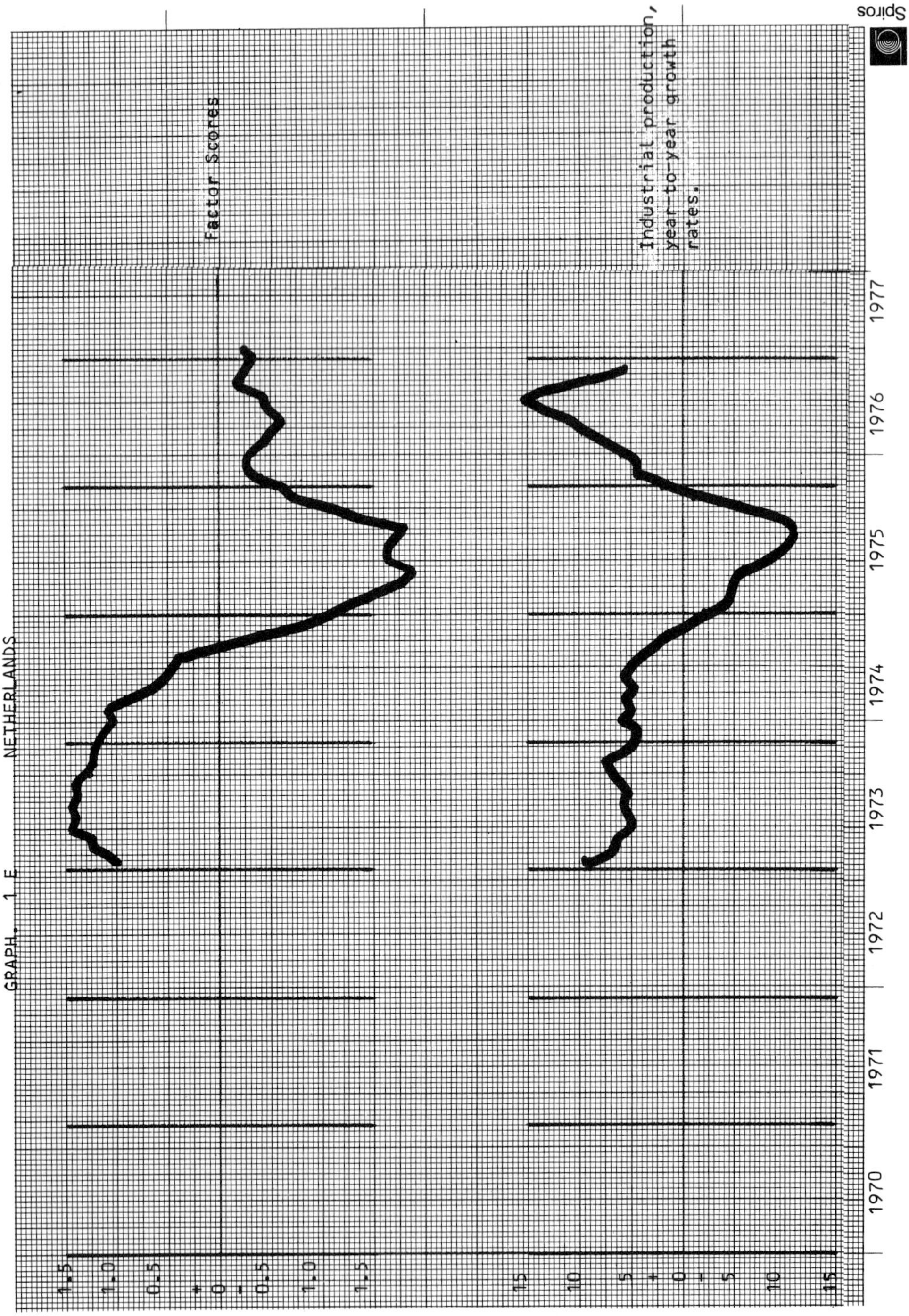
GRAPH. 1 E
NETHERLANDS
Factor Scores
Industrial production, year-to-year growth rates.
1970
1971
1972
1973
1974
1975
1976
1977
1.5
1.0
0.5
+ 0 -
0.5
1.0
1.5
15
10
5
+ 0 -
5
10
15

M = monthly, Q : quarterly and FM = four-monthly = January, May and October,
S = semestrial = May and October.

1. Judgment on the level of total order books (M).
2. Judgment on the level of stocks of finished products (M).
3. Production expectations over the next 3 to 4 months (M).
   Is production currently being held up by any of the following obstacles :
   4. Insufficient demand (FM),
   5. Labour shortage (FM),
   6. Lack of equipment (FM)?
7. Judgment on the sufficiency of production capacity (FM) (not sufficient - sufficient - more than sufficient).
8. Number of months accounted for by orderbook or production schedule.
9. Employment expectations (up - unchanged - down).

Series 1, 2, 3, 7, 9 are testbalances; 4, 5 and 6 are percentages of responses and 8 is expressed in number of months. The analysis has been applied to the data of four countries : the Federal Republic of Germany, France, Italy and Belgium.

A frequency distribution of the correlation coefficients gives a crude measure of the association between the nine variables in the analysis (see Table 1). (The correlation coëfficients themselves are given in Table A4 of the appendix).

TABLE 1 :

Relative Frequencies of zero order correlation coëfficients (%)
(absolute values)

Lower bound of interval	0.0	0.2	0.4	0.6	0.8
FR. of Germany	3	6	22	22	47
France	0	8	22	50	20
Italy	0	0	3	42	55
Belgium	0	3	5	28	64

From this table it is clear that the variables in the analysis are highly intercorrelated. The intercorrelation is, however, higher in Italy and Belgium than in the Federal Republic of Germany and France. We, therefore, expect only a few attitudinal clusters to account for the bulk of the total variation in the data-set. (See Table 2.)

.../...

TABLE 2 :

Percentage of variance explained by PC1 and PC2

	FR of Germany	France	Italy	Belgium
PC1	76.6	70.7	83.9	82.4
PC2	11.0	11.2	6.2	10.5
$\sum$	87.6	81.9	90.1	92.9

Furthermore, for most countries variables 1, 2, 3, 7, 9 load on the same component (see Appendix, Table A5). We may, therefore, interpret the first component as reflecting the factors related to capacity utilisation.* Indeed, the variables with highest correlation with Q7 (Entrepreneurs' judgment on capacity utilisation) are "lack of demand, orderbooks, stocks of finished products, production tendencies and hire of personel. (see also [9]). Although rotation of the factor matrix does not succeed in a very clear separation as between factors, graphs 2A and 2B (pp. 6a and 6b) show an interesting picture of the loadings in a two-factor plane. It suggests rather similar attitudinal clusters in the different member-countries.**

Summarizing, it results from the two preceding paragraphs that the different survey-questions, monthly as well as non-monthly questions, are highly correlated and that few attitude-dimensions are required to account for the entrepreneurs' opinions. Even more interesting is the fact that in the different member-countries a comparable judgmental pattern is registered, i.e. the business-environment is perceived in nearly the same way by entrepreneurs in different countries.

.../...

* For Belgium the second component is comparable to the first in the other countries.

** For France a difference in sign can be observed.

GRAPH 2A
FACTORSPACE

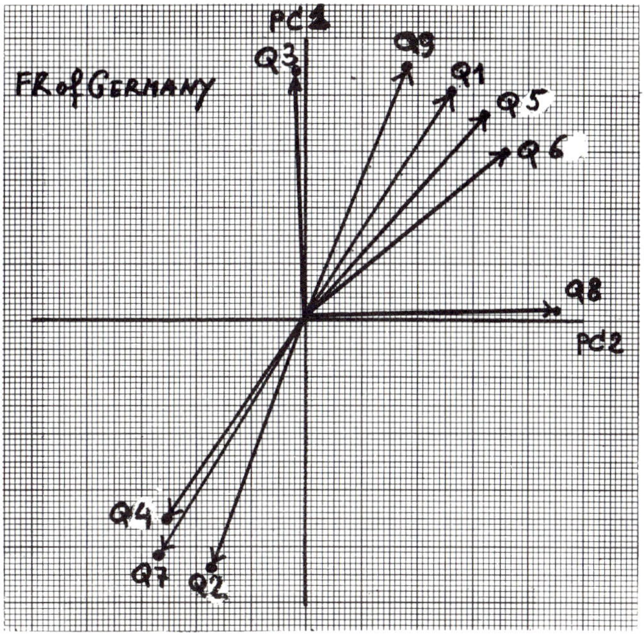

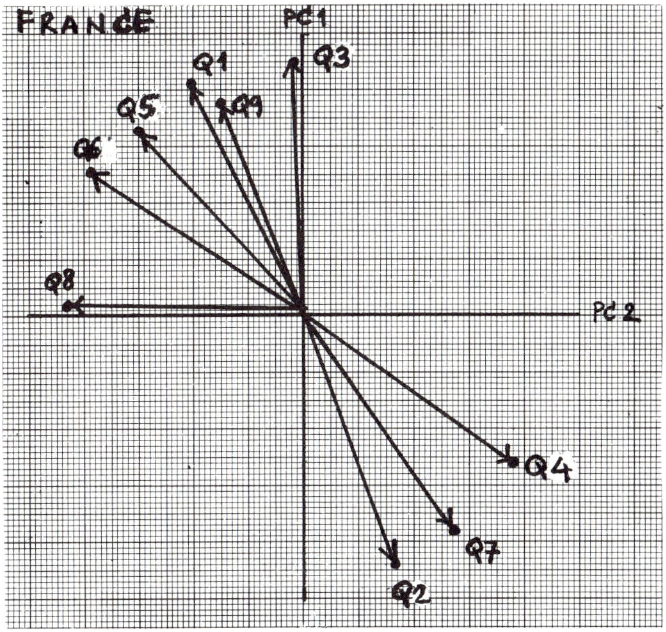

GRAPH 2B
FACTORSPACE

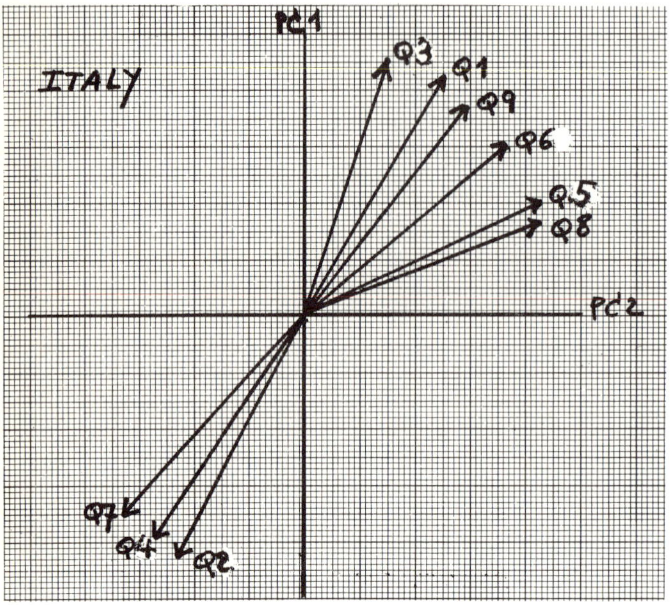

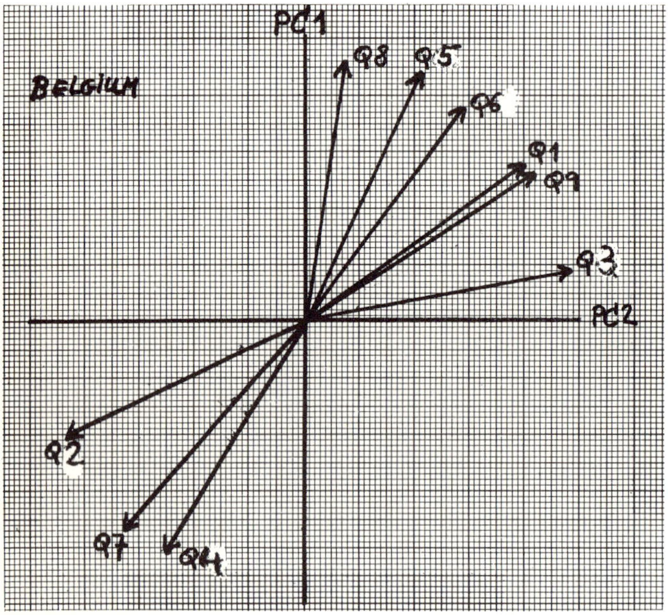

3. THE FOUR-MONTHLY CONSUMER SURVEY

Whereas the heads of enterprises or businessmen were the economic agents whose attitudes and expectations we looked at in the previous section, we now turn to the economic agents at the demand side, i.e. the consumers.

At the request of the Commission of the European Communities, a study was undertaken in 1975 with the twofold aim of (a) setting-up a data-base with the detailed information of the harmonised consumer survey and (b) analysing by means of the principal components technique the underlying dimensions in the answers of consumers to the survey-questionnaire.*

In the following paragraph we will comment on the outcome of (b) and briefly compare it with similar studies undertaken elsewhere. Furthermore, a closer look will be given to time-series analysis since the major purpose of the consumer survey is to provide an aid to short-term forecasting.

A. Cross-section principal components analysis :

The purpose of applying a principal components analysis to the cross-section data of the consumer survey is to understand the relationship between the replies to attitudinal and intentions questions on the micro-economic level and to see whether common dimensions can be found in the reply-pattern in different member-countries. Moreover, if ultimately one wanted to use these results for index construction, it is important to know in how far the relationship between variables at the cross-section level remains more or less stable over time.

The analysis covers the surveys carried out between 1972 and 1974 in five of the six original member countries (Luxembourg does not participate in the consumer survey programme). Because of lack of data at the time that the analysis started, the analysis was more limited for some countries (f.i. for Italy information on household income was incomplete). The analysis was carried

.../...

---

* Mariash, B. et G. Moutet, "Rapport pour la Commission sur les enquêtes conjoncturelles auprès des ménages : intentions d'achat et attitudes", IBM Belgique, 1976. Non-published report.

out on 20 variables (1 income variable, 12 attitudinal variables and 7 buying intentions for durable goods variables), using two alternative ways of weighting the answers to the attitudinal and intentions questions.*

The results of the analysis indicate that there is very little correlation between buying intentions on the one hand and attitudes on the other.** Buying intentions are highly correlated with each other, especially in the Federal Republic of Germany. However, the intention to buy a car is only slightly correlated with other durable-intentions in the Federal Republic of Germany and the Netherlands. Correlations in general are higher - for intentions as well as for attitudes - when using the more extended scaling system (see Appendix, tables A6 - A 13). Even then, for all four countries in the analysis, "intercorrelations among individuals' responses to various attitudinal questions are far lower in the corss-section than in the aggregative time series",*** as will be shown in the next section on time-series analysis (compare Tables A6 - A 13 with Table A 24) (see also [2]). This suggests that the informational content of the cross-section data will not highly load upon one component, but will be spread over several components. Indeed, the analysis lead to three, well identiable components. In order not to reproduce too great a mass of data, we will compare the stability of the components for May 1973 and May 1974.

.../...

* For income, the weights are based on the class-means, except for the extreme-classes, where the following rule was applied : 0.8 times the lower bound (i.e. income $\leq$ x, then the weight would be 0.8x) and 1.2 times the upper-bound (f.i. income $\geq$ Y, then the weight would be 1.2 Y). The attitudinal questions mostly have six reply possibilities, f.i. much better, better, the same, worse, much worse, don't know. The incisive scaling method consists of applying the weights : +2, +1, 0, -1, -2, 0, the less incisive method applies the weights +1, +1, 0, -1, -1, 0. The questions on prices are not symmetrical; the same principle, however, heas been applied. For the intentions questions, the reply-possibilities generally number five : yes, certainly, yes perhaps, probably not, certainly not, don't know. The incisive method (based on passed experience with the French surveys) gives the following weights : 1, 1/2, 1/3, 0, 1/3 whereas the second weighting method gives the weights : 1, 1/2, 0, 0, 0.

The discussion will mostly center around the more incisive scaling method.

** The correlation coëfficients (X 100) given in Tables A6 - A13 of the Appendix are those of the May 1974 survey.

*** Adams, F.G.; "Prediction with Consumer Attitudes : the time-series-cross section paradox", R.E.S., Nov. 1965.

Anticipating what will follow, we can conclude that - although some slight changes occurred and factor reversal as well - in general, the components remained remarkedly stable and, which is also of interest, they remain highly comparable as between countries.

We will start by giving the variance breakdown of the first three components (see Table 3), based on the rotated factor matrix. The factor matrix has been rotated in order to obtain a clearer separation as between the different dimensions.

Table 3 : Variance breakdown of first three components (PC1, PC2, PC3) (in %)

(after rotation)

	FR of Germany		France		Belgium		Netherlands	
	May 1973	May 1974	May 1973	May 1974	May 1973	May 1974	May 1973	May 1974
PC1	21.36	18.63	11.59	11.71	13.93	11.92	12.25	10.57
PC2	12.86	12.87	9.86	11.42	12.51	12.49	9.21	8.51
PC3	10.43	11.36	11.29	8.96	9.81	9.70	8.59	9.15
	44.65	42.86	32.74	32.09	36.25	34.11	30.05	28.23

Results from the above table show that the three components do not explain a high proportion of the total variance in the data-set. There is even a slightly decreasing trend over time in all four countries. Nevertheless, they form three quite distinct and important dimensions of consumer sentiment. More precise and interesting information can be gathered when comparing per country the factor loadings and their stability, both for May 1973 and May 1974. (see Appendix, Tables A15 - A22). (For the sake of easy comparability, the loadings are indicated with an X if they are $|\geq 0.50|$ in Table A23. This merely serves the purpose of clarity.)

.../...

First there appeared a buying intentions component. Five variables loaded heavily on this component: the intention to buy (1) a refrigerator, (2) a black and white TV, (3) a washing machine, (4) a fridge/freezer and (5) a dishwasher. The loadings were highest for the Federal Republic of Germany and lowest for France.

A second component related more specifically to the general economic situation. The variables on the past and expected economic situation loaded highest on this component. Price variables appear as well in this component.

A third component was more clearly linked to the interviewee's personal financial situation and highest correlations involved income, the present financial situation and saving.

It must be mentioned that the ordering of the components underwent some changes in the course of time, except in the Federal Republic of Germany. This is summarised in Table 4.

TABLE 4

Ordering of components (PCi)
Changes over time

	FR of Germany		France		Belgium		Netherlands	
	1973	1974	1973	1974	1973	1974	1973	1974
A. Buying Intentions Dimension	PC1	PC1	PC1	PC1	PC1	PC2	PC3	PC2
B. General Economic Dimension	PC2	PC2	PC2	PC3	PC3	PC3	PC2	PC3
C. Personal Financial Dimension	PC3	PC3	PC3	PC2	PC2	PC1	PC1	PC1

.../...

It becomes clear from Table A 23 in the Appendix that - apart from the sign of the loading coëfficients, which is less important as negative loadings can be converted to positive ones - a high degree of stability exists over time on the one hand, and that on the other hand , approximately the same three dimensions occur in consumers' minds in four different countries.

A detailed comparison of the results of this analysis with comparable studies in other countries is rather difficult as the variables appearing in the different studies often were different. Adams' [2] first component in a cross-section analysis of six attitudinal variables - based on data from the Survey Research Center (University of Michigan) - is very roughly comparable to the general economic situation component in our data. Other analyses have been carried out by Pickering for Great-Britain [14] and by the "Forschungsstelle Köln" in the Federal Republic of Germany ([3]) . Each of these studies have aspects that are in common with the EEC-cross section survey analysis and also some aspects that show differences. A point of principal interest remains the fact that consumer sentiment, at least part of it, consists of roughly the same dimensions in the EEC-member countries.

B. Time-series analysis

In this section we turn to the behaviour of the aggregate time-series, specifically of the data on various consumer attitudes. The purpose now is to analyse the evolution of consumer sentiment over time. Buying intentions will not be looked at as, since 1975, they only appear once a year in the 5,000 sample October survey. They are, therefore, less interesting from a conjunctural viewpoint. For this reason, eight attitudinal variables will be analysed, covering the period May 1972 - January 1977, totalling 15 observations. The original replies have been transformed to weighted testbalances, using the more incisive weighting scheme, i.e. the two extreme replies (much better, much worse) with 2 and -2 the two moderate replies (a little better, a little worse) with 1 and -1, and giving zero weight to the "remain the same" and "don't know" replies. The eight variables we plan to study concern (1) the respondent's perception of his personal financial situation as compared to last year (SFAD), (2) his personal financial expectations for the next 12 months (SFAP), (3) his assessment of the evolution of the general economic situation since a year (SEAD, (4) his expectations for next year (SEAP), (5) his unemployment expectations (CHOM), (6) his judgment if it is a good time to buy durables (ACHT), (7) if, in

.../...

view of the economic situation it is reasonable to save (EPAR) and (8) his saving expectations over the next 12 months (EPAP). Variables relating to consumers opinions on past price increases and expectations for the next 12 months have been left out, as the impact of such opinions on buying behaviour depends very much on particular situations.

The analysis has been carried out for five countries (the Federal Republic of Germany, France, Italy, Belgium and the Netherlands) as for the new countries (Denmark, the United Kingdom and Ireland) not yet enough data are available to perform time series analyses.

A first glance at the correlation matrix (for the five countries) shows that the correlation between attitudinal variables is much more important in time-series than in cross-section (see Appendix, Table A 24).

It also becomes clear that - although some differences can be observed - a high degree of similarity exists as between attitudes in the various countries : for all countries SFAD and SFAP are highly correlated suggesting that personal financial expectations of households over the coming 12 months are greatly extrapolated from past year's experience or that both judgments on the past and expectations for next year are originating from their opinions on the present situation. A steady relationship exists between SEAP and CHOM : this probably means that unemployment expectation is a crucial variable in expressing views about the general economic situation. Another point is the link between personal and more general variables : consumers' general economic expectations are fairly highly correlated with their personal financial expectations. This is less so in the Netherlands than in other countries. The relation between financial and savings variables is, however, not very clear cut : - For the Federal Republic of Germany, there exist virtually no links between consumers' judgments and expectations concerning their financial situation and their opinions on saving. In the other countries the correlation between the financial situation of households compared to last year and their judgment on the advisability of saving is very significant. In all countries, except the Netherlands, savings expectations seem to be influenced, partly, by unemployment expectations. Further details can be seen in Table A 24 of the Appendix.

.../...

The first two components explain between 77 % of total variation in the data in Belgium and 92 % in Italy (see Table 5). It therefore, seems that - generally speaking - two underlying dimensions determine to a great extent the consumers' perception of his socio-economic environment.

Table 5 : Variance breakdown in %

	PC1	PC2	PC1 + PC2
FR of Germany	65.3	21.3	86.6
France	67.2	20.0	87.2
Italy	77.1	14.8	91.9
Netherlands	47.6	32.0	79.6
Belgium	61.1	15.0	76.1

In Italy, the first principal component alone accounts already for 77 % of the variation in the data, against 48 % in the Netherlands. Consumer confidence, therefore, seems to be more concentrated in Italy than elsewhere.

A glance at the factor matrix shows differences as well as similarities : in all countries, except in the Netherlands, the personal financial and general economic variables load highest on the first component (see Appendix, Table A 25). Unemployment expectations are loading on both components in the Federal Republic of Germany, Italy and Belgium and the question concerning the opportunity of making major purchases is part of the second component in France, Italy and Belgium. Only in the Federal Republic of Germany do the savings questions form a dimension on their own, more related to unemployment expectations than to the general economic and personal financial variables. In the Netherlands, the savings questions are also loaded on the second component, but together with the questions on the personal financial situation. In France and - with a different sign- also in Belgium, savings expectations and consumers' judgment on the opportunity to make major purchases now, form a specific dimension. In Italy, households judgments on saving are made in the light of their personal financial situation and their opinions on the evolution of economic activity in general.

.../...

Summarising the differences and the similarities in attitudes between countries, the two principal components could be interpreted approximately as follows : the first component reflects opinions on the general economic situation and its relation to the personal financial situation of households; the second component might be described as reflecting more discretionary activities, like saving and/ or the purchase of durable goods. A summary picture of the relation between the first two components and the variables is given in graphs 3a and 3b (pp. 14a and 14b).

Comparison with other time-series principal components analyses for France [11], Great-Britain [5] and the United States [1], [2] shows correspondencies as well as differences, depending greatly on which variables were taken in the analysis. Furthermore, the periods over which the analyses extended were also different and a change in the pattern of sentiment is not a priori excluded in a ten-year period, in which important changes in the economies of the industrialised world have occurred, especially since the upsurge of inflation in the beginning of the seventies.

We think that the first principal component may serve as an indicator of consumer confidence as both general economic and personal financial variables load on this component (see also [5]).

The choice of this indicator is appealing; but a more precise analysis must be carried out in order to judge in how far this indicator is better than one based on e.g. equal weighting of attitude-variables or one taking only specific variables into account.

The two previous sections show that a much higher correlation exists between attitudinal variables in the time-series approach . This is because through time-series analysis much of the variation in the individual data is ironed out. Similar results have been obtained in other countries.

C. An indicator of consumer confidence

Summarising the mass of information resulting from the consumer survey into a single indicator, reflecting the evolution of consumer sentiment or confidence, has first been applied by the Survey Research Center (Michigan) (see [7], [12]). The S.R.C.-approach is based on an equal weighting of the attitudinal variables included. Although research in the field of indices of consumer confidence still is in a rather early stage, especially as far as the harmonised EEC-survey is concerned, alternative ways of

GRAPH 3a : Two Factor Space

FR of Germany

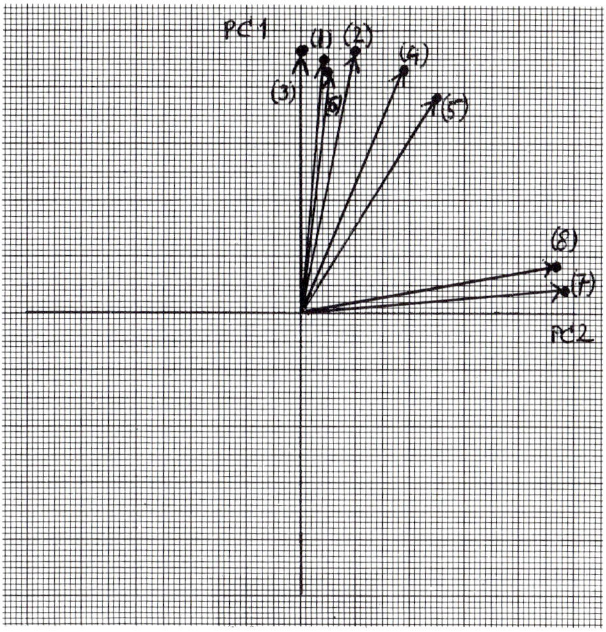

France

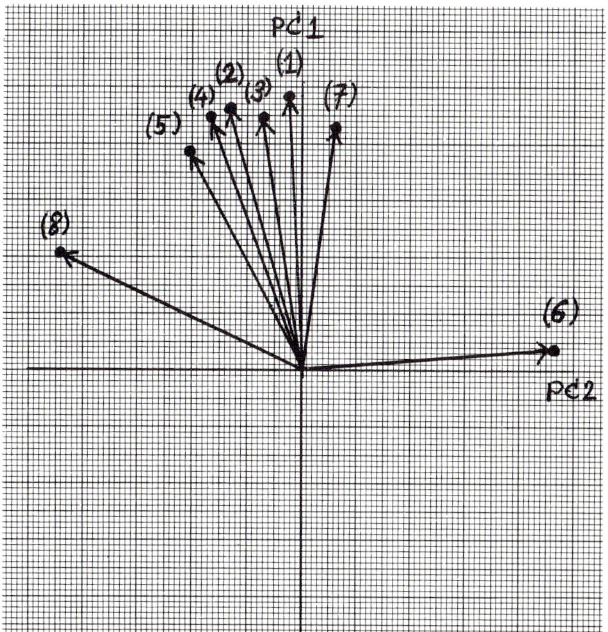

GRAPH 3b

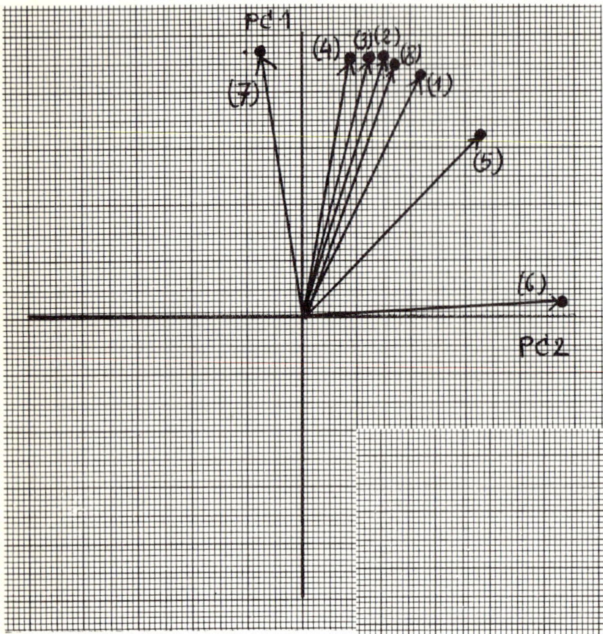

Italy

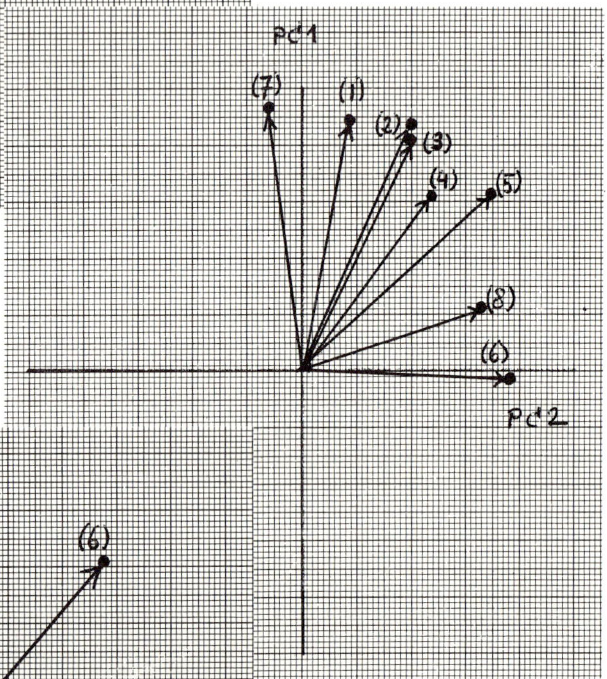

Belgium

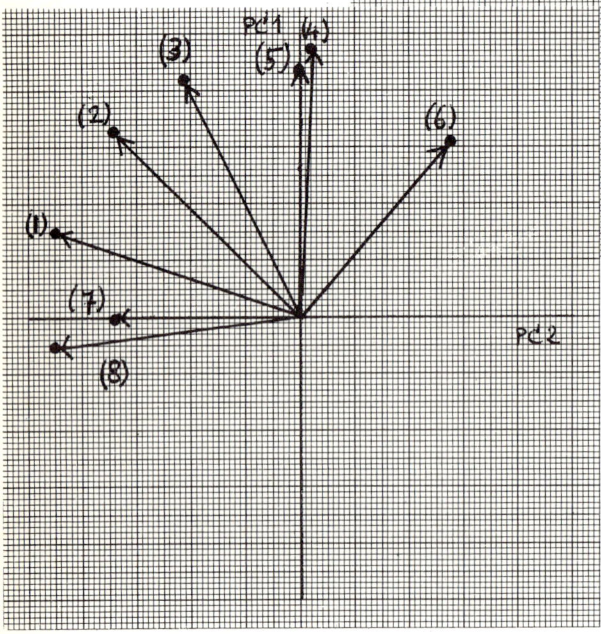

Netherlands

obtaining these indices have been tried on several occasions, based mainly on principal component analysis. One of such is the confidence index of the Gallup organisation (see [5]). This index is derived by summing thee weighted scores for each of five attitude questions, the weights being the loadings on the first component in a time-series principal component analysis. This component explained about 44 % of the variance in the data on these five attitude questions. A similar approach has been undertaken in France (see [11]).

In the previous section we analysed eight attitude questions for five EEC-countries. The first component was roughly similar in the different countries and could be used as an indicator of consumer confidence or consumer sentiment. Our approach is to use the factor scores - i.e. the value taken by a component for a given observation - which are based on the loadings. This method is, therefore, comparable to the one followed by Heald (see [5]). Our series, however, have not been corrected for seasonal factors. The resulting curves are depicted in graphs 4a and 4b (pp. 15a, 15b).

Other authors propose a different way of getting at a confidence index. Pickering (see [14]) suggests the use of cross-section results as a basis for building such an index, "since the concept relates to the structure of confidence in the mind of the individual consumer" ([5]). He is in favour of forming an index where the weights (the factor loadings of a cross-section principal component analysis) are allowed to change when "the structure of confidence changes".

The purpose of using such a synthesized indicator is mainly to obtain a better understanding of the fluctuations which characterise consumer expenditure on durable goods and total consumption of households. We, therefore, are interested in the predictive performance, which should be a criterion for choosing the best indicators. Irrespective of the discussion as to whether or not to include these indicators in regression equations or econometric models (see also [11], [12], [13], [15]),[16], the consumer survey should in any case be an additional instrument in short-term economic analysis.

.../...

GRAPH 4a Indicator of consumer confidence in 5 member countries
(Factor scores of first principal component)

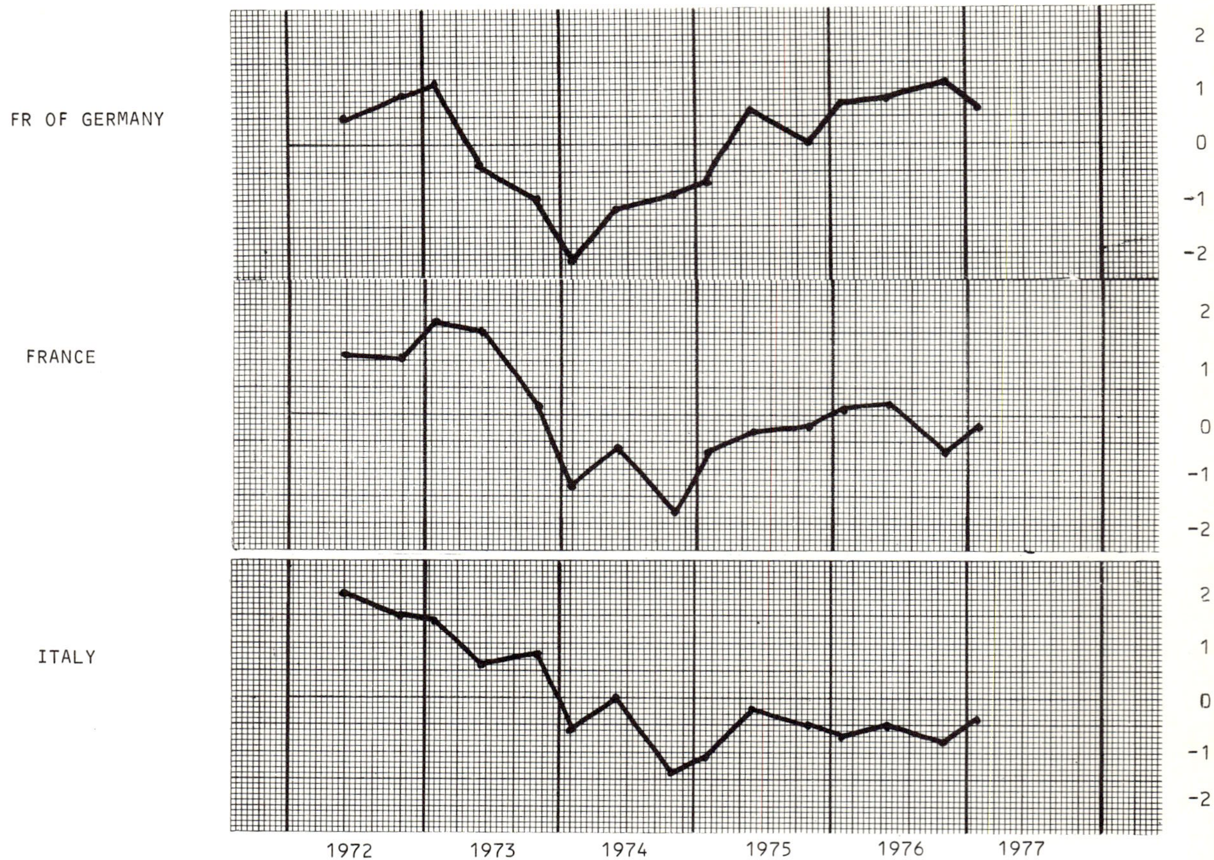

GRAPH 4b

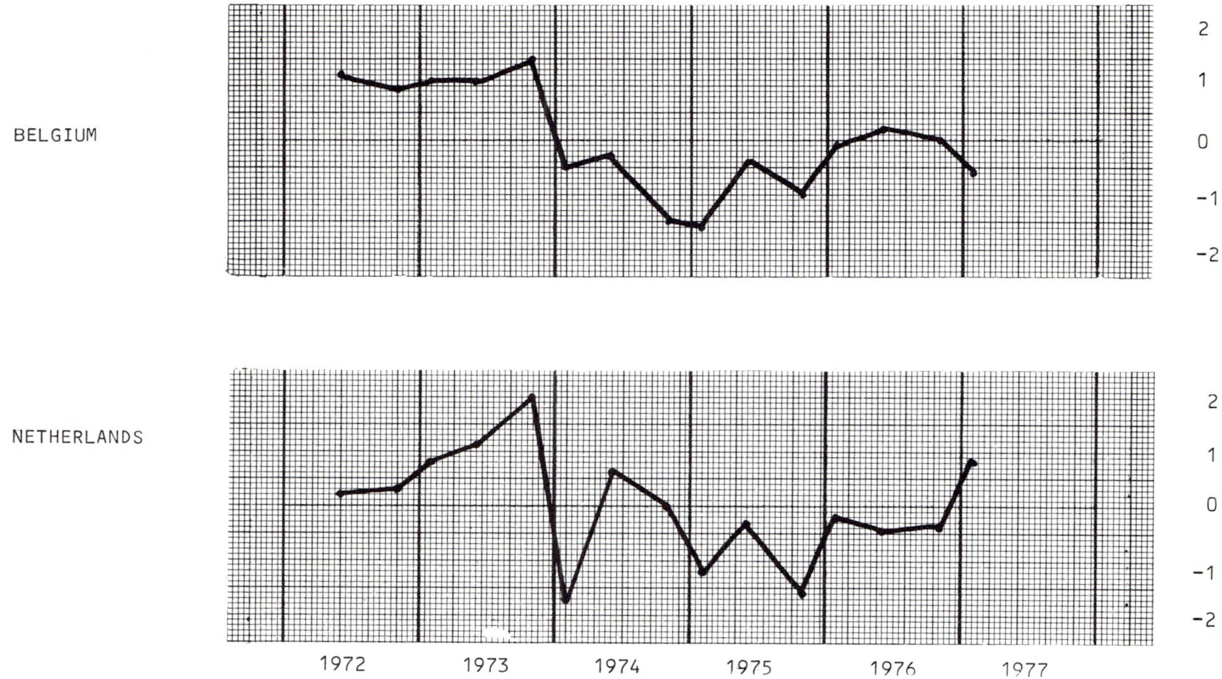

4. CONCLUDING REMARKS

In the previous sections we tried to present a concise picture of the attitudinal dimensions in the entrepreneurial and consumer surveys, without going into the problem of prediction. The aim of this paper was to see if, and in how far, differences exist in the perception of the economic environment between different countries. Application of the principal component technique allowed us to identify some basic attitudinal dimensions in the replies of businessmen and consumers throughout Europe.

The analyses show that there are similarities as well as differences between the different countries. The absence of differences in attitudes and relations between attitudes would have been suspicious. The countries, for which the surveys have been analysed are all in an economically difficult situation. They have some basic problems in common, but they suffer from them in different degrees. Everywhere unemployment is at an unacceptably high level, but inflation is less of a problem in the Federal Republic of Germany than in Italy. Consequently, consumers' and businessmens' judgments and expectations will show differences between countries. Still, we think that this paper has shown that a high degree of similarity exists in the pattern of judgments and expectations of economic agents in the EEC-member countries.

5. SUMMARY

In order to see in howfar differences and/ or similarities exist in the attitudinal pattern of consumers and entrepreneurs in different EEC-member states, the principal component technique was applied to the results of the monthly harmonised business survey and the four-monthly consumer survey.

The outcome of the exercise, indeed, showed similarities and differences. The replies to four monthly questions that are part of the business survey, are highly correlated and, as a consequence, the first component explains between 80 % of the variance in the data for Italy and 86 % for Belgium. This component can be used as an indicator of economic activity. However, the analysis shows that the weights of the four monthly variables are nearly equal, suggesting that simple averaging of the testbalances would give identical results. The non-monthly questions in the business survey are not only highly correlated among themselves, they are also highly correlated with the quarterised monthly questions. Here, differences between countries are more important. Nevertheless, nearly the same questions "cluster" together, as can be observed on graphs 2A and 2B.

Two principal component analyses have been applied on the weighted testbalances of 20 variables of the harmonised four-monthly consumer survey; one on the cross-section level and one on the time-series level. The cross-section analysis resulted in three quite distinct and clearly identifiable dimensions of consumer confidence. These three dimensions reflected first consumers' buying intentions, second, their opinion on the general economic situation and third, the way they perceive their personal financial situation. The components are highly similar for the different EEC member countries and they also remained rather stable over time. The proportion of variance explained by the three components together is slightly decreasing over time and ranges, on average, from about 30 % for the Netherlands to about 45 % for the FR of Germany. The time series analysis covers 15 surveys including January 1977. Only 8 attitudinal variables were taken into account. An important difference between the time series and the cross-section analysis is the much lower intercorrelation in the cross-section case. This is because much of the variation in the individual data is ironed out in the time series.

.../...

Two components suffise to account for the bulk of the variation in the data. In Italy, where the first component explains 77 % of the variation in the data, consumer confidence seems to be less diffuse than in the other countries, and particularly than in the Netherlands, where only 48 % is reached. The first component can be interpreted as consumers' views on the economic situation in general , as well as their personal financial situation. This interpretation applies less to the Dutch data than to the data on the other countries. The second component might be described as reflecting more discretionary activities, like saving and/ or the purchase of durable goods.

Consumer confidence is a notion which is hard to define in terms of specific variables from the consumer survey. In this paper we presented the first principal component as one possible indicator of consumer confidence. The discussion on indicators of consumer confidence is, however, far from closed and more extensive research is required in this field. It was not the aim of this paper to treat this subject in detail. The main purpose was comparing attitudes in different EEC-member countries and, although differences are clearly present, the general picture remains one of similarity.

6. REFERENCES

1. Adams, F.G., "Consumer Attitudes, Buying Plans, and Purchases of Durable Goods : A principal component's time series approach", R.E.S., November, 1964.

2. Adams, F.G., "Prediction with consumer Attitudes : The time series-cross section paradox", R.E.S., November 1965.

3. Biervert, B., Haarland, H.P., Niessen H.-J. : Bericht über ein Forschungs-Projekt der Forschungstelle für empirische Sozial-Ökonomik (Prof. Dr. G. Schmölders) e.V., Köln 1972.

4. Courtois, J.-M., Molitor, B., "Les enquêtes de conjoncture auprès des consommateurs de la CEE : Premières réflexions", paper read at the 11th Ciret-Conference, London, September 1973.

5. Heald, G., "Intentions and Attitude Data in Short-Term Forecasting of Consumer Durable Expenditures - A report of British experiences", paper read at the 10th Ciret-Conference, Brussels, September, 1971.

6. Johnston, J., "Econometric Methods", Sec. Ed., Mac Graw Hill, New-York, 1972, pp. 322 - 330.

7. Katona, G., "The powerful consumer", Mac Graw Hill, 1960.

8. Kloek, T., and Bannink, R., "Principal-component analysis applied to business test data", paper read at the 5th Ciret-Conference, Noordwijk, May, 1961 .

9. Liberatori, L., Pinca, F., "Factor Analysis and Results of Business Surveys", paper read at the 12th Ciret-Conference, Stockholm, June, 1975.

10. Mc Neil, J.M., "Census Bureau Programs to Measure Consumer Purchase Expectations, 1959-1973", U.S. Dep. of Commerce, Technical Paper 36, Dec. 1974.

.../...

11. Moutet, G., Vangrevelinghe, G., "Attitudes and Buying Intentions of Private Househols", paper read at the 9th Ciret-Conference, Madrid, September, 1969.

12. Mueller, E., "Ten years of consumer Attitude Surveys : Their Forcasting Record", J.A.S.A., vol. 58, 1963.

13. Nerb, G., "Konjunkturprognose mit Hilfe von Urteilen und Erwartungen der Konsumenten und der Unternehmer", Dunker & Humblot, Berlin,-München, 1975.

14. Pickering, J.F., Harrison, J.A., and Cohen, C.D., "Identification and Measurement of Consumer Confidence : Methodology and some Preliminary Results", J.R. Statist. Soc. A. (1973), 136.

15. Poser, G., "Die Verwendbarkeit von Urteilen und Erwartungen im Rahmen der Konjunktur-analyse", Ifo-Studien, 22, Jahrgang 1976, Heft 1/2.

16. Strümpel, B., "Consumer Attitudes during Prosperity and Recession - The questions of Symmetry and Generality in Predictive Relationships", 10th Ciret-Conference, Brussels, Sept., 1971.

17. "The Harmonized Business Surveys in the Community : Principles and Methods", CEE, November, 1967.

7. Appendix

Correlation coëfficiënts, eigenvalues, variance breakdown and factor equations of the monthly business survey results

TABLE A1

Correlation coëfficiënts

	FRG	FRA	ITA	NED	BEL
C Q1/Q2	0.668	0.899	0.768	0.722	0.773
C Q1/Q3	- 0.734	- 0.892	- 0.512	- 0.761	- 0.727
C Q1/Q4	0.805	0.824	0.568	0.808	0.810
C Q2/Q3	- 0.975	- 0.961	- 0.901	- 0.926	- 0.913
C Q2/Q4	0.697	0.751	0.832	0.693	0.858
C Q3/Q4	- 0.759	- 0.763	- 0.764	- 0.765	- 0.794

Table A2

	Eigenvalues				Cumulative proportion of eigenvalues			
	λ_1	λ_2	λ_3	λ_4				
FRG	3.322	0.465	0.193	0.020	0.831	0.947	0.995	1.000
FRA	3.550	0.307	0.105	0.039	0.887	0.964	0.990	1.000
ITA	3.191	0.532	0.246	0.031	0.798	0.931	0.992	1.000
NED	3.339	0.400	0.194	0.067	0.835	0.935	0.983	1.000
BEL	3.440	0.313	0.172	0.076	0.860	0.938	0.981	1.000

TABLE A3

Factor equations, first component

FRG : $PC_{1t} = 0.264\ z_1 + 0.277\ z_2 - 0.287\ z_3 + 0.268\ z_4$

FRA : $PC_{1t} = 0.271\ z_1 + 0.271\ z_2 - 0.271\ z_3 + 0.248\ z_4$

ITA : $PC_{1t} = 0.246\ z_1 + 0.308\ z_2 - 0.282\ z_3 + 0.279\ z_4$

NED : $PC_{1t} = 0.269\ z_1 + 0.274\ z_2 - 0.284\ z_3 + 0.267\ z_4$

BEL : $PC_{1t} = 0.259\ z_1 + 0.278\ z_2 - 0.270\ z_3 + 0.271\ z_4$

TABLE A4

Correlation between monthly and non-monthly variables in the business survey

	F.R. of Germany	France	Italy	Belgium
C 1,2	-0.882	-0.896	-0.950	-0.925
C 1,3	0.637	0.742	0.880	0.857
C 1,4	-0.831	-0.733	-0.947	-0.885
C 1,5	0.919	0.720	0.743	0.812
C 1,6	0.870	0.729	0.876	0.887
C 1,7	-0.966	-0.841	-0.931	-0.942
C 1,8	0.478	0.415	0.731	0.655
C 1,9	0.914	0.632	0.926	0.948
C 2,3	-0.738	-0.777	-0.850	-0.850
C 2,4	0.738	0.745	0.968	0.757
C 2,5	-0.830	-0.778	-0.731	-0.700
C 2,6	-0.741	-0.733	-0.798	-0.781
C 2,7	0.910	0.814	0.917	0.827
C 2,8	-0.382	-0.306	-0.695	-0.543
C 2,9	-0.875	-0.687	-0.833	-0.879
C 3,4	-0.519	-0.465	-0.786	-0.622
C 3,5	0.560	0.561	0.636	0.549
C 3,6	0.467	0.451	0.772	0.663
C 3,7	-0.651	-0.728	-0.810	-0.706
C 3,8	0.154	0.243	0.557	0.337
C 3,9	0.807	0.660	0.831	0.880
C 4,5	-0.815	-0.879	-0.744	-0.889
C 4,6	-0.745	-0.955	-0.805	-0.896
C 4,7	0.841	0.831	0.928	0.942
C 4,8	-0.429	-0.529	-0.749	-0.824
C 4,9	-0.774	-0.646	-0.851	-0.846
C 5,6	0.944	0.742	0.901	0.966
C 5,7	-0.937	-0.774	-0.841	-0.894
C 5,8	0.531	0.432	0.724	0.803
C 5,9	0.885	0.645	0.772	0.808
C 6,7	-0.871	-0.831	-0.864	-0.938
C 6,8	0.588	0.533	0.722	0.711
C 6,9	0.773	0.630	0.872	0.880
C 7,8	-0.485	-0.500	-0.796	-0.718
C 7,9	-0.919	-0.722	-0.888	-0.902
C 8,9	0.391	0.298	0.724	0.629

TABLE A5

Rotated Factor Matrix

	F.R. of Germany		France		Italy		Belgium	
	P C 1	P C 2	P C 1	P C 2	P C 1	P C 2	P C 1	P C 2
Q 1	0.810	0.530	0.816	-0.410	0.844	0.511	0.572	0.804
Q 2	-0.871	-0.343	-0.883	0.334	-0.846	-0.465	-0.413	-0.850
Q 3	0.896	-0.070	0.903	-0.044	0.898	0.289	0.167	0.960
Q 4	-0.693	-0.516	-0.555	0.775	-0.784	-0.542	-0.823	-0.505
Q 5	0.731	0.630	0.651	-0.592	0.402	0.846	0.866	0.422
Q 6	0.605	0.715	0.532	-0.765	0.591	0.727	0.768	0.576
Q 7	-0.823	-0.531	-0.759	0.556	-0.710	-0.661	-0.732	-0.638
Q 8	0.054	0.896	0.035	-0.846	0.339	0.842	0.920	0.149
Q 9	0.906	0.346	0.766	-0.294	0.736	0.580	0.534	0.812

TABLE A6 *

FACTOR ANALYSIS - ALLEMAGNE MAI74 (W1)

20 VARIABLES

.... STRUCTURE OF VARIABLES ....

LOADING ON FACTOR,%

	IREF	ITVN	IMLL	IMLV	ICON	AEQD	SEAP	SEAD	PRAP	SFAP	CHOM	SFAD	PRAD	EPAP	SFAC	REVN	EPAR	IAUT	ACHT	CAUT
LOADING %	89.5	88.3	87.7	81.8	79.6	11.1	70.6	61.1	59.9	58.4	57.1	53.6	52.6	76.7	69.9	56.5	51.9	38.6	32.1	18.3
IREF	1																			
ITVN	78	1																		
IMLL	79	74	1																	
IMLV	64	65	61	1																
ICON	62	61	60	63	1															
AEQD	8	4	7	8	8	1														
SEAP	-1	-4	-2	-3	-4	6	2													
SEAD	6	4	8	2	4	4	35	2												
PRAP	3	0	3	1	1	-1	27	22	2											
SFAP	0	-2	3	-2	0	7	42	28	16	2										
CHOM	5	3	5	4	4	4	34	20	27	22	2									
SFAD	0	-2	1	-2	3	6	32	33	16	44	21	2								
PRAD	-3	-5	-2	-4	-4	0	21	23	31	13	17	16	2							
EPAP	4	2	5	5	9	1	14	14	1	20	7	29	6	3						
SFAC	2	-1	1	5	8	5	13	16	4	19	9	33	6	49	3					
REVN	4	-3	4	7	9	6	3	2	1	9	4	14	-1	27	26	3				
EPAR	-2	-3	-1	-3	-1	1	16	14	7	19	11	19	10	44	29	10	3			
IAUT	12	12	14	16	17	6	2	0	-3	7	4	7	-5	15	9	27	4	3		
ACHT	1	-1	3	2	6	4	6	6	2	9	2	12	-1	18	15	9	6	4	3	
CAUT	0	0	0	2	3	0	1	3	-2	-1	1	4	0	6	4	7	4	11	1	3

* Table A6 - A13 give the correlation between the 20 variables, as well as the factor loadings. The questions corresponding to the four-letter variable-names are given in Table14.

W1 : uses the weights based on the more incisive scaling method.

Source : B. Mariash et G. Moutet, op. cit.

TABLE A7

FACTOR ANALYSIS - ALLEMAGNE MAI74 (W2)*

20 VARIABLES

.... STRUCTURE OF VARIABLES ....

	SEAP	SFAP	SEAD	CHOM	SFAD	PRAP	PRAD	EPAP	SFAC	EPAR	REVN	ACHT	IMLV	IAUT	ICON	IREF	AEQD	IMLL	CAUT	ITVN
LOADING ON FACTOR,%	70.1	59.5	57.0	54.2	53.4	50.4	47.0	78.6	73.4	59.0	42.8	32.1	50.5	50.4	47.5	43.2	41.4	39.6	11.9	5.5
SEAP	1																			
SFAP	42	1																		
SEAD	31	26	1																	
CHOM	30	19	15	1																
SFAD	31	45	29	19	1															
PRAP	19	11	15	19	10	1														
PRAD	16	9	18	14	11	23	1													
EPAP	11	18	11	5	24	-1	2	2												
SFAC	11	18	15	8	30	0	3	46	2											
EPAR	13	18	11	9	17	1	5	38	27	2										
REVN	4	8	3	3	14	1	-1	25	25	8	2									
ACHT	6	9	7	1	11	1	-4	17	16	5	9	2								
IMLV	2	4	3	1	3	1	2	6	5	-1	15	4	3							
IAUT	6	9	0	3	6	-2	-4	13	7	0	25	6	12	3						
ICON	2	3	2	0	4	-2	1	7	8	2	12	7	8	9	3					
IREF	2	2	0	2	5	1	0	2	5	-1	8	2	9	4	8	3				
AEQD	6	7	4	4	8	2	2	0	6	1	5	5	9	6	11	8	3			
IMLL	0	5	1	-3	5	-1	3	2	-1	1	1	4	5	8	11	11	5	3		
CAUT	1	-1	3	1	4	-2	-1	5	3	3	7	1	3	9	3	-1	0	-2	3	
ITVN	0	2	-2	1	2	-2	-2	2	-4	2	-1	-3	1	4	2	2	1	-1	1	3

* W2 uses the weights based on the more incisive scaling method.

TABLE A6

FACTOR ANALYSIS - FRANCE MAI74 (W1)

20 VARIABLES

.... STRUCTURE OF VARIABLES ....

LOADING ON FACTOR,%

66.1 65.8 65.3 55.1 53.9 52.5 18.3 72.1 71.5 67.3 49.1 41.3 40.8 60.2 51.6 50.0 48.8-37.2 30.1-12.1

	IREF	IMLL	ITVN	IAUT	IMLV	ICON	AEQD	EPAP	SFAC	SFAD	SFAP	REVN	SEAD	SEAP	PRAP	CHOM	EPAR	ACHT	PRAD	CAUT
IREF	1																			
IMLL	37	1																		
ITVN	35	33	1																	
IAUT	21	25	25	1																
IMLV	19	19	21	22	1															
ICON	18	17	18	24	35	1														
AEQD	7	9	6	9	5	6	1													
EPAP	11	12	13	16	11	12	6	2												
SFAC	3	4	6	9	7	6	6	52	2											
SFAD	5	6	6	12	8	7	7	31	33	2										
SFAP	6	9	8	13	9	9	8	29	13	37	2									
REVN	10	12	12	27	19	15	1	24	21	15	9	2								
SEAD	0	2	4	3	4	3	5	15	15	24	15	2	2							
SEAP	3	2	3	4	4	3	5	13	9	15	24	-2	37	3						
PRAP	2	1	0	-1	-2	-2	2	0	-2	0	8	-6	1	21	3					
CHOM	-1	-1	-1	-4	-1	-2	2	4	5	7	11	-8	11	23	17	3				
EPAR	0	-2	0	-7	-6	-4	1	11	7	3	3	-16	10	13	9	9	3			
ACHT	0	1	1	3	2	-2	0	1	3	3	-5	8	3	-5	-11	-3	-21	3		
PRAD	-2	-1	-3	-3	-1	-1	4	5	5	7	4	-4	13	8	8	9	8	-4	3	
CAUT	-1	1	3	14	7	1	0	4	4	2	2	6	1	1	-2	-2	-2	1	0	3

TABLE A9

FACTOR ANALYSIS - FRANCE MAI74 (W2)

20 VARIABLES

.... STRUCTURE OF VARIABLES ....

	IAUT	IMLL	IREF	ITVN	ICON	AEQD	IMLV	SEAP	PRAP	CHOM	EPAR	ACHT	REVN	PRAD	CAUT	SFAC	EPAP	SFAD	SFAP	SEAD
LOADING ON FACTOR,%	54.5	54.2	51.3	50.3	48.5	39.9	39.9	54.2	48.9	46.4	46.0	-41.6	-41.5	19.3	-12.4	-73.1	-71.7	-65.0	-48.1	-44.7
IAUT	1																			
IMLL	15	1																		
IREF	10	18	1																	
ITVN	18	16	17	1																
ICON	17	7	7	7	1															
AEQD	9	13	12	6	7	1														
IMLV	15	7	7	8	16	6	1													
SEAP	3	3	4	3	3	4	4	2												
PRAP	-3	-1	-1	-4	-2	3	-2	14	2											
CHOM	-3	0	-1	0	-2	2	-1	18	15	2										
EPAR	-7	-2	-1	-2	-3	1	-6	12	7	9	2									
ACHT	2	1	-1	0	-2	-1	2	-6	-11	-4	-21	2								
REVN	26	12	11	14	15	1	22	0	-8	-8	-15	8	2							
PRAD	-1	0	-1	0	-1	2	-1	3	8	3	2	-3	-3	2						
CAUT	17	-1	-1	3	0	-1	5	1	-1	-1	-3	1	6	-1	2					
SFAC	10	4	3	7	5	4	6	9	-6	3	6	4	22	0	3	3				
EPAP	14	10	8	11	9	5	8	12	-4	3	9	0	22	1	3	52	3			
SFAD	13	7	7	9	7	6	3	15	-2	5	3	2	14	2	2	33	78	3		
SFAP	13	11	9	9	9	7	10	23	2	8	3	-4	8	2	3	14	27	36	3	
SEAD	3	2	1	4	2	4	3	36	-1	7	9	3	3	3	1	13	12	23	14	3

TABLE A10

FACTOR ANALYSIS - BELGIQUE MAI74 (W1)

20 VARIABLES

.... STRUCTURE OF VARIABLES ....

LOADING ON FACTOR,%

	EPAP	SFAC	REVN	SFAD	SFAP	IAUT	ACHT	CAUT	IREF	IMLL	ITVN	ICON	IMLV	AEQD	SEAP	SEAD	CHOM	PRAP	EPAR	PRAD
LOADING ON FACTOR,%	77.6	69.9	67.0	56.6	45.5	40.7	23.1	8.6	74.5	71.5	70.7	65.9	58.8	21.4	74.9	66.2	51.0	38.3	34.8	18.6
EPAP	1																			
SFAC	53	1																		
REVN	39	29	1																	
SFAD	35	34	22	1																
SFAP	30	20	18	41	1															
IAUT	19	11	30	11	10	1														
ACHT	11	8	10	6	5	5	1													
CAUT	1	-2	7	2	2	7	3	1												
IREF	6	2	8	5	7	13	0	2	2											
IMLL	8	3	10	8	10	14	0	2	42	2										
ITVN	3	1	1	5	6	9	-1	2	48	39	2									
ICON	8	4	14	9	9	12	-1	0	35	36	31	2								
IMLV	7	2	15	8	9	13	0	3	28	30	26	33	2							
AEQD	12	9	7	14	13	9	9	5	12	13	7	12	10	2						
SEAP	10	8	-1	19	22	1	2	-1	2	3	3	5	3	8	3					
SEAD	9	9	1	24	15	-1	4	1	0	2	1	2	3	8	45	3				
CHOM	4	5	-3	7	9	-1	0	-2	0	4	1	3	0	8	22	15	3			
PRAP	4	1	1	3	9	3	0	-1	3	3	2	2	1	4	19	2	18	3		
EPAR	19	13	-2	9	12	-2	4	-1	0	1	2	-2	-3	7	13	13	7	7	3	
PRAD	4	3	-1	4	2	-1	-1	-2	-2	-1	-1	0	1	3	2	7	5	7	5	3

TABLE A11

FACTOR ANALYSIS - BELGIQUE MAI74 (W2)

20 VARIABLES

.... STRUCTURE OF VARIABLES ....

LOADING ON FACTOR,%
77.8 75.4 60.9 56.4 49.6 24.7 20.9 71.5 62.5 48.5 31.6 20.9 52.0 47.1 46.1 44.5 43.9 40.8 26.0 25.6

	EPAP	SFAC	SFAD	REVN	SFAP	EPAR	ACHT	SEAP	SEAD	CHOM	PRAP	PRAD	IMLL	IMLV	AEQD	ICON	IAUT	IREF	CAUT	ITVN
EPAP	1																			
SFAC	52	1																		
SFAD	33	35	1																	
REVN	37	31	21	1																
SFAP	28	22	39	17	1															
EPAR	17	12	9	-3	11	1														
ACHT	10	9	6	10	5	3	1													
SEAP	6	6	16	-1	19	10	1	2												
SEAD	5	7	21	2	13	9	4	38	2											
CHOM	1	3	7	-3	8	5	-2	19	11	2										
PRAP	-2	-3	-1	-2	1	2	-4	8	-1	8	2									
PRAD	-1	-3	-1	-3	-2	-2	-1	3	1	2	19	2								
IMLL	7	5	8	10	9	0	2	0	0	0	1	-1	3							
IMLV	5	4	6	14	7	-5	2	-2	-1	-2	1	-1	10	3						
AEQD	9	9	12	6	11	6	8	5	6	5	2	0	13	9	3					
ICON	8	5	6	15	9	-1	2	0	-1	-2	-2	0	10	11	12	3				
IAUT	14	9	7	26	9	-3	3	-1	1	-2	-2	-1	11	13	7	9	3			
IREF	6	2	3	7	6	0	2	-2	-2	0	2	-1	10	6	11	6	6	3		
CAUT	2	-1	2	7	1	-1	3	0	2	-1	0	-1	3	2	5	1	10	4	3	
ITVN	3	1	3	0	6	3	1	1	1	1	1	-1	10	0	7	5	2	2	5	3

TABLE A12

FACTOR ANALYSIS - HOLLANDE AVR74 (W1)

20 VARIABLES

.... STRUCTURE OF VARIABLES ....

LOADING ON FACTOR,%

	EPAP	SFAC	REVN	SFAD	IAUT	ACHT	CAUT	IREF	IMLL	ITVN	ICON	IMLV	AEQD	SEAP	SEAD	SFAP	CHOM	PRAP	EPAR	P
	76.3	74.0	56.7	48.6	41.1	18.9	14.0	-65.1	-64.2	-48.4	-42.5	-34.5	-33.7	66.3	63.7	50.3	47.3	26.9	22.0	1
EPAP	1																			
SFAC	51	1																		
REVN	27	25	1																	
SFAD	29	36	8	1																
IAUT	20	12	27	10	1															
ACHT	7	9	9	7	7	1														
CAUT	3	3	6	0	3	1	1													
IREF	4	2	7	4	8	8	0	2												
IMLL	3	2	6	4	8	5	4	29	2											
ITVN	1	1	-1	2	5	3	-3	18	17	2										
ICON	8	5	10	1	14	2	1	13	11	9	2									
IMLV	7	3	13	3	11	2	0	9	7	6	9	2								
AEQD	3	6	5	8	9	3	0	8	11	3	9	9	2							
SEAP	9	7	1	18	4	0	-2	0	3	1	3	2	0	3						
SEAD	6	8	-9	21	-4	-2	-4	-2	0	-2	0	-2	2	33	3					
SFAP	22	18	5	37	9	4	2	2	4	0	3	3	9	24	13	3				
CHOM	3	4	-2	7	0	-1	-1	-1	3	0	0	-1	2	19	12	11	3			
PRAP	0	3	-1	1	2	-4	-2	-3	-1	2	-1	2	0	9	1	5	14	3		
EPAR	21	13	-7	8	-3	-8	0	-3	-1	1	1	-3	0	4	6	7	5	4	3	
PRAD	2	4	-1	3	3	-4	-2	-3	-2	3	1	1	0	-2	4	2	5	12	4	

TABLE A13

FACTOR ANALYSIS - HOLLANDE AVR74 (W2)

20 VARIABLES

.... STRUCTURE OF VARIABLES ....

LOADING ON FACTOR, %

64.3 60.9 44.8 41.9 31.6 21.7-74.7-74.3-56.9-34.4 49.9 49.3 46.1 43.9 43.7 41.1 34.6 19.C 13.0 10.3

	SEAP	SEAD	CHOM	SFAP	PRAP	PRAD	EPAP	SFAC	SFAD	EPAR	IAUT	AEQD	IREF	IMLL	REVN	IMLV	ICON	ACHT	ITVN	CAUT
SEAP	1																			
SEAD	31	1																		
CHOM	16	10	1																	
SFAP	22	11	8	1																
PRAP	4	1	7	-1	1															
PRAD	1	1	1	-3	24	1														
EPAP	9	4	0	18	-5	-4	2													
SFAC	6	8	2	15	-2	-1	48	2												
SFAD	16	19	5	34	-3	0	25	32	2											
EPAR	3	3	3	7	1	-2	18	12	7	2										
IAUT	6	0	0	11	-3	0	16	11	11	-4	3									
AEQD	-1	-1	-1	7	2	2	3	4	7	0	12	3								
IREF	1	1	2	2	-2	0	6	3	4	-4	6	8	3							
IMLL	3	2	1	6	-1	-2	2	1	4	-3	5	13	12	3						
REVN	2	-7	-3	4	-5	-1	23	23	6	-7	24	4	7	5	3					
IMLV	1	-2	-1	2	-2	-1	4	1	0	-2	8	11	9	4	11	3				
ICON	4	-2	0	3	-5	-2	8	5	1	-1	12	8	8	3	9	2	3			
ACHT	-1	-3	-3	4	-4	-2	7	9	7	-8	5	3	2	1	9	2	2	3		
ITVN	0	-3	-3	3	-2	0	6	3	1	1	4	4	4	1	2	0	5	3	3	
CAUT	-2	-3	0	3	-2	-1	2	2	0	0	5	0	1	4	6	-1	0	1	-2	3

TABLE A14

VARIABLES USED IN THE CONSUMER SURVEY PRINCIPAL COMPONENTS ANALYSIS *

1. REVN : Income.

2. SEAD : Economic situation of household compared to 12 moths ago.
3. SEAP : Economic situation of household over the next 12 moths.
4. PRAD : Evolution of prices compared to 12 moths ago.
5. PRAP : Evolution of prices over the next 12 months.
6. SFAC : Present financial situation of household.
7. SFAD : Financial situation of household compared to 12 moths ago.
8. SFAP : Financial situation of household over the next 12 moths.
9. ACHT : Judgement on the opportunity to make major purchases now.
10. CHOM : Unemployment expectations over the next 12 months.
11. AEQD : The purchase of durable goods compared to last year.
12. EPAP : Household's saving expectations over the next 12 months.
13. EPAR : Is it a good time to save now ?

14. CAUT : Did you place an order for a new car ?
15. IAUT : Buying intention for a car.
16. IREF : Buying intention for a refrigerator.
17. ICON : Buying intention for a fridge/freezer.
18. IMLL : Buying intention for a washing machine.
19. ITVN : Buying intention for a black and white TV.
20. IMLV : Buying intention for a dish-washer.

* The precise wording of the survey questions can be found in (4).

TABLE A15

FACTOR ANALYSIS - GERMANY MAI73 (W1) *

20 VARIABLES

.... ROTATED FACTOR MATRIX (3 FACTORS).

		1	2	3
1	REVN	0.07527	-0.08854	**-0.58219**
2	SEAD	0.01598	**0.62737**	-0.09742
3	SEAP	0.02096	**0.66153**	-0.04052
4	PRAD	0.01970	**0.50595**	0.27263
5	PRAP	-0.01374	**0.55536**	0.33956
6	SFAC	-0.00965	0.32156	**-0.63904**
7	SFAD	-0.04777	**0.58424**	-0.38519
8	SFAP	-0.01411	**0.61780**	-0.23655
9	ACHT	-0.00750	0.02687	**-0.33438**
10	CHOM	-0.01747	**0.33333**	0.00385
11	AEQD	-0.00194	0.06806	**-0.13154**
12	EPAP	0.02560	0.24843	**-0.68893**
13	EPAR	0.00662	**0.39066**	-0.33950
14	CAUT	-0.02817	-0.06918	**-0.21173**
15	IAUT	0.11900	-0.08273	**-0.40319**
16	IREF	**0.93574**	0.00517	-0.00150
17	ICON	**0.90470**	-0.01355	-0.06299
18	IMLL	**0.93318**	-0.01161	-0.02011
19	ITVN	**0.93419**	0.00172	0.00038
20	IMLV	**0.89928**	-0.00112	-0.06055
	% TOTAL VARIANCE	21.36	12.86	10.43

* W1 means that the weights are based on the more incisive scaling methods

TABLE A16

FACTOR ANALYSIS - GERMANY - MAY 74 (W1)

20 VARIABLES .... ROTATED FACTOR MATRIX (3 FACTORS)

		1	2	3
1	REVN	0.04318	-0.06113	0.56548
2	SEAD	0.06542	0.61085	0.10644
3	SEAP	-0.03739	0.70632	0.09379
4	PRAD	-0.04928	0.52581	-0.09042
5	PRAP	0.03282	0.59891	-0.14570
6	SFAC	0.00005	0.16001	0.69920
7	SFAD	-0.01746	0.53647	0.41013
8	SFAP	-0.01503	0.58445	0.27376
9	ACHT	0.01533	0.04395	0.32091
10	CHOM	0.06432	0.57074	-0.00448
11	AEQD	0.11065	0.06133	0.09618
12	EPAP	0.02514	0.12896	0.76731
13	EPAR	-0.06445	0.21394	0.51852
14	CAUT	0.00986	-0.045[illegible]8	0.18327
15	IAUT	0.19751	-0.09185	0.38562
16	IREF	0.89542	0.02708	0.00517
17	ICON	0.79631	-0.02381	0.11923
18	IMLL	0.87694	0.03525	0.00780
19	ITVN	0.88296	-0.00861	-0.03857
20	IMLV	0.81800	-0.03223	0.05410
% TOTAL VARIANCE		18.63	12.87	11.36

TABLE A17

FACTOR ANALYSIS - FRANCE - MAY 73 (W1)

20 VARIABLES

.... ROTATED FACTOR MATRIX (3 FACTORS)

		1	2	3
1	REVN	0.27576	-0.17021	-0.53920
2	SEAD	0.06875	0.66292	-0.26279
3	SEAP	0.08336	0.71448	-0.23202
4	PRAD	0.03497	0.44819	-0.01792
5	PRAP	-0.00929	0.47287	0.20494
6	SFAC	-0.05884	0.08233	-0.71230
7	SFAD	0.08700	0.25867	-0.59456
8	SFAP	0.19885	0.26549	-0.41292
9	ACHT	0.02530	-0.15709	-0.19841
10	CHOM	-0.00506	0.42778	0.04652
11	AEQD	0.26618	0.08910	-0.14025
12	EPAP	0.10082	0.18412	-0.72571
13	EPAR	-0.10168	0.38547	-0.03197
14	CAUT	0.04582	-0.12510	-0.20904
15	IAUT	0.51686	-0.09017	-0.34227
16	IREF	0.64188	-0.00488	0.01765
17	ICON	0.58274	-0.03425	-0.07390
18	IMLL	0.62036	0.01998	0.00258
19	ITVN	0.61579	0.01663	-0.03276
20	IMLV	0.54916	-0.03886	-0.11503
% TOTAL VARIANCE		11.59	9.86	11.29

TABLE A18

FACTOR ANALYSIS - FRANCE MAI74 (W1)

20 VARIABLES

.... ROTATED FACTOR MATRIX (3 FACTORS)

		1	2	3
1	REVN	0.26816	0.41262	-0.38715
2	SEAD	-0.00734	0.40822	0.37629
3	SEAP	0.06264	0.28462	0.60239
4	PRAD	-0.05778	0.11297	0.30084
5	PRAP	0.06647	-0.07672	0.51646
6	SFAC	-0.00536	0.71455	-0.06134
7	SFAD	0.04747	0.67310	0.09612
8	SFAP	0.14967	0.49114	0.26013
9	ACHT	-0.04742	0.13993	-0.37174
10	CHOM	-0.02161	0.08503	0.50021
11	ALQD	0.18270	0.08668	0.11998
12	EPAP	0.15153	0.72091	0.00598
13	EPAR	-0.05355	0.02811	0.48780
14	CAUT	0.07453	0.11611	-0.12140
15	IAUT	0.55106	0.21734	-0.15663
16	IREF	0.66138	-0.05428	0.06132
17	ICON	0.52528	0.09584	-0.07116
18	IMLL	0.65805	-0.01509	0.04117
19	ITVN	0.65288	0.00840	0.03065
20	IMLV	0.53921	0.11874	-0.09614
% TOTAL VARIANCE		11.71	11.42	8.96

TABLE A19

FACTOR ANALYSIS BELGIUM - MAI73 (W1)

20 VARIABLES

.... ROTATED FACTOR MATRIX (3 FACTORS)

		1	2	3
1	REVN	0.14162	-0.64009	-0.14425
2	SEAD	0.00984	-0.20107	0.68435
3	SEAP	0.00071	-0.18339	0.74007
4	PRAD	0.06544	0.08583	0.46226
5	PRAP	0.05146	0.11801	0.49284
6	SFAC	-0.00705	-0.70054	0.05247
7	SFAD	0.01318	-0.61089	0.30214
8	SFAP	0.02251	-0.48728	0.28315
9	ACHT	-0.07150	-0.27168	-0.01191
10	CHOM	0.01300	-0.07830	0.47289
11	AECD	0.09228	-0.21267	0.05149
12	EPAP	0.06999	-0.75469	0.05903
13	EPAR	-0.00830	-0.15174	0.21963
14	CAUT	-0.01932	-0.11961	0.02362
15	IAUT	0.23207	-0.38928	-0.08844
16	IREF	0.74680	-0.03539	0.03758
17	ICON	0.74638	-0.03372	0.04337
18	IMLL	0.73622	-0.07422	0.04742
19	ITVN	0.73103	0.02432	0.02669
20	IMLV	0.70285	-0.05333	0.02688
	% TOTAL VARIANCE	13.93	12.51	9.81

TABLE A20

FACTOR ANALYSIS - BELGIUM - MA174 (h1)

20 VARIABLES

.... ROTATED FACTOR MATRIX (3 FACTORS)

		1	2	3
1	REVN	0.67036	0.12828	-0.16465
2	SEAD	0.06384	0.00312	0.66208
3	SEAP	0.02591	0.04148	0.74919
4	PRAD	0.00620	-0.02519	0.18556
5	PRAP	-0.04682	0.05558	0.38279
6	SFAC	0.69891	-0.04796	0.10331
7	SFAD	0.56565	0.06577	0.35096
8	SFAP	0.45528	0.10556	0.37485
9	ACHT	0.23140	-0.03803	0.00693
10	CHOM	-0.06458	0.03828	0.51029
11	AEQD	0.18556	0.21367	0.19232
12	EPAP	0.77574	0.02903	0.11681
13	EPAR	0.14696	-0.05035	0.34754
14	CAUT	0.08617	0.05108	-0.06412
15	IAUT	0.40675	0.23486	-0.14296
16	IREF	0.00678	0.74513	-0.00773
17	ICON	0.08540	0.65917	0.01284
18	IMLL	0.05300	0.71543	0.02452
19	ITVN	-0.05752	0.70728	0.03163
20	IMLV	0.10002	0.58809	-0.02359
% TOTAL VARIANCE		11.92	12.49	9.70

TABLE A21

FACTOR ANALYSIS - NETHERLANDS - AVR73 (WI)

20 VARIABLES

.... ROTATED FACTOR MATRIX (3 FACTORS)

		1	2	3
1	REVN	0.58492	-0.19468	0.11845
2	SEAD	0.16658	0.56307	-0.03397
3	SEAP	0.08930	0.67209	0.02199
4	PRAD	-0.08396	0.41774	0.03644
5	PRAP	-0.15856	0.53516	0.04158
6	SEAC	0.71597	0.10633	0.00519
7	SEAD	0.62669	0.25509	0.01627
8	SEAP	0.46068	0.34566	0.00961
9	ACHT	0.16722	-0.07786	0.12975
10	CHOM	-0.00954	0.50253	0.01603
11	AEOD	0.15389	0.06941	0.26605
12	EPAP	0.74493	0.16170	0.01323
13	EPAR	0.11636	0.25249	-0.09390
14	CAUT	0.13577	-0.10002	0.01234
15	IAUT	0.44964	-0.11071	0.27679
16	IREF	0.00266	-0.01180	0.67227
17	ICON	0.17362	-0.02419	0.43127
18	IMLL	-0.06555	0.01576	0.69280
19	ITVN	-0.11670	0.01696	0.52521
20	IMLV	0.18325	-0.04122	0.36404
% TOTAL VARIANCE		12.25	9.21	8.59

TABLE A22

FACTOR ANALYSIS - NETHERLANDS - AVR74 (W1)

20 VARIABLES

.... ROTATED FACTOR MATRIX (3 FACTORS)

		1	2	3
1	REVN	0.56739	-0.20126	-0.24599
2	SFAD	-0.03548	0.03304	0.63659
3	SEAP	0.02067	-0.07394	0.66287
4	PRAD	0.01056	0.02121	0.13691
5	PRAP	-0.06346	-0.00833	0.26903
6	SFAC	0.73955	0.02944	0.16034
7	SFAD	0.48587	-0.03704	0.46310
8	SFAP	0.32868	-0.07520	0.50259
9	ACHT	0.18901	-0.18505	-0.09112
10	CHCM	-0.07098	-0.04767	0.47299
11	AEQD	0.08580	-0.33650	0.07824
12	EPAP	0.76316	-0.00275	0.13146
13	EPAR	0.18909	0.16183	0.22036
14	CAUT	0.13959	0.00127	-0.11987
15	IAUT	0.41115	-0.31619	-0.10523
16	IREF	-0.01984	-0.65073	-0.01620
17	ICON	0.10861	-0.42496	-0.03070
18	IMLL	-0.05079	-0.64203	0.06236
19	ITVN	-0.09852	-0.48422	0.05642
20	IMLV	0.12250	-0.34532	-0.05151
% TOTAL VARIANCE		10.57	8.51	9.15

TABLE A23

STABILITY OF COMPONENTS BETWEEN MAY 73 AND MAY 74

	F.R.of Germany		France		Belgium		Netherlands	
	M 73	M 74	M 73	M 74	M 73	M 74	M 73	M 74
PC 1								
REVN	X	X	X		X	X	X	X
SEAD								
SEAP								
PRAD								
PRAP								
SFAC	X	X	X	X	X	X	X	X
SFAD			X	X	X	X	X	
SFAP								
ACHT								
CHOM								
AEQD								
EPAP	X	X	X	X	X	X	X	X
EPAR		X						
CAUT								
IAUT								
IREF								
ICON								
IMLL								
ITVN								
IMLV								
PC 2								
REVN								
SEAD								
SEAP								
PRAD								
PRAP								
SFAC								
SFAD								
SFAP								
ACHT								
CHOM								
AEQD								
EPAP								
EPAR								
CAUT								
IAUT			X	X				
IREF	X	X	X	X	X	X	X	X
ICON	X	X	X	X	X	X		
IMLL	X	X	X	X	X	X	X	X
ITVN	X	X	X	X	X	X	X	
IMLV	X	X	X	X	X	X		
PC 3								
REVN								
SEAD	X	X	X		X	X	X	X
SEAP	X	X	X	X	X	X	X	X
PRAD	X	X						
PRAP	X	X		X			X	
SFAC								
SFAD	X	X						
SFAP	X	X						
ACHT		X						X
CHOM				X		X	X	
AEQD								
EPAP								
EPAR								
CAUT								
IAUT								
IRLF								
ICON								
IMLL								
ITVN								
IMLV								

Source : B. Mariash et G. Moutet, op. cit.

TABLE A 24

CORRELATION BETWEEN ATTITUDINAL VARIABLES IN TIME SERIES ANALYSIS

CORR.	F.R. of Germany	France	Italy	Netherlands	Belgium
1,2	0.927	0.847	0.939	0.843	0.815
1,3	0.795	0.957	0.951	0.696	0.912
1,4	0.719	0.825	0.841	0.315	0.411
1,5	0.575	0.765	0.804	0.270	0.648
1,6	0.756	0.019	0.510	-0.196	0.299
1,7	0.152	0.825	0.738	0.760	0.825
1,8	0.234	0.497	0.917	0.624	0.267
2,3	0.864	0.739	0.950	0.822	0.860
2,4	-0.873	0.972	0.959	0.560	0.842
2,5	0.729	0.841	0.806	0.520	0.863
2,6	0.715	-0.188	0.359	0.005	0.224
2,7	0.264	0.779	0.792	0.533	0.713
2,8	0.290	0.575	0.893	0.539	0.463
3,4	0.812	0.743	0.913	0.754	0.534
3,5	0.724	0.740	0.761	0.670	0.743
3,6	0.702	-0.068	0.363	0.245	0.459
3,7	0.061	0.700	0.839	0.448	0.722
3,8	0.086	0.579	0.912	0.121	0.355
4,5	0.942	0.846	0.782	0.883	0.813
4,6	0.749	-0.267	0.235	0.546	0.104
4,7	0.440	0.760	0.823	-0.076	0.471
4,8	0.463	0.622	0.853	-0.068	0.473
5,6	0.742	-0.198	0.587	0.240	0.517
5,7	0.511	0.424	0.461	0.019	0.475
5,8	0.582	0.711	0.789	-0.199	0.480
6,7	0.047	0.024	-0.023	-0.573	-0.004
6,8	0.317	-0.769	0.395	-0.295	0.223
7,8	0.871	0.212	0.844	0.419	0.105

TABLE A25

ROTATED FACTOR MATRICES (time series analysis)

F.R. OF GERMANY

ROTATED FACTOR MATRIX

VARIABLE 1	0.89796	0.07688
VARIABLE 2	0.93032	0.18810
VARIABLE 3	0.93164	0.00410
VARIABLE 4	0.86727	0.38206
VARIABLE 5	0.76441	0.50455
VARIABLE 6	0.86320	0.09943
VARIABLE 7	0.07538	0.96640
VARIABLE 8	0.17601	0.93840

FRANCE

ROTATED FACTOR MATRIX

VARIABLE 1	0.97414	-0.04960
VARIABLE 2	0.91584	-0.25779
VARIABLE 3	0.89219	-0.14499
VARIABLE 4	0.89443	-0.32938
VARIABLE 5	0.78080	-0.41560
VARIABLE 6	0.07167	0.94131
VARIABLE 7	0.86457	0.12481
VARIABLE 8	0.42080	-0.88410

ITALY

ROTATED FACTOR MATRIX

VARIABLE 1	0.85883	0.44255
VARIABLE 2	0.92694	0.30020
VARIABLE 3	0.93439	0.27886
VARIABLE 4	0.93824	0.18788
VARIABLE 5	0.65387	0.64677
VARIABLE 6	0.06180	0.96430
VARIABLE 7	0.94510	-0.15330
VARIABLE 8	0.89421	0.32924

BELGIUM

ROTATED FACTOR MATRIX

VARIABLE 1	0.89483	0.17858
VARIABLE 2	0.88316	0.40507
VARIABLE 3	0.83445	0.39747
VARIABLE 4	0.62052	0.47514
VARIABLE 5	0.62424	0.70357
VARIABLE 6	-0.02452	0.76976
VARIABLE 7	0.92964	-0.12658
VARIABLE 8	0.22676	0.65989

NETHERLANDS

ROTATED FACTOR MATRIX

VARIABLE 1	0.29237	-0.89419
VARIABLE 2	0.66809	-0.68047
VARIABLE 3	0.84391	-0.42493
VARIABLE 4	0.97340	0.03701
VARIABLE 5	0.88211	0.00534
VARIABLE 6	0.61899	0.55129
VARIABLE 7	-0.11497	-0.88691
VARIABLE 8	0.01334	-0.68269

G. HEALD
SOCIAL SURVEYS (GALLUP POLL) LTD.
LONDON

WORLD-WIDE STUDY
ON SOCIAL INDICATORS AND QUALITY OF LIFE

WORLD-WIDE STUDY ON SOCIAL INDICATORS AND QUALITY OF LIFE

G. I. Heald - Social Surveys (Gallup Poll) Ltd., London and
Oxford Centre for Management Studies

This survey was conducted at two points in time, during late 1974-1975 and in the spring of 1976 by the thirty research organisations comprising Gallup International Research Institutes as part of a global research project sponsored by the Charles F. Kettering Foundation.

Questions were administered to nationally representative samples in more than 60 countries on six continents representing nearly two-thirds of the world's population - major exclusions were the Eastern Bloc countries and China. More than 10,000 interviews were completed and each interview took approximately one hour to administer and contained 100 questions, not including demographic and other information to be entered by the interviewer. The areas covered were as follows:

Hopes, aspirations, expectations, worries and fears, values. Perceptions regarding the ideal life - and the worst possible life.

Personal happiness - present, five years ago, five years hence.

Optimism - Pessimism (other than with respect to personal circumstances) - is life for the people of the world, the citizens of one's nation, and residents of one's community becoming better or worse?

Levels of personal satisfaction-dissatisfaction with key aspects of life - job, leisure and recreation, education, health, family life, standard of living, personal safety, etc..

Religion - its perceived importance in own life, specific religious beliefs.

Urban/Community problems - perceived most important problems; improvement or decline in community life; attitudes concerning crime; preferred size of community and attitudes toward industrialization, population, and conservation efforts; satisfaction with community life.

The Nation - perceived most important national problems, improvement or decline in national life, satisfaction with life in nation, desire to emigrate.

Internationalism and global problems, likelihood or world government, perceptions regarding wealth or own nation and desirability of increasing financial aid to poor nations, desire to visit other countries.

Women - attitudes toward housework, desire for job outside home, degree to which women's role perceived as changing, perceived existence of equal job and educational opportunities, and desirability of equal opportunities.

International organization - the United Nations, awareness of UN organization and of own nation's membership, rating of UN's overall performance, awareness of major UN agencies.

Interviewers were instructed to note and record the respondent's facial expression, personal neatness and cleanliness, interest in the interview, and cooperativeness. They also recorded such information about the physical environment as the condition of the respondent's housing, the character of the neighbourhood, the proximity of mountains, etc.. Careful attention was paid to maintaining the same meanings or semantic equivalents of the questions when they were translated into different languages.

Before the questionnaire was administered to the sample, it was pretested in the United States, Canada, several Western European nations, and in Uruguay and India. The last pretest was especially important, since it included a number of illiterate and very poor respondents. Final revisions were then made.

About 15 of the questions were of the open-end variety; the remainder were precoded. The organizations conducting the interviews took care of coding open-end questions, but keypunching and tabulations were handled centrally in the United States.

Sample Design

To design a sample that would permit reporting detailed findings from individual nations would be enormously costly. A total sample of somewhere between 70,000 and 100,000 would be necessary. The decision was therefore made to divide the world into major regions and to draw a sample that would accurately reflect the attitudes of adults fifteen years of age or older in each region. The regions were as follows:

Africa (Sub-Sahara)
Australia
Eastern Europe and USSR
Far East
Latin America
North Africa and Middle East
U.S. and Canada
Western Europe

Surveys have not been conducted in Eastern Europe and the Soviet Union, but negotiations are currently being conducted to persuade research organizations in this area to participate in the future. Data from the Far East do not include the People's Republic of China.

Drawing the sample for each region involved allocating cases based on the total adult population of all nations in that region. The participating survey organizations therefore first drew a sample of the sampling point included in their national master samples. Five to ten interviews were then allocated to each of the selected sampling points. In those few countries where in-place national samples were unavailable, the research organization concerned was asked to draw a national sample using established sampling procedures and the best available census data. The design that was adopted called for a global sample of approximately 7,500 cases, but some research organizations oversampled in order to be able to report separate findings for their own countries and the final number of interviews were approximately 10,000. In some developing countries, better educated and urban "elite" groups were oversampled so that their views could be reported separately.

Selected British Results

In an unprompted question, respondents were asked what they wanted out of life. The replies are shown in Table 1 - one's health and an improved standard of living were the two more important factors people claimed.

In terms of ranking objectives there were surprisingly little differences between males and females. Age and income group were more discriminating variables and these results are summarised in Table 2, which shows the five most frequently cited responses for each group.

This lack of discrimination by the different sexes has also been found in other studies [1].

Not unnaturally, as people became older, they increasingly cited health as the most important factor and women generally laid greater stress on wanting good health than men did.

On average, 30 per cent of respondent's mentioned "one's own health" and 20 per cent mentioned "improved standard of living", but for the lower social groups there was no significant discrimination between health (28 per cent) and living standards (27 per cent). Hence, for this group the desire for an improved standard of living is perhaps overwhelming. This is very much reinforced by their desire for their own home, which was mentioned by 19 per cent of this group, compared to 13 per cent on average.

Whilst 12 per cent of respondents wanted a happy family life, there was a far greater desire for this by women (15 per cent) than men (9 per cent). Perhaps one of the reasons for this is that men seek a good job and congenial work (9 per cent) compared to women (5 per cent). It is the younger people aged 16 - 34 who laid real stress on wanting a happy family life.

For young people the desire to have their own home was the most important aspect in their lives. They were the only group who did not list health at the top of their priorities. Again, this is understandable - and indicates how desirable are government schemes of special help to young couples wishing to purchase their own home.

As middle age approaches and families become more established, it is the wider issue of peace in the international situation and opportunities for offspring which become important after personal health.

As old age approaches and people's income diminishes, it is the economic issues (after health) which recur - improving their standard of living and owning their own home are the two most important factors. There is also emphasis on 'maintaining the status quo' - people are reluctant to adapt to change at this age.

For the upper income groups the emphasis lies in personal health and a family life which is happy and healthy.

Recreation and travel is cited fourth and perhaps surprisingly 'increasing wealth' is cited fifth. No doubt, this supports the old adage that once you acquire wealth it becomes like a disease.

The more ethereal concept of "happiness" is listed ninth in order of priorities in Table 1 and suggests that either it is relatively unimportant or perhaps it has already been largely subsumed in the previous eight categories.

TABLE 1 : All of us want certain things out of life. When you think about what really matters in your own life, what are your wishes and hopes for the future? If you imagine your future in the <u>best</u> possible light, what would your life look like then if you are <u>to be</u> happy?

		SEX		SOCIAL CLASS			AGE		
	TOTAL	Men	Women	Upper	Middle	Lower	16-34	35-54	55
BASE	307	144	163	30	150	127	107	95	98
	%	%	%	%	%	%	%	%	%
To be happy:									
One's own health	30	25	35	22	34	28	19	32	41
Improved standard of living	20	18	21	12	15	27	23	15	20
Own house, garden etc	13	15	12	8	9	19	26	5	8
Happy family life	12	9	15	14	13	11	22	9	4
International peace	11	10	11	2	11	12	7	19	[illegible]
Opportunities for children	9	9	8	11	11	6	5	17	[illegible]
Good job; congenial work	7	9	5	12	9	4	14	8	[illegible]
Health of family	7	3	11	14	9	3	8	9	
Happiness	6	4	8	9	5	7	8	6	[illegible]
Maintain status quo	6	4	8	0	8	6	4	6	[illegible]
Have wealth	5	6	5	13	5	4	7	4	
Economic security	5	6	4	0	6	5	6	5	
Success	4	6	3	9	5	3	10	1	
Happy old age	4	6	2	2	2	7	1	5	
Recreation, travel etc	4	4	4	14	2	3	4	3	

TABLE 2 : The five most important priorities in a respondent's life

AVERAGE - ALL RESPONDENTS:
One's own health
Improved standard of living
Own house, garden
Happy family life
International peace

UPPER INCOME:	MIDDLE INCOME:	LOWER INCOME:
One's own health	One's own health	One's own health
Happy family life	Improved standard of living	Improved standard of living
Health of family	Happy family life	Own house, garden
Recreation, travel	International peace	International peace
Have wealth	Opportunities for children	Happy family life

YOUNG PEOPLE 16 - 34:	MIDDLE AGE 35 - 54:	OLD AGE 55+:
Own house, garden etc.	One's own health	One's own health
Improved standard of living	International peace	Improved standard of living
Happy family life	Opportunities for children	Own house, garden
One's own health	Improved standard of living	Maintain status quo
Good job, congenial work	Family life - happy, healthy	International peace

Respondents were also asked about their fears and worries for the future. Generally these answers were the negatives to their previously expressed hopes. They can be summarised as follows:

	Percentage of respondents mentioning the factor	Upper income	16-34	55+
Ill-health; accident; death of self	26	39	21	30
Deterioration in standard of living	12	4	17	15
Unemployment	12	7	18	4
Ill-heath for family	10	2	6	8
Economic instability generally	10	8	11	8
Loneliness	6	19	6	9

Perhaps not expected was the finding that as people grew older they feared for their health and a deterioration in their standard of living.

One unusual feature was the very high fear of unemployment and a deterioration in standard of living by young people aged 16 - 34. This finding may be an indication of the effect of the economic recession at the time of the survey period - December, 1974.

Loneliness was also a great fear - particularly amongst the upper income group (19 per cent). Care must be exercised in this result because of the small sample size of this group.

The Mountain Scale

In the early 1960s, the Institute for International Social Research directed by Hadley Cantril and Lloyd A. Free, interviewed national samples in 13 countries representing more than one third of the world's population. One of the major purposes of this group of surveys was to determine how satisfied people were with their indivdual situations and which qualities of life were most important to them. (Results of this research were presented in Cantril, 1965.) One of the instruments they used was called a self-anchoring striving scale.

The more recent Gallup survey differed from the one conducted by the Institute for International Social Research in a number of respects. For one thing, Cantril had found in the course of his research that in some parts of the world, ladders were not commonly used and the idea of using the rungs on a ladder to indicate degrees of satisfaction was not easily understood. In these countries Cantril had substituted for the ladder a diagram of a mountain with 11 ascending steps. Guided by Cantril's experience, the mountain scale was used exclusively and found to work satisfactorily as a scaling device in all parts of the world.

The British results are shown in Table 3 and can be briefly summarised as follows:

- Respondents are optimistic about the next five years compared to the present time and the last five years. The only exception is older people who become more pessimistic about their life as time goes by. Young people are the most optimistic about the future (with a rating 7.79).

- Respondents family life was rated the highest of the factors questioned. This result is largely confirmed by other studies (M. Abrahams, S.S.R.C. - Quality of Life Study).

TABLE 3 : Respondents mean ratings on the mountain scale (0 - 10)

		SEX		SOCIAL CLASS			AGE		
	TOTAL	Men	Women	Upper	Middle	Lower	16-34	35-54	55+
BASE	307	144	163	30	150	127	107	95	98
Striving Scale (0-10)									
Life in 5 years time	7.23	6.99	7.45	7.35	7.53	6.84	7.79	7.48	6.40
Life at the moment	6.79	6.59	6.97	7.04	7.15	6.31	6.61	6.98	6.79
Life 5 years ago	6.06	6.13	6.01	6.57	6.19	5.78	5.53	5.87	6.86
Satisfaction Scale (0-10)									
Family life	8.02	7.99	8.05	7.76	8.32	7.73	7.96	8.07	8.11
Free time activities	7.64	7.75	7.55	7.09	7.89	7.47	7.45	7.74	7.78
Health	7.59	7.81	7.40	7.66	7.93	7.17	8.57	7.61	6.65
Life today	7.53	7.36	7.67	7.28	7.74	7.33	7.50	7.52	7.58
Housing	7.20	7.15	7.25	7.48	7.37	6.93	6.86	7.22	7.61
Present work)	6.91	6.84	7.05	5.86	7.17	6.84	6.91	6.82	7.12
Housewives only)	7.02	-	(7.05	(7.55)	(6.79)	(7.17)	(6.36)	(7.13)	(7.39)
Standard of living	6.79	6.73	6.84	7.44	7.04	6.33	6.90	6.80	6.68
Community	6.77	6.80	6.76	6.97	6.73	6.78	6.31	7.00	7.12
Education in preparing for work	6.08	5.96	6.19	6.46	6.35	5.69	6.73	5.81	5.74
Education in preparing for life	5.93	5.77	6.07	6.71	6.09	5.56	6.07	5.69	6.09
Life in Britain today	5.82	5.68	5.94	5.39	5.85	5.87	5.83	5.55	6.08

International Results

One of our principal conclusions is that economic privation seems to affect the spirit as well as the body. Poverty adversely colours attitudes and perceptions. Although one probably could find isolated places in the world where the inhabitants are very poor but happy, this study failed to discover any area that met this test. The nations with the highest per capita income almost invariably top every test of psychological well-being and satisfaction in major aspects of life. People in industrialized nations, compared with those who live in the developing nations, find their lives more interesting, worry less, and would like fewer changes. They are almost more satisfied with their family life, their health, their jobs, their community, their education, and with themselves.

Some hopeful signs are found in the nations of the third and fourth worlds. People there believe that their lot will improve with time-and, in fact, they are relatively more optimistic in this respect than those living in the industrialized nations. Attitudes toward the role of women are undergoing a marked change in the developing nations. In addition, even those countries with the lowest level of formal education are beginning to recognize the interdependece among nations and the need for mutual co-operation and assistance.

There are advance signs also. The impoverished people of the third world quite naturally wish to emulate the more advanced nations and believe that the way to a better life is to follow the example set by these nations. They want growth and development, industrial growth, population growth and urban growth. In direct contrast to those who live in the more advanced societies, the people of the developing countries would like more factories and greater industrialization not only in their nation but in their own communities.

Present birth control efforts are likely to meet with little success in the developing nations until the standard of living is improved, thereby lessening the economic motivation for having large families, and until religious attitudes change.

Inhabitants of the small towns and rural areas in the developing nations, in disturbing number, would like to move to the cities and urban centres. This desire to leave the land contrasts sharply with the desire of many city residents of the advanced nations who would like to escape from the city and move to towns and rural areas. This trend to the cities in developing nations is contributing to the alarming growth of slums in all the cities of the third and fourth world countries.

These are but a few of the findings of this survey which sought to embrace the world's population living where surveys of a social, economical, or cultural nature can be conducted.

In some cases, the regional percentages mask wide differences among countries or areas within the region. This is especially true in the Far East, for which national figures are available in the case of India and Japan. In India, only 35 percent of the respondents said that their lives were "Very Interesting" or "Fairly Interesting," while in Japan the percentage was 73 (Table 4). There are also appreciable differences among the countries of Western Europe.

As for the question of personal happiness (Table 5), again, within the Far East, the differences between Japan and India are very large, although it is remarkable that the proportion of those saying "Very Happy" is not much higher in Japan than in India (9 percent as opposed to 6 percent)

When the inhabitants of the major regions of the world are asked about their hopes and aspirations, their main desires center about their economic welfare, their health, and family life. Economic well-being plays a far more important role in the hopes of those who live in the developing nations. Jobs, a higher standard of living, the chance to own a business, a farm or land, and to have "wealth"-these take precedence over everything.

While economic security, the health of oneself and family, and a happy family life are almost important to those who live in the advanced industrial states, the range of hopes and aspirations is far wider. Such things as "self development," "public service,"

Table 4: "Would You Say That Your Life at This Time Is Very Interesting, Fairly Interesting, Fairly Dull, or Very Dull?"

	Very Interesting	Fairly Interesting	Fairly Dull	Very Dull
North America	35%	53%	8%	4%
Australia	30	62	6	2
Western Europe	20	57	20	3
Latin America	22	44	26	8
Africa	17	57	19	7
Far East	11	38	35	16

Table 5: "Generally Speaking, How Happy Would You Say You Are-Very Happy, Fairly Happy, or Not Too Happy"

	Very Happy	Fairly Happy	Not Too Happy	DK NA
North America	40%	51%	8%	1%
Australia	37	57	18	*
Western Europe	20	60	18	2
Latin America	32	38	28	2
Africa	18	50	31	1
Far East	7	41	50	2

"religion," the "desire for peace and a better world," seldom mentioned by those in developing nations, are often cited by those in the developed nations.

Conversely, when asked to name their fears and worries for the future-the worst possible situation for themselves-opinions in the developing nations tend to center on the loss of jobs, a lowering of their standard of living. These are also important for the inhabitants of the advanced nations, but to these economic and health worries are added many other concerns such as "war," "the deterioration of the international situation," "spiritual and moral breakdown of society," "injustice in society," "political instability," "lack of freedom," etc.

As far as perceptions of the past and hopes for the future are concerned, people in most of the developing countries seem to feel that their lot has improved substantially in recent years and is likely to improve much more in the next few years. This is especially true in Africa and Latin America, as can be seen from Table 6. The reasons for the lack of optimism in Western Europe and the perceived decline in the goodness of life in the Far East during the past five years must await further analysis.

Although Cantril was studing nations while we were basically interested in regions, for a limited number of countries it is possible to make direct comparisons between the ratings from the "ladder" striving scale that Cantril obtained 15 years ago (Table 7) and those that were revealed by the "mountain" scale (Table 8). In the case of West Germany and Brazil the "Now" ratings are higher in the Gallup survey than in the Cantril study. For the United States and India the "Now" ratings are almost the same. Judging by the answers to the "5 Years Hence" rating for the earlier study compared to the "Now" ratings in Table 8, it is apparent, however, that life has not improved as rapidly as had been hoped. Only West Germany has exceeded its expectations.

In order to compare the satisfaction with various aspects of life that was reported in the five regions, we calculated the proportion of those in each region who pointed to the top three

Table 6: Mean Step Ratings on Mountain "Striving Scale"

	5 Years Ago	Now	5 Years Hence
North America	5.8	6.5	7.1
Western Europe	5.7	6.3	6.3
Latin America	4.9	6.1	7.6
Africa	3.7	4.6	6.1
Far East	4.4	4.1	4.6

Table 7: Mean Step Ratings On "Ladder" Striving Scale as of Early 1960's"

	5 Years Ago	Now	5 Years Hence
United States	5.9	6.6	7.8
West Germany	4.1	5.3	6.2
Brazil	4.1	4.6	7.3
Nigeria	2.8	4.8	7.4
India	3.4	3.7	5.1

Table 8: Mean Step Ratings on Mountain "Striving Scale," by Country

	5 Years Ago	Now	5 Years Hence
United States	6.0	6.7	7.5
West Germany	5.9	6.6	6.9
Brazil	4.7	6.1	8.2
India	4.0	3.4	3.4

steps of the "mountain" scale when asked about their family life, health, leisure time, and so on. The results for each aspect are shown in Table 9. This table raises more questions than it answers. It supports the hypothesis that the more affluent populations enjoy most aspects of life more than those that are disadvantaged, but it also points to areas that call for further investigation. Why are the less wealthy Latin Americans so happy? Indeed, in some respects they are more satisfied than the more wealthy West Europeans and almost as happy as the North Americans. Why are people in the Far East more satisfied with their standard fo living than people in Africa, but less satisfied in most other respects?

We cannot answer these questions on the basis of analyses made thus far, but perhaps further analysis of the data will shed light on them. We feel that measures of subjective satisfaction can make an important contribution to efforts of improve the well-being of the peoples of the world, and hope that this survey will help to establish some benchmarks with which the results of future surveys can be compared. Economic statistics have their place, of course, but they mean more in conjunction with data about subjective satisfaction.

[1] *Cantril, Hadley*
1965 The Patterns of Human Concerns. New Brunswick, N.J.: Rutgers University Press

Table 9: Proportion of Respondents Who Are "High Satisfied" with Various Aspects of Theri Lives

	North America	Western Europe	Latin America	Africa	Far East
Your family life	73%	64%	60%	18%	18%
Your present health	63	51	48	33	18
Your leisure time	58	48	51	30	13
Your housing	55	49	37	14	14
Your work	49	40	22	7	7
Your community	47	42	38	17	13
Your standard of living	46	35	36	5	8
Yours education-for work	40	28	26	6	6
Your education-for life	36	25	32	4	4
Life in nation today	36	29	38	18	12

R. EISNER
NORTHWESTERN UNIVERSITY
EVANSTON

MORE ON CAPITAL EXPENDITURE ANTICIPATIONS

More on Capital Expenditure Anticipations*

6.0 Introduction

We turn now to analysis of investment realizations functions, beginning with the one-year ahead, or short run capital expenditure anticipations, based upon McGraw-Hill data over the fourteen year period, 1955-68. The picture to emerge is one of considerable forecasting inaccuracy for individual firm observations but substantial if varying accuracy in annual means or aggregates. For both individual firms and, a fortiori, for all firms of a given industry or a given year or both, the gap between actual capital expenditures and anticipations can be accounted for in part by changes in current sales, by the difference between current and anticipated sales, and by current and immediately past profits.

Capital expenditure plans expressed by each firm at the beginning of the year are related to the actual capital expenditures for that year, which it reports at the beginning of the following year, as expected percent changes in sales expressed at the beginning of the year have been related to the change in sales shown by later accounting data to have actually occurred. Fourth quarter figures of the previous year were used for capital expenditure anticipation price deflation, on the assumption that capital expenditure anticipations were measured in prices at the time anticipations were formed. Expected sales changes were again taken as expressed implicitly or explicitly in physical terms, and were not deflated for price changes from the year from which the sales change was expected. Depreciation charges and capital stock were not price deflated at all for the purposes of this section.

*This paper is taken, with a number of deletions, from Chapters 6 and 7 of a forthcoming volume, entitled Factors in Business Investment, to be published by the National Bureau of Economic Research, New York, 1977.

Chapter 6 is an updated and revised version of "Investment Anticipations and Realizations: Cross Sections and Time Series of Data of the McGraw-Hill Surveys, 1955-66," presented to the Ninth CIRET Conference, in Madrid, in 1969.

In cross section and time series regressions, observations which were incomplete because of missing information in the observation vector on any one variable were again eliminated. Also, where the variables were (as was usual) taken as ratios of measures of either capital stock or sales, one or two percent of the observations were generally excluded because of "extreme values" (values outside of the pre-set intervals for one or more of the variables, as indicated below in the "Definitions and Sources of Variables and Intervals for Accepted Values"). The number of firms with usable information therefore varied from year to year as well as from regression to regression.

6.1 Means of Expenditures, Anticipations, Sales and Profits Changes

In the most inclusive observation set (involving current and previous capital expenditures, previous anticipations of current capital expenditures, gross fixed assets at the end of 1953 and at the end of 1957, and 1953 depreciation charges), 4698 observations were available, as indicated in Table 6.1.1. Over the fourteen years, the average annual increase in price deflated capital expenditures amounted to 0.56 percent of 1957 gross fixed assets. The corresponding mean anticipated increase in capital expenditures was 0.87 percent, indicating that the ratios of capital expenditures to gross fixed assets for this data set, at least on the basis of the price deflation we have undertaken, tended to be less than anticipated. The differences between the actual and anticipated capital expenditure ratios were not consistently negative, however. A comparison of columns (4) and (5) indicates that in 1955, 1956 and 1965, mean capital expenditure-to-gross-fixed-assets ratios exceeded mean anticipated ratios of expenditures to assets while in 1964 they were almost exactly equal.

Definitions and Sources of Variables and Intervals for Acceptable Values

Symbol[1]	Description	Source[2]	Acceptable Interval[3]
$i_t = \frac{I_t}{K_{57}}$	Capital Expenditures in 1954 Dollars as Ratio of 1957 Gross Fixed Assets	MH/FD	[.6,0]
$i_t^* = \frac{I_t}{K_{t-1}}$	Capital Expenditures in 1954 Dollars as Ratio of Previous Gross Fixed Assets	MH/FD	[.6,0]
$i_t^{t-1} = \frac{I_t^{t-1}}{K_{57}}$	Capital Expenditure Anticipations for the year t, in 1954 Dollars, as Ratio of 1957 Gross Fixed Assets	MH/FD	[.6,0]
$\Delta s_t = \frac{3(S_t - S_{t-1})}{S_{56}+S_{57}+S_{58}}$	Relative Sales Change Ratio, Price Deflated, 1956-58 Denominator	FD	[.7,-.6]
$\Delta s_t^* = \frac{3(S_t - S_{t-1})}{S_t+S_{t-1}+S_{t-2}}$	Relative Sales Change Ratio, Price Deflated, Previous Three-year Denominator	FD	[.7,-.6]
$p_t = \frac{P_t}{K_{57}}$	Net Profits in 1954 Dollars as Ratio of 1957 Gross Fixed Assets	FD	[.7,-.4]
$p_t^* = \frac{P_t}{K_{t-1}}$	Net Profits in 1954 Dollars as Ratio of Previous Price-Deflated Gross Fixed Assets	FD	[.7,-.4]
$d_{53} = \frac{D_{53}}{K_{53}}$	1953 Depreciation Charges as Ratio of 1953 Gross Fixed Assets	FD	[.2,0]
$s_t^{t-1} = \frac{S_t^{t-1} - S_{t-1}}{S_{t-1}}$	Short Run Sales Expectations for the year t = Expected Percent Change in Physical Volume of Sales from McGraw-Hill Surveys, Converted to Pure Decimal	MH	[.7,-.6]

[1] All flow variables (I, I_{t+1}^{t}, S and P) except depreciation charges (D) are price deflated.

[2] MH = McGraw-Hill surveys.
FD = Financial data, generally from Moody's.
MH/FD = Numerator from McGraw-Hill and denominator from financial data.

[3] [U,L] = Closed interval, including upper and lower bounds.
[U,L) = Interval including upper bound but not lower bound.

Table 6.1.1 Capital Expenditures, Change in Capital Expenditures and Anticipated Change in Capital Expenditures, Measured as Ratios of 1957 Gross Fixed Assets, Firm Means by Year, 1955-68

(1) Year	(2) Number of Observations	(3) i_t	(4) Δi_t	(5) $i_t^{t-1} - i_{t-1}$
1955	324	.073	.011	.005
1956	461	.094	.018	.014
1957	503	.092	-.003	.001
1958	399	.075	-.019	-.013
1959	359	.082	.004	.006
1960	363	.087	.006	.017
1961	361	.080	-.004	.002
1962	345	.084	.003	.008
1963	309	.091	.010	.012
1964	303	.108	.019	.019
1965	268	.132	.024	.022
1966	283	.150	.027	.031
1967	240	.142	-.004	.005
1968	180	.142	-.005	.005
All Years	4698	.098	.0056	.0087

In Table 6.1.2 observations are normalized over firms and time periods by dividing capital expenditures, capital expenditure anticipations, and profits by gross fixed assets at the end of the previous year. Changes in sales are analogously deflated by the simple average of current, previous, and two years previous sales. The overall results again indicate an excess of capital expenditure anticipations over capital expenditures of between 3 and 4 percent. But again capital expenditures exceeded or kept roughly even with previously expressed anticipations in boom years such as 1955, 1956, 1964, 1965 and 1966, but were sharply under anticipations in recession periods such as 1958 and 1960.

Table 6.1.2 Capital Expenditures, Capital Expenditure Anticipations, Previous Capital Expenditures, Capital Expenditure Realizations, Change in Capital Expenditures, Anticipated Change in Capital Expenditures, Profits, and Change in Sales, All Measured as Ratios of Previous Year's Gross Fixed Assets or Previous Three Year Sales Average, Firm Means by Year, 1955-68

(1) Year	(2) Number of Observat.	(3) i^*_t	(4) ${}_{t-1}i^*_t$	(5) i^*_{t-1}	(6) $i^*_t - {}_{t-1}i^*_t$	(7) $i^*_t - i^*_{t-1}$	(8) ${}_{t-1}i^*_t - i^*_{t-1}$	(9) p^*_t	(10) Δs^*_t
1955	203	.096	.091	.087	.005	.009	.004	.146	.093
1956	278	.113	.112	.099	.001	.014	.013	.118	.068
1957	283	.106	.111	.117	-.005	-.011	-.006	.101	.037
1958	250	.074	.083	.111	-.009	-.037	-.028	.081	-.044
1959	333	.075	.077	.077	-.002	-.002	-.000	.093	.088
1960	345	.075	.084	.077	-.009	-.002	.007	.077	.027
1961	343	.064	.069	.072	-.005	-.008	-.003	.070	.024
1962	317	.061	.066	.065	-.005	-.004	.001	.078	.080
1963	277	.061	.063	.059	-.001	.002	.004	.080	.067
1964	280	.071	.071	.062	.000	.009	.008	.091	.086
1965	256	.082	.082	.072	.000	.010	.010	.087	.087
1966	279	.092	.092	.079	.000	.014	.014	.092	.083
1967	177	.083	.086	.096	-.003	-.012	-.009	.074	.039
1968	182	.073	.077	.083	-.004	-.010	-.006	.069	.067
All Years	3803	.080	.083	.081	-.003	-.002	.001	.089	.057

6.2 Determinants of Anticipations and Expenditures

Short run capital expenditure anticipations, as pointed out by Eisner [1958c, 1962, 1963a, and 1965] and Jorgenson [1963 and 1965], have essentially the same determinants as the actual expenditures which they anticipate. In Table 6.2.1, we note in fact a relation and sets of parameters for anticipations of subsequent capital expenditures very similar to those for actual capital expenditures. [See Eisner, 1977, Table 1.1.] The sum of sales change coefficients, .548 as against .486, and values of di/ds .630 compared to .559, were both somewhat higher. This reflects the secular growth in capital expenditures and the fact that the anticipations relation refers to the subsequent year, along with some tendency for anticipations to exceed actual expenditures. The mean capital expenditures ratio, i_t, was .096 while the mean capital expenditure anticipations ratio was .106.

Anticipations or plans may be presumed to adapt, however, and with them actual expenditures, to changes in circumstances subsequent to the time of their formulation. We may hypothesize an adaptive mechanism whereby capital expenditure anticipations from year to year are adjusted to the experienced error in anticipations,[1] to sales changes in part or entirely

[1] I am again indebted to Paul Wachtel for this suggestion.

Table 6.2.1 Capital Expenditure Anticipations as a Function of Sales Changes, Profits and Depreciation, Firm Overall Regression, 1955-1968

$$i^{t}_{t+1} = b_0 + \sum_{j=1}^{7} b_j \Delta s_{t+1-j} + \sum_{j=8}^{9} b_j p_{t+8-j} + b_{10} d_{53} + u_t$$

(1) Variable or Statistic	(2) Regression Coefficients and Standard Errors	(3) Means and Standard Deviations and Products
Constant or i^{t}_{t+1}	.021 (.002)	.106 (.087)
Δs_t	.112 (.009)	.064 (.131)
Δs_{t-1}	.082 (.009)	.054 (.130)
Δs_{t-2}	.080 (.009)	.049 (.129)
Δs_{t-3}	.093 (.009)	.045 (.122)
Δs_{t-4}	.073 (.009)	.044 (.119)
Δs_{t-5}	.058 (.009)	.045 (.118)
Δs_{t-6}	.050 (.009)	.037 (.122)
p_t	.130 (.027)	.110 (.107)
p_{t-1}	-.008 (.028)	.105 (.102)
d_{53}	.826 (.041)	.053 (.028)
$\Sigma\Delta s$ coefficients	.548 (.023)	
Σp coefficients	.122 (.012)	
$di/d\Delta s$	.630	
n (-244)	4534	
r.d.f	4523	
$\hat{R}^2$	.314	
F	208.28	

subsequent to the time of anticipations and, particularly, to unexpected sales changes.

Results of estimation of such a relation are shown in Table 6.2.2. They confirm amply the adaptive hypothesis we have suggested. Anticipations shift rapidly indeed with actual expenditures and are generally tied more closely to them than to previous anticipations (as can be noted by subtracting b_2 from b_1 in the regressions reported). There is a greater residual role for the earlier anticipations in the cross sections, however, as may be expected in view of the greater component of permanent variance of anticipations there. Subsequent sales changes and, in the time series, the error in sales anticipations, also emerge as significant variables. We shall note their role again when we analyze realizations, or errors in anticipations, below.

Whatever the divergences between actual and anticipated capital expenditures relating to pervasive movements of the economy, a substantial amount of individual firm variation in capital expenditures is accounted for by capital expenditure anticipations, as is made clear in Table 6.2.3. In regressions based upon pooled individual firm time series of 4674 observations, it is found that over 64% of the variance over time of the capital expenditure ratio is accounted for by the ratio of capital expenditure anticipations to 1957 gross fixed assets. By way of contrast, only 15 percent of the variance in capital expenditures over time is accounted for by previous capital expenditures. Further, the addition of lagged capital expenditures does nothi[ng] to improve the fit already obtained using capital expenditure anticipations, a[nd] its regression coefficient is virtually zero. The major role of capital expenditure anticipations in explaining time series variance in capital expenditures is further confirmed by a coefficient of determination of .664 in the relation between actual and anticipated changes in capital expenditures also shown in Table 6.2.2.

Table 6.2.2 Short Run Capital Expenditure Anticipations as a Function of Previous Anticipations, Error in Previous Anticipations, Sales Changes and Sales Realizations, Firm and Industry Time Series and Cross Sections, 1955-1968

$$i_{t+1}^{t} = b_0 + b_1 i_t^{t-1} + b_2(i_t - i_t^{t-1}) + b_3\Delta s_t + b_4\Delta s_{t-1} + b_5(\Delta s_t - s_t^{t-1}) + u_t$$

(1) Variable or Statistic	(2) Time Series Firm	(3) Time Series Industry	(4) Cross Sections Firm	(5) Cross Sections Industry
	Regression Coefficients and Standard Errors			
Constant	.052 (.002)	.029 (.013)	.022 (.002)	-.004 (.008)
i_t^{t-1}	.497 (.019)	.788 (.059)	.796 (.014)	1.035 (.049)
$i_t - i_t^{t-1}$	.374 (.027)	.647 (.143)	.405 (.025)	.645 (.136)
Δs_t	.056 (.012)	.013 (.039)	.065 (.012)	.130 (.054)
Δs_{t-1}	.030 (.008)	-.020 (.024)	.013 (.008)	-.020 (.035)
$\Delta s_t - s_t^{t-1}$	.046 (.014)	.203 (.044)	.017 (.013)	-.018 (.059)
$b_1 + b_2$	.870 (.038)	1.435 (.171)	1.201 (.032)	1.679 (.153)
$b_3 + b_4 + b_5$	.133 (.012)	.196 (.039)	.095 (.011)	.092 (.046)
n	3268	125	3329	125
$\hat{R}^2$	.283	.814	.536	.852
F	219	101	768	129

Table 6.2.3 Capital Expenditures and Change in Capital Expenditures as Functions of Previous Capital Expenditures, Capital Expenditure Anticipations and Anticipated Change in Capital Expenditures, Measured as Ratios of 1957 Gross Fixed Assets, Pooled Individual Firm Time Series, 1955-68

(A) $i_t = b_0 + b_1 i_t^{t-1} + u_t$

(B) $i_t = b_0 + b_1 i_{t-1} + u_t$

(C) $i_t = b_0 + b_1 i_{t-1} + b_2 i_t^{t-1} + u_t$

(D) $\Delta i_t = b_0 + b_1 (i_t^{t-1} - i_{t-1}) + u_t$

(1) Variable or Statistic	(2) Regression (A)	(3) Coefficients (B)	(4) and Standard (C)	(5) Errors (D)	(6) Means and Stand[ard] Deviations
Constant or i_t	.018 (.001)	.060 (.002)	.018 (.001)	-.002 (.001)	.098 (.063)
i_{t-1}	--- ---	.412 (.015)	.001 (.011)	--- ---	.092 (.059)
i_t^{t-1}	.790 (.009)	--- ---	.790 (.011)	--- ---	.101 (.063)
$i_t^{t-1} - i_{t-1}$	--- ---	--- ----	--- ---	.880 (.010)	.009 (.062)
n (-87)	4674	4674	4674	4674	
r.d.f.	4108	4108	4107	4108	
$\hat{R}^2$	.642	.151	.642	.664	
F	7361	733	3680	8105	

The pooled cross sections of Table 6.2.4 further demonstrate the dominant role of capital expenditure anticipations as opposed to previous capital expenditures in explaining the variance of actual capital expenditures. The coefficient of determination is markedly higher in the regression involving anticipations than in that involving previous capital expenditures; with the fit only trivially improved when lagged capital expenditures are added to capital expenditure anticipations. Indeed, Table 6.2.5 reveals that a substantial portion of the role of lagged capital expenditures in explaining current expenditures relates to the varying normal investment-to-capital-stock ratio, or replacement requirements across firms. The 1953 ratio of depreciation charges to gross fixed assets, a proxy for (the inverse of) durability or replacement requirements, is markedly significant, and improves the fit otherwise obtained by anticipations alone by as much as does lagged investment.

Table 6.2.5 permits a somewhat closer examination of the underlying time series relation among capital expenditures, capital expenditure anticipations and lagged capital expenditures. Here we have results of pooled time series, still of individual firms, but pooled by each of our ten industry groups. While the broad outlines of the results already observed in the pooling of firms for all industries is confirmed, significant differences appear among industries. In each industry, it may be noted, the simple coefficient of determination between capital expenditures and capital expenditure anticipations is almost as high as that in the multiple regression. As might be expected, the coefficient of determination is highest among utilities, where capital expenditure plans are probably better formulated and involve firmer commitments. That the differences in coefficients among regressions are significant is confirmed by the F ratio involving the reduction in residual variance from having separate regression planes for each industry rather than a single regression plane for pooled observations of all industries.

Table 6.2.4 Capital Expenditures and Changes in Capital Expenditures as Functions of Previous Capital Expenditures, Capital Expenditure Anticipations and Anticipated Change in Capital Expenditures, Measured as Ratios of 1957 Gross Fixed Assets, Pooled Firm Cross Sections, 1955-68

(A) $$i_t = b_0 + b_1 i_{t-1} + b_2\, i_t^{t-1} + u_t$$

(B) $$\Delta i_t = b_0 + b_1(i_t^{t-1} - i_{t-1}) + u_t$$

(1) Variable or Statistic	(2)	(3)	(4)	(5)	(6) Means and Standard Deviations
	Regression Coefficients and Standard Errors				
	(A)	(A)	(A)	(B)	
Constant or i_t	.016	.040	.013	-.001	.098
	(.001)	(.001)	(.001)	(.001)	(.071)
i_{t-1}	---	.624	.108	---	.092
	---	(.013)	(.011)	---	(.066)
i_t^{t-1}	.807	---	.747	---	.101
	(.008)	---	(.010)	---	(.073)
$i_t^{t-1} - i_{t-1}$	---	---	---	.800	.009
	---	---	---	(.010)	(.061)
n (-87)	4697	4697	4697	4697	
r.d.f.	4558	4558	4557	4558	
$\hat{R}^2$	.700	.340	.706	.605	
F	10,656	2345	5488	6971	

Table 6.2.5 Capital Expenditures and Change in Capital Expenditures as a Function of Previous Capital Expenditures, Capital Expenditure Anticipations, and Anticipated Change in Capital Expenditures, Measured as Ratios of 1957 Gross Fixed Assets, and Ratio of 1953 Depreciation to 1953 Gross Fixed Assets, Pooled Annual Firm Cross Sections, 1955-68

(A) $$i_t = b_0 + b_1 d_{53} + b_2\, i_{t-1} + b_3\, i_t^{t-1} + u_t$$

(B) $$\Delta i_t = b_0 + b_1 (i_t^{t-1} - i_{t-1}) + b_2 d_{53} + u_t$$

(1) Variable or Statistic	(2)	(3)	(4)	(5)	(6) Means and Stand. Deviations
	Regression Coefficients and Standard Errors				
	(A)	(A)	(A)	(B)	
Constant or i_t	.007 (.002)	.009 (.002)	.023 (.002)	-.001 (.001)	.098 (.082)
d_{53}	.122 (.026)	.155 (.026)	.392 (.038)	-.010 (.025)	.053 (.023)
i_{t-1}	.101 (.011)	--- ---	.586 (.013)	--- ---	.092 (.066)
i_t^{t-1}	.740 (.010)	.794 (.008)	--- ---	--- ---	.101 (.073)
$i_t^{t-1} - i_{t-1}$	--- ---	--- ---	--- ---	.800 (.010)	.009 (.061)
n (-87)	4697	4697	4697	4697	
r.d.f.	4556	4557	4557	4557	
$\hat{R}^2$	.708	.703	.354	.605	
$\hat{r}^2_{i_t, i_t^{t-1}}$	.700	.700	.700	.700	
$r_\cdot^2$	.025	.007			
F	3683	5387	1252	3485	

N.B. "F" relates to multiple regression.

$\hat{R}^2$ = Adjusted or Unbiased Coefficient of Determination

$$r_\cdot^2 = (R^2 - r^2_{i_t, i_t^{t-1}}) / (1 - r^2_{i_t, i_t^{t-1}})$$

"F" relates to multiple regression.

Table 6.2.6 Capital Expenditures as a Function of Previous Capital Expenditures and Capital Expenditures Anticipations, Measured as Ratios of 1957 Gross Fixed Assets, Pooled Individual Firm Time Series by Industry, 1955-68

$$i_t = b_0 + b_1 i_{t-1} + b_2 i_t^{t-1} + u_t$$

(1)	(2)	(3)	(4)	(5)	(6)	(7)	(8)	(9)	(10)	(11)	(12)
	Regression Coefficients and Standard Errors										
Variable or Statistic	Primary Metals	Metal Working	Chemical Processing	Other Manufacturing	Mining	Utilities	Petroleum	Railroads	Stores	Comm. and Transportion (Excluding RR)	All Industries
Constant	.006	.021	.012	.018	.009	-.005	.005	.002	.041	.054	.018
	(.003)	(.002)	(.003)	(.003)	(.005)	(.002)	(.005)	(.001)	(.007)	(.018)	(.001)
i_{t-1}	.014	.005	-.062	.070	.054	.043	-.111	.084	.047	-.109	.001
	(.029)	(.025)	(.025)	(.028)	(.049)	(.022)	(.063)	(.042)	(.044)	(.067)	(.011)
i_t^{t-1}	.831	.761	.875	.762	.775	.988	1.023	.858	.645	.886	.790
	(.028)	(.022)	(.023)	(.025)	(.058)	(.019)	(.072)	(.042)	(.042)	(.065)	(.011)
$b_1 + b_2$	.846	.766	.814	.832	.829	1.031	.913	.943	.692	.776	.791
	(.033)	(.021)	(.024)	(.028)	(.056)	(.018)	(.056)	(.043)	(.048)	(.078)	(.011)
n (-87)	330	1255	690	791	136	485	198	250	420	119	4674
r.d.f.	297	1099	599	684	117	440	169	222	360	102	4107
$\hat{R}^2$	.773	.633	.751	.638	.675	.914	.640	.721	.449	.644	.642
$\hat{r}^2_{i_t, i_t^{t-1}}$	.773	.633	.749	.635	.674	.913	.636	.718	.449	.639	.642
$r^2_{\cdot}$	-.003	-.001	.008	.008	.002	.006	.012	.014	.000	.016	-.000
F	509	950	907	606	125	2345	153	291	148	95	3680

F(all-individual industries) = 4.74; $F_{.01}$ = 1.93.

6.3 Realizations Functions with Deflated (Normalized) Investment and Sales Changes

In Table 6.3.1 we turn again to variables deflated by lagged capital stock or the lagged average of sales. In this relatively normalized and less heteroscedastic set of relations, we find clearer confirmation of both the prime explanatory role of capital expenditure anticipations, and the further contribution of current values of sales change and profits variables which presumably post-date the anticipations. Both sales change and profits variables are positive and clearly significant in the firm and industry time series. The relative effect of sales change and profits variables, however, is not clearly indicated by the relative size of their coefficients, inasmuch as the variance of sales changes is considerably greater than that of profits, in these time series relations.

The major role of capital expenditure anticipations is underlined by the very small, and negative. coefficients of lagged capital expenditures. It is clear that the substantial explanatory power of capital expenditure anticipations cannot be explained by viewing them as merely a projection of previous capital expenditures. And one may note again that the coefficient of determination rises substantially if we move from observations involving individual firms to observations which are means of the individual firm observations within each industry. Along with this, it may be seen that the coefficient of capital expenditure anticipations in the industry time series is close to unity, perhaps again reflecting a washing-out of errors of individual firm anticipations.

Table 6.3.1 Capital Expenditures as a Function of Sales Changes, Profits, Capital Expenditure Anticipations, and Lagged Capital Expenditures, Measured as Ratios of Previous Year's Gross Fixed Assets or Previous Three Year Sales Average. 1955-68

$$i_t^* = b_0 + b_1 \Delta s_t^* + b_2 p_t^* + b_3 i_t^{t-1*} + b_4 i_{t-1}^* + u_t$$

(1) Variable or Statistic	(2) Regression Coefficients and Standard Errors: Firm Time Series	(3) Industry Time Series	(4) Aggregate Time Series	(5) Means and Standard Deviations From Firm Time Series
Constant	.003 (.001)	-.009 (.003)	-.013 (.004)	
i_t^*				.080 (.050)
Δs_t^*	.026 (.005)	.028 (.014)	.057 (.028)	.057 (.109)
p_t^*	.093 (.011)	.113 (.027)	.107 (.046)	.089 (.047)
i_t^{t-1*}	.823 (.011)	1.022 (.040)	.978 (.088)	.083 (.048)
i_{t-1}^*	-.016 (.010)	-.086 (.037)	-.005 (.088)	.082 (.051)
$b_1 + b_2$	.118 (.011)	.141 (.026)	.163 (.041)	
$b_3 + b_4$	.806 (.012)	.936 (.030)	.973 (.056)	
n (-75)	3766	139	14	
r.d.f.	3293	125	9	
$\hat{R}^2$	.687	.926	.983	
$\hat{r}^2_{i_t^*, i_t^{t-1*}}$	.674	.903	.943	
$r.^2$	.039	.244	.705	
F	1808	407	191	

Finally, in Table 6.3.1, we may note the results of our "aggregate time series" regression. Here observations are the means for all individual firms for each year; we treat these in effect as fourteen weighted observations. The fit is good -- the adjusted coefficient of determination is .983 -- and the parameter estimates are consistent with those obtained in the individual firm and industry time series relations. The underlying factors at work appear to be economy-wide in nature.

Table 6.3.2 treats cross section relations using the same data, but with the addition of the 1953 depreciation-to-gross fixed assets ratio which, as a constant over time could not be used in the time series. We may note first that in all cases, but particularly in the industry cross section, the great bulk of the variance in capital expenditures is accounted for by capital expenditure anticipations. Further, as we move from the firm cross section within industries to the industry cross section, the coefficient of capital expenditure anticipations rises sharply, to the neighborhood of unity. As we have noted previously, regressions on industry means may generally involve a washing out of errors or transitory factors found in variance within industries. The differences among regressions is highly significant, as indicated by the F ratio derived from the reduction of residual variance with separate planes for the within-industry and across-industry-mean regressions.

Table 6.3.3 returns to time series analysis on an individual industry basis. While results follow a pattern fairly similar to that already noted in the pooled regressions for firms in all industries in Table 6.3.1, differences between industries are statistically significant. As noted

Table 6.3.2

Capital Expenditures as a Function of Sales Changes, Profits, Depreciation, Capital Expenditure Anticipations and Previous Capital Expenditures, All Except Depreciation Measured as Ratios of Previous Year's Gross Fixed Assets or Previous Three Year Sales Average, 1955-68

$$i_t^* = b_0 + b_1 \Delta s_t^* + b_2 p_t^* + b_3 d_{53} + b_4 i_t^{t-1*} + b_5 i_{t-1}^* + u_t$$

(1)	(2)	(3)	(4)	(5)
	Regression Coefficients and Standard Errors			Means and Standard Deviations From Firm Cross Sections Across Industries
Variable or Statistic	Firm Cross Sections: Within Industries	Firm Cross Sections: Across Industries	Industry Cross Section	
Constant	.005	.001	-.003	
	(.001)	(.001)	(.002)	
				.080
				(.061)
Δs_t^*	.029	.029	.013	.057
	(.005)	(.005)	(.019)	(.106)
p_t^*	.040	.032	.019	.089
	(.006)	(.006)	(.018)	(.087)
d_{53}	.049	.069	-.035	.053
	(.023)	(.019)	(.058)	(.029)
i_t^{t-1*}	.781	.810	1.046	.083
	(.010)	(.010)	(.049)	(.062)
i_{t-1}^*	.035	.040	-.056	.081
	(.010)	(.010)	(.046)	(.062)
$b_1 + b_2$	.069	.061	.032	
	(.007)	(.007)	(.025)	
$b_4 + b_5$	.816	.850	.991	
	(.010)	(.010)	(.032)	
n (-75)	3803	3803	139	
r.d.f.	3659	3784	120	
$\hat{R}^2$	.713	.774	.954	
$\hat{r}^2_{i_t^*, i_t^{t-1*}}$	.704	.766	.954	
$r_.^2$	.031	.035	.007	
F	1818	2603	520	

$F[(3)-(2)-(4)] = 15.61; \quad F_{.01} = 3.02.$

Table 6.3.3 Capital Expenditures as a Function of Sales Changes, Profits, Capital Expenditure Anticipations and Previous Capital Expenditures, All Measured as Ratios of Previous Year's Gross Fixed Assets or Previous Three Year Sales Average, Firm Time Series by Industry, 1955-68

$$i_t^* = b_0 + b_1 \Delta s_t^* + b_2 p_t^* + b_3 i_t^{t-1*} + b_4 i_{t-1}^* + u_t$$

(1)	(2)	(3)	(4)	(5)	(6)	(7)	(8)	(9)	(10)	(11)
	Regression Coefficients and Standard Errors									
Variable or Statistic	Primary Metals	Metal Working	Chemical Processing	All Other Manu-facturing	Mining	Utilities	Petro-leum	Rail-roads	Stores	Transportation and Communication
Aggregate Dummy	.001	.000	-.000	.004	.001	.007	.003	.004	.007	.033
	(.002)	(.002)	(.002)	(.002	(.003)	(.002)	(.002)	(.002)	(.002)	(.003)
Constant Term	-.002	.003	-.003	.008	.014	-.005	-.013	.003	.000	.011
	(.003)	(.003)	(.003)	(.004)	(.009)	(.003)	(.005)	(.002)	(.013)	(.016)
Δs_t^*	.006	.034	.019	.043	.008	-.001	.024	.016	.009	.105
	(.010)	(.008)	(.009)	(.014)	(.027)	(.005)	(.015)	(.006)	(.036)	(.079)
p_t^*	.092	.094	.079	.072	.046	.129	.152	-.047	.203	.432
	(.043)	(.017)	(.030)	(.023)	(.077)	(.100)	(.095)	(.057)	(.083)	(.238)
i_t^{t-1*}	.826	.790	.840	.760	.737	.946	1.041	.846	.806	.853
	(.024)	(.025)	(.026)	(.030)	(.075)	(.018)	(.056)	(.040)	(.055)	(.059)
i_{t-1}^*	.040	-.022	.024	.006	-.038	.026	-.059	.100	-.055	-.046
	(.025)	(.022)	(.024)	(.030)	(.055)	(.013)	(.043)	(.040)	(.047)	(.059)
$b_1 + b_2$	.098	.128	.098	.115	.054	.128	.175	-.031	.213	.537
	(.041)	(.017)	(.029)	(.025)	(.077)	(.100)	(.094)	(.055)	(.085)	(.219)
$b_3 + b_4$	.866	.768	.865	.766	.699	.972	.982	.947	.751	.806
	(.025)	(.025)	(.030)	(.038)	(.079)	(.017)	(.047)	(.046)	(.052)	(.076)
n (-75)	306	948	580	554	101	460	169	239	294	115
r.d.f.	271	819	503	476	82	413	142	209	244	98
$\hat{R}^2$	.874	.661	.739	.636	.541	.902	.825	.752	.529	.723
$r^2_{i_t^*, i_t^{t-1*}}$	.872	.634	.733	.622	.552	.902	.819	.744	.518	.707
$r_.^2$	.020	.072	.025	.039	-.023	.005	.031	.031	.022	.055
F	478	402	361	211	26	965	173	162	71	68

F (All Minus Individual Industries) = 2.34; $F_{.01} = 1.65$

earlier in Table 6.2.4, coefficients of determination, along with the regression coefficients of capital expenditure anticipations, differ from industry to industry. Both are again high for utilities, and this time for primary metals and petroleum as well. Curiously, the utilities results include a high coefficient for current profits along with a coefficient of virtually zero for current sales change.

For highly demand-motivated utility capital expenditure programs, changes in sales of a short run nature might do little to modify predominantly long run capital expenditure plans. The somewhat high current profit coefficient of .129 reflects the relatively low variance over time in profits, which also contributes to a large standard error; the coefficient of determination is no higher for the multiple regression than it is for the relation involving only capital expenditures and capital expenditure anticipations.

6.4 The Role of Sales Expectations and Realizations

Table 6.4.1 summarizes the underlying data used in relations involving capital expenditures, capital expenditure realizations, sales realizations, and sales and profits changes. By including the McGraw-Hill responses regarding expected sales changes, we may test the hypothesis that the difference between capital expenditures and capital expenditure anticipations relates to the difference between actual and expected sales changes.[1] A comparison of columns (4) and (5) in Table 6.4.1 lends credence to the hypothesis that there is a positive relation between these variables. The regression results in Table 6.4.2 offers a more precise view.

---

[1] cf. Eisner [1962 and 1965].

Table 6.4.1 Capital Expenditures, Capital Expenditure Realizations, Sales Realizations, Sales and Profits Changes, Measured as Ratios of Previous Year's Gross Fixed Assets or Previous Three Year Sales Average, Means by Years, 1955-68

(1) Year (t)	(2) n	(3) i^*_t	(4) $i^*_t - i^{t-1*}_t$	(5) $\Delta s^*_t - s^{t-1}_t$	(6) Δs^*_t	(7) Δp^*_t
1955	131	.101	.004	.028	.099	.019
1956	159	.122	.000	-.023	.065	-.013
1957	163	.109	-.007	-.040	.038	-.025
1958	133	.069	-.015	-.048	-.044	-.033
1959	264	.074	-.002	-.007	.089	.007
1960	203	.071	-.007	-.054	.024	-.016
1961	201	.057	-.005	-.019	.024	-.006
1962	263	.061	-.006	-.002	.075	.005
1963	254	.063	-.003	.015	.066	.005
1964	254	.072	-.000	.023	.085	.008
1965	213	.086	.002	.025	.087	.001
1966	240	.095	.000	.011	.085	.004
1967	143	.083	-.002	-.017	.043	-.018
1968	148	.073	-.004	-.012	.066	-.005
All Years	2769	.079	-.003	-.006	.061	-.003

Table 6.4.2 Capital Expenditure Realizations as a Function of Sales Realizations, Measured as Ratios of Previous Three Year Sales Average, 1955-68

$$i^*_t - i^{t-1*}_t = b_0 + b_1 (\Delta s^*_t - s^{t-1}_t) + u_t$$

(1)	(2)	(3)	(4)	(5)	(6)	(7)
Variable	Regression Coefficients and Standard Errors					
or	Time Series			Firm Cross	Firm	Industry
Statistic	Firm	Industry	Aggregate	Section	Overall	Overall
Constant	-.003	-.003	-.002	-.003	-.003	-.003
	(.001)	(.001)	(.001)	(.001)	(.001)	(.001)
$\Delta s^*_t - s^{t-1}_t$	.037	.062	.123	.022	.029	.059
	(.007)	(.018)	(.029)	(.006)	(.006)	(.018)
n (-70)	2707	116	14	2769	2769	116
r.d.f.	2301	105	12	2754	2767	114
$\hat{R}^2$	.013	.093	.569	.004	.007	.077
F	31.48	11.85	18.16	11.80	21.38	10.57

Table 6.4.2 relates capital expenditure realizations to sales realizations; that is, the difference between capital expenditures and capital expenditure anticipations is taken as a function of the difference between actual and expected sales changes. Results are compared for a considerable number of regressions involving firms in all industries, all industries in the economy, and all years in the sample. First, in the individual firm time series, there is a significant positive coefficient of .037 for the sales realization variable, but a very low coefficient of determination, .013. Only a small portion of the time series variance in capital expenditure realizations can be explained by sales realizations. The industry time series indicates both a somewhat higher coefficient of the sales realization variable, and a higher coefficient of determination, .093. Finally, the aggregate time series shows a still higher coefficient of sales realization variable, .122, and a likewise higher coefficient of determination, .569.

Turning to cross sections, we find a significant but very small coefficient for sales realizations, and a very small coefficient of determination. The coefficients are similarly small in the overall individual firm regression, but somewhat higher in the overall industry regression, which again presumably tends to wash out some of the errors or erratic components of the variables.

Further light on the relation is thrown, however, when we include actual sales changes along with the sales realization variable. The results of a set of regressions for firm time series, firm cross sections and industry time series involving actual sales change and profits are presented in Table 6.4.3. It may be noted immediately, in the firm time series, that the positive role of the sales realization variable is now taken over by current sales changes and current and lagged profits. By

Table 6.4.3 Capital Expenditures or Capital Expenditure Realizations as a Function of Sales Changes, Sales Anticipations, Sales Realizations, Profits and Capital Expenditure Anticipations, Measured as Ratios of Previous Year's Gross Fixed Assets or Previous Three Year Sales Average, Firm and Industry Time Series and Firm Cross Section, 1955-68

$$\text{(F)}\quad i_t^* = b_0 + b_1\Delta s_t^* + b_2\Delta s_{t-1}^* + b_3 s_t^{t-1} + b_4 p_t^* + b_5 p_{t-1}^* + b_6 i_t^{t-1*} + u_t$$

$$\text{(I)}\quad i_t^* = b_0 + b_1\Delta s_t^* + b_2\Delta s_{t-1}^* + b_3 s_t^{t-1} + b_4 p_t^* + b_5 i_t^{t-1*} + u_t$$

$$\text{(H)}\quad i_t^* - i_t^{t-1*} = b_0 + b_1\Delta s_t^* + b_2(\Delta s_t^* - s_t^{t-1}) + b_3 p_t^* + u_t$$

(1) Variable or Statistic	(2)	(3)	(4)	(5)	(6)	(7)	(8)	(9)	(10)
	Regression Coefficients and Standard Errors								
	Firm Time Series			Industry Time Series			Firm Cross Section		
	(F)	(I)	(H)	(F)	(I)	(H)	(F)	(I)	(H)
Constant	-.002	.001	-.009	-.013	-.013	-.013	.004	.005	-.007
	(.002)	(.001)	(.001)	(.003)	(.003)	(.003)	(.001)	(.001)	(.001)
Δs_t^*	.034	.026	.026	.054	.056	.064	.030	.026	.022
	(.007)	(.007)	(.009)	(.022)	(.018)	(.022)	(.007)	(.006)	(.008)
Δs_{t-1}^*	.001	.005	---	.011	.010	---	.005	.007	---
	(.005)	(.005)	---	(.011)	(.011)	---	(.005)	(.005)	---
s_t^{t-1}	.003	.004	---	.010	.009	---	.015	.015	---
	(.009)	(.009)	---	(.026)	(.026)	---	(.009)	(.009)	---
$\Delta s_t^* - s_t^{t-1}$	---	---	.010	---	---	-.003	---	---	.000
	---	---	(.010)	---	---	(.026)	---	---	(.009)
p_t^*	.069	.114	.049	.102	.091	.068	.015	.047	.022
	(.016)	(.014)	(.013)	(.064)	(.035)	(.029)	(.015)	(.007)	(.008)
p_{t-1}^*	.080	---	---	-.014	---	---	.036	---	---
	(.016)	---	---	(.063)	---	---	(.014)	---	---
i_t^{t-1*}	.784	.801	---	.961	.958	---	.811	.815	---
	(.013)	(.013)	---	(.038)	(.034)	---	(.010)	(.010)	---
$\Sigma\, \Delta s^*$ coeff.	.035	.032	---	.064	.066	---	.034	.032	---
	(.009)	(.009)	---	(.023)	(.021)	---	(.008)	(.008)	---
$\Sigma\, p^*$ coeff.	.149	---	---	.089	---	---	.051	---	---
	(.015)	---	---	(.036)	---	---	(.008)	---	---
n (-70)	2707	2707	2707	116	116	116	2769	2769	2769
r.d.f.	2296	2297	2299	100	101	103	2749	2750	2752
$\hat{R}^2$	.691	.688	.024	.929	.930	.221	.734	.734	.010
$r_{p_t^*, i_t^{t-1*}}$	.671	.671	.671	.909	.909	.909	.725	.725	.725
r^2	.062	.052	-1.967	.218	.226	-7.554	.035	.033	2.600
F	860	1016	19.60	232	281	11.01	1271	1521	10.04

way of possible explanation, while it is the difference between actual experience and expectations regarding the determining variables which properly relates to the difference between actual and anticipate capital expenditures, there is some tendency to anticipate that "tomorrow will be like today." Given the fair amount of inaccuracy in the sales expectation variable, it is perhaps not very surprising that the differences between current and previous actual sales prove more relevant than those between the current level of actual sales and the level previously announced as expected. Similarly, the positive coefficients of profits variables would suggest that when profits are high they tend to be higher than expected, and capital expenditures then turn out to be somewhat higher than anticipated.

Generally similar results are to be noted in the industry time series, except that the coefficient of capital expenditure anticipations and the coefficient of determination are higher. In the firm cross section we note fairly corroborative results, with a somewhat lesser role for profits. This finding is roughly consistent with results noted elsewhere with regard to arguments of the investment function itself, where past profits had less of a role in cross sections than in time series.

Table 6.4.4 compares results among overall regressions with various combinations of current and lagged sales change and profits variables and the depreciation ratio. It is apparent that current rather than lagged sales changes improve the fit of the relation including capital expenditure anticipations. Lagged profits, however, while fairly substitutable with current profits, seem to perform at least trivially better. This may relate to a tendency for higher current capital expenditures to depress the accountin

Table 6.4.4 Capital Expenditures as a Function of Sales Changes, Profits, Depreciation, Sales Expectations and Capital Expenditure Anticipations, All Except Depreciation Measured as Ratios of Previous Year's Gross Fixed Assets or Previous Three Year Sales Average, Firm Overall Regression, 1955-68

$$i_t^* = b_0 + b_1 \Delta s_t^* + b_2 \Delta s_{t-1}^* + b_3 p_t^* + b_4 p_{t-1}^* + b_5 d_{53} + b_6 s_t^{t-1} + b_7 i_t^{t-1*} + u_t$$

(1) Variable or Statistic	(2)	(3)	(4)	(5)	(6)
	Regression Coefficients and Standard Errors				
Constant	.000	.000	.001	.003	.003
	(.001)	(.001)	(.001)	(.001)	(.001)
Δs_t^*	.034	.038	.031	.038	.031
	(.006)	(.006)	(.006)	(.006)	(.006)
Δs_{t-1}^*	.007	.006	---	.006	---
	(.005)	(.005)	---	(.005)	---
p_t^*	.022	---	.049	---	.052
	(.014)	---	(.007)	---	(.007)
p_{t-1}^*	.029	.047	---	.051	---
	(.014)	(.007)	---	(.007)	---
d_{53}	.073	.073	.076	---	---
	(.023)	(.023)	(.023)	---	---
s_t^{t-1}	.014	.014	.013	.015	.015
	(.009)	(.009)	(.009)	(.009)	(.009)
i_t^{t-1*}	.811	.810	.817	.820	.828
	(.011)	(.011)	(.010)	(.010)	(.010)
$\Sigma \Delta s^*$ coefficients	.041	.044	---	.044	---
	(.008)	(.008)	---	(.008)	---
$\Sigma\, p^*$ coefficients	.051	---	---	---	---
	(.007)	---	---	---	---
n (-70)	2769	2769	2769	2769	2769
r.d.f.	2761	2762	2763	2763	2764
$\hat{R}^2$	.754	.754	.754	.753	.753
$\hat{r}^2_{i_t^*, i_t^{t-1*}}$	.742	.742	.742	.742	.742
$r_.^2$	.047	.047	.045	.043	.042
F	1213	1414	1694	1689	2106

measure of current profits as start-up costs and initial depreciation are charged against income. The 1953 depreciation ratio, taken as a measure of durability, apparently does little to improve the fit although its significantly positive coefficient suggests some tendency for capital expenditures to be higher relative to anticipations to the extent that they involve capital of shorter than average life -- perhaps equipment as opposed to plant.

Table 6.4.5 taken from regressions excluding the sales expectations variable, is otherwise comparable to Table 6.4.1 but deals with a greater body of data. It may again be noted that capital expenditures, this time over 3756 observations, were slightly less than capital expenditure anticipations. And there appears to be some positive relation between changes in sales and/or changes in profits and the excess of capital expenditures over capital expenditure anticipations.

This relation may be seen more clearly in the regressions summarized in Table 6.4.6. Here the firm time series reveals distinctly positive coefficients for current sales changes and current and, to a lesser extent, past profits variables. Higher coefficients of determination and higher regression coefficients are to be found in the industry time series. In the industry time series,even after adjustment for lost degrees of freedom, some 21 percent of the variance in capital expenditures not explained by capital expenditure anticipations is explained by the addition of current sales change and profit variables. The result is again less marked in the firm cross sections but here, once more, the current sales change and profits

Table 6.4.5 Capital Expenditures, Capital Expenditure Realizations, Sales Changes and Profits Changes, Measured as Ratios of Previous Year's Gross Fixed Assets or Previous Three Year Sales Average, Means by Years, 1955-68

(1) Year (t)	(2) n	(3) i^*_t	(4) $i^*_t - {}_t i^{t-1*}$	(5) Δs^*_t	(6) Δp^*_t
1955	199	.096	.006	.095	.019
1956	276	.114	.001	.067	-.010
1957	284	.106	-.005	.038	-.018
1958	250	.074	-.009	-.042	-.024
1959	323	.075	-.002	.086	.007
1960	344	.075	-.009	.028	-.016
1961	339	.064	-.006	.025	-.005
1962	317	.061	-.006	.080	.004
1963	276	.061	-.003	.067	.005
1964	276	.071	.000	.086	.008
1965	245	.083	.001	.086	.001
1966	276	.093	.001	.082	.004
1967	171	.084	-.003	.041	-.018
1968	180	.073	-.004	.067	-.005
All Years	3756	.080	-.003	.057	-.003

Table 6.4.6 Capital Expenditures as a Function of Sales Changes, Profits and Capital Expenditure Anticipations, Measured as Ratios of Previous Year's Gross Fixed Assets or Previous Three Year Sales Average, Firm and Industry Time Series and Firm Cross Sections, 1955-68

$$(F)\quad i^*_t = b_0 + b_1\,\Delta s^*_t + b_2\Delta s^*_{t-1} + b_3\,p^*_t + b_4\,p^*_{t-1} + b_5\,i^{t-1*}_t + u_t$$

$$(I)\quad i^*_t = b_0 + b_1\,\Delta s^*_t + b_2\Delta s^*_{t-1} + b_3\,i^{t-1*}_t + u_t$$

$$(H)\quad i^*_t = b_0 + b_1\,\Delta s^*_t + b_2\Delta p^*_t + b_3\,i^{t-1*}_t + u_t$$

(1)	(2)	(3)	(4)	(5)	(6)	(7)	(8)	(9)	(10)
Variable	Regression Coefficient and Standard Errors								
or	Firm Time Series			Industry Time Series			Firm Cross Section		
Statistic	(F)	(I)	(H)	(F)	(I)	(H)	(F)	(I)	(H)
Constant	.000	.010	.002	-.012	-.007	-.012	.005	.008	.005
	(.001)	(.001)	(.001)	(.003)	(.003)	(.003)	(.001)	(.001)	(.001)
Δs^*_t	.028	.035	.021	.029	.060	.042	.032	.035	.030
	(.005)	(.005)	(.005)	(.017)	(.014)	(.014)	(.005)	(.005)	(.005)
Δs^*_{t-1}	-.000	.006	---	.009	-.002	---	.006	.010	---
	(.004)	(.004)	---	(.011)	(.012)	---	(.005)	(.005)	---
p^*_t	.086	---	.124	.190	---	.118	.021	---	.042
	(.014)	---	(.012)	(.059)	---	(.030)	(.013)	---	(.006)
p^*_{t-1}	.066	---	---	-.084	---	---	.022	---	---
	(.013)	---	---	(.061)	---	---	(.012)	---	---
i^{t-1*}_t	.779	.821	.793	.970	1.005	.951	.829	.841	.834
	(.011)	(.010)	(.011)	(.037)	(.030)	(.030)	(.008)	(.008)	(.008)
$\Sigma\Delta s^*$ coeff	.027	.041	---	.038	.058	---	.038	.045	---
	(.007)	(.007)	---	(.020)	(.019)	---	(.007)	(.007)	---
$\Sigma\ p^*$ coeff	.152	---	---	.107	---	---	.043	---	---
	(.013)	---	---	(.033)	---	---	(.006)	---	---
n (-98)	3715	3715	3715	139	139	139	3756	3756	3756
r.d.f.	3249	3251	3251	124	126	126	3737	3739	3739
$\hat{R}^2$	.678	.665	.676	.915	.904	.915	.763	.760	.763
$\hat{r}^2_{i^*_t,\,i^{t-1*}_t}$	.660	.660	.660	.891	.891	.891	.757	.757	.757
$r^2_{.}$	.054	.016	.048	.215	.119	.214	.028	.015	.027
F	1373	2156	2264	277	407	461	2415	3956	4019

variables contribute to the explanation of variance of capital expenditures beyond what can be accounted for by capital expenditure anticipations. Overall regressions analogous to those reported in Table 6.4.4, but excluding the sales realizations variable, generally confirm this contribution of current sales change and profits variables.

The utility of current sales changes as opposed to sales realizations in accounting for the difference between capital expenditures and capital expenditure anticipations is further confirmed by regressions using the same observations as Table 6.4.2. In firm time series, where the coefficients of determination are very low in the regressions involving either sales changes or sales realizations, there is little basis for choice between these two variables. In both the industry and aggregate time series the fit is considerably better in the case of sales changes; in the industry time series the sales change regression coefficient is somewhat higher, but in the aggregate time series the coefficient of the sales change variable is somewhat lower than that of the sales realization variable. The sales change variable is trivially better in the firm cross section and firm overall regressions where the fits are very poor, and somewhat better in the industry overall regression.

The fairly poor firm time series relation involving sales realizations is further explored for individual industries. The generally poor fits at the individual industry level do (barely) differ significantly at the .05 probability level, apparently because of the relatively high regression coefficient and coefficient of determination in the large group of metal working firms.

6.5. Accuracy of Anticipations, By Year and Industry

A measure of the accuracy of short anticipations as a forecast of actual expenditures is to be found in the Theil inequality coefficients for individual firms by years and industries, shown in Table 6.5.2. The overall coefficient was .538, varying by industry from a low of .280 in utilities to a high of .648 in "stores." Differences by year varied from a recession low of .415 in 1958 to a Viet-Nam escalation high of .719 in 1965. Firms were perhaps better in anticipating cutbacks than booms. In only six of the 139 industry-years for which observations were available were the inequality coefficients greater than unity, that is, would a naive forecast that expenditures would remain the same in the coming year have been more accurate than the capital expenditure anticipations.

Table 6.5.2 makes clear that departures from equality (unity) can be ascribed overwhelmingly to covariance components. Individual firm errors in anticipations were to a very considerable extent offsetting however, so that means and variance components were low and inequality coefficients themselves were lower when observations consisted of group means.

Table 6.5.1 Short Run Capital Expenditure Realizations: Inequality Coefficients (U), by Year and Industry, 1962-68

$$U = \left[\frac{\Sigma(a-p)^2}{\Sigma a^2}\right]^{\frac{1}{2}}, \quad \text{where } a = i_t - i_{t-1} \text{ and } a - p = i_t - i_t^{t-1}$$

(1) Year	(2) Primary Metals	(3) Metal Working	(4) Chemical Process.	(5) All Other Mfg.	(6) Mining	(7) Utilities	(8) Petroleum	(9) Rail-Roads	(10) Stores	(11) Transportation	(12) All Indust
1955	.801	.801	.626	.584	.604	---	.479	.778	1.121	.305	.594
1956	.383	.521	.450	.507	.471	.371	.549	.507	.607	.244	.466
1957	.457	.513	.391	.323	.547	.419	.233	.511	.484	.318	.453
1958	.183	.465	.400	.681	.318	.385	.377	.231	.518	.470	.415
1959	.347	.637	.726	.863	.857	.272	.889	.343	.362	.387	.524
1960	.396	.780	.464	.509	.580	.129	.962	.658	.620	.617	.590
1961	.466	.614	.517	.486	.669	.465	1.458	.284	.703	.606	.605
1962	.366	.482	.430	.771	.708	.456	.937	.593	.652	.193	.519
1963	.656	.682	.659	.716	1.324	.571	.443	.714	.655	.707	.677
1964	.433	.686	.533	.682	.389	.390	.797	.351	.908	.634	.662
1965	.416	.812	.673	.654	.976	.462	.507	.647	.864	.702	.719
1966	1.107	.458	.553	.331	.311	.366	.568	.566	1.646	.384	.496
1967	.679	.530	.502	.555	.121	.417	.672	.325	.432	1.933	.460
1968	.517	.641	.511	.832	.184	.285	.309	.262	.760	.350	.582
All Years	.432	.592	.507	.588	.479	.280	.499	.478	.648	.439	.538

Table 6.5.2 Short Run Capital Expenditure Realizations: Inequality Coefficients (U) and Bias (U^m), Variance (U^s) and Co-variance (U^c) Proportions, Individual Firms by Industry and Years, Overall Groups,* 1955-68

(1) Individual Firms	(2)	(3)	(4)	(5)
By Industry	U	U^m	U^s	U^c
Primary Metals	.432	.086	.013	.901
Metal Working	.592	.013	.021	.966
Chemical Processing	.507	.048	.000	.952
All Other Manufacturing	.588	.004	.000	.996
Mining	.479	.016	.017	.967
Utilities	.280	.086	.000	.914
Petroleum	.499	.052	.093	.855
Railroads	.478	.002	.000	.998
Stores	.648	.004	.044	.952
Transportation	.439	.001	.024	.975
By Years				
1955	.594	.012	.039	.949
1966	.466	.001	.002	.997
1957	.453	.026	.000	.974
1958	.415	.082	.014	.904
1959	.524	.004	.001	.995
1960	.590	.056	.036	.907
1961	.605	.034	.001	.965
1962	.519	.037	.002	.960
1963	.677	.004	.009	.987
1964	.662	.000	.025	.975
1965	.719	.000	.008	.992
1966	.496	.000	.008	.992
1967	.460	.014	.014	.972
1968	.582	.020	.062	.917
All Years and Industries	.538	.009	.011	.980
Group Means				
Industry-Years	.401	.122	.155	.722
Years	.368	.380	.286	.334

*

$$U = \left[\frac{\Sigma(a-p)^2}{\Sigma a^2}\right]^{\frac{1}{2}}, \qquad U^m = \frac{(\bar{a} - \bar{p})^2}{\frac{1}{n}\Sigma(a-p)^2}$$

$$U^s = \frac{(\sigma_a - \sigma_p)}{\frac{1}{n}\Sigma(a-p)^2}, \qquad U^c = \frac{2(1-r)\sigma_a\sigma_p}{\frac{1}{n}\Sigma(a-p)^2},$$

where $a = i_t - i_{t-1}$ and $p = i_t^{t-1} - t_{t-1}$.

Longer Term Capital Expenditure Anticipations*

7.0 Introduction

What are the determinants of long run capital expenditure anticipations? How well can we explain their variance over time? What accounts for differences between firms and between industries? What role do long run capital expenditure anticipations have in the determination of eventual actual expenditures? How accurate are long run capital expenditure anticipations? --We focus on these questions in the analysis of data built around McGraw-Hill capital expenditure surveys of the years 1959-69.

The underlying data consist of responses to survey questionnaires sent out generally in March of each year. At this time firms are asked, "How much did you invest in new plant and equipment in United States in" the recently completed year, which we designate as the year t. They are also asked how much they "now plan to invest in new plant and equipment in" the immediately ensuing year, t + 1, and in the three subsequent years, t + 2, t + 3, and t + 4. The focus of our inquiry is the anticipations of the year t + 4, designated I^t_{t+4}, the superscript referring to the year for which the survey collects information on actual expenditures. (It should be recognized that the anticipations are actually expressed early in the year t + 1.)

Along with the survey data on capital expenditures and capital expenditure anticipations, we utilize responses to questions regarding expected percent changes in the physical volume of sales over the ensuing year and the subsequent three year period,

*This chapter stems from but is a substantially revised version of "Longer Term Capital Expenditure Anticipations: A Micro-Economic Analysis," presented to the Tenth CIRET Conference in Brussels, September 1971.

$$s^t_{t+1} = \frac{S^t_{t+1} - S_t}{S_t} \quad \text{and} \quad s^t_{t+1,4} = \frac{S^t_{t+4} - S^t_{t+1}}{S^t_{t+1}}$$

as well as the ratio of the operating rate of capacity to the preferred utilization of capacity, u^c.

We again make use of data from financial sources, particularly Moody's Manuals, to supplement McGraw-Hill survey responses with further information as to actual sales, profits after taxes, P, depreciation charges, D, and gross fixed assets, K, which last is used as a deflator for profits, depreciation, and capital expenditure variables. Complete observations are available for over 400 firms involving capital expenditures of two or more of each of the 11 years from 1958 to 1968, but some observations have been eliminated because of variables which as transformed for use in the regressions had "extreme values" outside of acceptable intervals. A full set of "Definitions and Sources of Variables and Intervals for Acceptable Values" is to be found below.

7.1 Determinants of Long Run Capital Expenditure Plans

As we shall note below, the long run capital expenditure plans, which we take to be the four year ahead anticipations, i^t_{t+4} $(=I^t_{t+4}/K_{57})$, are in large part incomplete. Respondents do not know four years in advance, or do not report, about a third of capital expenditures ultimately undertaken. Yet these plans reveal essentially the same determinants as those found in our studies of current capital expenditures and the much fuller short run anticipations. In a pooled individual firm time series regression[1] of long run capital expenditure plans on sales changes and profits (column 4 of Table 7.1.1), the coefficient of determination is .251, and there is again substantial evidence of an accelerator effect in a sum of sales change coefficients of .319. Similarly, there is once more a strong positive role for current and immediate past profits, if anything greater than for current expenditures, in determining the timing of long run anticipations of capital expenditures. The role of both sets of variables and the coefficient of determination are again considerably greater in industry time series, where individual firm errors and disturbances would appear to wash out.

Cross sections which use as observations the means of each firm's observations over all years as well as cross sections which use means of observations of all firms within an industry within a given year, with observations in the latter case pooled for all years, also appear to wash out errors and random disturbances. In particular, they show higher coefficients for sales change or accelerator coefficients, as was noted in relations seeking to explain actual capital expenditures. Profits coefficients, however, are markedly smaller in the cross sections, again suggesting that interfirm differences in profits do not explain much of the long run or "permanent" rate of investment.

---

[1]See Appendix for statement of deviations used in the various regressions.

Definitions and Sources of Variables and Intervals for Acceptable Values

Symbol	Description[1]	Source[2]	Acceptable Interval[3]
$i_t = \frac{I_t}{K_{57}}$	Capital Expenditures in 1954 Dollars as Ratio of 1957 Gross Fixed Assets	MH/FD	[.6,0)
$i_{tAV} = (i_{t+1} + 2i_t + i_{t-1})/4$	Weighted, Centered Average Capital Expenditure Ratio		
$i^t_{t+1} = \frac{I^t_{t+1}}{K_{57}}$	Capital Expenditure Anticipations One Year Ahead as Ratio of 1957 Gross Fixed Assets	MH/FD	[.6,0)
$i^t_{t+4} = \frac{I^t_{t+4}}{K_{57}}$	Capital Expenditure Anticipations Four Years Ahead as Ratio of 1957 Gross Fixed Assets	MH/FD	[.7,0)
$\Delta s_t = \frac{3(S_t - S_{t-1})}{S_{56} + S_{57} + S_{58}}$	Relative Sales Change Ratio, Price Deflated, 1956-58 Denominator	FD	[.7,-.6]
$p_t = \frac{P_t}{K_{57}}$	Net Profits in 1954 Dollars as Ratio of 1957 Gross Fixed Assets	FD	[.7,-.4]
$d_{53} = \frac{D_{53}}{K_{53}}$	Depreciation Charges as Ratio of 1953 Gross Fixed Assets	FD	[.2,0]
$s^t_{t+1,4} = \frac{S^t_{t+4} - S^t_{t+1}}{S^t_{t+1}}$	Long Run Expected Sales Change Over Three Years. (See Summary Symbols and Descriptions List at End of Text.)	MH	[1,-.6]
$s^t_{t+1} = \frac{S^t_{t+1} - S_t}{S_t}$	Short Run Sales Expectations = Expected Percent Change in Physical Volume of Sales from McGraw-Hill Survey, Converted to Pure Decimal	MH	[.7,-.6]
$u^c_t = \frac{u^a_t}{u^p_t}$	Ratio of Actual to Preferred Rate of Utilization of Capacity	MH	[1.3,.3]

Footnotes see next page

[1]The variables I_t and I^t_{t+4}, except where indicated otherwise, and I^t_{t+1}, P and S were price deflated, all except the last by a capital goods price index relating to the period of the ex post variable or, in the case of anticipatory variables, to the period in which the anticipations were formulated. Sales (S) were deflated by indices relevant to the industry-group in which firms were classified. The survey questions as to expected sales changes relate to the "physical volume of sales" and responses were therefore not price-deflated. Depreciation charges (D) and gross fixed assets (K) were also not price deflated.

[2]MH = McGraw-Hill surveys; FD = Financial data, generally from Moody's; MH/FD = Numerator from McGraw-Hill denominator from financial data.

3 [U,L] = Closed interval, including upper and lower bounds.
[U,L) = Interval including upper bound but not lower bound.

Table 7.1.1 - Determinants of Long Run Capital Expenditure Plans

$$i^{t}_{t+4} = b_0 + \sum_{j=1}^{7} b_j \Delta s_{t+1-j} + \sum_{j=8}^{9} b_j p_{t+8-j} + b_{10} d_{53} + u_t \qquad t = 1958 \text{ to } 1968$$

(1)	(2)	(3)	(4)	(5)	(6)	(7)	(8)
	Regression Coefficients and Standard Errors						
	Firms			Industry	Firm Cross Sections		Industry
Variable or Statistic	Overall	Cross Section of Firm Means	Time Series	Time Series	Across Industries	Within Industries	Cross Section
Constant	.051 (.002)	.053 (.018)	.040 (.003)	.011 (.013)	.024 (.003)	.022 (.004)	.025 (.013)
Δs_t	.080 (.012)	.027 (.077)	.061 (.010)	.082 (.045)	.061 (.012)	.062 (.012)	.049 (.077)
Δs_{t-1}	.076 (.012)	.033 (.088)	.039 (.010)	.073 (.040)	.051 (.012)	.047 (.012)	.103 (.076)
Δs_{t-2}	.105 (.012)	.219 (.082)	.063 (.009)	.081 (.038)	.081 (.012)	.076 (.012)	.057 (.072)
Δs_{t-3}	.086 (.012)	.008 (.080)	.050 (.010)	.073 (.035)	.065 (.012)	.063 (.012)	.042 (.069)
Δs_{t-4}	.085 (.012)	-.015 (.076)	.049 (.010)	.081 (.034)	.072 (.012)	.062 (.012)	.120 (.061)
Δs_{t-5}	.102 (.012)	.315 (.085)	.044 (.010)	.139 (.041)	.087 (.012)	.073 (.012)	.205 (.070)
Δs_{t-6}	.057 (.012)	.110 (.074)	.013 (.010)	.090 (.041)	.047 (.012)	.034 (.012)	.170 (.076)
p_t	.111 (.035)	.348 (.230)	.195 (.027)	.302 (.164)	.088 (.033)	.089 (.032)	.213 (.249)
p_{t-1}	.075 (.036)	-.213 (.241)	.206 (.028)	.226 (.172)	.045 (.034)	.059 (.034)	-.125 (.262)
d_{53}	--- ---	--- ---	--- ---	--- ---	.751 (.054)	.797 (.065)	.592 (.181)
$\Sigma\Delta s$ Coeff.	.591 (.029)	.696 (.074)	.319 (.034)	.618 (.114)	.465 (.029)	.416 (.030)	.746 (.133)
Σp Coeff.	.187 (.015)	.135 (.032)	.401 (.027)	.528 (.102)	.132 (.014)	.148 (.015)	.088 (.061)
n (-220)	2591	410	2591	108	2656	2653	108
r.d.f.	2581	400	2172	89	2635	2538	87
$\hat{R}^2$	.278	.327	.251	.754	.277	.223	.539
F	111.54	23.11	82.11	34.29	102.23	73.94	12.35

F[(2)-(3)-(4)]= 11.98; $F_{.01}$ = 2.41. F[(6)-(7)-(8)]= 2.86; $F_{.01}$ = 2.32.

Table 7.1.2 Role of Current Capital Expenditures

$$i^t_{t+4} = b_0 + \sum_{j=1}^{7} b_j \, \Delta s_{t+1-j} + \sum_{j=8}^{9} b_j \, p_{t+8-j} + b_{10} \, d_{53} + b_{11} \, i_t + u_t$$

t = 1958 to 1968

(1)	(2)	(3)	(4)	(5)	(6)	(7)	(8)
	Regression Coefficients and Standard Errors						
	Firms				Firm Cross Sections		
Variable or Statistic	Overall	Cross Section of Firm Means	Time Series	Industry Time Series	Across Industries	Within Industries	Industry Cross Section
Constant	.020 (.002)	.009 (.011)	.026 (.003)	.003 (.011)	.013 (.003)	.008 (.003)	.013 (.009)
Δs_t	.027 (.010)	-.020 (.049)	.038 (.009)	.041 (.038)	.026 (.010)	.026 (.010)	.064 (.050)
Δs_{t-1}	.016 (.009)	-.081 (.056)	.018 (.009)	-.004 (.035)	.009 (.010)	.011 (.010)	-.024 (.051)
Δs_{t-2}	.050 (.009)	.096 (.053)	.043 (.009)	.026 (.033)	.040 (.010)	.039 (.010)	.011 (.047)
Δs_{t-3}	.051 (.010)	.033 (.051)	.040 (.009)	.011 (.030)	.047 (.010)	.049 (.010)	.008 (.045)
Δs_{t-4}	.050 (.010)	.031 (.049)	.038 (.009)	.028 (.029)	.049 (.010)	.043 (.010)	.077 (.040)
Δs_{t-5}	.053 (.010)	.094 (.055)	.033 (.009)	.073 (.035)	.052 (.010)	.044 (.010)	.141 (.046)
Δs_{t-6}	.028 (.010)	.015 (.047)	.010 (.009)	.049 (.034)	.027 (.010)	.020 (.010)	.104 (.050)
p_t	.103 (.027)	.432 (.147)	.150 (.025)	.149 (.139)	.094 (.027)	.093 (.027)	.005 (.164)
p_{t-1}	-.049 (.029)	-.451 (.154)	.100 (.027)	.103 (.144)	-.048 (.028)	-.054 (.029)	.129 (.173)
d_{53}	--- ---	--- ---	--- ---	--- ---	.240 (.047)	.373 (.056)	-.331 (.146)
i_t	.611 (.016)	.848 (.035)	.355 (.018)	.588 (.092)	.578 (.016)	.566 (.017)	.727 (.067)
$\Sigma\Delta s$ Coeff.	.275 (.024)	.168 (.052)	.219 (.032)	.225 (.113)	.249 (.025)	.232 (.026)	.380 (.093)
Σp Coeff.	.053 (.012)	-.019 (.022)	.251 (.026)	.252 (.095)	.046 (.012)	.040 (.013)	.134 (.040)
n (-220)	2591	410	2591	108	2656	2653	108
r.d.f.	2580	399	2171	88	2634	2537	86
$\hat{R}^2$	.545	.726	.370	.830	.508	.453	.803
$\hat{r}^2_{i_t, i^t_{t+4}}$	.509	.711	.287	.811	.469	.414	.752
F	312	110	129	49	249	193	37

$F[(2)-(4)-(3)] = 32.38$; $F_{.01} = 2.32$. $F[(6)-(7)-(8)] = 4.34$; $F_{.01} = 2.25$.

Expressed capital expenditure anticipations are not merely a projection of current or immediately past actual expenditures. We note in Table 7.1.2 in the firm time series, that while the simple coefficient of determination, $\hat{r}^2_{i_t, \hat{i}_{t+4}}$, involving only current expenditures and anticipations of the future, is .287, the coefficient of determination in the multiple regression is .370, reflecting significant positive regression coefficients for both sales change and profits variables. At the level of the individual firm, immediately past capital expenditures and past sales changes and profits all contribute to the explanation of anticipations of capital expenditures four years hence. When we turn to industry time series which pool the individual firm observations in each year, we find a larger portion of capital expenditure anticipations explained by past expenditures, but a role for past sales changes and profits remains. In industry cross sections, the profits coefficients are again lower but coefficients of determination and regression coefficients of past capital expenditures and past sales changes are high. Past changes in sales, and to a lesser extent profits, consistently show positive effects on capital expenditure anticipations over and above the role of past actual capital expenditures (which of course themselves are influenced by past sales changes and profits). This is what might be expected from our underlying distributed lag model. The effects of current and some past sales changes and profits will be embodied partly in current capital expenditures and partly in future expenditures, and hence in anticipations of those expenditures.[1]

---

[1]The regressions based on the cross section of firm means seem to indicate that those firms which invest more over the entire period also expect to invest more in almost as large measure and that the systematic components of sales changes and profits which might affect expenditure anticipations are fully accounted for (or more than fully accounted for) in actual expenditures. This result may be treated with some reserve, though, since in observations which involve means of expenditures and anticipations over eleven years, mean current expenditures relate in large part to the same years as mean forward anticipations.

In Table 7.1.3 we introduce short run capital expenditure anticipations as an independent variable. They show substantial correlations with the long run capital expenditure anticipations in individual firm regressions. In the industry regressions, however, both time series and cross sections, short run anticipations have little or nothing to add to the positive relation between actual expenditures and long run anticipations. The short run anticipations apparently involve only firm-related variance; they have nothing to add to systematic differences among observations which are means for broad industry groups.

Some further explanatory value is found in the utilization-of-capacity and expected sales change variables introduced in the regressions shown in Table 7.1.4. At least this is true in the firm time series. In the industry time series they seem to offer little explanation not already accounted for by either past actual sales change or capital expenditure variables.

Table 7,1.3 Role of Current Capital Expenditures and Short Run Capital Expenditure Plans

$$i^t_{t+4} = b_0 + \sum_{j=1}^{7} b_j \Delta s_{t+1-j} + \sum_{j=8}^{9} b_j p_{t+8-j} + b_{10} d_{53} + b_{11} i_t + b_{12} i^t_{t+1} + u_t$$

t = 1958 to 1968

(1)	(2)	(3)	(4)	(5)	(6)
	Regression Coefficients and Standard Errors				
Variable or Statistic	Time Series		Firm Cross Sections		Industry Cross Section
	Firm	Industry	Across Industries	Within Industries	
Constant	.015	.006	.004	-.004	.013
	(.003)	(.013)	(.003)	(.003)	(.009)
Δs_t	.034	.041	.017	.018	.060
	(.009)	(.038)	(.009)	(.010)	(.052)
Δs_{t-1}	.018	-.005	.011	.012	-.022
	(.009)	(.035)	(.009)	(.009)	(.052)
Δs_{t-2}	.044	.027	.042	.043	.010
	(.009)	(.033)	(.009)	(.010)	(.048)
Δs_{t-3}	.041	.010	.049	.050	.011
	(.009)	(.031)	(.010)	(.010)	(.046)
Δs_{t-4}	.039	.026	.047	.042	.077
	(.009)	(.030)	(.010)	(.010)	(.040)
Δs_{t-5}	.035	.071	.052	.045	.140
	(.009)	(.036)	(.010)	(.010)	(.046)
Δs_{t-6}	.010	.047	.023	.017	.102
	(.009)	(.035)	(.009)	(.010)	(.051)
p_t	.135	.148	.056	.049	.006
	(.025)	(.139)	(.026)	(.026)	(.165)
p_{t-1}	.110	.096	-.010	-.015	.130
	(.026)	(.146)	(.027)	(.027)	(.174)
d_{53}	---	---	.140	.313	-.346
	---	---	(.045)	(.054)	(.153)
i_t	.331	.603	.451	.436	.708
	(.018)	(.098)	(.018)	(.018)	(.090)
i^t_{t+1}	.188	-.045	.358	.395	.039
	(.023)	(.099)	(.023)	(.024)	(.120)
$\Sigma\Delta s$ Coeff.	.221	.218	.241	.225	.380
	(.031)	(.115)	(.024)	(.025)	(.094)
Σp Coeff	.245	.244	.046	.035	.136
	(.025)	(.097)	(.012)	(.013)	(.041)
n (-220)	2591	108	2656	2653	108
r.d.f.	2170	87	2633	2536	85
$\hat{R}^2$	.388	.828	.548	.506	.801
F	126.47	43.91	268.14	218.47	33.58

$F[(4)-(5)-(6)] = 6.25$ $F_{.01} = 2.18$.

Table 7.1.4 - Role of Utilization of Capacity and Expected Sales Changes

$$i^t_{t+4} = b_0 + \sum_{j=1}^{7} b_j \Delta s_{t+1-j} + \sum_{j=8}^{9} b_j p_{t+8-j} + b_{10} i_t + b_{11} s^t_{t+1} + b_{12} s^t_{t+1,4} + b_{13} u^c_{t-1} + u_t$$

t = 1958 to 1968

(1) Variable or Statistic	(2) Regression Coefficients and Standard Errors: Firm Time Series	(3)	(4) Industry Time Series	(5)
Constant	-.020 (.013)	-.001 (.013)	-.067 (.046)	-.002 (.045)
$\Sigma\Delta s$ Coefficients	--- ---	.239 (.043)	--- ---	.247 (.135)
p_t	.217 (.028)	.100 (.029)	.450 (.124)	.125 (.151)
p_{t-1}	.173 (.030)	.087 (.030)	.147 (.148)	.001 (.164)
s^t_{t+1}	--- ---	.023 (.021)	--- ---	.025 (.092)
$s^t_{t+1,4}$	.049 (.014)	.042 (.013)	.121 (.086)	-.064 (.084)
i_t	--- ---	.264 (.025)	--- ---	.578 (.121)
u^c_{t-1}	.067 (.015)	.030 (.014)	.075 (.050)	.032 (.047)
Σp Coefficients	.390 (.029)	.188 (.032)	.597 (.079)	.126 (.111)
$\Sigma p, u^c_{t-1}$ Coefficients	.458 (.028)	.217 (.034)	.672 (.072)	.157 (.124)
$\Sigma p, u^c_{t-1}, s^t_{t+1,4}$ Coef.	.507 (.031)	.260 (.036)	.793 (.104)	.093 (.161)
$\Sigma s^t_{t+1}, s^t_{t+1,4}$ Coef.	--- ---	.065 (.022)	--- ---	.039 (.095)
n (-85)	1013	1013	64	64
r.d.f.	823	814	54	45
$\hat{R}^2$	.252	.384	.652	.808
F	70.61	40.65	28.16	19.81

7.2 The Role of Long Run Capital Expenditure Plans as Determinants or Forecasts of Actual Expenditures

The next question we try to answer is whether long run capital expenditure plans show any effect, beyond those of exogenous sales changes and profits, upon the capital expenditures finally undertaken. This relates partly to the forecasting value of anticipations because of their embodiment of information which we are unable to find in readily measurable determinants of investment. It also may relate to the question of whether there is something sufficiently rigid about the planning process so that plans once made (and expressed) will affect ultimate expenditures independently of the exogenous determinants of such expenditures. Evidence on this matter from the time series, which would be particularly relevant, is positive, as seen in Table 7.2.1. We may observe that the coefficient of long run capital expenditure anticipations in the firm time series regression is a quite significant .241, and .331 in the industry time series, in regressions including the full set of past sales change and profits variables. The cross section results show still larger coefficients of long run capital expenditure anticipations. Further, the sales change and profits coefficients are smaller in the cross sections. The long run anticipations apparently pick up more in the way of factors in inter-firm differences in expenditures which are not embodied in the ex post variables in the regressions.

Table 7.2.1- Role of Long Run Capital Expenditure Plans

$$i_t = b_0 + \sum_{j=1}^{7} b_j \Delta s_{t+1-j} + \sum_{j=8}^{9} b_j p_{t+8-j} + b_{10} d_{53} + b_{11} i_t^{t-4} + u_t$$

t = 1962 to 1968

(1)	(2)	(3)	(4)	(5)	(6)	(7)	(8)
	Regression Coefficients and Standard Errors						
	Time Series		Firm Overall,	Firm Cross Sections			Firm
Variable or Statistic	Firm	Industry	Time Series Observations Only	Across Industries	Within Industries	Industry Cross Section	Overall, All Observations
Constant	.014 (.007)	-.004 (.019)	.016 (.004)	-.000 (.005)	-.001 (.006)	.001 (.010)	-.004 (.005)
Δs_t	.084 (.019)	.183 (.071)	.075 (.018)	.061 (.017)	.053 (.017)	.122 (.073)	.063 (.017)
Δs_{t-1}	.080 (.019)	.120 (.079)	.084 (.018)	.069 (.017)	.069 (.017)	.044 (.090)	.085 (.017)
Δs_{t-2}	.082 (.020)	.193 (.083)	.058 (.018)	.038 (.017)	.031 (.018)	.106 (.091)	.059 (.017)
Δs_{t-3}	.027 (.019)	.104 (.070)	.019 (.018)	.007 (.017)	.014 (.018)	-.083 (.081)	.020 (.017)
Δs_{t-4}	.049 (.018)	.061 (.055)	.039 (.018)	.008 (.018)	.010 (.019)	-.003 (.073)	.033 (.017)
Δs_{t-5}	.055 (.019)	.055 (.072)	.061 (.019)	.047 (.019)	.048 (.019)	.006 (.086)	.049 (.018)
Δs_{t-6}	.048 (.017)	.082 (.057)	.049 (.018)	.028 (.017)	.028 (.018)	-.013 (.081)	.031 (.017)
p_t	.094 (.047)	.056 (.218)	-.080 (.044)	-.091 (.042)	-.084 (.043)	-.057 (.253)	-.098 (.043)
p_{t-1}	.363 (.050)	.232 (.218)	.272 (.047)	.255 (.045)	.292 (.046)	.027 (.265)	.279 (.046)
d_{53}	--- ---	--- ---	--- ---	.733 (.080)	.692 (.100)	1.018 (.239)	.638 (.081)
i_t^{t-4}	.241 (.048)	.331 (.213)	.660 (.034)	.536 (.033)	.517 (.034)	.628 (.139)	.545 (.034)
$\Sigma\Delta s$ Coeff.	.425 (.069)	.798 (.171)	.384 (.038)	.258 (.038)	.253 (.041)	.178 (.130)	.341 (.037)
Σp Coeff.	.457 (.058)	.287 (.178)	.192 (.020)	.164 (.020)	.208 (.021)	-.030 (.063)	.182 (.020)
(-107)	1172	68	1172	1225	1223	68	1225
d.f.	893	48	1161	1207	1146	50	1213
R^2	.275	.774	.484	.475	.410	.749	.499
	35.19	20.85	110.85	101.02	74.00	17.55	111.82

$F[(5)-(6)-(7)] = 2.69; \quad F_{.01} = 2.25.$

It is illuminating to eliminate variables measuring sales changes and profits variables subsequent to expression of expenditure anticipations. As shown in Table 7.2.2, coefficients of determination are much lower. It is clear that firms subsequently tailor actual expenditures to circumstances not reflected in their long run anticipations.

In Table 7.2.3 we present direct measures of the forecasting accuracy of long run capital expenditure plans of individual firms; they prove almost worthless as forecasts of actual expenditures. The adjusted coefficient of determination in the individual firm time series relating capital expenditures to their anticipations some three or four years previously is only .039, and the regression coefficient, while quite significantly positive, is only .342. When we turn to the industry time series, we find a coefficient of determination of .404 and high regression coefficient, 1.593.

The beginning of an explanation may be found in the fact that means of reported plans were only about two-thirds of the actual expenditures to which they purported to relate. The variation of plans, as measured by their standard deviation was in the firm time series also about two-thirds of actual expenditures. In the industry time series observations, the standard deviation was only .016 for anticipations and .040 for the actual expenditures. In the aggregate time series, where each observation is the mean of observations for all firms, the standard deviation of the anticipations variable was only .010, as against .032 for actual expenditures, and the regression coefficient as even higher 2.338. Aggregate or mean expenditure plans, after washing out individual firm differences, varied in the same direction but clearly much less than the actual expenditures they anticipated.

Table 7.2.2- Forecasting Accuracy of Long Run Capital Expenditure Plans, Given Previous Sales Changes

$$i_t = b_0 + \sum_{j=1}^{3} b_j \Delta s_{t-3-j} + b_4 d_{53} + b_5 i_t^{t-4} + u_t \qquad t = 1962 \text{ to } 1968$$

(1)	(2)	(3)	(4)	(5)	(6)	(7)
	Regression Coefficients and Standard Errors					
	Time Series		Firm Cross Sections			
Variable or Statistic	Firm	Industry	Across Industries	Within Industries	Industry Cross Section	Firm Overall, All Observations
Constant	.089 (.005)	.018 (.022)	.015 (.005)	.021 (.006)	.005 (.010)	.014 (.005)
Δs_{t-4}	.101 (.019)	.247 (.064)	.053 (.018)	.055 (.020)	.039 (.063)	.103 (.018)
Δs_{t-5}	.086 (.021)	.216 (.080)	.080 (.019)	.083 (.020)	.058 (.077)	.100 (.019)
Δs_{t-6}	.058 (.020)	.129 (.073)	.047 (.018)	.054 (.019)	-.022 (.078)	.057 (.018)
d_{53}	--- ---	--- ---	.997 (.082)	.880 (.106)	1.114 (.195)	.916 (.086)
i_t^{t-4}	.284 (.054)	.920 (.286)	.566 (.035)	.555 (.036)	.660 (.137)	.588 (.037
$\Sigma\Delta s$ Coeff	.245 (.043)	.592 (.164)	.180 (.033)	.193 (.035)	.075 (.117)	.260 (.034)
n (-107)	1172	68	1225	1223	68	1225
r.d.f.	899	54	1213	1152	56	1219
$\hat{R}^2$	.072	.497	.404	.317	.741	.404
F	18.58	15.34	165.91	108.16	35.82	167.02

$F[(4)-(5)-(6)] = 1.11; \quad F_{.01} = 3.02; \; F_{.1} = 1.85.$

Table 7.2.3 - Forecasting Accuracy of Long Run Capital Expenditure Plans, Price Deflated and Undeflated Data

$$i_t^* = b_0 + b_1 i_t^{t-4} + u_t \qquad t = 1962 \text{ to } 1968$$

(1) Variable or Statistic	(2) Time Series: Firm	(3) Time Series: Industry	(4) Time Series: Aggregate	(5) Firm Cross Sections: Across Industries	(6) Firm Cross Sections: Within Industries	(7) Industry Cross Section	(8) Firm Overall, All Observations	(9)
A. Deflated								
	Regression Coefficients and Standard Errors							
Constant	.096 (.005)	-.014 (.022)	-.079 (.081)	.059 (.003)	.067 (.003)	.024 (.010)	.056 (.004)	
i_t^{t-4}	.342 (.051)	1.593 (.247)	2.338 (.926)	.757 (.031)	.670 (.033)	1.155 (.107)	.788 (.032)	
$\hat{R}^2$	.039	.404	.473	.290	.229	.648	.292	
F	45.80	41.71	6.38	601.40	417.97	117.19	608.91	
	Standard Deviations							Means*
i_t^{t-4}	.041	.016	.010	.068	.063	.030	.068	.087
i_t	.069	.040	.032	.095	.088	.043	.100	.125

B. Undeflated

	Regression Coefficients and Standard Errors							
Constant	.115 (.006)	-.040 (.027)	-.128 (.089)	.075 (.004)	.085 (.005)	.032 (.013)	.070 (.005)	
i_t^{t-4}	.434 (.054)	1.880 (.248)	2.705 (.832)	.798 (.033)	.709 (.035)	1.205 (.112)	.846 (.034)	
$\hat{R}^2$	.054	.486	.615	.289	.229	.646	.296	
F	64.17	57.63	10.59	599.35	417.98	115.80	621.79	
	Standard Deviations							Means*
i_t^{t-4}	.050	.021	.014	.083	.076	.037	.084	.107
i_t	.093	.056	.047	.123	.113	.055	.130	.161
n (-39)	1413	70	7	1477	1475	70	1477	
r.d.f.	1102	59	5	1469	1406	62	1475	

*For observations in firm overall regressions.

$F[(5)-(6)-(7)] = 37.43$; $F_{.01} = 6.63$.

The cross sections (and the overall regressions, reflecting largely cross sectional variance and covariance) reveal coefficients of long run anticipated expenditures closer to unity and higher coefficients of determination. These results suggest that though the incomplete capital expenditure plans of firms and industries are of little value in forecasting fluctuation of actual expenditures, they differ from each other at any point in time in about the same measure as subsequent expenditures.

It was thought that our poor results in firm time series might reflect the fact that expressed expenditure plans do not relate correctly to the dates to which they are presumed to apply. Perhaps firms indicating that expenditures will be higher some four years from now are not really wrong in their anticipation that expenditures will be higher but are quite unable to predict the timing of anticipated expenditures, so that their "four year plans" prove to be quite inaccurate forecasts of the specific year, four years hence, to which they are deemed to relate. To evaluate this possibility we constructed a capital expenditure variable which was a weighted, moving average of three years of expenditures and related this variable to the anticipations formulated four years before the year on which the moving average was centered.

However, regressions of this moving average capital expenditure variable on long run anticipations and on previous sales changes and the depreciation ratio as reported in Table 7.2.4, did not markedly alter the picture. In the firm time series, the coefficient of determination and the regression coefficient of capital expenditure anticipations remain small. In the industry time series, the coefficient of capital expenditure anticipations is brought closer to unity but the coefficient of determination is also reduced.

Table 7.2.4- Moving Average Forecasting Accuracy of Long Run Capital Expenditure Plans

$$i_{tAV} = b_0 + b_1 d_{53} + b_2 i_t^{t-4} + u_t \qquad t = 1962 \text{ to } 1967$$

(1)	(2)	(3)	(4)	(5)
	Regression Coefficients and Standard Errors			
			Cross Sections	
Variable or Statistic	Time Series Firm	Time Series Industry	Firm Within Industries	Industry
Constant	.098	.008	.030	.008
	(.005)	(.022)	(.005)	(.006)
d_{53}	---	---	.707	1.128
	---	---	(.091)	(.135)
i_t^{t-4}	.219	1.303	.596	.606
	(.054)	(.261)	(.034)	(.083)
n (-36)	956	59	1015	59
r.d.f.	712	48	955	51
$\hat{R}^2$	.021	.329	.336	.863
F	16.34	25.00	242.70	167.52

It also seemed possible that our price deflation was causing some havoc. We had implicitly assumed that capital expenditure anticipations were expressed in terms of prices at the time the anticipations were formulated. This led us to use for anticipations a capital goods price deflator relating to the quarter before the anticipations were revealed, while using for the actual capital expenditures four years later the price deflator relating to the year of those expenditures. But perhaps our price deflators, involving averages of indices for different components of the broad industry groups into which firms were categorized, were inappropriate. Perhaps, indeed, respondents' answers incorporated anticipated price changes and these anticipations were correct. It would then be appropriate to use the same deflator for both actual and anticipated expenditures or use no deflator at all, thus measuring the usefulness of long run capital expenditure anticipations as forecasts of the money value of capital expenditures.

This latter relation between undeflated variables as shown in section B of Table 7.2.3. Coefficients of determination in the time series do prove generally higher. But at the individual firm level the great bulk of the time series variance in capital expenditures remains unexplained by capital expenditure plans.

Confirmation and some detail regarding the poor quality of long run plans as direct forecasts of capital expenditures are offered in Table 7.2.5 which presents Theil inequality coefficients by industry-year, by year, by industry, and for all observations. In each year, the inequality coefficient was less than unity when all of the observations were included, but not usually by much. In three of the ten industries the inequality coefficients for all years were actually slightly above unity and only in two industries, primary metals and utilities, were they substantially below unity. In no less than 19 of the 70 industry-years the inequality coefficients were greater than one. Overall it was a scantily encouraging .953.

A major source of difficulty should have been recognized in the information as to means and standard deviations presented in Table 7.2.3. Since reported anticipations of capital expenditures four years in the future understated by about one-third the actual expenditures subsequently reported, there is a substantial "bias" component to the inequality coefficients, which becomes relatively larger as observations are grouped into means for industry-years or for years. The smaller standard deviation of anticipations similarly contributes to substantial variance components which also become relatively larger where grouping lowers the covariance components. In general, however, the incompleteness of reported plans for capital expenditures four years ahead is apparently not consistent and on the individual firm level the bulk of the large inequality coefficients is to be accounted to low covariance of plans and expenditures, as already shown.

Table 7.2.5 - Long Run Capital Expenditure Realizations: Inequality Coefficients (U), By Year and Industry

$$U = \left[\frac{\Sigma(a-p)^2}{\Sigma a^2}\right]^{\frac{1}{2}}, \text{ where } a = i_t - i_{t-4} \text{ and } a - p = i_t - i_t^{t-4}$$

(1) Year	(2) Primary Metals	(3) Metal Working	(4) Chemical Processing	(5) All Other Mfg.	(6) Mining	(7) Utilities	(8) Petro-leum	(9) Railroads	(10) Stores	(11) Trans-portation	(12) All Industries
1962	.542	.861	.945	1.260	.978	.865	1.148	.836	1.188	1.368	.979
1963	.624	1.061	.797	1.159	.729	.605	2.462	1.580	1.086	.899	.988
1964	.828	.877	1.046	1.065	1.243	.867	.843	.994	.962	1.259	.965
1965	.917	.921	.982	.942	1.383	.820	.971	.994	.907	1.117	.951
1966	.918	.970	.920	.936	.893	.660	.910	.972	1.077	1.307	.966
1967	.766	.919	.935	.842	1.015	.813	.962	1.003	.604	7.131	.895
1968	.903	.973	.884	.864	.058	.848	.800	.688	.990	2.175	.956
All Years	.763	.935	.926	.976	1.012	.787	1.007	1.018	.998	1.173	.953

Table 7.2.6- Long Run Capital Expenditures Realizations: Inequality Coefficients (U) and Bias (U^m), Variance (U^s) and Covariance (U^c) Proportions, Individual Firms by Industry and Years, Overall and Groups*

(1)	(2)	(3)	(4)	(5)
Individual Firms By Industry	U	U^m	U^s	U^c
Primary Metals	.763	.236	.058	.706
Metal Working	.935	.223	.156	.621
Chemical Processing	.926	.160	.197	.642
All Other Manufacturing	.976	.226	.162	.612
Mining	1.012	.247	.136	.616
Utilities	.787	.071	.132	.797
Petroleum	1.007	.099	.159	.742
Railroads	1.018	.359	.045	.596
Stores	.998	.053	.062	.855
Transportation	1.173	.243	.004	.753
By Years				
1962	.979	.011	.017	.972
1963	.988	.047	.012	.941
1964	.965	.118	.055	.827
1965	.951	.299	.068	.633
1966	.966	.397	.112	.491
1967	.895	.311	.188	.501
1968	.956	.147	.142	.711
All years and Industries	.953	.164	.096	.740
Group Means				
Industry-Years	.964	.549	.103	.348
Years	1.617	.716	.251	.033

*

$$U = \left[\frac{\Sigma(a-p)^2}{\Sigma a^2}\right]^{\frac{1}{2}}, \qquad U^m = \frac{(\bar{a} - \bar{p})^2}{\frac{1}{n}\Sigma(a-p)^2}$$

$$U^s = \frac{(\sigma_a - \sigma_p)}{\frac{1}{n}\Sigma(a-p)^2}, \quad \text{and} \quad U^c = \frac{2(1-r)\sigma_a\sigma_p}{\frac{1}{n}\Sigma)a-p)^2},$$

where $a = i_t - i_{t-4}$ and $p = i_t^{t-4} - i_{t-4}$.

Eisner, R. "Expectations, Plans, and Capital Expenditures: A Synthesis of Ex Post and Ex Ante Data." In M. J. Bowman, ed., Expectations, Uncertainty and Business Behavior. New York, Social Research Council (1958c): 165-188.

________. "Investment Plans and Realizations." American Economic Review 52 (May 1962): 190-203.

________. "Investment: Fact and Fancy." American Economic Review 53 (May 1963a): 237-246.

________. "Realization of Investment Anticipations." In L.R. Klein, et al., eds., The Brookings Quarterly Econometric Model of the United States. Chicago, Rand McNally (1965): 95-128.

________. "Cross Section and Time Series Estimates of Investment Functions," INSEE-CNRS Symposium on the Econometrics of Panel Data, Paris, 1977.

Holt, C.C. and F. Modigliani. "Firm Cost Structures and the Dynamic Responses of Inventories, Production, Work Force, and Orders to Sales Fluctuations." In Inventory Fluctuations and Economic Stabilization Part II. Joint Economic Committee, 87th Congress, 1st Session, 1961.

Jorgenson, D.W. "Capital Theory and Investment Behavior." American Economic Review 53 (May 1963): 247-259.

________. "Anticipations and Investment Behavior." In J. S. Dusenberry, E. Kuh, G. Fromm, and L.R. Klein, eds. The Brookings Quarterly Econometric Model of the United States. Chicago, Rand-McNally (1965):35-94.

Modigliani, F. and K.J. Cohen. "The Significance and Uses of Ex Ante Data." In M.J. Bowman, ed., Expectations, Uncertainty and Business Behavior. New York, Social Science Research Council (1958): 151-164.

________. The Role of Anticipations and Plans in Economic Behavior and Their Use in Economic Analysis and Forecasting. Urbana, University of Illinois Press (1961).

Modigliani, F. and F.E. Hahn. "Production Planning Over Time and the Nature of the Expectation and Planning Horizon." Econometrica 23 (Jan. 1955): 46-66.

Modigliani, F. and Owen H. Sauerlander. "Economic Expectations and the Plans of Firms in Relation to Short-Term Forecasting." In Short-Term Economic Forecasting, Studies in Income and Wealth, Vol. 17. Princeton, NBER (1955): 261-351.

Summary and Conclusions

1. Short run capital expenditure anticipations, sharing common determinants with the actual expenditures to which they relate, adapt to both errors in previous expenditure anticipations and to changes in sales and errors in expectations of sales.

2. Capital expenditure anticipations account for a major share of the variance in capital expenditures, far more than do previous capital expenditures or other variables.

3. Variance of capital expenditure realizations (the difference between capital expenditures and capital expenditure anticipations) is far greater on an individual firm basis than for means of observations within years or industries.

4. Perhaps because of the tendency for errors to wash out in aggregation, the time series regressions show generally higher coefficients of determination and higher regression coefficients of relevant variables the greater the degree of aggregation involved in the observations. Higher coefficients were thus found in the industry time series than in the firm time series, and the highest regression coefficients and coefficients of determination were generally found in the aggregate time series. Similar effects of aggregation were noted in cross sections and overall regressions.

5. While there was some general tendency for capital expenditure anticipations to exceed actual capital expenditures (although this conclusion should be tempered by recognition of its sensitivity to our methods of price deflation), there was some evidence that the capital expenditure realizations variable tended to be positively associated with generally favorable economic circumstances as measured by sales changes, sales realizations (the difference between actual and expected sales), and profits.

6. This last point was confirmed in various regressions, especially time series, in which current sales change, sales realizations, and profits all manifested significant coefficients in relations where capital expenditures or capital expenditure realizations were dependent variables. Variables reflecting conditions that should have been taken into account in capital expenditure anticipations usually had coefficients close to zero or slightly negative. Current variables, which post-dated the information entering into anticipations, generally contributed significantly to the explanation of capital expenditure realizations. To the extent that firms experienced conditions in sales or profits that were better than at the time anticipations were formed, or better than expected, capital expenditures tended to exceed capital expenditure anticipations.

We may see in all this confirmation of the realizations function proposed by Modigliani.[1] The confirmation, while small in terms of predictive power for individual firms, is distinct even there, and takes greater weight at more aggregative levels.

---

[1] See Modigliani and Hahn [1955], Modigliani and Cohen [1958] and [1961], Modigliani and Sauerlender [1955] and Holt and Modigliani [1961].

7. Reported long run (four year ahead) capital expenditure plans are seriously incomplete and understate actual expenditures by almost a third. Thus, without blow-up by use of regression estimates or otherwise tney are hardly better than current expenditures as predictors of future expenditures of individual firms. Errors tend to wash out somewhat however in industry and aggregative averaging.

8. Current and past sales changes and profits account for much more of the variance over time of firms' capital expenditures than do their long run anticipations of their expenditures. Expenditures are clearly related much more closely to these sales and profits variables than to the long previously expressed capital expenditure anticipations.

9. Previous long run anticipations do continue to evidence some relation to actual capital expenditures in time series regressions including a complete set of past sales change and profits variables. Past plans thus apparently embody information of commitment or independent influence on expenditures beyond that found in past sales and profits variables. Previous plans account most substantially for capital expenditure differences in cross sections between firms and industries.

10. Longer term capital expenditure anticipations may be explained, like actual capital expenditures, in terms of actual and expected sales changes, profits and utilization of capacity. Accelerator coefficients are generally significant but profits variables show a larger role in the timing of capital expenditure

anticipations, as evidenced by their higher coefficients in individual firm time series.

Past actual capital expenditures as well as short run anticipations add significantly to the explanation of long run anticipations. Sales change and profits variables in their turn contribute to the explanation of long run capital expenditure anticipations over and above the explanation offered by actual expenditures and short run anticipations.

11. One may conclude from all this that long run capital expenditure plans offer little security against the winds of change in the economic climate. Firms adjust their actual expenditures to recent sales change and profits experience whatever their previous plans. It is perhaps recognition that actual expenditure will be tailored to later developments that leads firms to fail to articulate or fail to report long run plans for major, and apparently varying portions of the capital expenditures which they ultimately undertake.

A.G. HART/J.W. ALBRECHT
COLUMBIA UNIVERSITY
NEW YORK

SOME USES OF THE CAPACITY CONCEPT IN UNDERSTANDING INVESTMENT BEHAVIOR

SOME USES OF THE CAPACITY CONCEPT IN UNDERSTANDING INVESTMENT BEHAVIOR

Introduction

What is the proper framework for an econometric investigation of investment in fixed capital? The answer depends upon which investment phenomena one wishes to analyze. Our interests are in the expectational aspects of investment--in the questions of how businessmen forecast, how plans are drawn based on forecasts, and how plans are modified as expectations change. Despite the importance of these expectational phenomena (the phrase "animal spirits" might be invoked here), the conventional capital stock adjustment model of investment (typified by JORGENSON [1971]) downgrades them in favor of other factors. The fact that considerable expectational (*ex ante*) data exist for the U.S. manufacturing sector makes it possible to rectify the relative neglect of these phenomena.

As a long term project we are attempting to specify and estimate a model that allows the fullest possible exploitation of these data. The bulk of the present paper consists of data analysis. This corresponds to our intuition that while the reader will have little difficulty accepting our model, he may feel that the data we intend to use are too "soft."

The reader may be disconcerted to find our model organized around the adjustment of a stock of capacity rather than of capital. Our approach is a natural outgrowth of our decision to explore the *ex ante* data since

Table A1

BASIC STRUCTURE OF STUDY ON PLANNING AND EXECUTION
OF FINED INVESTMENT IN U.S. MANUFACTURING

Dependent variable in each equation is indicated by corresponding line-number in stub.

Symbole: . located principal diagonal

+? and -? indicate likelihood of influence

+ denotes presumed positive influence

- denotes presumed negative influence

blank indicates presumed absence of influence

	Variable	Equation 1	2	3	4	5	6	7	8	9	1o	11	12	13	14
Explicit ex ante variables	1. Sales forecast	.	+								–				
	2. Capacity target		.	+											
	3. Capital-expenditure plan			.	+										
	4. Realized capital expenditure				.										
"Prospect" (Expectations proxy) variables	5. Capacity-replacement requirement			+		.									
	6. Capital-goods price		-?	–			.					–			
	7. Wage rate		-?	+				.					–		
	8. Cash flow		+?	+					.					–	
	9. Interest rate		-?	–						.					–
Surprise variables	1o. Sales-surprise				+						.				
	11. Capital-goods-price surprise				–							.			
	12. Wage-rate surprise				+								.		
	13. Cash-flow surprise				+									.	
	14. Interest-rate surprise				–										.

Table A2

BASIC STRUCTURE OF STUDY ON PLANNING AND EXECUTION
OF FINED INVESTMENT IN U.S. MANUFACTURING

Dependent variable in each equation is indicated by corresponding line-number in stub.

Symbole: . located principal diagonal

+? and -? indicate likelihood of influence

\+ denotes presumed positive influence

\- denotes presumed negative influence

blank indicates presumed absence of influence

	Variable	Equation 1	2	3	4	5	6	7	8	9	1o	11	12	13	14
Exogenous or fully-predetermined variables	15. Sales-history	+							+		+				
	16. Orders for produce	+													
	17. Economic indicators	+													
	18. Preferred operating rate		+												
	19. Index of uncertainty		+	-?											
	2o. Capacity history					+									
	21. Capital-goods-price history						+					+			
	22. Capital-goods queuing						+								
	23. Wage-rate history							+					+		
	24. Unemployment rate							-							
	25. Cash-flow history								+					+	
	26. Interest-rate history									+					+
	27. Bank-reserve position			+?						-					

agh/jwa 28 March 1977

capacity is the pivotal variable in the underlying survey. It is our view that capacity data are not inferior to capital-quantum data and will bear the weight of econometric analysis. We do not insist that the capital stock adjustment approach be abandoned--rather, that the alternative capacity adjustment approach should also be examined.

A Capacity Stock Approach to Investment

Our framework is based on Franco Modigliani's division of the investment process into the forecasting function, the planning function and the realization function (MODIGLIANI [1960]). The linkage among these functions is outlined in Table A. Each column corresponds to a proposed equation; thus, for example, reading down the first column shows that we hypothesize that the sales forecast depends upon sales history (i.e., a distributed lag of realized sales), upon an orders variable and upon an index of economic indicators.[1] The equations and variables fall into several broad groups. The first set (variables 1-4) corresponds to Modigliani's three functions except that the structure of the *ex ante* data leads us to split the planning function into the determination of capacity targets and the setting

1. We might write this as $S(t,t+k) = \mu_k + \sum_{i=0}^{t} \beta_{k,i} S^*_{t-i} + \gamma_k O_t + \delta_k E_t + u(t,t+k)$, where S(t,t+k) denotes the sales forecast as of viewpoint date t for a horizon date k years in the future. Parameters are subscripted by k to indicate that forecasts of different lengths are determined differently.

of expenditure plans. The second group (variables 5-9) consists of variables which are in principle forecasting variables but for which *ex ante* data are lacking or fragmentary. We use realized (*ex post*) data to construct "expectation proxies" or "prospects" for these variables. The third group (variables 10-14) deals with the "surprise" variables used in the fourth equation. These are generated as identities; surprise is defined as the difference between the *ex post* realization and the *ex ante* forecast or prospect. (The process of expectation revision has been omitted in the tabular display to keep the design as transparent as possible.) Finally, the last group (variables 15-27) is the exogenous or pre-determined variables which enter one or more of the equations 1-14.

This approach offers great advantages in bringing available information to bear on investment problems. The capital stock adjustment model may be viewed as a variant of the Modigliani model in which all the expectational variables are substituted out, leaving realized investment expenditure as the sole dependent variable and making no place for observed values of the variables (1-3). Further, the "desired stock" of capital in the capital stock adjustment model has no observational counterpart but must be an expectations proxy. A waste of valuable information is avoided by shifting to the capacity adjustment approach.

The basic expectational data that will be used to apply this approach are generated by the McGraw-Hill (MGH) Company's investment plan surveys of U.S. manufacturing (supplemented by various other MGH surveys). The annual "spring survey," which has had a reasonably stable structure since 1955, asks for *ex ante* information on (1) capital expenditures for the survey ("viewpoint") year and for each of the ensuing three years; (2) capacity (stated in terms of percent changes) for the base year (completed just before the viewpoint), the viewpoint year, and the ensuing three year span; and (3) sales (again in percent changes) for the viewpoint year compared with the base year, and for a horizon year three years later as compared with viewpoint year. Supplementary questions cover the proportion of expenditures for "structures" (as against equipment) and for "expansion" (as against "replacement and modernization"), capacity utilization in December of the base year, and (often, but not always) a "preferred operating rate." In addition, there are supplementary surveys which give information over part of the period about expenditures for pollution control, about the age distribution of existing capacity, and (with a one year horizon) about expected cash flows and expected capital capital goods prices. Finally, there is an "autumn survey" of investment

2. The Conference Board's quarterly appropriations series provides another source of *ex ante* expenditure data.

plans, giving preliminary estimates three months earlier than the spring survey.

The full range of *ex post* data on sales, capital expenditures, etc., is, of course, also available for an *ex ante* study. There are many problems with these data, involving deflation and industrial classification in particular, but these problems are present also in a capital stock adjustment approach. Rather than rehash these difficulties, we prefer to devote our attention to the capacity data.

The MGH Capacity Data

The basic stock variable is represented *ex post* by a time series of capacity in being at the opening of each year from 1951 through 1977. These series are presented in Table 5 appended to the paper. They appear also in Charts 2 and 3, to be examined shortly.

The industrial classification used is conventional for U.S. investment statistics. It differs from a "2-digit" classification by splitting into two components both the primary metals industry (Standard Industrial Classification 33) and the transport equipment industry (SIC 37) while combining fabricated metal products (SIC 34) with instruments (SIC 38). The total includes several 2-digit industries for which separate data are not provided by MGH, and petroleum is excluded from the total (and from the bulk of our study) because of problems with the coverage of non-manufacturing (i.e., distribution and extractive) activities.

The series are derived from MGH figures on the annual realized percent change in capacity for each of the industries. Our procedure is as follows:

(a) To obviate the rounding errors that have entered MGH's cumulative index we replicate the cumulation operation, using all the available source detail.

(b) We estimate the ratio of 1967 year-end capacity to 1967 output by applying the "Wharton method" (see KLEIN/SUMMERS 1966) of making a semi-log interpolation between the "unsubmerged peaks" of the relevant component of the Federal Reserve Board's production index on each side of 1967.

(c) A relatively minor adjustment is introduced to correct for the difference between the log-linear expansion implied by the Wharton procedure and any upward or downward concavity between "unsubmerged peaks" indicated by the basic index referred to in (b).

(d) The adjusted capacity in 1967 value-added dollars in each industry is then obtained by multiplying together:

The MGH capacity index (1968.0 = 1.00), as adjusted in (a)
The capacity/output ratio derived in (b)
The correction coefficient derived in (c)
1967 value added (output) taken from the U.S. Census Bureau's publication Enterprise Statistics.[3]

We should now ask whether this procedure has produced a coherent, believable set of time series. A first check can be made by comparing these capacity

3. The value added data are for industries classified on the basis of principal products of companies rather than of component establishments. However, since the FRB production index is used in (b) some data used in the process are unavoidably collected on an establishments basis. Also, since the Wharton method is used to derive the 1967 capacity/output ration the result is an effective measure, i.e., one that does not include any reserve of unused capacity that may be held at peaks.

USA: Total manufacturing

Chart 1

CAPACITY, OUTPUT AND QUANTUM OF CAPITAL

VIEWPOINTS 1951.0-1976.0

[Unit: 1 billion 1967 dollars]

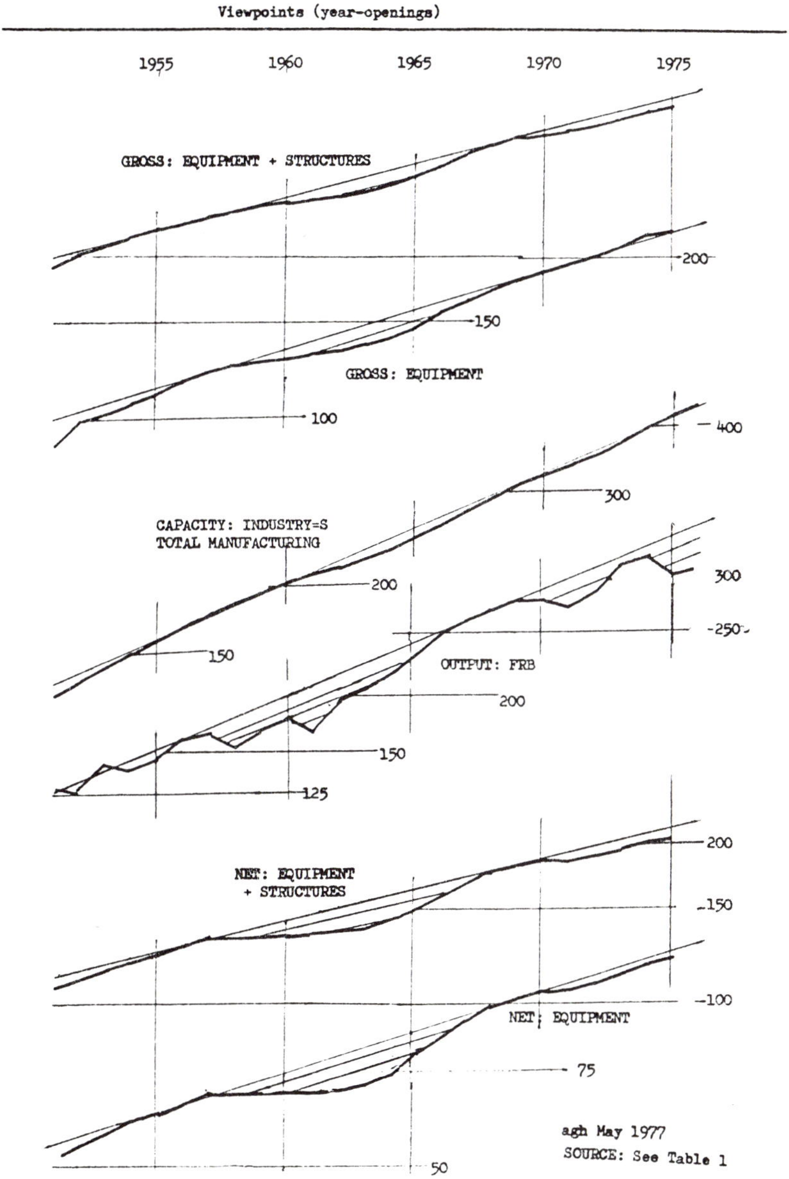

agh May 1977

SOURCE: See Table 1

data with concurrent output and capital stock data. This is done for total manufacturing in Chart 1 with capital stock data taken from MUSGRAVE [1976]. The two top curves trace the gross capital stock over time--first equipment plus structures (ESG) and then equipment alone (EG). The middle two curves trace our version of MGH capacity (CAPA) and the FRB production index (Q) over time. Finally, the lower two curves trace the net capital stocks of equipment plus structures (ESN) and of equipment alone (EN) over time. To guide the eye we have linked the unsubmerged peaks in each of the series (disregarding the 1953 peak in Q as a Korean War aberration) with thin lines and have drawn parallels to the thin lines 5% and 10% lower.

In broad terms these series all tell a consistent story. The lines linking the unsubmerged peaks show almost identical growth rates for capacity and for the FRB production index, while the growth rates for the various capital stocks are somewhat less, as one would expect given technological change and expansion in "human capital." The growth rates for capacity and for the capital stocks agree over shorter periods as well--both show a deceleration in the late 1950's and an acceleration in the late 1960's.

A second check on the coherence of the capacity data can be carried out using a separate body of MGH data, the "How Modern is American Industry?" series, which presents age distributions of capacity at six different dates.

USA: Manufac-
turing by
industries

Chart 2

LEVEL, "MORTALITY" AND SURVIVAL OF CAPACITY
1951-1977

[Unit: billion value-added dollars of 1967]

Conventions of graph: Actual capacity is shown by top curve in each industry-panel; fat dots represent survivals, <u>to</u> viewpoint-date shown by longitude of the point, <u>from</u> base-date shown by longitude of left-hand end of diagonal. Slopes of diagonals correspond to "mortality rates" of capacity between these two dates; cf. scale of mortllity-rate gradients at foot of chart.

Base-dates and viewpoints Base-dates and viewpoints Base-dates and viewpoints

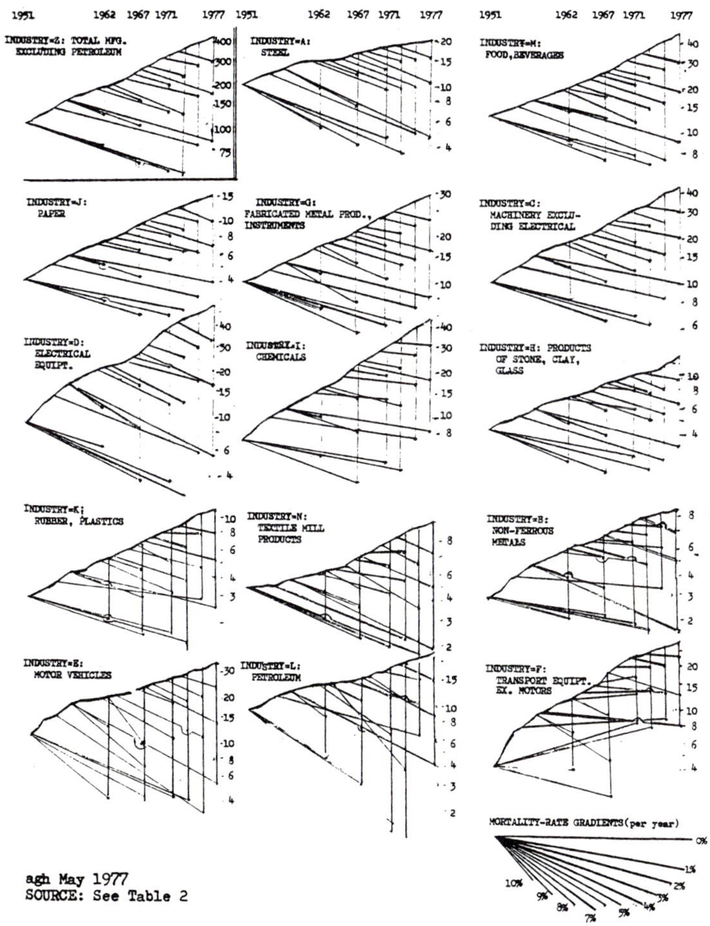

agh May 1977
SOURCE: See Table 2

Response in this survey takes the form of percentage allocations of capacity at the survey's viewpoint date into age brackets. For each of the dates 1962, 1967, 1971, 1973, 1975, 1977 we multiply the total amount of capacity in each industry by that industry's allocation into capacity of age less than 5 years, 5-10 years, 10-20 years, and over 20 years.

This test operation is presented in Chart 2 with data in the Appendix, Table 2. Each industry has a panel in the chart--beginning at the upper left with a panel for total manufacturing (excluding petroleum). Industries are sequenced by the apparent degree of coherence of their "mortality."

In each panel the top curve traces the level of actual capacity in 1967 value-added dollars. With only one or two exceptions, all component industries show the pattern of deceleration in the 1950's followed by acceleration in the 1960's--not without some interesting differences of timing. Some but not all show deceleration again in the 1970's.

Below the total capacity point for each of the six survey dates is a column of points representing capacity over 5 years old, over 10 years old, and over 20 years old.[4] Each point is then linked back to the level of

4. The "over 20" allocation actually has a boundary of 16 years for the 1967 viewpoint and 22 years for the 1973 viewpoint, and the "over 10" allocation is actually 11 years for the 1962 viewpoint. These dates are correctly placed in the chart, so that the descriptive inexactitude does not distort the slopes of the diagonals in the charts. Also, we have omitted the oldest category for the 1962 viewpoint because its base date is 1946, and we have completely ignored the first of the "How Modern..." surveys, with a 1958 viewpoint, as a trial run, since it contained many entries implying negative mortalities between the base dates and 1958. With these exceptions all of the "How Modern..." data are embodied in the chart and table.

capacity at its base date, and the slope of each linking line represents the rate of capacity mortality between the two dates. For convenience, we include a scale of mortality rate gradients in the lower right-hand corner of the chart. The "coherence" of the data can be tested informally by examining the consistency of these gradients in each industry.

There are a number of reasons to expect distortions in these slopes. First, the responses in the "How Modern..." surveys could be very impressionistic since companies have no obvious incentive to keep records of capacity by age cohorts; besides piecemeal additions and replacements may introduce important ambiguities. Second, the percentages assigned to the youngest and oldest age groups are often small, so MGH rounding errors may be significant. Third, the viewpoint and base years are far enough apart so that changes in the industrial classification of companies may have blurred comparability. We are thus pleasantly surprised by the coherence shown by most of the industries. Only the three in the bottom row of the chart seem incoherent, and special reasons can be cited for each. Motor vehicles (E) reported in 1962 an astounding 58% of capacity aged under 5 years (point indicated by a star); petroleum (L) is plagued by a non-uniform inclusion of non-manufacturing facilities; and transportation equipment (F) has undergone a massive shift in composition from railroad equipment and shipbuilding to aerospace.

Each industry has a characteristic pattern. Very rapid capacity mortality can be seen in petroleum (L), motor vehicles (E), steel (A) and electrical equipment (D) whereas slow capacity mortality is seen in chemicals (K), paper (J) and non-ferrous metals (B). But within each industry there seem to be few systematic differences in slopes between diagonals. Those starting further to the right on the historical curves (representing more modern "vintages" of capacity) do not appear to be systematically steeper or flatter than those starting towards the left. Nor are the longer diagonals, representing attrition over longer periods, steeper or flatter than the short diagonals. This last result is interesting in relation to the problem of capital consumption since it indicates that attrition of the capacity represented by given facilities starts very soon after installation--and far too soon for actual retirements to have occurred. This supports the result of FELDSTEIN/FOOT 1971) using MHG data on "expansion" versus "replacement and modernization," that "one-hoss-shay" phenomena are not common and that the rental value of facilities declines from very soon after installation. An intuitive explanation of this almost immediate fall in rental value is product obsolescence.[5]

---

5. The official survey (CENSUS [1973]) obtained results much like those of MGH for capacity utilization under a definition of capacity which rests on the expansion of output feasible with existing facilities assuming sufficient labor and materials and a steady product mix. Fading of the market for an established product (or failure of a new product to generate the expected sales volume) results in a reduction of the amount of capacity attributed to stated facilities under such a definition.

These age distribution figures also give us a tool to remedy the discrepancy between the inherently gross MGH data for capital expenditure and the inherently net capacity increment series obtained (*ex post*) by differencing the historical capacity level index or (*ex ante*) by using the data on plans for capacity expansion. This net/gross problem is the counterpart of the familiar problem of allowing for capital consumption in the capital-stock adjustment approach. In that approach gross expenditure is treated as dependent on two variables--the excess of desired over actual stock and the rate at which the stock is "consumed."

One way to bring the MGH data to bear on the capital consumption problem is to use the data on the proportion of expenditures devoted to "expansion." Using these data (FELDSTEIN/FOOT 1971) indicates that both net and replacement expenditure are responsive to accelerator and price/finance influences. These data are suspect, however, because the alternative to expansion is replacement and modernization. It is hard to imagine modernization that does not also expand facilities.

Since capacity increments are net estimates, a promising approach in the context of our model is to try to gross up capacity increments to comparability with gross expenditures. The MGH materials used for this purpose are given in Tables 3 and 4 in the Appendix. In Table 4, part iii, we present mortality rates corresponding to the slopes of the diagonals in chart 2 based on the data for 10 year spans. Given the series for net increments of capacity (ex post or ex ante), we can generate a series of gross capacity increments by adding to each net increments by adding to each net increment a proportion of viewpoint date capacity sufficient to offset the indicated mortality.[6]

An alternative approach using the age distribution data is to estimate the original installations represented by survivals of capacity under 5 years old. To standardize the list of quinquennia for which such estimates can be made, we have adopted reference dates of 1952, 1957, 1962, 1967, 1972 and 1975. This requires merging the results of the 1971 and 1973 surveys to simulate a 1972 survey and disregarding the survey of 1975. Except for the 1952-56 quinquennium, the average time from installation to survey is only 2½ years, so that the gross installation estimates of Table 3 are not very sensitive to possible errors in mortality rates. Subtracting net increments from gross installations yields residual estimates of replacement. In parts i, ii and iv of Table 4 net increments, replacements and gross increments are stated as percents of mean levels of capacity during the quinquennia. The replacement proportions in part ii confirm rather well the mortality coefficients in part iii, particularly if we disregard the estimates for 1952-56, of lower quality than those for later quinquennia.

---

6. An advantage of the capacity adjustment approach is that one can see that both the net increment and the replacement estimate will have positive partial correlations with expenditure. In the capital stock adjustment approach the appropriate sign of the partial correlation between the existing capital stock and expenditure is ambiguous.

turing, by
industries

Chart 5 d

CAPACITY LEVELS: ACTUALS AND TARGETS FOR HORIZONS ONE
AND FOUR YEARS AFTER VIEWPOINT,
VIEWPOINTS 1953.0-1976.0
[Unit: 1 billion value-added dollars of 1967]

Conventions of graph: In each industry-panel:

Bottom curve traces actual (ex post) capacity.
Top curve traces targeted (ex ante) capacity for horizon four years later than viewpoint-date shown by longitude of column of points.
Middle curve shows targeted capacity for horizon one year later than viewpoint.

Vertical distances within columns of points represent capacity-target ratios (MGH survey data)

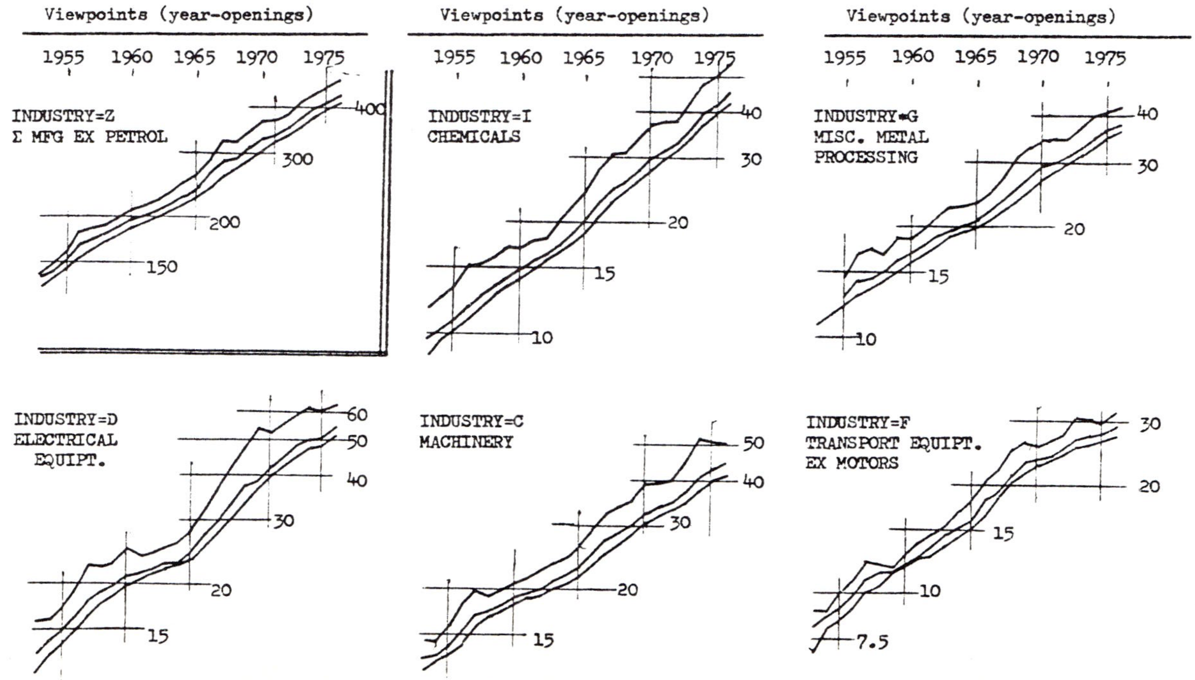

Chart b

Conventions of graph: In each industry-panel:

Bottom curve traces actual (<u>ex post</u>) capacity.
Top curve traces targeted (<u>ex ante</u>) capacity for horizon four years later than viewpoint-date shown by longitude of column of points.
Middle curve shows targeted capacity for horizon one year later than viewpoint.

Vertical distances within columns of points represent capacity-target ratios (MGH survey data)

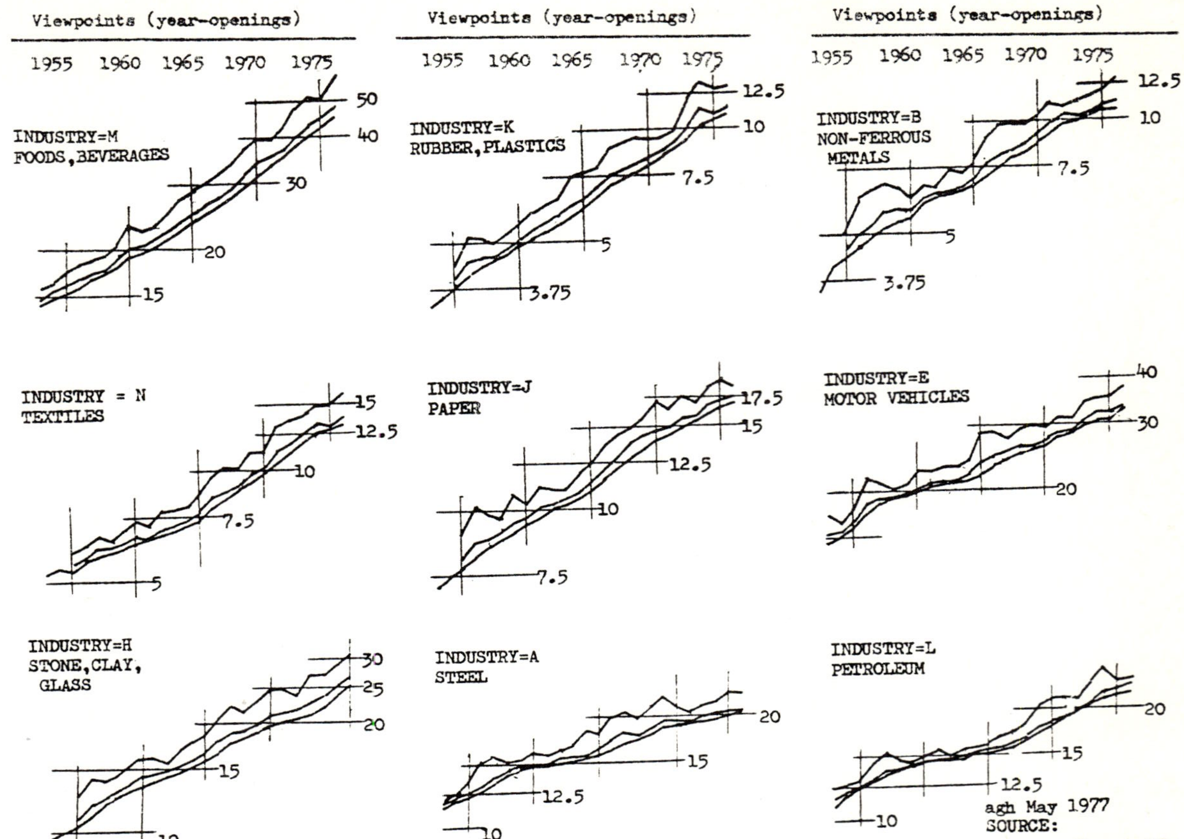

agh May 1977
SOURCE: See tables 5-7

These procedures for grossing up the increments of capacity do not lead to reliable time series of the replacement component. If we doubt the significance of movements between quinquennia, we can scarcely rely on interpolation to individual years. From this standpoint the alternative of decomposing expenditures into components for expansion and replacement has at least the attraction of generating distinct replacement requirements for each industry in each year. We are perhaps better off on a capacity stock adjustment basis than on a capital stock adjustment basis in handling these gross versus net problems; but on either basis, replacement is a weak link in the chain.

Finally, we turn our attention to the ex ante capacity data, i.e., the capacity targets. For each industry in each year the available data include the actual level of capacity at the year-opening viewpoint, together with targeted expansion percentages for the viewpoint year and for the three year span starting at the end of the viewpoint year. Capacity target levels for dates one and four years later than the year-opening viewpoint are of course generated by calculating planned capacity increments and adding them to the viewpoint level.[7] We exhibit time series for "Industry Z" and for all the component industries in Chart 3. Industry panels are sequenced in order

7. It is often convenient to derive implicit capacity targets for intermediate horizons. For this purpose we use log-linear interpolations between the one year and four year target levels.

of the average rate of expansion from 1955 to 1976. In each panel the bottom curve again traces the level of actual capacity (ex post); the top curve traces the ex ante series of four year targets; the middle curve traces the ex ante series for one year targets. Vertical distances between the curves represent the numerators of capacity target ratios.

The "accuracy" of capacity targeting can be visually assessed by a one or four year horizontal movement from the relevant target curve towards the historical curve. Inspection tells us at once that the one year targets are very "accurate," but this is a trivial result. Deviations between targeted and actual percent changes over one year are, however, far from small--although close analysis would not be rewarding because of rounding error problems. Larger and more interesting discrepancies arise if we compare targeted and actual levels or increments for the longer four year span.

The question of "accuracy," however, is not the crucial one. Decision-makers can revise their expansion plans during execution and such revisions are likely to be worthwhile. Given that capacity targets are provisional and conditional, the more interesting question is whether the stated targets represent an image of the future on which decision-makers are acting by designing installations, acquiring sites, making preliminary arrangements with suppliers of equipment, etc. Whether capacity targets are meaningful in this sense must be determined by studying their relations with sales forecasts in one direction and with expenditures in the other. For lack of space in this paper we cannot demonstrate the character of these relations, but our preliminary impression is that they are illuminating.[8]

A striking visual feature of the capacity target data is the presence of sharp saw-teeth in the curves for the four year capacity target levels. In the slower-growing industries these take the form of absolute reductions in the four year target level stated at date (t) as compared with date (t-1); in the more rapidly-growing industries the form is more one of "growth cycle" movements. In almost all industries the movements are sharp enough to indicate important changes in expectations. We emphasize that this restructuring testifies to the contingent and conditional character of medium-term investment decisions, which can scarcely be understood without exploitation of *ex ante* data.[9]

Uses of capacity data

We have indicated how capacity data can be used in our own study. Specifically:

(a) We propose to use capacity as the basic stock variable that is "adjusted" by investment.

---

8. Our impressions rest on preliminary runs in our major study which did not take full account of company/establishments effects in the data and of other considerations that we are now in the process of systematizing.

9. In a paper for the Stockholm meeting of CIRET in 1975 Hart suggests that the readiness of planners to modify forecasts and plans over short periods may be a way in which they map out contingent aspects of their future prospects within the confines of reporting only single-valued estimates at each viewpoint. See also HART [1976].

(b) We propose to deal with the question of gross versus net in investment by using the capacity data themselves to gauge replacement requirements, grossing up capacity increments to match gross expenditures.

But there are also several ways in which capacity data can be used in studies differently oriented, notably in studies that use the stock of capital rather than capacity as their organizing principle. Specifically:

(c) Capacity can be used as a basis for estimating replacement requirements, obviating the ambiguity as to whether existing capital should have a negative partial effect on investment (because it competes with new capital for an economic niche) or a positive effect (because it generates replacement requirements).

(d) If sales forecasts are integrated into a capital stock adjustment model, capacity may be considered as an alternative for sales forecast estimation. It could well be interpreted as a Shackle-type "focus-gain estimate", representing *the highest level of possible sales worth taking into account for estimating desired capital* and used to supplement the ordinary sales forecast data which may be taken as an expectation.

(e) If expenditure plans are integrated into a capital stock adjustment model, capacity may be used as a basis for an alternative expenditure plan series, correcting for possible biases in the MGH expenditure plan series.

(f) Capacity may be used jointly with capital-quantum and capital-expenditure data to cast light on capital-intensity in the production function (a matter with which we had hoped to deal in this paper, but which proved unexpectedly difficult). The MGH data permit dealing with capital in the putty stage, comparing *increments* of capacity (*ex ante* or *ex post*) with comparable flows of expenditure. Since new capacity is presumably intended to be fully utilized in its first few years, the gross increment of capacity (less allowance for attrition) can be used as a proxy for the output to which incremental capital corresponds.

In broader terms capacity target data will have to be taken into account in any study that considers interaction among decision-makers in the field of fixed investment. Each firm's decision-makers are presumably concerned with the question of whether other firms in the industry are over-expanding or undervaluing investment opportunities. For such an evaluation, the McGraw-Hill surveys represent a data pool into which each firm feeds its provisional intentions and from which each firm can draw off information about aggregates of intentions.

References

CENSUS [1973]. United States Bureau of the Census, Survey of Plant Capacity 1973 Series MQ-Cl(73-1.

FELDSTEIN/FOOT [1971]. M. Felstein and D. Foot, "The Other Half of Gross Investment: Replacement and Modernization Expenditures," Review of Economics and Statistics 53 (February 1971) pp 49-58.

HART [1976]. A. Hart, "The Multiple Futures," in Martin Pfaff (ed), Frontiers in Social Thought: Essays in Honor of Kenneth Boulding, North-Holland Publishing, 1976.

JORGENSON [1971]. D. Jorgenson, "Econometric Studies of Investment Behavior: A Survey," Journal of Economic Literature IX (December 1971), pp 1111-1147.

KLEIN/SUMMERS [1966]. L. Klein and R. Summers, The Wharton Index of Capacity Utilization, University of Pennsylvania, Wharton School of Finance and Commerce, Economics Research Unit, 1966.

MODIGLIANI [1960]. F. Modigliani, "Introduction," in A. Hart, F. Modigliani, and G. Orcutt (eds), Quality and Economic Significance of Anticipations Data, Princeton University for the National Bureau of Economic Research, 1960.

MUSGRAVE [1976]. J. Musgrave, "Fixed Nonresidential Business and Residential Capital in the United States, 1925-75," Survey of Current Business (April 1976).

Summary

For the study of fixed-investment decisions, we propose a capacity-stock-adjustment model as an alternative to the conventional capital-stock-adjustment model. Our approach lends itself to the exploitation of the rich collection of *ex ante* data on sales, capacity and capital expenditure available for US manufacturing and component industries, obviating the enormous waste of relevant information in the conventional approach.

Our paper stops short of econometric treatment of the data, being devoted to the often-neglected preliminary phase of preparing the data for analysis and carrying out various informal tests of their validity as measures of the phenomena they purport to represent. We focus on the data (both *ex ante* and *ex post*) on manufacturing capacity, and the question whether these data can be regarded as "hard" economic statistics.

Confrontation of capacity data with date for output and for the "physical quantum" of equipment and structures in manufacturing (Chart 1) leads to the inference that our capacity series has better credentials as a measure of available productive facilities than the capital-quantum series underlying the revised National Accounts of USA. The series for "equipment, net, in 1967 dollars", which in principle might be regarded as the best measure of available capital services, has a much less reasonable time-shape than does capacity.

Capacity data are subjected to a severe trial in a comparison (Chart 2) of survivals at a series of survey-dates of capacity installed prior to stated base-dates. The capacity-level series used derive from McGraw-Hill's regular "spring survey" of investment plans, while the complementary age-distributions of capacity arise from a separate series of surveys entitled "HOW MODERN IS AMERICAN INDUSTRY?" The extraordinary coherence of the picture of "mortality gradients" in almost all of the component industries suggests strongly that corporate managements maintain a quantitative picture of capacity that can properly be treated as yielding "hard" statistics. Incidentally, this branch of our study yields very revealing images of the replacement aspect of fixed investment.

The *ex ante* data on capacity expansion (Chart 3) give a very interesting picture of the business view of the future. It is plain that the medium-term (4-year horizon) data on targeted levels of capacity lacks "accuracy" as a predictor of future capacity: the sawteeth exhibited by the targets have no counterpart in the *ex post* data for actual capacity. But taking into account the relations of capacity targets to sales-forecasts and to capital-expenditure plans (not presented in this paper), we form the impression that the capacity targets are probably a very good measure of the image of the future on which business men are placing their investment bets.

The paper ends with an extensive list of uses we see for capacity data. While it is obvious that investment studies cannot rest all their weight on the capacity variable, it seems plain also that capacity data will enormously enrich the study of investment decision, and especially of its contingent aspects.

TABLE 1-7

VIEWPOINTS 1951.0-1976.0

[Unit: 1 billion 1967 dollars]

View-point	Levels: FRB Out-put (1)	Levels: FRB Capa-city (2)	Levels: Capacity Industry =S, agh/jwa (3)	Levels: Capital quantum, Commerce, Gross E+S (4)	Levels: Capital quantum, Commerce, Gross E (5)	Levels: Capital quantum, Commerce, Net E+S (6)	Levels: Capital quantum, Commerce, Net E (7)	Ratios to agh/jwa capacity: FRB series Out-put (1/3) (8)	Ratios to agh/jwa capacity: FRB series capa-city (2/3) (9)	Ratios to agh/jwa capacity: Capital quantum Gross E+S (4/3) (10)	Ratios to agh/jwa capacity: Capital quantum Gross E (5/3) (11)	Ratios to agh/jwa capacity: Capital quantum Net E+S (6/3) (12)	Ratios to agh/jwa capacity: Capital quantum Net E (7/3) (13)	Ratios to FRB output: Capacity FRB (2/1) (14)	Ratios to FRB output: Capacity agh/jwa (3/1) (15)	Ratios to FRB output: Capital quantum Gross E+S (4/1) (16)	Ratios to FRB output: Capital quantum Gross E (5/1) (17)	Ratios to FRB output: Capital quantum Net E+S (6/1) (18)	Ratios to FRB output: Capital quantum Net E (7/1) (19)
1951.0	126.8	145.4	122.8	194.2	86.9	107.4	51.5	1.03	1.18	1.58	0.71	0.87	0.41	1.15	0.97	1.53	0.69	0.85	0.41
1952.0	127.1	151.7	130.1	202.0	93.3	111.5	54.4	0.98	1.17	1.55	0.72	0.86	0.42	1.19	1.02	1.59	0.73	0.88	0.43
1953.0	140.7	157.7	139.2	209.4	99.5	115.1	57.1	1.01	1.13	1.50	0.72	0.83	0.41	1.12	0.99	1.49	0.71	0.82	0.41
1954.0	138.3	165.0	147.6	216.9	105.6	118.6	59.7	0.94	1.12	1.47	0.72	0.80	0.41	1.19	1.07	1.57	0.76	0.86	0.43
1955.0	142.3	171.3	155.0	224.7	110.5	121.9	61.5	0.92	1.11	1.43	0.71	0.79	0.40	1.20	1.09	1.58	0.78	0.86	0.43
1956.0	156.9	178.9	165.8	233.0	117.2	127.5	65.2	0.95	1.08	1.41	0.71	0.77	0.39	1.14	1.06	1.49	0.75	0.81	0.42
1957.0	160.3	187.8	175.8	242.6	123.3	132.7	68.4	0.91	1.07	1.38	0.70	0.76	0.39	1.17	1.10	1.51	0.77	0.83	0.43
1958.0	150.9	195.2	184.6	247.3	125.8	133.9	68.3	0.82	1.06	1.34	0.68	0.73	0.37	1.29	1.22	1.64	0.83	0.89	0.45
1959.0	161.4	201.7	191.9	250.3	128.0	133.7	68.1	0.84	1.05	1.31	0.67	0.70	0.36	1.25	1.19	1.55	0.79	0.83	0.42
1960.0	170.0	209.1	199.6	254.4	130.5	134.7	68.5	0.85	1.05	1.28	0.65	0.68	0.34	1.23	1.17	1.50	0.77	0.79	0.40
1961.0	166.6	218.5	207.6	257.8	132.1	135.1	68.4	0.80	1.05	1.24	0.64	0.65	0.33	1.31	1.25	1.55	0.79	0.81	0.41
1962.0	181.6	225.8	213.8	261.6	134.1	135.9	68.9	0.85	1.06	1.22	0.63	0.64	0.32	1.24	1.18	1.44	0.74	0.75	0.38
1963.0	192.3	233.4	222.4	266.1	136.8	137.0	70.1	0.87	1.05	1.20	0.62	0.62	0.32	1.21	1.16	1.38	0.71	0.71	0.37
1964.0	204.9	242.6	231.3	271.9	141.1	141.1	73.0	0.89	1.05	1.18	0.61	0.61	0.32	1.18	1.13	1.33	0.69	0.69	0.36
1965.0	222.9	254.1	240.5	281.6	147.9	148.3	78.2	0.93	1.06	1.17	0.62	0.62	0.33	1.14	1.08	1.26	0.66	0.67	0.35
1966.0	246.3	271.4	257.4	294.8	157.0	158.5	85.4	0.96	1.06	1.15	0.61	0.62	0.33	1.10	1.05	1.20	0.64	0.64	0.35
1967.0	259.9	291.3	275.4	308.5	166.0	168.3	92.0	0.94	1.06	1.12	0.60	0,61	0.33	1.12	1.06	1.19	0.64	0.65	0.35
1968.0	270.1	311.0	289.1	319.7	173.8	175.3	96.9	0.93	1.08	1.11	0.60	0.61	0.34	1.15	1.07	1.18	0.64	0.65	0.36
1969.0	285.3	328.8	306.5	331.4	182.0	182.1	101.7	0.93	1.07	1.08	0.59	0.59	0.33	1.15	1.07	1.16	0.64	0.64	0.36
1970.0	287.1	345.0	324.9	340.8	188.9	186.5	105.0	0.88	1.06	1.05	0.58	0.57	0.32	1.20	1.13	1.19	0.66	0.65	0.37
1971.0	278.9	357.9	341.1	346.8	193.9	187.9	106.3	0.82	1.05	1.02	0.57	0.55	0.32	1.28	1.22	1.24	0.70	0.67	0.38
1972.0	295.0	368.3	354.8	353.5	200.1	190.0	108.8	0.83	1.04	0.98	0.55	0.53	0.30	1.25	1.20	1.20	0.68	0.64	0.37
1973.0	327.7	381.2	372.5	363.8	209.1	195.3	113.9	0.88	1.02	0.98	0.56	0.52	0.31	1.16	1.14	1.11	0.64	0.60	0.35
1974.0	343.2	395.9	398.6	373.5	218.6	201.6	119.4	0.86	0.99	0.94	0.55	0.51	0.30	1.16	1.16	1.09	0.64	0.59	0.35
1975.0	314.4	409.2	418.5	383.8	223.4	204.1	120.9	0.75	0.98	0.92	0.53	0.49	0.29	1.30	1.33	1.22	0.71	0.65	0.39
1976.0	326.2	419.2	431.1	*	*	*	*	0.76	0.97	*	*	*	*	1.29	1.32	*	*	*	*

Notes (by columns) to Table 1.   *: not available.

(1)-(2). Four-quarter means, centered at year-openings to correspond to dating of capital-quantum data, of indexes given in Federal Reserve Bulletin, November 1976, p. 903, multiplied by a constant to make 1967 output equal the $261.98 billion of value added by manufacture.

(3) Based on MGH survey materials; for construction see notes to Table 2. Figures for "Industry S" ("total manufacturing") are not given in Table 2, but are equal to the sum of the columns for industries Z and L in that table.

(4)-(7) Data for "constant-dollar" gross stocks" and "Constant-dollar net stocks" for manufacturing, from John C. Musgrave, "Fixed Nonresidential Business and Residential Capital in the United States, 1925-75", Survey of Current Business, April 1976, pp. 48-49. Mnemonics "E+S" and "E" in heading denote respectively "Equipment and Structures" and "equipment" in the Musgrave tables.

(8)-(13). Data of columns (1)-(2) and (4)-(7) with column (3) as common denominator. Downtrend in column (9) presumably reflects differences in methodology-- compounded probably by understatement of FRB output index in recent years resulting from use of KWH as proxy for output. Downtrends in columns (10)-(13) presumably reflect embodied and unembodied technical progress. Cyclical movements visible when columns (12)-(13) are charted are suspect: to the degree that technical progress is "embodied", decline of these ratios (of the nature of capital-intensity measurements) should be slowed down rather than accelerated when recession slows down investment embodying new methods.

(14)-19). Data of columns (2)-(7) with column (1) as common denominator. Downtrends in columns (16)-(19) again presumably reflect technical progress. Cyclical movements visible when columns (18)-(19) are again suspect. In the expansion from the trough of output in the year centered at viewpoint 1961.0, the quantum of capital per unit of output should be reduced by fuller utilization of the slack which existed at the trough and also be embodiment of new methods at an accelerating rate.

Whereas on methodological grounds the best proxy for capacity among the capital-quantum series should be equipment net, this series is the one which misbehaves worst. Equipment plus structure, net, behaves better than equipment net; so does equipment gross; and equipment plus structures gross has the most reasonable time-shape of all the capital-quantum series. Daniel Creamer at the Conference Board suggests that all the quantum series behave more reasonably if longer service lives are used; those assumed by Musgrave are "85 per cent of the lives specified in the 1942 edition of IRS Bulletin F."

USA: Manufacturing, by industry

Table 2

ACTUAL (EX POST) CAPACITY: SURVIVALS TO STATED SURVEY VIEWPOINTS FROM STATED BASE-DATES, 1951.0-1977.0

[Unit: 1 billion value-added dollars of 1967]

Survey viewpoint		Base date prior to which capacity in question was installed											
Date	Capacity	1972.0	1970.0	1968.0	1967.0	1966.0	1965.0	1963.0	1962.0	1961.0	1957.0	1955.0	1951.0
		Industry = Z: Total manufacturing excluding petroleum											
1977.0	429.5	292.2			180.7						86.0		
1975.0	396.7		273.4				170.1					82.6	
1973.0	352.1			230.4				131.5					49.9
1971.0	322.3					209.6				135.8			55.3
1967.0	259.7								165.7		111.3		62.5
1962.0	199.2										133.7		80.1
Base-date		335.2	307.3	272.7	259.7	241.9	225.2	207.8	199.2	193.0	162.5	142.7	112.8

Table 2, page 2

Date	Capa-city	1972.0	1970.0	1968.0	1967.0	1966.0	1965.0	1963.0	1962.0	1961.0	1957.0	1955.0	1951.0
Industry = A: Primary iron and steel													
1977.0	20.34	15.67			10.78				4.68				
1975.0	19.93		15.35				9.97					4.98	
1973.0	19.16			14.75				9.77					3.64
1971.0	18.79					12.96				9.58			4.51
1967.0	17.02								12.08		7.66		4.08
1962.0	14.98										9.87		5.54
Base-date		19.16	18.60	17.36	17.02	16.37	15.59	15.13	14.98	14.84	13.07	12.20	10.24
Industry = M: Food, beverages													
1977.0	47.56	30.43			19.02						9.03		
1975.0	42.34		27.53				16.52					6.78	
1973.0	37.33			23.90				14.94					6.35
1971.0	33.54					21.13				14.42			7.38
1967.0	26.08								17.72		12.52		6.79
1962.0	20.25										14.37		9.11
Base-date		34.88	31.64	27.38	26.08	25.08	23.44	21.26	20.25	19.66	16.65	15.25	13.29
Industry = J: Paper													
1977.0	14.91	10.72			7.00						4.02		
1975.0	14.06		9.99				6.32					3.09	
1973.0	12.87			9.01				6.56					2.57
1971.0	11.90					8.09				5.60			2.38
1967.0	9.70								5.41		4.36		2.43
1962.0	7.54										5.22		2.96
Base-date		12.38	11.45	10.28	9.70	8.98	8.39	7.76	7.54	7.18	5.91	5.21	4.17

Table 2, page 3

Date	Capacity	1972.0	1970.0	1968.0	1967.0	1966.0	1965.0	1963.0	1962.0	1961.0	1957.0	1955.0	1951.0
		Industry = G: "Miscellaneous metal processing" = Fabricated metal products + Instruments											
1977.0	38.13	25.93			16.77						8.00		
1975.0	35.26		24.00				14.12					6.70	
1973.0	31.38			21.34				13.17					5.34
1971.0	28.74					17.53				10.63			5.17
1967.0	22.34								13.41		7.37		4.69
1962.0	17.51										11.74		6.66
Base-date		29.89	26.86	23.46	22.34	20.88	19.89	18.39	17.51	16.84	13.59	12.10	9.96
		Industry = C: Machinery, excluding electrical											
1977.0	44.54	31.18			20.49						10.25		
1975.0	40.42		26.67				15.76					8.09	
1973.0	34.65			24.26				14.56					5.20
1971.0	32.04					19.22				12.49			6.09
1967.0	24.91								15.44		10.46		5.73
1962.0	19.17										13.04		7.36
Base-date		33.00	30.52	26.65	24.91	23.10	21.56	20.12	19.19	18.79	15.61	13.03	10.13

Table 2, page 4

Date	Capacity	1972.0	1970.0	1968.0	1967.0	1966.0	1965.0	1963.0	1962.0	1961.0	1957.0	1955.0	1951.0
							Industry = D: Electrical equipment						
1977.0	54.90	31.84			16.47						5.49		
1975.0	47.86		28.72				17.71					5.74	
1973.0	45.15			24.83				12.64					3.16
1971.0	39.44					21.69				12.22			3.55
1967.0	27.44								15.91		8.51		3.84
1962.0	21.35										11.75		6.41
Base-date		42.20	36.86	29.91	27.44	25.18	23.10	22.21	21.35	20.53	16.27	13.69	9.11
							Industry = I: Chemicals						
1977.0	45.11	30.22			18.04						8.12		
1975.0	40.15		26.50				16.86					7.23	
1973.0	34.11			21.83				12.28					4.43
1971.0	29.51					19.48				13.28			5.02
1967.0	22.52								13.74		8.10		3.83
1962.0	15.63										10.47		5.63
Base-date		31.58	27.84	24.09	22.52	20.66	18.61	16.41	15.63	14.74	11.57	10.11	7.10
							Industry = H: Products of stone, clay and glass						
1977.0	13.30	9.31			6.39						3.33		
1975.0	11.84		8.05				5.09					2.61	
1973.0	10.44			7.52				5.01					2.30
1971.0	10.04					7.93				5.92			2.81
1967.0	8.83								5.92		3.97		2.21
1962.0	7.13										4.85		2.71
Base-date		10.24	9.94	9.01	8.83	8.26	7.79	7.34	7.13	6.92	5.92	5.22	4.30

Table 2, page 5

Date	Capa-city	1972.0	1970.0	1968.0	1967.0	1966.0	1965.0	1963.0	1962.0	1961.0	1957.0	1955.0	1951.0
						Industry = K: Rubber, plastics							
1977.0	11.21	8.07			5.16						2.47		
1975.0	10.46		7.74				4.71					2.72	
1973.0	9.32			5.97				3.82					1.49
1971.0	8.45					4.98				3.30			1.69
1967.0	6.96								4.52		3.06		1.67
1962.0	5.35										3.64		2.14
Base-date		8.79	7.90	7.31	6.96	6.56	6.13	5.56	5.35	5.14	4.36	3.77	2.99
						Industry = N: Textile mill products							
1977.0	13.78	8.68			5.10						1.93		
1975.0	12.74		7.26				3.69					1.78	
1973.0	11.68			8.64				5.61					2.34
1971.0	10.40					7.07				4.68			2.08
1967.0	8.24								5.11		3.87		2.39
1962.0	6.65										4.86		3.26
Base-date		10.92	9.72	8.73	8.24	7.85	7.20	6.79	6.65	6.46	5.85	5.31	5.16
						Industry = B: Primary non-ferrous metals							
1977.0	11.07	7.73			4.98						1.66		
1975.0	10.65		8.83				6.18					3.19	
1973.0	9.85			7.49				4.73					1.77
1971.0	9.11					6.92				5.10			1.91
1967.0	7.50				6.92				5.40		3.45		1.72
1962.0	6.29										4.09		2.14
Base-date		9.75	8.76	8.03	7.50	7.08	6.68	6.42	6.29	6.05	4.93	4.31	3.08

Table 2, page 6

Date	Capa-city	1972.0	1970.0	1968.0	1967.0	1966.0	1965.0	1963.0	1962.0	1961.0	1957.0	1955.0	1951.0
						Industry = E: Motor vehicles and parts							
1977.0	33.37	23.69			13.68						5.34		
1975.0	30.84		20.05				11.10					3.08	
1973.0	29.65			19.57				12.45					4.15
1971.0	27.96					18.83				10.90			4.47
1967.0	24.15								10.14		7.00		4.35
1962.0	20.86										14.81		4.38
Base-date		28.24	26.13	25.12	24.15	23.45	21.91	21.06	20.86	20.45	18.71	15.89	11.40
						Industry = L: Petroleum							
1977.0	23.16	15.29			8.80						4.17		
1975.0	21.84		15.51				10.48					6.65	
1973.0	20.39			11.21				3.87					1.22
1971.0	18.85					12.06				6.79		7.52	1.70
1967.0	15.67								11.28		7.52		3.13
1962.0	14.62										9.06		4.68
Base-date		19.60	17.62	16.45	15.67	15.51	15.36	14.62	14.62	14.62	13.25	12.25	9.98
						Industry = F: Transport equipment other than motor vehicles							
1977.0	28.86	21.36			12.70						7.79		
1975.0	26.69		20.02				13.34					8.81	
1973.0	25.16			19.88				13.84					7.80
1971.0	23.48					17.37				13.38			8.45
1967.0	18.27								9.51		4.93		2.74
1962.0	12.69										7.49		4.19
Base-date		24.19	22.58	20.10	18.27	16.31	14.97	13.58	12.69	12.44	10.05	8.38	4.64

agh May 1977. SOURCE: MGH: capacity index and "HOW MODERN..." surveys; see text.

USA: Manufacturing, by industries

Table 3

GROSS INSTALLATIONS, NET GROWTH AND APPARENT REPLACEMENT OF CAPACITY: ESTIMATES USING McGRAW-HILL DATA ON AGE-DISTRIBUTION OF CAPACITY IN BEING, TRANSFORMED TO "STANDARD" VIEWPOINT DATES 1962.0, 1967.0, 1972.0 AND 1977.0: EX POST DATA

[Unit: 1 billion value-added dollars of 1967]

Quinquennium	Industry														
	Steel	Non-ferrous metals	Machinery	Electrical equipt.	Motor vehicles	Other transport	Misc. metal processing	Stone, clay, glass	Chemicals	Paper	Rubber, plastics	Food, beverages	Textiles	Total excluding petroleum	Petroleum
	A	B	C	D	E	F	G	H	I	J	K	M	N	Z	L
i. Gross installations during quinquennium estimated by reversing "mortality" of youngest capacity age-group.															
1952-56[a]	5.42	2.10	5.67	6.58	14.76	3.54	6.00	2.42	4.97	2.42	1.68	5.82	1.87	60.19	6.56
1957-61	5.74	2.36	6.63	10.78	7.02	5.52	6.60	2.49	5.44	2.50	1.86	6.43	1.99	70.99	6.64
1962-66	5.56	2.33	10.23	12.93	16.25[b]	9.54	9.90	3.18	9.26	3.53	2.65	9.05	3.47	103.47	5.24
1967-71	6.60	2.82	13.37	21.15	10.58	8.38	13.06	2.41	11.45	4.15	3.74	13.50	3.98	125.16	8.75
1972-76	5.27	3.80	14.46	25.87	11.23	9.42	13.09	4.36	15.70	4.47	3.42	18.57	5.66	149.57	9.41
ii. Net expansion during quinquennium estimated by differencing capacity levels															
1952-56	2.52	1.54	4.77	6.34	6.05	4.76	3.24	1.28	3.76	1.57	1.25	2.83	0.64	42.78	10.14
1957-61	1.91	1.36	3.55	5.08	2.15	2.64	3.92	1.21	4.06	1.63	0.99	3.60	0.80	36.68	1.37
1962-66	2.04	1.21	5.75	6.09	3.29	5.58	4.83	1.71	6.89	2.17	1.61	5.83	1.59	60.50	10.46
1967-71	2.14	2.25	8.09	14.75	4.09	5.92	7.55	1.40	9.06	2.68	1.84	8.81	2.68	75.46	3.94
1972-76	1.17	1.32	11.54	12.70	5.13	4.67	8.24	3.07	13.53	2.52	2.42	12.68	2.86	94.29	3.56
iii. Replacement during quinquennium estimated as residual: gross installations less net expansion															
1952-56	2.89	0.56	0.89	0.24	8.71	-1.22	2.76	1.14	1.20	0.84	0.43	3.02	1.23	17.41	3.70
1957-61	3.83	1.00	3.08	5.70	4.87	2.88	2.48	1.28	1.38	0.87	0.87	2.83	1.19	34.31	5.27
1962-66	3.52	1.12	4.49	6.84	12.96[b]	3.95	5.07	1.48	2.37	1.37	1.04	3.22	1.89	42.96	4.20
1967-71	4.46	0.58	5.28	6.40	6.49	2.46	5.52	1.01	2.39	1.47	1.90	4.70	1.40	49.67	4.82
1972-76	4.10	2.48	2.90	13.17	6.10	4.75	4.85	1.30	2.17	1.94	1.00	5.89	2.79	55.27	5.88

agh April 1977. a. Estimated from next-to-youngest group in 1962 survey. b. Distorted by exaggeration of youngest group in 1967 survey.
To simulate 5-year survey intervals, 1975 survey is ignored, and "1972" is estimated by averaging 1971 and 1963 data. Survivals from base-dates not used in surveys are estimated by log-linear interpolation.

USA: Manufacturing, by industry

Table 4

RATIOS TO AVERAGE LEVEL OF CAPACITY IN BEING DURING QUINQUENNIUM OF NET INCREMENTS, APPARENT REPLACEMENT AND GROSS INSTALLATIONS OF CAPACITY, 1952-1977

(Annual rates-- per cent)

Quinquennium	Industry (coded as in Table 3) A	B	C	D	E	F	G	H	I	J	K	M	N	Z	L
	i. Per cent of capacity represented by net increments														
1952-56	4.8	7.5	7.4	9.7	7.7	11.9	5.4	4.9	7.7	6.1	6.8	3.8	2.4	6.1	4.8
1957-61	2.6	4.9	4.0	5.2	2.2	4.6	5.1	3.7	6.0	4.9	4.1	4.9	2.6	4.0	2.0
1962-66	2.6	3.6	5.3	5.2	3.0	7.5	4.9	4.4	7.5	5.2	5.3	5.1	4.4	5.4	1.4
1967-71	2.4	5.3	5.5	8.5	3.1	5.4	5.8	2.9	6.8	4.8	4.7	5.8	5.6	5.1	4.5
1972-76	1.2	2.5	5.9	5.2	3.3	3.6	4.9	5.3	7.1	3.7	4.8	6.2	4.6	4.9	3.3
	ii. Per cent of capacity represented by apparent replacement														
1952-56	4.2	2.7	1.4	0.4	11.1	-3.1	0.6	4.4	2.5	3.3	2.3	4.0	4.5	2.5	6.2
1957-61	5.3	3.6	3.5	5.8	4.9	5.0	3.2	3.9	2.0	2.6	3.7	3.1	3.8	3.8	7.5
1962-66	4.5	3.4	4.2	5.8	11.8[a]	5.3	5.2	3.8	2.6	3.3	3.5	2.8	5.2	3.8	5.5
1967-71	4.9	1.4	3.6	3.7	5.0	2.3	4.2	2.1	1.8	2.7	4.9	3.1	2.7	3.3	5.5
1972-76	4.2	4.8	1.5	5.4	3.9	3.6	2.9	2.2	1.1	2.8	2.0	2.9	4.5	2.9	5.5
	iii. Memorandum: Mortality rate indicated by 10-year survival rates														
	4.7	2.7	3.1	4.5	5.8	3.3	4.0	3.4	2.1	2.7	3.3	3.2	4.1	3.5	6.9
	iv. Per cent of capacity represented by gross installations														
1952-56	9.0	10.2	8.8	10.0	18.8	8.9	10.1	9.3	10.2	9.4	9.1	7.8	6.9	8.6	11.1
1957-61	7.9	8.4	7.5	11.0	7.1	9.6	8.3	7.6	8.0	7.5	7.8	7.0	6.4	7.8	9.4
1962-66	7.1	7.0	9.5	11.0	14.8[a]	12.8	10.1	8.2	10.1	8.5	8.8	7.9	9.6	9.2	6.9
1967-71	7.3	6.6	9.1	12.1	8.1	7.7	10.0	5.1	8.5	7.5	9.6	8.9	8.4	8.4	10.0
1972-76	5.4	7.3	7.4	10.6	7.2	7.2	7.7	7.6	8.2	6.5	6.7	9.1	9.0	7.8	8.8

agh April 1979 a. Distorted by exaggeration of youngest age-group in 1967 survey.

Numerators of percentages are corresponding entries in Table 3. Denominators are sums (because quinquennial [illegible] 2 are sums) of capacity-level figures at opening of years during quinquennia, from Table 5.

USA: Manufacturing, by industry

Table 5

ACTUAL (EX POST) LEVELS OF CAPACITY IN BEING, YEAR-OPENINGS, 1951-1976

[Unit: 1 billion valued-added dollars of 1967]

Date	Industry														
	Steel A	Non-ferrous metals B	Machinery C	Electrical equipt. D	Motor vehicles E	Other transport equipt. F	Misc. metal processing G	Stone, clay, glass H	Chemicals I	Paper J	Rubber, plastic K	Food, beverages M	Textiles N	Total, excluding petroleum Z	Petroleum L
1951.0	10.24	3.08	10.13	9.11	11.40	4.64	9.96	4.30	7.10	4.17	2.99	13.29	5.16	112.77	9.98
1952.0	10.55	3.39	10.84	9.93	12.66	5.29	10.35	4.64	7.81	4.33	3.11	13.82	5.21	119.74	10.38
1953.0	11.40	3.46	11.82	11.22	14.56	6.83	10.87	4.87	8.67	4.68	3.33	14.23	5.26	128.33	10.91
1954.0	11.96	4.10	12.53	12.68	14.99	7.99	11.52	5.02	9.53	4.96	3.53	14.66	5.42	135.93	11.66
1955.0	12.20	4.31	13.03	13.69	15.89	8.38	12.10	5.22	10.11	5.21	3.77	15.25	5.31	142.72	12.25
1956.0	12.57	4.61	13.94	14.78	17.16	9.05	12.95	5.53	10.81	5.57	4.11	15.86	5.63	153.19	12.62
1957.0	13.07	4.93	15.61	16.27	18.71	10.05	13.59	5.92	11.57	5.91	4.36	16.65	5.85	162.52	13.25
1958.0	13.99	5.23	16.71	17.57	19.27	10.45	14.27	6.27	12.50	6.26	4.45	17.15	5.97	170.91	13.64
1959.0	14.69	5.49	17.21	18.45	19.46	11.39	14.99	6.46	13.25	6.51	4.58	17.83	6.15	177.88	14.05
1960.0	14.83	5.66	18.07	19.74	19.85	11.74	15.89	6.72	13.91	6.90	4.90	19.08	6.39	185.27	14.33
1961.0	14.84	6.05	18.79	20.53	20.45	12.44	16.84	6.92	14.74	7.18	5.14	19.66	6.46	192.97	14.62
1962.0	14.98	6.29	19.17	21.35	20.86	12.69	17.51	7.13	15.63	7.54	5.35	20.25	6.65	199.20	14.62
1963.0	15.13	6.42	20.12	22.21	21.06	13.58	18.39	7.34	16.41	7.76	5.56	21.26	6.79	207.75	14.62
1964.0	15.28	6.48	20.93	22.43	21.27	14.39	19.31	7.56	17.39	8.00	5.84	22.32	6.99	216.06	15.21
1965.0	15.59	6.68	31.56	23.10	21.91	14.97	19.89	7.79	18.61	8.39	6.13	23.44	7.20	225.16	15.36
1966.0	16.37	7.08	23.10	25.28	23.45	16.31	20.88	8.26	20.66	8.98	6.56	25.08	7.85	241.85	15.51
1967.0	17.02	7.50	24.91	27.44	24.15	18.27	22.34	8.83	22.52	9.70	6.96	26.08	8.24	259.70	16.45
1968.0	17.36	8.03	26.65	29.91	25.12	20.10	23.46	9.01	24.09	10.28	7.31	27.38	8.73	272.69	16.45
1969.0	17.89	8.19	28.25	33.21	25.62	21.51	25.10	9.37	25.78	10.78	7.60	29.30	9.17	189.21	17.27
1970.0	18.60	8.76	30.52	36.86	26.13	22.58	26.86	9.84	27.84	11.45	7.90	31.64	9.72	307.26	17.62
1971.0	18.79	9.11	32.04	39.44	27.96	23.48	28.74	10.04	29.51	11.90	8.45	33.54	10.40	322.27	18.85
1972.0	19.16	9.75	33.00	42.20	28.24	24.19	29.89	10.24	31.58	12.38	8.79	34.88	10.92	335.16	19.60
1973.0	19.16	9.85	34.65	45.15	29.65	25.16	31.38	10.44	34.11	12.87	9.32	37.33	11.68	352.16	20.39
1974.0	19.35	10.24	37.42	47.86	30.84	25.91	32.95	10.96	37.18	13.52	10.16	39.94	12.62	377.38	21.20
1975.0	19.93	10.65	40.42	47.86	30.84	26.69	35.26	11.84	40.15	14.06	10.46	42.34	12.74	396.66	21.84
1976.0	20.13	10.55	41.63	52.29	32.71	27.22	36.32	12.67	42.16	14.34	10.78	44.45	13.13	409.00	22.06

agh April 1977

SOURCE: MGH; see notes on ensuing page.

USA: Manufacturing, by industry

Table 3

TARGETED (EX ANTE) LEVELS OF CAPACITY FOR HORIZON

ONE YEAR FROM VIEWPOINT, 1953-1976

[Unit: 1 billion value-added dollars of 1967]

Viewpoint	Industry														
	Steel A	Non-ferrous metals B	Machinery C	Electrical equipt. D	Motor vehicles E	Other transport equipt. F	Misc. metal processing G	Stone, clay, glass H	Chemicals I	Paper J	Rubber, plastic K	Food, beverages M	Textiles N	Total, excluding petroleum Z	Petroleum L
1953.0	11.88	*	12.88	12.68	15.58	8.13	*	*	9.54	*	*	14.80	*	137.52	11.56
1954.0	12.20	*	13.03	13.82	15.59	8.55	*	*	10.20	*	*	15.54	*	141.36	12.13
1955.0	12.44	4.48	13.81	14.65	16.53	9.05	12.83	5.48	10.82	5.57	3.96	16.01	5.53	150.35	12.37
1956.0	12.95	4.98	15.19	16.11	18.53	9.77	14.25	5.97	11.78	6.13	4.44	16.65	5.74	166.07	13.00
1957.0	13.98	5.32	16.86	17.90	19.27	10.85	14.40	6.22	12.61	6.26	4.58	17.32	6.20	172.41	13.91
1958.0	14.41	5.75	17.38	18.80	19.46	11.29	14.98	6.52	13.38	6.51	4.54	17.49	6.23	179.02	13.91
1959.0	14.84	5.87	17.90	19.56	19.65	11.50	16.19	6.72	14.31	6.97	4.72	18.54	6.33	185.42	14.19
1960.0	14.98	5.72	18.97	20.92	20.45	12.09	16.84	7.12	14.61	7.11	5.05	20.22	6.71	195.11	14.47
1961.0	14.84	6.17	19.54	21.35	20.86	12.69	17.51	7.20	15.62	7.61	5.40	20.45	6.52	201.27	14.62
1962.0	15.43	6.42	19.94	21.99	21.28	13.45	18.74	7.34	16.41	7.77	5.67	21.26	6.98	207.60	14.77
1963.0	15.58	6.55	21.12	22.88	21.27	14.33	19.49	7.63	17.23	7.99	5.89	22.32	7.06	216.35	14.91
1964.0	15.59	6.67	21.77	22.88	21.91	15.11	20.08	7.86	18.61	8.32	6.31	23.88	7.27	227.47	15.36
1965.0	16.21	7.01	22.85	24.02	23.66	15.72	20.69	8.18	20.10	8.89	6.50	24.85	7.70	239.44	15.51
1966.0	17.35	7.72	24.95	27.45	24.86	18.27	21.92	8.92	22.52	9.52	7.02	26.33	8.40	262.28	15.67
1967.0	18.31	8.18	27.15	29.91	25.12	19.09	23.68	9.45	24.77	10.38	7.59	27.38	8.73	284.01	16.14
1968.0	17.71	8.35	28.32	33.20	26.12	21.31	25.34	9.46	25.78	10.79	7.82	28.75	8.99	289.71	16.78
1969.0	18.43	8.60	29.95	37.53	26.13	23.02	27.11	9.84	27.33	11.32	8.06	31.35	9.72	309.97	17.96
1970.0	19.53	9.20	32.35	38.33	26.91	23.26	29.01	10.53	30.07	12.02	8.37	34.17	10.11	325.87	18.50
1971.0	19.35	9.93	33.96	42.20	28.52	24.18	30.18	10.64	31.28	12.26	8.62	35.55	11.23	337.82	20.36
1972.0	19.16	10.14	34.65	45.15	28.52	25.16	31.09	10.75	32.84	13.12	9.14	36.28	11.68	349.35	19.60
1973.0	19.73	10.24	37.08	48.76	30.84	26.67	32.64	11.28	35.82	13.13	10.07	39.57	12.50	374.06	20.80
1974.0	20.12	10.44	41.16	50.25	32.38	27.21	34.93	11.62	39.78	14.06	11.38	43.53	13.25	400.23	22.26
1975.0	20.33	10.86	43.25	50.25	31.46	27.49	37.02	12.55	41.76	14.62	10.88	44.46	12.99	412.74	22.50
1976.0	20.33	11.08	44.54	54.90	33.36	28.85	38.14	13.30	45.11	14,91	11.21	47.56	13.82	429.45	23.16

* No capacity-target ratios reported by MGH. 1955-56 ratios for industry N lacking in source, estimated by agh.

SOURCE: viewpoint levels from Table 1, plus percentages reported by MGH for viewpoint-year expansion.

agh 30 May 1977

turing, by
industry

TARGETED (EX ANTE LEVELS OF CAPACITY FOR HORIZON

FOUR YEARS FROM VIEWPOINT, 1953-1976

[Unit: 1 billion value-added dollars of 1967]

View-point	Industry														
	Steel	Nonferrous metals	Machinery	Electrical equipt.	Motor vehicles	Other transport equipt.	Misc. metal processing	Stone, clay, glass	Chemicals	Paper	Rubber, plastics	Food, beverages	Textiles	Total, excluding petroleum	Petroleum
	A	B	C	D	E	F	G	H	I	J	K	M	N	Z	L
1953.0	11.98	*	14.43	15.72	17.45	8.94	*	*	11.64	*	*	15.84	*	140.10	12.36
1954.0	12.44	*	14.20	15.75	16.37	8.81	*	*	12.44	*	*	16.16	*	148.74	12.62
1955.0	13.31	5.02	15.61	16.85	18.18	10.05	14.37	6.25	13.20	6.46	4.36	17.45	6.03	159.28	12.86
1956.0	15.15	6.37	18.23	19.17	21.87	10.84	16.82	7.04	15.20	7.79	5.24	18.48	6.26	181.78	14.30
1957.0	15.66	6.65	19.73	22.55	21.39	12.37	17.12	6.97	15.38	7.32	5.18	18.88	6.70	187.43	15.44
1958.0	15.13	6.90	19.12	22.18	20.24	12.08	16.78	7.17	15.92	7.10	4.95	16.09	6.45	188.69	14.61
1959.0	15.29	6.75	19.87	22.69	20.63	11.73	18.46	7.59	17.03	8.29	5.29	20.39	6.90	198.85	14.33
1960.0	16.03	6.29	20.68	24.69	22.50	12.82	17.85	8.05	16.95	7.68	5.56	23.25	7.38	208.79	14.90
1961.0	15.58	6.79	21.49	23.70	22.53	13.71	19.61	7.99	17.81	8.68	5.99	22.70	6.98	212.85	15.50
1962.0	16.36	6.68	22.33	24.19	23.41	14.53	21.36	7.71	18.05	8.55	6.35	23.17	7.82	220.43	14.92
1963.0	16.67	7.40	23.45	25.17	23.40	15.33	22.61	8.39	19.99	8.47	6.48	25.00	7.84	233.70	15.66
1964.0	18.08	7.20	24.38	26.08	24.10	16.77	22.89	8.88	21.96	9.40	7.51	27.46	7.92	248.14	15.67
1965.0	17.67	7.92	26.05	28.10	28.63	17.92	23.17	9.16	24.12	9.96	7.67	29.07	8.62	260.78	15.98
1966.0	19.78	9.11	28.94	32.12	28.84	20.83	24.33	10.35	27.92	11.14	7.86	30.28	9.58	281.79	16.92
1967.0	20.58	9.82	32.31	36.79	27.38	21.76	27.00	11.25	30.96	11.94	8.96	32.03	10.21	324.69	17.27
1968.0	19.66	10.02	33.94	42.16	28.99	25.15	30.66	10.60	30.68	12.30	9.23	33.93	10.16	320.52	18.12
1969.0	20.64	9.80	34.74	47.66	30.05	26.24	32.80	11.41	33.89	13.02	9.51	36.99	11.28	342.13	20.29
1970.0	22.46	10.21	39.79	53.66	29.60	25.59	34.23	12.32	36.99	14.78	9.37	39.98	11.12	363.27	21.09
1971.0	21.09	11.12	39.73	52.33	31.37	26.36	35.00	12.34	37.54	13.85	9.57	39.46	13.03	368.90	21.58
1972.0	20.31	11.36	39.85	55.08	31.09	27.17	34.82	11.83	38.09	15.22	9.87	41.72	13.67	383.26	21.17
1973.0	21.31	11.26	44.13	58.51	34.54	30.94	37.54	13.65	42.98	14.18	12.18	47.88	13.92	413.21	23.09
1974.0	21.53	11.80	52.27	61.31	35.29	30.48	40.52	13.48	48.13	15.89	13.54	51.80	14.97	437.76	25.82
1975.0	23.20	12.05	51.03	60.30	35.55	29.69	41.83	14.31	50.95	16.67	12.73	51.13	14.94	458.35	23.63
1976.0	22.97	12.74	50.33	62.04	37.70	31.45	42.34	15.16	54.58	15.95	12.89	58.02	16.05	473.00	23.85

* No capacity-target ratios reported by MGH. 1955-56 ratios for industry N lacking in source, estimated by agh.

agh 30 May 1977

SOURCE: (v+1) levels from Table 4, plus percentages reported by MGH for expansion from (v+1) to (v+4).

A N N E X

A. List of Papers presented at the 13th CIRET Conference 14-16 September 1977 in Munich

B. List of CIRET Studies

ANNEX A: List of Papers presented at the 13th CIRET Conference 14-16 September 1977 in Munich

1st Session

Chairman: W.H. STRIGEL, IFO-Institut für Wirtschaftsforschung, Munich

W.A. JÖHR Universität St. Gallen	Psychological Infection, A Cause of Business Fluctuations
G. KATONA/B. STRÜMPEL University of Michigan Ann Arbor Freie Universität Berlin Berlin	Consumer Sentiment and Economic Trends

2nd Session

Chairman: Å. LÖNNQVIST, Statistiska Centralbyrån, Stockholm

B.A. PERSSON Konjunkturinstitutet Stockholm	Balance Series as True and False Indicators of Quantitative Change: Theory and Practice
K. AIGINGER Österreichisches Institut für Wirtschaftsforschung Vienna	Micro-Economic Tests of Macro-Economic Investment Theories by Means of Entrepreneurial Surveys
J.T. BRIMER University of Nigeria Nsukka	The Causal Structure of Expectations in The Confederation of British Industry Industrial Trends Survey
K. VOGLER IFO-Institut für Wirtschaftsforschung Munich	Content and Determinants of Judgemental and Expectational Variables in the IFO Business Survey
A. NYSSENS/R. REYNDERS Banque Nationale de Belgique Brussels	Signification of the Price Development "ex ante" and "ex post" in the Business Survey

3rd Session

Chairman: V. ZARNOWITZ, University of Chicago, Chicago

J. LEYLAND Organisation for Economic Co-operation and Development (OECD) Paris	Qualitative Indicators in International Business Cycle Analysis
G.H. MOORE/Ph.A. KLEIN National Bureau of Economic Research New York The Pennsylvania State University Pennsylvania	Forecasting Foreign Trade Flows with Leading Indicators
M. HANADA/E. SASAKI The Bank of Japan Tokyo	A Study in the Bank of Japan's Investment Survey
W.C. HUG Eidgenössische Technische Hochschule Zürich Zurich	Diffusion Indexes as Leading Indicators in Different Branches
W. SIMON/G. LANGHANS/ R. BAUMGÄRTNER Siemens AG Erlangen	Application of Leading Indicators with Regard to Industrial Planning
J. RODRIGUEZ/V. POVEDA Banco de Espana Madrid	An Approximation to the Reference Cycle for the Spanish Economy, 1965-75

4th Session

Chairman: M. BABA, Kyoto Institute of Economic Research, Kyoto

M. DEVILLIERS Institut National de la Statistique et des Etudes Economiques (INSEE) Paris	An Appraisal of the Corporate Liquidity and the Profitability of Firms by Means of Business Surveys as well as of the Consequences on the Firms' Behaviour
J. GARCIA VALVERDE Ministerio de Industria Madrid	Forecasting of Cycles by Means of Industrial Business Surveys of the Ministerio de Industria
G.B. KEATING Confederation of British Industry (CBI) London	The Use of the CBI Survey Data for Measuring Constraints to Fixed Investment Authorization
A.J.M. de VRIES Bureau for Economic Research Stellenbosch	An Evaluation of the Annual Forecast of the Bureau for Economic Research, University of Stellenbosch
R. KRC/M. KODAJ Slovenska Akademia Vied Ekonomicky Ustav Bratislava	Economic Tendency Surveys in Czechoslovakia

5th Session

Chairman: J. GARCIA VALVERDE, Ministerio de Industria, Madrid

G. NERB/W.H. STRIGEL IFO-Institut für Wirtschaftsforschung Munich	Entrepreneurs' Perception of Social Environment and its Influence on Growth Expectations
E.J. van der LINDEN Commission of the European Communities Brussels	Principal Component Analyses with Data from EEC-Entrepreneurial and Consumer Surveys
C.R. WESTON/R.A. McDONNEL La Trobe University Bundoora	Consumer Attitudes in a Dynamic Demand Theory
G. POSER/Z.E. SHIPCHANDLER Technische Hochschule Darmstadt Indiana University - Purdue University Fort Wayne	Impact of Inflation on Consumer Life Style
G. HEALD Social Surveys (Gallup Poll) Ltd. London	World-wide Study on Social Indicators and Quality of Life

6th Session

Chairman: M. WEGNER, Commission of the European Communities, Brussels

R. EISNER Northwestern University Evanston	More on Capital Expenditure Anticipations
A.G. HART/J. ALBRECHT Columbia University New York	Some Uses of the Capacity Concept in Understanding Investment Behavior
M. GERARD Université de Namur Namur	Investment and Capacity Utilization Optimal Decision and Econometric Approach; the Case of Some Belgian Industrial Sectors
K. CHANG/T. SHU Graduate School of Economics College of Chinese Culture Taipei	Experience with Tendency Surveys in Taiwan

ANNEX B: **List of CIRET Studies**

No. 1 H. HELMSCHROTT, Estimation of Stocks as a Cyclical Indicator. April 1963, DM 15.--. (a) (b)

No. 2 S. RÖDIG, Record of the Actual and Anticipated Development of Producer Prices in the Business Survey. April 1964, DM 10.--. (b)

No. 3 W. STRIGEL, The Business Surveys of the IFO-Institute for Economic Research. December 1954, DM 20.--. (a) (b)

No. 4 O. ANDERSON jr. and W. STRIGEL, Significance and Determination of Businessmen's Opinions and Expectations. April 1965, DM 10.--. (b)

No. 5 J.P. PETERSEN and R. PETERSEN, Entrepreneurial Reaction Patterns over Time. October 1965, DM 15.--. (b)

No. 6 F.O. BONHOEFFER, The Investment Plans of Industrial Firms and their Contribution to the Forecast of Capital Expenditures. July 1966, DM 15.--. (a) (b)

No. 7 M. ZIEGLER, Significance of Changes and Estimations of Stocks for Business-cycle Research. August 1966, DM 15.--. (b)

No. 8 J.D. LINDLBAUER, On the Informative Value of Demand Variables in the IFO Business Survey. March 1967, DM 20.--. (b)

No. 9 F.O. BONHOEFFER and W.H. STRIGEL, Investment Planning and the Quality of Investment Anticipations in German Industry. April 1967, DM 15.--. (b)

No. 10 M. ZIEGLER, A Bibliography of Business Surveys. July 1968, DM 25.--. (a) (b)

No. 11 J.D. LINDLBAUER, Estimation of the Production Index with the Help of ex post and ex ante Data from the Business Survey. February 1969, DM 20.--. (a) (b)

No. 12 G. POSER, The Contribution of Consumer Research to the Analysis and Forecast of Business Trends. August 1969, DM 25.--. (b)

No. 13 F.O. BONHOEFFER and W.R. STRECK, The IFO Institute's Investment Test. A Survey of its Evolution and its Present Status. 1969, DM 20.--.

No. 14 G. NERB, W. GERSTENBERGER and S. SCHITTENHELM, Entrepreneurial Opinions and Anticipations Regarding Labour Requirements. September 1969, DM 20.--. (b)

(a) out of print
(b) only published in German

No. 15 W. GERSTENBERGER, J.D. LINDLBAUER, G. NERB and W.H. STRIGEL, Downswing and Recession in the Light of Quantitative and Qualitative Statistics. August 1969, DM 25.--. (b)

No. 16 J.D. LINDLBAUER, Seasonal Adjustment of IFO Business Test Series. September 1971, DM 20.--. (b)

No. 17 J.M. COURTOIS, G. GOLDRIAN and S. RICHTER, Indicators Derived from Trade Cycle Surveys in the European Communities. 1972, DM 25.--. (b)

No. 18 J.D. LINDLBAUER and J. PUHANI, Extrapolation of Entrepreneurial Investment Plans by Means of the IFO Business Survey. 1972, DM 25.--. (b)

No. 19 W.H. STRIGEL, Trade Cycle Indicators Derived from Qualitative Data. 1972, DM 25.--.

No. 20 J.D. LINDLBAUER, G. NERB and Ch.C. ROBERTS, An Indicator System of the West German Economy Employing Tendency Data and Official Statistics. 1973, DM 30.--. (b)

No. 21 G. NERB and W.H. STRIGEL, Consumer Surveys in Different Countries. 1974, DM 35.--. (b)

No. 22 Ch.C. ROBERTS, Macro-economic Indicators of the Trade Cycle. 1975, DM 35.--. (b)

No. 23 E. LANGMANTEL, Late Phases of the Economic Boom. 1976, DM 35.--. (b)

No. 24 K. AIGINGER, The Use of Survey Data for the Analysis of Business Cycles. 1977, DM 30.--.

No. 25 Summary Booklet, 13th CIRET Conference 1977. 1978, DM 20.--.

(a) out of print
(b) only published in German

CIRET Studies can be obtained at the CIRET Secretariate (Poschingerstr 5, 8000 München 80).

Vol. 59: J. A. Hanson, Growth in Open Economies. V, 128 pages. 1971.

Vol. 60: H. Hauptmann, Schätz- und Kontrolltheorie in stetigen dynamischen Wirtschaftsmodellen. V, 104 Seiten. 1971.

Vol. 61: K. H. F. Meyer, Wartesysteme mit variabler Bearbeitungsrate. VII, 314 Seiten. 1971.

Vol. 62: W. Krelle u. G. Gabisch unter Mitarbeit von J. Burgermeister, Wachstumstheorie. VII, 223 Seiten. 1972.

Vol. 63: J. Kohlas, Monte Carlo Simulation im Operations Research. VI, 162 Seiten. 1972.

Vol. 64: P. Gessner u. K. Spremann, Optimierung in Funktionenräumen. IV, 120 Seiten. 1972.

Vol. 65: W. Everling, Exercises in Computer Systems Analysis. VIII, 184 pages. 1972.

Vol. 66: F. Bauer, P. Garabedian and D. Korn, Supercritical Wing Sections. V, 211 pages. 1972.

Vol. 67: I. V. Girsanov, Lectures on Mathematical Theory of Extremum Problems. V, 136 pages. 1972.

Vol. 68: J. Loeckx, Computability and Decidability. An Introduction for Students of Computer Science. VI, 76 pages. 1972.

Vol. 69: S. Ashour, Sequencing Theory. V, 133 pages. 1972.

Vol. 70: J. P. Brown, The Economic Effects of Floods. Investigations of a Stochastic Model of Rational Investment. Behavior in the Face of Floods. V, 87 pages. 1972.

Vol. 71: R. Henn und O. Opitz, Konsum- und Produktionstheorie II. V, 134 Seiten. 1972.

Vol. 72: T. P. Bagchi and J. G. C. Templeton, Numerical Methods in Markov Chains and Bulk Queues. XI, 89 pages. 1972.

Vol. 73: H. Kiendl, Suboptimale Regler mit abschnittweise linearer Struktur. VI, 146 Seiten. 1972.

Vol. 74: F. Pokropp, Aggregation von Produktionsfunktionen. VI, 107 Seiten. 1972.

Vol. 75: GI-Gesellschaft für Informatik e.V. Bericht Nr. 3. 1. Fachtagung über Programmiersprachen · München, 9.–11. März 1971. Herausgegeben im Auftrag der Gesellschaft für Informatik von H. Langmaack und M. Paul. VII, 280 Seiten. 1972.

Vol. 76: G. Fandel, Optimale Entscheidung bei mehrfacher Zielsetzung. II, 121 Seiten. 1972.

Vol. 77: A. Auslender, Problèmes de Minimax via l'Analyse Convexe et les Inégalités Variationelles: Théorie et Algorithmes. VII, 132 pages. 1972.

Vol. 78: GI-Gesellschaft für Informatik e.V. 2. Jahrestagung, Karlsruhe, 2.–4. Oktober 1972. Herausgegeben im Auftrag der Gesellschaft für Informatik von P. Deussen. XI, 576 Seiten. 1973.

Vol. 79: A. Berman, Cones, Matrices and Mathematical Programming. V, 96 pages. 1973.

Vol. 80: International Seminar on Trends in Mathematical Modelling, Venice, 13–18 December 1971. Edited by N. Hawkes. VI, 288 pages. 1973.

Vol. 81: Advanced Course on Software Engineering. Edited by F. L. Bauer. XII, 545 pages. 1973.

Vol. 82: R. Saeks, Resolution Space, Operators and Systems. X, 267 pages. 1973.

Vol. 83: NTG/GI-Gesellschaft für Informatik, Nachrichtentechnische Gesellschaft. Fachtagung „Cognitive Verfahren und Systeme", Hamburg, 11.–13. April 1973. Herausgegeben im Auftrag der NTG/GI von Th. Einsele, W. Giloi und H.-H. Nagel. VIII, 373 Seiten. 1973.

Vol. 84: A. V. Balakrishnan, Stochastic Differential Systems I. Filtering and Control. A Function Space Approach. V, 252 pages. 1973.

Vol. 85: T. Page, Economics of Involuntary Transfers: A Unified Approach to Pollution and Congestion Externalities. XI, 159 pages. 1973.

Vol. 86: Symposium on the Theory of Scheduling and its Applications. Edited by S. E. Elmaghraby. VIII, 437 pages. 1973.

Vol. 87: G. F. Newell, Approximate Stochastic Behavior of n-Server Service Systems with Large n. VII, 118 pages. 1973.

Vol. 88: H. Steckhan, Güterströme in Netzen. VII, 134 Seiten. 1973.

Vol. 89: J. P. Wallace and A. Sherret, Estimation of Product. Attributes and Their Importances. V, 94 pages. 1973.

Vol. 90: J.-F. Richard, Posterior and Predictive Densities for Simultaneous Equation Models. VI, 226 pages. 1973.

Vol. 91: Th. Marschak and R. Selten, General Equilibrium with Price-Making Firms. XI, 246 pages. 1974.

Vol. 92: E. Dierker, Topological Methods in Walrasian Economics. IV, 130 pages. 1974.

Vol. 93: 4th IFAC/IFIP International Conference on Digital Computer Applications to Process Control, Part I. Zürich/Switzerland, March 19–22, 1974. Edited by M. Mansour and W. Schaufelberger. XVIII, 544 pages. 1974.

Vol. 94: 4th IFAC/IFIP International Conference on Digital Computer Applications to Process Control, Part II. Zürich/Switzerland, March 19–22, 1974. Edited by M. Mansour and W. Schaufelberger. XVIII, 546 pages. 1974.

Vol. 95: M. Zeleny, Linear Multiobjective Programming. X, 220 pages. 1974.

Vol. 96: O. Moeschlin, Zur Theorie von Neumannscher Wachstumsmodelle. XI, 115 Seiten. 1974.

Vol. 97: G. Schmidt, Über die Stabilität des einfachen Bedienungskanals. VII, 147 Seiten. 1974.

Vol. 98: Mathematical Methods in Queueing Theory. Proceedings 1973. Edited by A. B. Clarke. VII, 374 pages. 1974.

Vol. 99: Production Theory. Edited by W. Eichhorn, R. Henn, O. Opitz, and R. W. Shephard. VIII, 386 pages. 1974.

Vol. 100: B. S. Duran and P. L. Odell, Cluster Analysis. A Survey. VI, 137 pages. 1974.

Vol. 101: W. M. Wonham, Linear Multivariable Control. A Geometric Approach. X, 344 pages. 1974.

Vol. 102: Analyse Convexe et Ses Applications. Comptes Rendus, Janvier 1974. Edited by J.-P. Aubin. IV, 244 pages. 1974.

Vol. 103: D. E. Boyce, A. Farhi, R. Weischedel, Optimal Subset Selection. Multiple Regression, Interdependence and Optimal Network Algorithms. XIII, 187 pages. 1974.

Vol. 104: S. Fujino, A Neo-Keynesian Theory of Inflation and Economic Growth. V, 96 pages. 1974.

Vol. 105: Optimal Control Theory and its Applications. Part I. Proceedings 1973. Edited by B. J. Kirby. VI, 425 pages. 1974.

Vol. 106: Optimal Control Theory and its Applications. Part II. Proceedings 1973. Edited by B. J. Kirby. VI, 403 pages. 1974.

Vol. 107: Control Theory, Numerical Methods and Computer Systems Modeling. International Symposium, Rocquencourt, June 17–21, 1974. Edited by A. Bensoussan and J. L. Lions. VIII, 757 pages. 1975.

Vol. 108: F. Bauer et al., Supercritical Wing Sections II. A Handbook. V, 296 pages. 1975.

Vol. 109: R. von Randow, Introduction to the Theory of Matroids. IX, 102 pages. 1975.

Vol. 110: C. Striebel, Optimal Control of Discrete Time Stochastic Systems. III. 208 pages. 1975.

Vol. 111: Variable Structure Systems with Application to Economics and Biology. Proceedings 1974. Edited by A. Ruberti and R. R. Mohler. VI, 321 pages. 1975.

Vol. 112: J. Wilhlem, Objectives and Multi-Objective Decision Making Under Uncertainty. IV, 111 pages. 1975.

Vol. 113: G. A. Aschinger, Stabilitätsaussagen über Klassen von Matrizen mit verschwindenden Zeilensummen. V, 102 Seiten. 1975.

Vol. 114: G. Uebe, Produktionstheorie. XVII, 301 Seiten. 1976.

Vol. 115: Anderson et al., Foundations of System Theory: Finitary and Infinitary Conditions. VII, 93 pages. 1976

Vol. 116: K. Miyazawa, Input-Output Analysis and the Structure of Income Distribution. IX, 135 pages. 1976.

Vol. 117: Optimization and Operations Research. Proceedings 1975. Edited by W. Oettli and K. Ritter. IV, 316 pages. 1976.

Vol. 118: Traffic Equilibrium Methods, Proceedings 1974. Edited by M. A. Florian. XXIII, 432 pages. 1976.

Vol. 119: Inflation in Small Countries. Proceedings 1974. Edited by H. Frisch. VI, 356 pages. 1976.

Vol. 120: G. Hasenkamp, Specification and Estimation of Multiple-Output Production Functions. VII, 151 pages. 1976.

Vol. 121: J. W. Cohen, On Regenerative Processes in Queueing Theory. IX, 93 pages. 1976.

Vol. 122: M. S. Bazaraa, and C. M. Shetty, Foundations of Optimization VI. 193 pages. 1976

Vol. 123: Multiple Criteria Decision Making. Kyoto 1975. Edited by M. Zeleny. XXVII, 345 pages. 1976.

Vol. 124: M. J. Todd. The Computation of Fixed Points and Applications. VII, 129 pages. 1976.

Vol. 125: Karl C. Mosler. Optimale Transportnetze. Zur Bestimmung ihres kostengünstigsten Standorts bei gegebener Nachfrage. VI, 142 Seiten. 1976.

Vol. 126: Energy, Regional Science and Public Policy. Energy and Environment I. Proceedings 1975. Edited by M. Chatterji and P. Van Rompuy. VIII, 316 pages. 1976.

Vol. 127: Environment, Regional Science and Interregional Modeling. Energy and Environment II. Proceedings 1975. Edited by M. Chatterji and P. Van Rompuy. IX, 211 pages. 1976.

Vol. 128: Integer Programming and Related Areas. A Classified Bibliography. Edited by C. Kastning. XII, 495 pages. 1976.

Vol. 129: H.-J. Lüthi, Komplementaritäts- und Fixpunktalgorithmen in der mathematischen Programmierung. Spieltheorie und Ökonomie. VII, 145 Seiten. 1976.

Vol. 130: Multiple Criteria Decision Making, Jouy-en-Josas, France. Proceedings 1975. Edited by H. Thiriez and S. Zionts. VI, 409 pages. 1976.

Vol. 131: Mathematical Systems Theory. Proceedings 1975. Edited by G. Marchesini and S. K. Mitter. X, 408 pages. 1976.

Vol. 132: U. H. Funke, Mathematical Models in Marketing. A Collection of Abstracts. XX, 514 pages. 1976.

Vol. 133: Warsaw Fall Seminars in Mathematical Economics 1975. Edited by M. W. Loś, J. Loś, and A. Wieczorek. V. 159 pages. 1976.

Vol. 134: Computing Methods in Applied Sciences and Engineering. Proceedings 1975. VIII, 390 pages. 1976.

Vol. 135: H. Haga, A Disequilibrium – Equilibrium Model with Money and Bonds. A Keynesian – Walrasian Synthesis. VI, 119 pages. 1976.

Vol. 136: E. Kofler und G. Menges, Entscheidungen bei unvollständiger Information. XII, 357 Seiten. 1976.

Vol. 137: R. Wets, Grundlagen Konvexer Optimierung. VI, 146 Seiten. 1976.

Vol. 138: K. Okuguchi, Expectations and Stability in Oligopoly Models. VI, 103 pages. 1976.

Vol. 139: Production Theory and Its Applications. Proceedings. Edited by H. Albach and G. Bergendahl. VIII, 193 pages. 1977.

Vol. 140: W. Eichhorn and J. Voeller, Theory of the Price Index. Fisher's Test Approach and Generalizations. VII, 95 pages. 1976.

Vol. 141: Mathematical Economics and Game Theory. Essays in Honor of Oskar Morgenstern. Edited by R. Henn and O. Moeschlin. XIV, 703 pages. 1977.

Vol. 142: J. S. Lane, On Optimal Population Paths. V, 123 pages. 1977.

Vol. 143: B. Näslund, An Analysis of Economic Size Distributions. XV, 100 pages. 1977.

Vol. 144: Convex Analysis and Its Applications. Proceedings 1976. Edited by A. Auslender. VI, 219 pages. 1977.

Vol. 145: J. Rosenmüller, Extreme Games and Their Solutions. IV, 126 pages. 1977.

Vol. 146: In Search of Economic Indicators. Edited by W. H. Strigel. XVI, 198 pages. 1977.

Vol. 147: Resource Allocation and Division of Space. Proceedings. Edited by T. Fujii and R. Sato. VIII, 184 pages. 1977.

Vol. 148: C. E. Mandl, Simulationstechnik und Simulationsmodelle in den Sozial- und Wirtschaftswissenschaften. IX, 173 Seiten. 1977.

Vol. 149: Stationäre und schrumpfende Bevölkerungen: Demographisches Null- und Negativwachstum in Österreich. Herausgegeben von G. Feichtinger. VI, 262 Seiten. 1977.

Vol. 150: Bauer et al., Supercritical Wing Sections III. VI, 179 pages. 1977.

Vol. 151: C. A. Schneeweiß, Inventory-Production Theory. VI, 116 pages. 1977.

Vol. 152: Kirsch et al., Notwendige Optimalitätsbedingungen und ihre Anwendung. VI, 157 Seiten. 1978.

Vol. 153: Kombinatorische Entscheidungsprobleme: Methoden und Anwendungen. Herausgegeben von T. M. Liebling und M. Rössler. VIII, 206 Seiten. 1978.

Vol. 154: Problems and Instruments of Business Cycle Analysis. Proceedings 1977. Edited by W. H. Strigel. VI, 442 pages. 1978.